A Nation of Religions

EDITED BY STEPHEN PROTHERO

SOCIAL SCIENCES DIVISION
CHICAGO PUBLIC LIBRARY
400 SOUTH STATE STREET
CHICAGO, IL 60605

A Nation of Religions

The Politics of Pluralism in Multireligious America

The University of North Carolina Press Chapel Hill

© 2006 The University of North Carolina Press
All rights reserved
Manufactured in the United States of America
Designed by Eric M. Brooks
Set in Quadraat by Keystone Typesetting, Inc.

The paper in this book meets the guidelines for permanence
and durability of the Committee on Production Guidelines for
Book Longevity of the Council on Library Resources.

The publication of this book was supported by a grant from
the Smith Richardson Foundation.

Library of Congress Cataloging-in-Publication Data
A nation of religions: the politics of pluralism in multireligious
America / edited by Stephen Prothero.
    p. cm.
Includes bibliographical references and index.
ISBN-13: 978-0-8078-3052-9 (cloth: alk. paper)
ISBN-10: 0-8078-3052-6 (cloth: alk. paper)
ISBN-13: 978-0-8078-5770-0 (pbk.: alk. paper)
ISBN-10: 0-8078-5770-X (pbk.: alk. paper)
1. United States—Religion. 2. Religious pluralism—United
States. 3. Religion and politics—United States. I. Prothero,
Stephen R.
BL2525.N36   2006
222.973'09051—dc22   2006011156

cloth   10 09 08 07 06   5 4 3 2 1
paper   10 09 08 07 06   5 4 3 2 1

R0409211327

CONTENTS

SOCIAL SCIENCES DIVISION
CHICAGO PUBLIC LIBRARY
400 SOUTH STATE STREET
CHICAGO, IL 60605

A Nation of Religions

Introduction

In the United States, religion matters. In overwhelming numbers, Americans believe in God, pray, and contribute their time and money to churches, synagogues, mosques, and temples. As much as race, gender, ethnicity, or region, religious commitments make individual Americans who they are. The significance of religion is not confined, however, to self-identity and the private sphere. In the United States, religion is as public as it is pervasive, as political as it is personal. And so it has been for a long, long time.

Some Puritans, no doubt, came to the New World just to catch fish, but many more came to build a biblical commonwealth, to construct, inhabit, and defend what the first Massachusetts governor, John Winthrop, called a "city upon a hill." Nineteenth-century Americans reinterpreted that spiritual errand as an errand to the West, but as they pushed the frontier across the Mississippi and over the Rockies, they too saw themselves as doing God's work. In the 1980s, Governor Winthrop's evocative phrase became the centerpiece of President Ronald Reagan's struggle to rid the world of godless communism (and win evangelicals to the Republican Party).

Well into that decade, most American intellectuals remained convinced that religion was collapsing under the weight of modernity or at least was retreating meekly to the private sphere—convinced, in other words, that religion played no more important a role in the life of the nation than it did in their own lives. These intellectuals were wrong. Faith may be fading in the ivory tower and among other partisans of what sociologist Peter Berger has termed "Eurosecularity," but it is vibrant in virtually every other quarter of the United States.[1] Faith remains so vibrant, in fact, that any attempt to understand the nation without understanding its believers is bound to fail. If you want to know what moves America, you need to know what moves Americans. And here a prime mover is God in many guises, religion in its many manifestations.

The First Amendment, of course, prohibits the federal government from establishing religion but says nothing about religious groups consecrating the state. Nation-states typically legitimate their regimes through myths, rites, and theologies, and the United States is no exception. But Americans have put their own spin on that ancient tradition of the sociopolitical construction of reality. From the Revolutionary War to the new millennium, Americans have interpreted the saga of the United States as a gospel of sorts—good news to the Puritans, the Protestants, or the pluralists. In fact, one source of the country's political and social stability is Americans' willingness to anoint their nation with God's favor—to see themselves as God's chosen people and their march to freedom as an Exodus tale.

This theological legitimation of America was from the start a Protestant endeavor. One popular myth of the nation was that God had held the New World in abeyance until after the Protestant Reformation, lest it be populated by the ungodly. Or, as one American put it, "The Reformation had taught the Christian world afresh the value of the individual man, standing erect, the Bible in his hand, fearless before priest and king, reverent before God. . . . When a new light for the social and political life of mankind began to ray out from the open Bible in the hands of Luther, God opened the way to the new continent."[2]

Such myths of America, while never uncontested, remained plausible as long as virtually all Americans were Protestants—plausible in 1776, for example, when there were fewer than one hundred Roman Catholic churches in the colonies and only a handful of synagogues, meager numbers compared with the two-thousand-plus churches controlled by the top four Protestant denominations (Congregationalists, Presbyterians, Baptists, and Anglicans). During the 1830s, however, Roman Catholic immigrants from western Europe began to flood the country, followed in the late nineteenth century by a new wave of immigrants from eastern Europe, many of them Jews. At first, few of the nation's handlers believed that these immigrants and their religions could be integrated into the Protestant myth of America as God's promised land. Conversions, after all, were few, and accommodation was never as rapid as the nativists would have liked.

In the 1930s, however, an intrepid few began to refer to Protestants, Catholics, and Jews as roughly equal partners in a nation that was no longer Protestant or even Christian but instead Judeo-Christian.[3] During World War II, that formulation became commonplace, and by the early 1950s President Dwight D. Eisenhower was famously tracing "our form of government" to what he called the "Judeo-Christian concept."[4]

This concept burst onto the public stage with the publication of *Protestant, Catholic, Jew* (1955) by sociologist Will Herberg. Now a classic in the study of American religion, this book epitomized even as it scrutinized the new Judeo-Christian consensus. Herberg (a Jew) began by observing immigrants' tendency to hold fast to their parents' faiths even as they forgot their parents' languages. In the United States, he argued, speaking Yiddish or Polish marked one as un-American, but observing the Passover Seder or attending Mass did not. In fact, religion acted as the primary vehicle for self-identity and social location for immigrants in this new land. "It was largely in and through his religion," Herberg argued, that the immigrant crafted an American identity.[5]

There are always limits, however, to acceptable religious identification, and in postwar America the Judeo-Christian tradition demarcated them. Herberg saw a "fundamental tripartite division" of postwar America into Protestants, Catholics, and Jews, all of which practiced a common patriotic piety Herberg called the "American way of life." To be sure, these traditions differed in some matters of belief and practice, but all three shared certain basic theological and political convictions that bound the nation together in the face of the ethnic, racial, and class divisions ever threatening to tear it apart. According to Herberg, all championed the fatherhood of God and the brotherhood of humanity, all affirmed human rights and democracy, and all stood fast against godless communism. At least in the 1950s, to be American was to be committed to one God, to listen to his voice in the Bible, and to try to follow his commandments. "Not to be . . . either a Protestant, a Catholic, or a Jew," he wrote, "is somehow not to be an American."[6]

Herberg's reinvigoration of melting pot theory circulated widely during the 1950s and gained traction as the words "under God" made their way into the Pledge of Allegiance (in 1954) and as "In God We Trust" became the country's official motto (in 1956). By the mid-1960s, however, both his "triple melting pot" theory in particular and assimilationist theorizing in general were beginning to seem stale. In 1965, new immigration legislation opened the borders to another wave of newcomers. That year, U.S. Supreme Court Justice William Douglas observed that the United States was no longer merely a Judeo-Christian country. It had become, he wrote, "a nation of Buddhists, Confucianists, and Taoists, as well as Christians."[7]

In the United States today, the Asian American population is growing more rapidly than any other ethnic group. In 2002, 12.5 million Asian and Pacific Islanders were living in the United States. This figure amounted to roughly 4.4

percent of all Americans and had risen from 7.3 million (2.9 percent) in 1990. The U.S. Census expects this population to more than triple by 2050, climbing to just under 40 million, or nearly 10 percent of the overall population.[8]

Buddhism, Hinduism, and Sikhism have all benefited from these demographic shifts, but Islam in particular has been buoyed by the new immigration. An April 2001 study found 1,209 mosques in the United States. Of these Islamic centers, 30 percent were established in the 1990s, and 32 percent were founded in the 1980s. The number of mosques jumped 25 percent between 1994 and 2000, while the number of Muslims associated with each mosque rose even more dramatically: 235 percent. The study concluded by estimating the total American Muslim population at 6 to 7 million. That figure is likely inflated, but even so Islam appears to be close to surpassing Judaism as the nation's second-most-popular religion—if it has not already done so.[9]

The Buddhist figure is particularly dicey. It depends heavily, for example, on whether the count includes only people who respond "Buddhist" when asked, "What is your religion?" or whether sympathizers are included as well: people who may not self-identify as Buddhists but who might nonetheless participate in a weekly Zen meditation group or subscribe to the Buddhist magazine Tricycle. One recent study found 4 million Americans who call themselves Buddhists but 25 million (roughly one-eighth of the adult population) who say that Buddhism has significantly influenced their religious lives.[10]

Because Hinduism and Sikhism have few white adherents, their numbers are much easier to figure. The United States has roughly 1 million Hindus and 250,000 or so Sikhs.

From Protestantism to Pluralism

Over the past two decades, scholars of American religion have begun to explore the lives of U.S. practitioners of all these religions. After focusing for more than a century on Protestantism, scholars trained in history, sociology, anthropology, and religious studies turned their collective attention after World War II to Roman Catholics and Jews and more recently to religious traditions that have prospered in the wake of the "new immigration." Today, the Protestant paradigm that informed works from Robert Baird's Religion in America (1844) to Sydney Ahlstrom's A Religious History of the American People (1972) has given way to a new pluralist paradigm that sees the United States as a nation of religions whose skyline is punctuated not only by church spires but also by onion domes and minarets.

Nowhere is this new paradigm (and this new nation) more in evidence than in Professor Diana Eck's ambitious and influential Pluralism Project at Harvard University. Through her book, *A New Religious America* (2001), her CD-ROM, *On Common Ground: World Religion in America* (2002), and her Pluralism Project Web site, Eck and her collaborators have demonstrated convincingly that the United States is among the most religiously diverse countries on the globe. It is, in short, a very different nation from the one Herberg mapped fifty years ago.

But what are we to make of all this diversity? How is it transforming the public square? And what pressures is that public square bringing to bear on America's newest religions? The short answer is that we do not yet know.

Four decades after the liberalization of immigration laws in 1965, scholars of American religion continue to obsess on overturning the old Protestant paradigm. This work has proceeded on two fronts. First, ethnographers have produced many fine microstudies on topics such as the Italian Catholic Festa of the Madonna of 115th Street in Harlem, Vodou priestess initiation in Brooklyn, and Cuban Catholic patriotic piety in Miami, teasing out in each case the multiple meanings participants make out of these religious practices—how ordinary Americans draw on religious resources not only to make sense of the world but also to make a home in it. Alongside these ethnographers, Eck and others at the Pluralism Project have been mapping the post-1965 religious landscape, conducting microstudies of urban areas from Boston to Los Angeles. And their model has been replicated elsewhere. This mapping project will never be complete, but it is nevertheless quite advanced. We now know how many Hindu temples Houston has, how many mosques Miami has, and how many Buddhist centers Atlanta has. The cumulative effect of all these efforts is to demonstrate that U.S. religions are many, not one; that American religious experience comes in all shapes and sizes; and that the meanings of each are polysemous and contested. All this local work generally neglects, however, the national frame: how the new religious realities are transforming American political and social life, and how activities in the public square are changing the rules of engagement in the new spiritual marketplace.[11]

Scholars have also produced good studies of individual conversions—for example, from Protestantism to Buddhism. They have explored how denominations such as Soka Gakkai International and congregations such as the Ganesha Temple in Flushing, New York, have accommodated themselves to Christian norms and organizational forms. So we understand something of how the new pluralism has transformed individual immigrants who, like the earlier immigrants Herberg scrutinized, seem to be making their religious congregations the primary context for self-identification and social location. We know almost nothing, however, about how those individuals and their congregations are affecting politics in the United States and how American social life is impinging on our newest "mediating structures"—the Muslims' mosques, the Buddhists' centers, and the Hindus' temples that now dot this nation of religions.

Volumes that attend to religion in American public life typically follow the Judeo-Christian model, focusing on Christians and Jews, while volumes that deal with religious diversity rarely expand their horizons beyond congregational life. To put it another way, recent scholarship on religious diversity in the United States has focused on the cultivation of "lived religion" inside the *domus* of families and neighborhoods, for example, or in particular religious congregations.[12] The scholarship in this volume seeks to broaden that field of vision, scrutinizing the contributions of particular individuals, congregations, and religious traditions to the polis.

The Politics of Pluralism

This book begins by taking U.S. religious diversity not as a proposition to be proved but as the truism it has become. Instead of attempting to drive yet another nail in the coffin of the old Protestant paradigm, our authors start by acknowledging religious diversity as an undeniable fact. Our question is not whether the United States is a Christian or a multireligious nation—it is clearly both—but how religious diversity is changing the values, rites, and institutions of the nation and how those values, rites, and institutions are changing American religions.

Consider for a minute the nation's ninety-two thousand public schools. Inaugurated in the early nineteenth century as a way to inculcate in young Americans both Protestant and civic virtues, public schooling (or "common schooling," as it was called at the time) remains an important vehicle for making and shaping citizens and legitimating the nation-state. The students in these schools, however, look very different from their predecessors in the 1850s or even the 1950s. Today in many high schools in Hawaii, Buddhists routinely outnumber Protestants, Catholics, and Jews. Some elementary schools in California have more Hindus than Baptists, more Sikhs than Methodists. What myths of America are taught in these schools? What political values are inculcated? What rites of the nation are practiced?

Imagine that you are a Jewish civics teacher at a high school in Honolulu, a city that boasts at least forty-five different Buddhist centers. Do you tell your students that the God of the Bible set aside the New World as virgin land until after the Protestant Reformation so that his pure church could be transplanted here? Do you claim that the United States is a Judeo-Christian nation in which all good citizens bow down before one God? Do you celebrate the Buddha's birthday along with the birthday of George Washington?

Now imagine you are an imam in a mosque of the Muslim American Society, the largest group of African American Sunni Muslims. What do you tell the young people in your community about the proper relationship between church and state? How do you reconcile the discrepancies between Quranic teaching and constitutional law? How (if at all) do you celebrate the Fourth of July?

Or perhaps you are a counselor at a summer camp for Gujarati American Hindu students. How do you reconcile the legacy of caste with your commitment to democracy? What do you say about school prayer or women's rights?

Finally, consider President George W. Bush's efforts to provide faith-based groups with government funding for social service projects. We know that the First Amendment prohibits giving preference to Christian or Jewish groups in the distribution of government funds. However, a poll conducted in 2001 by the Pew Forum on Religion and Public Life found that while about 75 percent of Americans favored government funding to faith-based organizations, only half of those in favor of such funding wanted to see money provided to mosques or Buddhist temples.[13] And recent investigations into the billions of dollars the Bush administration has allocated to this effort have found little evidence that funds are flowing with any force to groups that fall outside the "Judeo-Christian concept."

Are religions such as Islam and Buddhism making their way into the American mainstream, or is this integration still decades (or centuries) away? When will the United States be led by its first Muslim president? Its first Hindu? Do Protestantism, Catholicism, and Judaism remain the only three religious options for Americans? Or is Herberg's "Protestant, Catholic, Jew" model giving way to something new?

From the White House to public schools in Hawaii, an important contest is taking shape: the American values of the Enlightenment and the Judeo-Christian tradition are bumping up against the values of Islam, Buddhism, Hinduism, and Sikhism. Jewish schoolteachers, Hindu camp counselors, and Muslim imams are weighing American narratives of freedom, equality, and sacrifice against the teachings of the Quran and the Upanishads, bringing Abraham Lincoln and Malcolm X into conversation with the Buddha and

Muhammad. In these many and varied encounters between East and West, new myths and new rites are taking shape.

The twelve essays in this volume were solicited expressly to examine these rich encounters from a variety of disciplinary perspectives—to ask first how religious diversity is changing the values and institutions of the United States and second how those values and institutions are transforming American religious organizations and congregations. The lines of influence no doubt run in both directions—from politics to religion and from religion to politics —so these essays attempt to explore both dynamics.

Our authors consider, second, whether these new American religions are working to legitimate the nation-state and cultivate citizenship. Are Hinduism, Buddhism, Islam, and Sikhism continuing to do the work in the twenty-first century that Protestantism, Catholicism, and Judaism did in the twentieth? Are they binding together the nation? Or, as some conservative critics fear, are they undermining American values and institutions, setting the country up for a Babel-like fall?

Until fairly recently, many scholars believed that religious diversity destabilized religious faith and with it the social and political order. Only in societies with a common faith would religion function as a sort of social glue, binding a nation and its people around shared myths, theologies, and rites. In modern societies, where religions compete like so many products on a supermarket shelf, any given religion would suffer from a debilitating crisis of credibility. Religions can legitimate the state and stabilize the social order only when they carry with them the transcendent power of the sacred, and they can do that work only when their reality appears to be given rather than chosen, locked into the order of the universe rather than patched together willy-nilly by the individual whims of this citizen and that. Or so the old argument goes. Today, most scholars of the American scene understand that religious diversity does not lead inevitably to secularization, that pluralism and plausibility can go hand in hand and have in fact done so, at least in the United States. Moreover, some evidence indicates that this view is fairly widely accepted among the population. For example, in a survey conducted in 2002 for *Religion and Ethics NewsWeekly* and *U.S. News and World Report*, only 13 percent of the Americans surveyed called "America's growing religious diversity" "a threat to individual religious beliefs." By contrast, 76 percent saw that diversity as "a source of strength and vitality to individual religious beliefs."[14]

When Herberg surveyed the U.S. religious and political scene after World War II, he saw three great religions supporting with one voice the bedrock principles of the American way of life. These essays consider how these bed-rock principles are being tested and transformed in the new religious land-scape. How is monotheism faring in the face of growing numbers of Bud-dhists who affirm no God and Hindus who affirm many? How is the growing presence of Islam testing and transforming the principle of the separation of church and state? How is the growing presence of Hinduism affecting com-mitments to the proposition that all people are created equal? Are America's newest mediating structures enhancing or undermining civility and demo-cratic citizenship?

The Judeo-Christian-Islamic Tradition

The past two decades—particularly after September 11, 2001—have seen fit-ful efforts to answer at least some of these questions by updating Herberg's thesis. As early as 1988, a spokesperson for the Muslim Political Action Com-mittee urged his fellow Americans "to start thinking of the U.S. as a Judeo-Christian-Muslim society," and in 1992 scholar of Islam John L. Esposito used the phrase "Judeo-Christian-Islamic heritage."[15] Today, some see Amer-ica's fundamental tripartite division not in Protestantism, Catholicism, and Judaism but in Judaism, Christianity, and Islam. And Americans increasingly are invoking, however haltingly, an "Abrahamic" or a "Judeo-Christian-Islamic" tradition that undergirds and legitimates American society. U.S. Mus-lim groups, including the Council on American-Islamic Relations, the Muslim American Society, and the American Muslim Council, have been promoting this view for some time, and key players in Washington, D.C., appear to be listening. President Bill Clinton and Vice President Al Gore both spoke regu-larly during their administration of the important faith-based social work being done in American churches, synagogues, and mosques. In his January 2001 inaugural address, President George W. Bush invoked this same Abra-hamic structure, remarking that "church and charity, synagogue and mosque lend our communities their humanity, and they will have an honored place in our plans and in our laws." After 9/11, he attempted to adopt American Muslims into the Judeo-Christian family, describing Islam as a "religion of peace," visiting mosques, and describing Muslims as partners rather than antagonists in the war on terrorism.[16]

Predictably, some observers were alarmed by this new public theology, which surfaced (among other places) in a December 2001 *National Geographic* cover story, "Abraham: Father of Three Faiths," and in a September 30, 2002, *Time* cover story on Abraham. Some Jews were concerned that the demise of Herberg's triple-melting-pot metaphor would take away the status they gained in American society during and after World War II as the number one religious minority. On the Christian right, evangelicals such as Billy Graham's son Franklin Graham, televangelist Jerry Falwell, and Ted Haggard of the National Association of Evangelicals argued forcefully that President Bush had gone too far—that the United States was a Christian country and Islam a religion of war. Echoing this line, conservative Catholic Richard John Neuhaus spoke out forcefully in First Things magazine for drawing a line in the sand at "Judeo-Christian." Otherwise, people would in no time be talking blithely about the United States as a "Judeo-Christian-Buddhist-Hindu-Islamic-Agnostic-Atheist society," he remarked.[17]

On the left, mainline Protestants such as Eck insisted that the Abrahamic canopy was far too skimpy to cover a nation now bulging with Sikh gurdwaras and Hindu temples, Jain centers and Buddhist retreats. Offering a multicultural twist on the metaphor of the "city upon a hill," a shining example for all the world to see, they contended that the example America has to offer the world is not its crusading Puritanism but its irenic pluralism. America's destiny, this line of reasoning goes, is not to purify Protestantism but to manifest the widest range of religious commitments and thus to offer the broadest platform for interreligious dialogue.

This book subjects to scholarly scrutiny the "new pluralism" and the myths and rites it is producing. Is religious diversity contributing, as Arthur Schlesinger Jr. intimated in The Disuniting of America (1992), to the splintering of American public life into ever-smaller, self-interested groups? Are new immigrants from Asia and the Middle East jettisoning their religious commitments to become more American? Or are they, like Herberg's immigrants, locating themselves in American society largely in and through their religious commitments? Finally, is there some new American way of life afoot that incorporates not only Protestants, Catholics, and Jews but also Muslims and perhaps even Buddhists, Sikhs, and Hindus?

Muslims-Buddhists-Hindus-Sikhs

To address these questions, this volume gathers an interdisciplinary group of distinguished scholars in sociology, political science, anthropology, history, and religious studies. A key focus of the book is religions that originated in south and east Asia—that is, Buddhism, Hinduism, and Sikhism. One issue concerning the adaptation of these religions to U.S. soil is the problem of God. As the Pledge of Allegiance and the official motto of the United States

("In God We Trust") indicate, God is a key national symbol. How do Buddhists, who have traditionally denied a personal God, negotiate this key element in the American way of life? Are they accommodating themselves to it by finding ways to affirm a God of some sort? Or are they making efforts to modify American conceptions of divinity (to proffer an impersonal rather than a personal God)? And if so, how are those efforts faring? Finally, how are Hindus, many of whom are polytheistic, navigating their way in a nation that purports to act under and trust in God? (In a course I teach on Hinduism in America, my Hindu students routinely inform me that they are monotheists, not polytheists.)

A second preoccupation of the book is Islam, which by many accounts is among the fastest-growing religions in the United States and one of the most resistant to Americanization. Here our authors seek to illuminate to what extent American political culture is at odds with Islam and to what extent Islam is becoming an American faith. Is the United States experiencing on its own soil the battle between Christianity and Islam that Samuel Huntington foresaw in The Clash of Civilizations (1996)? Or is the United States becoming a "Judeo-Christian-Islamic" nation in which Muslims are partners rather than antagonists? How do American Muslims accommodate themselves to American norms and organizational forms? (Do they fly American flags? Piously recite the Pledge of Allegiance?) How, if at all, are American political institutions accommodating themselves to Islam?

Ihsan Bagby's essay, based on a major study of U.S. mosques, explores three attitudes of American Muslims toward American society—isolation, insulation, and assimilation—before concluding that Muslims as a whole strongly favor engagement with American political processes. Bagby's piece finds a major racial divide between African American Muslims, on the one hand, and south Asian American and Arab American Muslims, on the other hand (plus major differences among African American Muslims). Omid Safi's chapter on progressive Islam constitutes both an analysis of that movement and something of a manifesto for it. Surveying part of the ground covered in Bagby's essay but from a very different perspective, Safi argues for a modern understanding of Islam that is critical not only of Islam's varied fundamentalisms but also of American colonialism.

Together, these essays on Islam present, not surprisingly, a spectrum of religious responses to America and a variety of American responses to religious diversity. There is some consensus among our authors that U.S. Muslims are both the most politically engaged of the religious traditions we considered and the most wary about marking the sacred places and sacred times of American civil religion with a Muslim stamp of approval. In his study of Italian Catholics in Harlem, Robert Anthony Orsi observed that Italians manifested their ambivalence about their new country by seeking "half-citizenship"—applying to be U.S. citizens but never making it happen. Muslims seem to be in a similar position today. Rather than seeing Islam as a way to articulate their American identities, many Muslims seem to be seeing the Americanization proposition as tantamount to forgetting their faith. Still, American Islam has produced a number of highly visible political organizations. During the 2004 presidential election, volunteers from the Islamic Society of Nevada, for example, attempted to call each and every Muslim in that battleground state to urge him or her to vote.

As this volume's three essays on Buddhism make clear, Buddhists are also active in the public square but are less organized when it comes to political campaigning. Over the past decade, Buddhists have been most visible on the issue of Tibetan independence, thanks to some high-profile celebrity activists (for example, Richard Gere) and to organizations such as Tibet House and Students for a Free Tibet. The Buddhist Churches of America, the closest U.S. Buddhism gets to a mainline denomination, has also ventured into the public square on issues such as school prayer (against) and gay marriage (for). And during the debate over the Elk Grove v. Newdow Pledge of Allegiance case, twenty-three Buddhist groups weighed in against the current Pledge on the grounds that the words "under God" endorsed monotheistic religions and stigmatized Buddhist schoolchildren as unpatriotic.[18]

Duncan Ryûken Williams's historical work on the internment of Japanese American Buddhists during World War II makes important contributions to our understanding of this key moment in the life of the nation and the lives of American Buddhists, focusing on "modes of accommodation and resistance." Documented with an array of new sources, including interviews, private papers, letters, and Federal Bureau of Investigation documents, this chapter concludes with some provocative comparisons between the experiences of Japanese Americans during World War II and the experiences of Muslims, Sikhs, and south Asian Americans in the months and years following 9/11. Hien Duc Do's case study of a Vietnamese American temple in San Jose, California, presents a finer-grained study of how one refugee community, led in this case by a talented and creative nun named Dam Luu, somehow manages both to replicate key elements of Vietnamese culture in the United States and to help its members adjust to American culture. A key factor here is intergenerational conflict, to which the Perfect Harmony Temple attends (among other means) by offering English language classes to adults and Vietnamese language classes to children. Finally, Robert A. F. Thurman's chapter focuses on the American peregrinations of Tibetan Buddhism—in his words, "a monastic, messianic, and apocalyptic tradition that seeks via ethics, religion, science, and technology to turn an entire culture into a theater for enlightenment." The United States, of course, has thus far resisted becoming that venue; in fact, many Americans seem to take Tibetan Buddhism more as a theater for entertainment than a theater for enlightenment (to view the Dalai Lama as a celebrity more than a bodhisattva). But Thurman's impassioned piece challenges readers to understand the ongoing American encounter with Tibetan Buddhism as the grand civilizational challenge that it is becoming. According to Thurman, because of its history as a mainstream religious, cultural, and political force in Tibet, Tibetan Buddhism is particularly well suited to contribute to America's "sacred canopy."

On the scale of political involvement, Hindus lag far behind Buddhists. Though one of the wealthiest and the most highly educated religious groups in the country (ranking at or near the top, alongside Unitarian-Universalists, in per capita income and graduate degrees), Hindus are also among the least mobilized politically. (Tellingly, the first Indian American politician to gain national prominence—Bobby Jindal, a Republican who narrowly lost a runoff election for governor of Louisiana in 2003 and then won a seat in the U.S. House of Representatives in 2004—is a convert to Roman Catholicism.) Hindus have organized American Hindus against Defamation, an organization modeled after the Anti-Defamation League that has met with some notable successes. In 1997, its protesters convinced the rock band Aerosmith to change the cover of its Nine Lives CD, which had depicted the Hindu god Krishna with breasts and a cat's head. More recently, the Indian American Center for Political Awareness has attempted to mobilize this community's electorate. But Muslims and Buddhists have a far more formidable array of pressure groups, and Hindus contribute very little to political campaigns. So while imams are invited to the White House and the Dalai Lama receives a royal welcome when he comes to Washington, D.C., Hindus occupy something of a political Neverland. Only 30 percent of Indian Americans voted in the 2004 presidential election, and more than 90 percent of those who did not vote were not even registered.[19]

Prema A. Kurien, a sociologist with an expertise on Hindu organizations in the United States, explores in her chapter how Hindus responded to the rapid legitimation of a Judeo-Christian-Islamic tradition in the United States after the events of 9/11. Hindu Americans are a particularly Web-savvy group, so Kurien focuses on how the intra-Hindu contest between "genteel multiculturalism" and "militant nationalism" is playing out on Internet groups, Web sites, and e-zines. More specifically, Kurien explores the "external negotiations" of U.S. Hindus—their ongoing efforts to gain for Hinduism recognition (alongside Judaism, Christianity, and Islam) as a legitimate American religion. Vasudha Narayanan's essay, also on U.S. Hindus, transports us from cyberspace to sacred space, documenting how Hindus are making the American landscape holy—transforming, by the powers of imagination and ritual, American rivers into the sacred Ganges and American mountains into the Himalayan abodes of the gods. Along the way, she includes a wonderfully creative interpretation of the architecture of the first Hindu temple in the United States and documents a second form of accommodation—in this case to the American Protestant Social Gospel tradition, as U.S. Hindus seek not only to build and consecrate temples but also to feed and clothe the needy.

U.S. Sikhism presents a particularly intriguing case study. More than any of the other believers surveyed here, U.S. Sikhs are at peace with American values and institutions; as contributor Gurinder Singh Mann puts it in his essay in this volume, they are "at home in America." Perhaps because they have had relatively little to complain about, Sikhs have remained aloof from politics and largely absent from the public square. The events of 9/11 shined a glaring spotlight on their community, however, bringing their leaders out from the shadows of invisibility. The murder of coreligionist Balbir Singh Sodhi in Mesa, Arizona, on September 15, 2001 (by an assassin who wrongly believed that Sodhi was a Muslim), led Sikhs to launch a public relations campaign outlining the differences between Sikhism and Islam. And the spate of interfaith gatherings that followed brought Sikhs into the public spotlight as never before, in part because their trademark turbans signified in stark visual form America's religious diversity.

The Myth of the Wall

Among the most cherished U.S. myths is the view that church and state are utterly separate—that Thomas Jefferson's famous metaphor of a wall of separation between the two is somehow written into the Constitution and thereby into American law and life. Yet U.S. presidents from George Washington forward have placed their hands on the Bible during their inaugurations and used their bully pulpit to weigh in on matters from the biblical view of slavery to the Quranic view of war. Moreover, both congressional legislation and the courts' interpretations of that legislation have dramatically shaped the course of U.S. religious history. As is well known, the signing of the Immigration Act of 1965 ushered in a new era in American religion. (*Life* magazine would not have declared 1968 the "Year of the Guru" without the new measure.) But that law was necessary only because of the exclusionary acts Congress passed between 1882 and 1924.

In an effort to shed some light on such supply-side effects on the spiritual marketplace, this volume includes two very different essays on what has classically been termed the church/state question. First, Courtney Bender and Jennifer Snow examine the circumstances under which Muslims, Buddhists, Hindus, or Sikhs literally made federal cases out of religion (and in so doing helped to change the course of U.S. constitutional law). One of the major themes of this essay is how, even in the post-1965 era, federal judges continue to define religion largely in Protestant terms. Stephen Dawson has a very different view of the Free Exercise and Establishment Clauses of the First Amendment from that of Bender and Snow. His chapter on Alabama's Ten Commandments controversy presents a novel argument for what he calls agonistic federalism, all in service of what he hopes will be a broader recognition of religion in the public square. Rejecting a one-size-fits-all approach to the church/state question, Dawson argues on behalf of the wisdom of a "plurality of solutions"—allowing different levels of public recognition of religion in different states. Both of these thought-provoking essays broaden the old-fashioned church/state discussion to include a wide variety of religious congregations. What is the proper relationship between mosque and state? Temple and state? How has the Supreme Court decided cases involving the rights of Muslim and Buddhist inmates? The public display of the Ten Commandments? How should it decide those cases?

The volume concludes with an essay by James Davison Hunter and David Franz proposing what might be called a natural history of the public lives of immigrant religions in the United States. Hunter and Franz posit, largely on the shoulders of prior work on Catholic and Jewish immigration, a four-stage trajectory among these groups from invisibility to recognition to internal negotiation (accommodations they make within their community) to external negotiation (adaptations to the broader society) and finally to establishment as a "legitimate" American religion. Some of the contributors to this volume view Hunter's typology as tilted too heavily toward outmoded assumptions of assimilation. In an era in which it is not only permissible but in some cases cool to be a Buddhist or a Hindu, can we assume that these groups will follow in the footsteps of Catholics and Jews? And won't their trek be quite different, given the realities of transnationalism—the ability of Hindus and Sikhs, for example, to return repeatedly to India and in fact to maintain India and the United States as dual homelands? Despite these reservations, many of the authors whose works appear here found Hunter's suggestions helpful and have integrated his insights into their analyses.

To conclude, this volume seeks to subject the cliché of American religious pluralism to scholarly scrutiny, particularly where it shows its public face. But the volume does not look at U.S. Muslims, Buddhists, Hindus, and Sikhs in splendid isolation. As R. Stephen Warner's essay, "The De-Europeanization of American Christianity," shows, the new immigration is in many respects making the country more rather than less Christian. And Christian norms and organizational forms repeatedly factor into the accommodations U.S. Buddhists, Muslims, Sikhs, and Hindus are making to American circumstances. In this way, *A Nation of Religions* hopes not only to open up the public side of the new pluralism paradigm but also to bring that paradigm into conversation with old Protestant-centered narratives.

NOTES

1. Peter L. Berger, "Religion and the West," *National Interest* 80 (Summer 2005): 112–19.

2. Merrill Edwards Gates, "The Significance of Christianity to the Discovery and the History of America," paper presented at the Congress of the Evangelical Alliance, World's Columbian Exposition, Chicago, 1893, quoted in Judith Snodgrass, *Presenting Japanese Buddhism to the West: Orientalism, Occidentalism, and the Columbian Exposition* (Chapel Hill: University of North Carolina Press, 2003), 46.

3. The classic source is Mark Silk, "Notes on the Judeo-Christian Tradition in America," *American Quarterly* 36.1 (Spring 1984): 65–85. Silk traces this tradition to Christian thinkers. My discussion in *American Jesus: How the Son of God Became a National Icon* (New York: Farrar, Straus, and Giroux, 2003), 258–61, credits Jewish thinkers with the genesis of the concept.

4. The full quote is typically given as: "In other words, our form of government has no sense unless it is founded in a deeply felt religious faith, and I don't care what it is. With us of course it is the Judeo-Christian concept, but it must be a religion that all men are created equal." For a New Testament scholar's witty take on the vexed transmission history of these remarks, see Patrick Henry, " 'And I Don't Care What It Is': The Tradition-History of a Civil Religion Proof-Text," *Journal of the American Academy of Religion* 49.1 (March 1981): 35–49.

5. Will Herberg, *Protestant-Catholic-Jew: An Essay in American Religious Sociology* (Chicago: University of Chicago Press, 1983), 28.

6. Ibid., 256–57.

7. *United States v. Seeger*, 380 U.S. 163 (1965).

8. "The White House Initiative on Asian Americans and Pacific Islanders," <http://www.aapi.gov/resources.htm>; Terrance Reeves and Claudette Bennett, "The Asian and Pacific Islander Population in the United States: March 2002," U.S. Census Bureau (May 2003), <http://www.census.gov/prod/2003pubs/p20-540.pdf>; Claudette E. Bennett and Barbara Martin, "The Asian and Pacific Islander Population," U.S. Census Bureau, <http://www.census.gov/population/www/pop-profile/apipop.html>.

9. Ihsan Bagby, Paul M. Perl, and Bryan T. Froehle, *The Mosque in America: A National Portrait* (Washington, D.C.: Council on American-Islamic Relations, 2001). See also Bagby, this volume. For a much lower figure for U.S. Muslims (1.9 million), see Tom W. Smith, *Estimating the Muslim Population in the United States* (New York: American Jewish Committee, 2001).

10. Robert Wuthnow and Wendy Cadge, "Buddhists and Buddhism in the United States: The Scope of Influence," *Journal of the Scientific Study of Religion* 43.3 (September 2004): 361–78.

11. Classic examples of the ethnographic turn in the study of American religion are Robert Anthony Orsi, *The Madonna of 115th Street: Faith and Community in Italian Harlem, 1880–1950* (New Haven: Yale University Press, 1985); Karen McCarthy Brown, *Mama Lola: A Vodou Priestess in Brooklyn* (Berkeley: University of California Press, 1991); Thomas A. Tweed, *Our Lady of the Exile: Diasporic Religion at a Cuban Catholic Shrine in Miami* (New York: Oxford University Press, 1997).

12. On congregations, see R. Stephen Warner, *Gatherings in Diaspora: Religious Communities and the New Immigration* (Philadelphia: Temple University Press, 1998); Helen Rose Ebaugh and Janet Saltzman Chafetz, *Religion and the New Immigrants: Continuities and Adaptations in Immigrant Congregations* (Walnut Creek, Calif.: AltaMira, 2000). See also a follow-up study by Helen Rose Ebaugh and Janet Saltzman Chafetz, *Religion across Borders: Transnational Immigrant Networks* (Walnut Creek, Calif.: AltaMira, 2002). Another volume with some essays of this sort is Robert A. Orsi, ed., *Gods of the City: Religion and the American Urban Landscape* (Bloomington: Indiana University Press, 1999). Less useful is Bruce B. Lawrence's *New Faiths, Old Fears: Muslims and Other Asian Immigrants in American Religious Life* (New York: Columbia University Press, 2002). The Pew Charitable Trusts have launched a massive Religion and the New Immigrants Initiative that aims to study the role played by religion in seven urban "gateways"—Los Angeles, San Francisco, Chicago, Houston, Miami, New York, and Washington, D.C. With the exception of Ebaugh and Chafetz's work (which focuses on Houston), these studies are in process, and it remains to be seen how much any of them will attend to the polis. One new project that does appear to have the public square firmly in its sights is the Religious Pluralism in Southern California Project, centered at the University of California at Santa Barbara and funded by the Ford Foundation. According to its Web site (<http://www.religion.ucsb.edu/projects/newpluralism/project.htm>), this project seeks to understand "the impact that religious pluralism is having on civic life in Southern California."

13. "Faith-Based Funding Backed, but Church-State Doubts Abound," Pew Re-

search Center for the People and the Press, April 10, 2001, <http://people-press.org/reports/display.php3?ReportID=15>.

14. "Exploring Religious America, 2002," <http://www.thearda.com/FR_Index.html?/archive/codebooks/RELIGN02CB.HTML>. In that same survey, 62 percent of respondents said that "having many different religions in the United States" did not "make it harder to keep the country united," while only 29 percent said that religious diversity did make it more difficult.

15. Richard N. Ostling, "Americans Facing toward Mecca," Time, May 23, 1988, 50, quoted in Jonathan D. Sarna, "Jewish Identity in the Changing World of American Religion," in Jewish Identity in America, edited by David M. Gordis and Yoav Ben-Horin (Los Angeles: University of Judaism, 1991), 97; John L. Esposito, Islam the Straight Path (New York: Oxford University Press, 1992), quoted in "The Judeo-Christian-Islamic Heritage," <http://www.islamfortoday.com/esposito01.htm>.

16. This phrase received a powerful imprimatur when the usage maven William Safire took it up in his "On Language" column in 1995. Quoting Daniel Patrick Moynihan, Safire wrote, "It's now official. Ours is a Judeo-Christian-Islamic heritage" ("Goo-Goo Eyes," New York Times, May 7, 1995, SM32). See also Russell Baker's reference to America's "Judeo-Christian-Islamic culture" in his "Except for the Pentagon" (New York Times, September 24, 1996, A25), and a grateful letter to the editor by M. A. Cheema, president of the American Muslim Council ("Muslim Music," New York Times, September 27, 1996, A32). The earliest usage of this neologism that I have been able to locate came at the Thirty-sixth Annual National Prayer Breakfast in Washington, D.C., on May 12, 1988. The speaker was Prince Bandar of Saudi Arabia, who, after affirming his belief in both Moses and Jesus, said, "I would like to commend to this distinguished gathering this morning that it is long past time to cease talking about just the Judeo-Christian tradition and make it Judeo-Christian-Islamic tradition" (134 Cong. Rec. S 5663). Prince Bandar's remarks indicate that this may well have been the first time that a Muslim had been invited to address this gathering. For a related though less mellifluous neologism, see the Reverend Walter Fauntroy's reference to "my Judeo-Christian-Muslim heritage" in his May 14, 2002, testimony before the Subcommittee on Oversight of the Committee on House Ways and Means (supporting an amendment to the tax code, H.R. 2357, that would permit political activism by tax-exempt religious organizations).

Referring to Judaism, Christianity, and Islam as "Abrahamic" faiths is more common. In 1990, Aly Y. Massoud, while contending that the National Conference of Christians and Jews should be renamed the National Conference of Christians, Jews, and Muslims, referred to Islam as "the completion of the Abrahamic religions" (Ari L. Goldman, "No Matter What Americans Think about Going to Church, They Admire Religious Figures," New York Times, April 7, 1990, 11). In 1995 testimony before the House Committee on the Judiciary, Azizah Y. Al-Hibri of the American Muslim Council called Islam "one of the three Abrahamic religions" ("Prepared Statement of Azizah Al-Hibri," Federal News Service, June 14, 1995). A 1998 Senate concurrent resolution supporting "religious tolerance toward Muslims" referred to Islam as "one of the great Abrahamic faiths" (S. Con. Res. 94). Official prayers offered in both the House and the

Senate referred fairly regularly in the early-twenty-first century to "Abrahamic faith." (See, e.g., 149 *Cong. Rec.* H. 9823, October 28, 2003).

17. Richard John Neuhaus, "While We're at It," *First Things* 135 (August–September 2003), <http://www.firstthings.com/ftissues/ft0308/public.html>.

18. The Buddhists' amicus curiae brief in the "under God" case, dated February 12, 2004, can be viewed at <http://pewforum.org/religion-schools/pledge/docs/Buddhist Temples.pdf>.

19. "Indian American Political Participation," *Hindustan Times*, November 24, 2004, <http://www.hindustantimes.com/news/181_900801,001301190000.htm>.

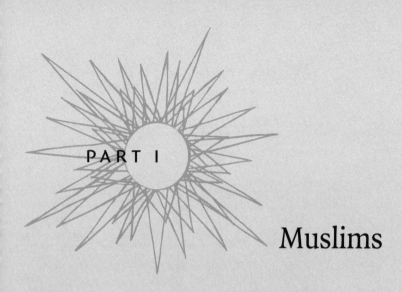

PART I

Muslims

IHSAN BAGBY

1

Isolate, Insulate, Assimilate

Attitudes of Mosque Leaders toward America

American Muslims' attitudes toward the United States and participation in American society are key factors in determining their future. In the aftermath of the 9/11 terrorist attacks, the relationship between the American Muslim community and American society has taken on even greater importance. What path will that community take as it seeks its place in a culture that differs dramatically from Islamic cultures? Will Muslims seek isolation or involvement, accommodation or resistance? Peter Berger has argued that religion historically has served as an effective tool for legitimizing the institutions of a society by bequeathing to them a sacred purpose.[1] Immigrant religious groups such as Catholics and Jews have struggled for acceptance in the American mainstream and in so doing came to adopt America's patriotic myths, thereby stretching their sacred canopy over the United States and its political canopy over themselves. Involvement, therefore, leads to accommodation, and isolation leads to resistance and fanaticism.[2]

This essay explores American Muslim attitudes toward America and involvement in American society primarily by using the results from the Mosque in America: A National Study (MIA), a comprehensive survey of mosque leaders conducted in 2000.[3] Analysis of the data has been supplemented by comments from interviewees at the time of the interviews, follow-up interviews conducted in 2002 with mosque leaders who participated in the MIA study, and a review of recent American Muslim literature relevant to these issues.

Emerging from the data is a picture of a religious community virtually unanimous in its desire to be involved in society—to be recognized as a respected part of the mosaic of American life. Muslim leaders clearly have opted to seek a place in mainstream America rather than to entrench themselves behind the walls of rejectionism and fanaticism. But as Muslims stand on this threshold, they harbor doubts and misgivings. Although they accept the pluralist ideal, they reject much in U.S. society. A palpable tension exists between the ideals of this self-confident body of believers and (as the Muslims see it) secular American culture. From the Muslim point of view, involvement in American society should not entail the surrender or compromise of Islamic beliefs and practices. Muslims are disquieted by what they see as the immorality of American culture and its hostility toward Islam and Muslims. In their minds, secularism, materialism, and an unfair foreign policy remain unacceptable.

So Muslim leaders are pulled in two directions. They want involvement in American society but are nervous about the possible erosion of Islamic identity and practice that might result. This concern is common among faith groups, who have long weighed the effects of a supposedly secular society on their beliefs and practices. Muslim leaders also want to have a seat at the table of mainstream America, but many are not comfortable appropriating the rhetoric and symbolism of American patriotism. The U.S. Muslim community is changing, however, and 9/11 has propelled it toward a greater commitment to involvement and accommodation. Since 9/11, the pull of those two forces has become overpowering.

This position of Muslim leaders—committed to but uneasy about involvement and accommodation—is captured by an African American Muslim in Indianapolis who remarks that the Muslim has three choices in facing America: isolate, insulate, or assimilate. The best choice, he believes, is to insulate —retain Islamic values and practices as protection against the immorality of America and anti-Islamic sentiments while remaining active in society. The metaphor of a coat as protection against wintry weather might be appropriate —the individual engages the world but is protected from harmful elements. This approach sees the importance—the necessity, even—of Muslim involvement in American society yet recognizes the dangers of identity loss such involvement portends. How else to change negative attitudes toward Islam, America's moral standards, and its government's policies? The middle path of insulation envisions full partnership with America, but this position implies a reluctance to embrace fully the patriotic ideals and rhetoric of America—the faithful hesitate to use Islam to pull a sacred canopy over the nation.

The MIA survey asked mosque leaders if they agreed or disagreed with the statement "America is an immoral, corrupt society" (see table 1.1). More than two-thirds (67 percent) of the respondents agree that America is immoral. Mosque leaders clearly are troubled by the U.S. moral climate. When talking about America's immorality, they most often refer to the sexual mores and the

TABLE 1.1 ∘ "America Is an Immoral, Corrupt Society"
(Percentage Giving Each Response; "Don't Know" Excluded from Percentages)

Strongly agree	28%
Somewhat agree	39
Somewhat disagree	27
Strongly disagree	6

prevalence of alcohol and drug consumption. Muslims feel great tension between normative Islamic culture and American society, especially in the arena of popular culture. And no wonder. Normative Islamic culture forbids premarital sex, dating, casual social interaction and touching between the sexes, homosexuality, alcohol and drug consumption, and the public show of a woman's body. Muslims need to be insulated from America's immorality.

Muslims' objections to this perceived immorality are not accompanied by a hatred and rejection of American society. In this regard, Muslim views resemble those of Christian evangelicals and fundamentalists who are concerned about the country's deteriorating moral climate.

Important gradations of responses exist. Leaders who say that they "somewhat agree" that America is immoral qualify their response with various points. The most common qualification is that there are a lot of good, decent American people—in other words, not all Americans are immoral. Another qualification is expressed by a Pakistani mosque leader in New York City: "In sexual matters, America is much more immoral than the Muslim world, but when it comes to business, I think America is more moral than Pakistan." Other comments mention that political corruption is worse in Muslim lands— in other words, not all segments of American society are immoral. Those mosque leaders who respond that they "somewhat agree" constitute the largest category—39 percent.

Those who "somewhat disagree" that American society is immoral and corrupt accentuate the positive about the United States. Most point to the highly moral people they know through their jobs, their neighborhoods, and even interfaith activities. This group seems to recognize the darker side of popular culture but to minimize its scope.

Those who "strongly agree" see immorality throughout America. One Arab mosque leader (a professional) points to America's foreign policy ("We don't take into account who is hurt"), high schools and teenage culture ("Look at the dress code, and then the best thing they can teach in high school

TABLE 1.2 ○ Mosques Grouped according to Dominant Ethnic Groups
(Percentage of Mosques in Each Category)

South Asian	28%
African American	27
Arab	15
Mixed evenly South Asian and Arab	16
All other combinations	14

Note: Dominant groups have 35–39 percent of participants in one group, and all other groups less than 20 percent; 40–49 percent of one group and all others less than 30; 50–59 percent of one group and all others less than 40; or any group over 55 percent. Mixed groups have two groups with at least 30 percent of participants each.

is how to use a condom, and we end up with children with no parents"), and business ("When a woman has to go back to work after giving birth, that's immoral"). A full 28 percent of all mosque leaders hold this strong criticism of American society.

Only 8 percent of mosque leaders "strongly disagree" that America is immoral. Explaining his response, one leader says that people cannot be outright condemned as immoral. After a thoughtful pause, possibly realizing the moral relativism implied in his remarks, the leader explains that what he means is that people cannot be dealt with effectively if they think that they are being condemned as immoral.

A number of variables will be used to analyze responses. One of the most important variables is ethnicity. Most U.S. mosques are dominated by one of three ethnic groups: African American, south Asian, or Arab (see table 1.2). The large presence of African American Muslims means that the Muslim view of America is not purely an immigrant view. The differences in opinions between the immigrant and African American leaders are distinct, and because mosque leaders are not completely isolated in ethnic enclaves, these differences have an impact and influence throughout the Muslim community.

African American mosque leaders are, in general, more critical of America's perceived immorality than are immigrants (see table 1.3). In the MIA survey, 70 percent of African American leaders agree that America is immoral; more significantly, 39 percent "strongly agree" that America is immoral, compared to 24 percent for all immigrant mosque leaders. The more critical stance of African American leaders can be explained by the fact that most of them converted to Islam, often because they were unhappy with American culture and politics. Most African American leaders, in other words, came to

TABLE 1.3 ○ "America Is Immoral" by Predominant Ethnicity
(Percentage Agreeing/Disagreeing with Statement)

	Ethnicity of Mosque				
	African American	South Asian	Arab	South Asian and Arab	All Others
Strongly agree	39%	23%	20%	26%	28%
Somewhat agree	31	42	48	41	39
Somewhat disagree	26	29	24	27	27
Strongly disagree	4	6	8	6	6

Note: N = 402. Not statistically significant.

Islam in part because they were repulsed by the racism they experienced and the spiritual vacuum that they saw in American society.

The African American Muslim community contains sharp internal differences between the American Society of Muslims (ASM), which constitutes approximately 56 percent of all African American mosques, and the historically Sunni African American mosques (HSAAM), which constitute about 44 percent of African American mosques. The ASM follows the leadership of Imam W. Deen Mohammed, who took over leadership of the Nation of Islam in 1975 and has transformed it into a mainstream Islamic organization. Imam Mohammed has come to champion patriotism, interfaith dialogue, and working within the system. The American flag has appeared on the masthead of the ASM monthly journal since 1975, and in some cities since the late 1980s, ASM mosques have organized "new world patriotism" parades on July 4.

The HSAAMs are mosques that do not belong to ASM—most never were a part of the Nation of Islam. The HSAAMs are a fractured group that have turned away from the syncretism of the Nation of Islam and sought a more authentic, normative form of Islam. I have used the phrase "historically Sunni" following Muslim leader K. Ahmad Tawfiq, who in the 1960s started using the phrase "Sunni Muslim" to distinguish between followers of the Nation of Islam and the African American Muslims who tried to follow the sunna (normative practice) of the Prophet Muhammad. HSAAMs are much more critical of the American political system, and some of them eschew interfaith dialogue (see table 1.4). They also have been more intent on digesting normative Islamic practice. Although not united in any one group, the National Umma, led for many years by Imam Jamil Al-Amin (the former H. Rap Brown), has previously had the largest group. A new organization, the Muslim Alliance in

TABLE 1.4 ∘ "America Is Immoral," by African American and Immigrant Mosques (Percentage Agreeing/Disagreeing with Statement)

	American Muslim Society	Historically Sunni Mosques	Immigrant Mosques
Strongly agree	18%	66%	24%
Somewhat agree	42	17	43
Somewhat disagree	36	13	26
Strongly disagree	4	4	7

Note: N = 401 African American mosques, 112 immigrant mosques, and 289 historically Sunni mosques. Statistically significant at .016.

North America, has recently initiated attempts to unite HSAAM mosques and other indigenous Muslims.

Two-thirds (66 percent) of all HSAAM leaders "strongly agree" that America is immoral, while only 18 percent of ASM leaders and 24 percent of immigrant leaders strongly agree. One HSAAM leader remarks in exasperation, "You can't turn on the radio, watch a video or TV, and not hear a whole bunch of cursing and sex. It's ridiculous." Overall, 83 percent of HSAAM mosque leaders, 60 percent of ASM leaders, and 67 percent of immigrant leaders agree that America is immoral. Of all mosque leaders, HSAAM leaders clearly have the most sharply negative view of America's morality, and ASM leaders have the least negative view.

Another variable measures the level of conservatism/traditionalism in mosque leaders. The MIA study delineated three categories: (1) those who interpret texts literally, without necessarily referring to the classical legal schools, including leaders who follow the highly conservative interpretation of Salafi thought, which is found largely in the Arabian Gulf region; (2) those traditionalists who follow one of the classical legal schools (madhhabs); and (3) those who follow the basic texts of Islam (Quran and sunna) but employ contextual interpretations, a category that includes a wide spectrum of leaders, some fairly liberal and a majority who adhere closely to the fairly conservative classical consensus of the great scholars (see table 1.5).

Thirty-nine percent of mosque leaders who favor a literal approach "strongly agree" that America is immoral, while that number was only 26 percent for leaders who favor the contextual approach (see table 1.6). Although the differences are not overwhelming, the more conservative mosques are more likely to be highly critical of American culture.

TABLE 1.5 ∘ "In Trying to Make Islamic Decisions, Which of the Following Do You Believe Is the Most Proper Approach?" (Percentage Giving Each Response)

Refer directly to the Quran and sunna and follow an interpretation that takes into account its purposes and modern circumstances	71%
Refer directly to the Quran and sunna and follow a literal interpretation	21
Follow the well-established views of a particular *madhhab* (legal school)	6
None of the above	2

TABLE 1.6 ∘ "America Is Immoral" by Islamic Approach (Percentage Agreeing/Disagreeing with Statement)

	Islamic Approach		
	Contextual	Literal	Madhhab
Strongly agree	26%	39%	13%
Somewhat agree	41	33	48
Somewhat disagree	29	16	39
Strongly disagree	5	13	0

Note: N = 390. Statistically significant at .004.

Leaders who follow a traditional *madhhab* are less likely to "strongly agree" that America is immoral. The *madhhabis* might be expected, like the conservative literalists, be more critical of American society. This finding seems to be an anomaly. Its resolution may lie in the fact that most U.S. *madhhabis* are either members of Tablighi Jamaat (a south Asia–based group dedicated to calling Muslims back to the practice of Islam) or, to a lesser extent, Sufis: both of those groups avoid harsh rhetoric against the societies in which they find themselves, focusing on the task of changing the hearts of their people rather than opposing perceived societal ills.

Mosque leaders who "strongly agree" that America is immoral are the only leaders more likely to reject participation in American society. This small group tends to advocate a more isolationist and rejectionist posture. Nevertheless, the responses to the question of America's immorality demonstrate clearly that the vast majority of America's mosque leaders are not opting for either isolation or assimilation.

The MIA study asked mosque leaders whether they agreed with the statement that "American society is hostile to Islam" (see table 1.7). A majority

TABLE 1.7 ∘ "American Society Is Hostile to Islam"
(Percentage Giving Each Response; "Don't Know" Excluded from Percentages)

Strongly agree	15%
Somewhat agree	41
Somewhat disagree	32
Strongly disagree	12

56 percent) believes that American society in general is hostile to Islam. Respondents comment on three components of that society: the American people, media, and government. Those who "strongly agree" that America is hostile believe that all components of American society are hostile. Mosque leaders who "somewhat agree" almost invariably argue that hostility is real but that the American people are good-hearted and reasonable. One leader explains his answer by saying, "I think if they are hostile, it is because of lack of information. They see negative images and think this way. If they knew us, they wouldn't believe that. It's not their fault." From this point of view, hostility exists but is not intrinsic—there is a hope and expectation that, with information and contact, the American people's hostility toward Islam will evaporate.

Those leaders who "somewhat disagree" that American society is hostile to Islam feel that the American people are not hostile to Islam. Some add that the media and government are not entirely hostile. One leader remarks, "You can't say all the media is bad. There's really an element that is against Islam, that promotes a bad picture of Islam." Those who "strongly disagree" feel that, overall, the American people, media, and government are not against Islam. One leader comments, "I don't think they are hostile to Islam. It is all national interest."

Unlike the immorality issue, this question elicits few differences among ethnic groups: African American and immigrant mosque leaders have virtually the same responses. The only significant differences occur among the HSAAM leaders, 30 percent of whom "strongly agree" that America is hostile, compared to only 8 percent for ASM mosques and 14 percent for immigrant mosques. One HSAAM leader remarks, "Those people know Islam—better than most of us. And they're scared to death to see Islam grow in America because they know that Islam is going to challenge their system."

When the responses to America's immorality and hostility to Islam are compared to attitudes toward involvement and political and community par-

TABLE 1.8 ∘ "Muslims Should Participate in the Political Process"
(Percentage Giving Each Response; "Don't Know" Excluded from Percentages)

Strongly agree	72%
Somewhat agree	17
Somewhat disagree	6
Strongly disagree	5

ticipation, a clear correlation can be seen between those who "strongly agree" that America is immoral/hostile and low levels of involvement and negative attitudes toward involvement. Greater alienation and tension are thus associated with a greater degree of isolation and rejection of involvement in America's public square. Only a small number (approximately 12 percent) of mosque leaders strongly agree that America is both immoral and hostile toward Islam, so the Muslim community at large does not exhibit a high degree of alienation. Rather, alienation is most typically found in mosques whose leaders are literalists or African Americans who do not belong to the ASM. This finding is borne out in other measures, to which we now turn.

The MIA study asked respondents if they agree or disagree with the statement that Muslims should participate in the political process (see table 1.8). Almost 90 percent of mosque leaders agree. America's Muslims want unequivocally to be political players. Isolationism and rejection of the U.S. system are not popular strategies among mosque leaders.

The primary motivation underlying mosque leaders' desire for political participation is the protection of Muslim rights and promotion of Muslim interests. One leader, Ahmad Kobeisy, argues for a paradigm of "interaction," which he describes as "the way of protecting the necessities without which Muslims cannot survive, let alone prosper. These necessities include: proper representation, protection of civil rights, protection of their Islamic identity, uplifting society from moral decay (drugs and violence), the elimination of prejudice and bias against Islam and Muslims, and, finally, the prevention and delay of the widely publicized and eminent conflict between Muslims and the West."[4]

In a *Boston Globe* article, a reporter describes a lecture encouraging Muslims to vote:

The Iraqi-born Muslim cleric paces across the university classroom, his green tunic and black cape sweeping across the floor, as, spicing his adopted English with phrases from his native Arabic, he urges the students to vote. How else can they persuade the U.S. government to reduce its support for Israel? To halt the alleged singling out of Muslims and Arab-Americans for interrogation at U.S. airports? To stop the use of secret evidence to justify the detention of suspected terrorists? "We should pursue our rights in a society we choose to live in," said Imam Hassan Qazwini. "If I keep myself excluded, I am not influencing anybody."[5]

This urgent need to protect Muslim civil rights, reduce prejudice against Muslims, and change American foreign policy drives Muslim involvement and best explains Muslims' tendency to be more politically active than other recent immigrant groups.

Another motivation for political action springs from a religious impulse found in the Quranic ideals of doing good (2:82), cooperating with others in righteousness (5:3), commanding good and forbidding evil (3:110), protecting the weak (107:2), feeding the poor (76:8–9), and standing up for justice (4:135). Javeed Akhter, a Muslim leader in Chicago, expresses this vision by saying that Muslims "must resist the understandable tendency towards self imposed isolation and avoid a retreat into the mosques and community centers. Moreover, if they isolate themselves, they will merely succeed in creating their own ghetto. They cannot ignore the problems around them, hoping to remain immune to them. Muslims must remember the Quranic injunctions to be a people of knowledge, compassion and patience, striving for positive change in the communities in which they live."[6]

Almost three out of four (72 percent) of all mosque leaders "strongly agree" that Muslims should participate in politics. Their comments echo the arguments given earlier. One African American leader offers an argument based on civic responsibility: "We're citizens. It doesn't make any sense for us to let other people make decisions for us." A few leaders reason that if they have to pay taxes, they should have some say about how the taxes are used.

Those mosque leaders who "somewhat agree" with Muslim participation in politics sound a cautionary note regarding the proper place of politics in Muslim life. One leader agrees with political involvement but thinks that Muslims should not invest much time and energy in it. Some leaders worry about usefulness: "Are we really going to get something out of it?" Many leaders, even those who strongly agree with political involvement, express concerns about the dirtiness of politics—involving their community in a game that seems to be about buying politicians and making deals with unsavory people.

Ethnicity (Percentage Agreeing/Disagreeing with Statement)

	Ethnicity of Mosque				
	African American	South Asian	Arab	South Asian and Arab	All Others
Strongly agree	66%	76%	82%	68%	71%
Somewhat agree	11	19	16	19	20
Somewhat disagree	10	4	0	10	7
Strongly disagree	13	1	2	3	2

Note: N = 410.

Those who "somewhat" and "strongly disagree" object to political involvement based on the strong feeling that politics corrupts while religion is pure. Their arguments will be discussed later in the chapter.

Parsing the responses based on the ethnicity of mosques, virtually all the ethnic groups agree with political involvement, but a significant minority of African American mosque leaders objects (see table 1.9). As in the question of America's immorality and hostility to Islam, a substantial portion of African American mosque leaders do not hold a positive view of America. Twenty-three percent of African American leaders disagree with the proposition that Muslims should participate in the political process.

Looking more closely at the African American Muslim community, the ASM mosques are strongly committed to political participation—90 percent strongly agree, compared to 74 percent of immigrant mosque leaders (see table 1.10). The HSAAM mosque leaders are much more evenly divided on this issue—59 percent agree and 41 percent disagree with political participation.

The HSAAMs have been greatly influenced by the Black Power movement of the 1960s and deeply distrust politics and politicians. Most of their leaders became Muslims in the 1960s and 1970s. Many believe that the U.S. political system is oppressive, suppressing poor and black people and hating Islam for opposing the ruthlessness of American politics. One leader comments apocalyptically, "We live in the belly of the beast." From this point of view, politics has won little for poor people and certainly have not abated the plight of African Americans. These leaders believe that political involvement represents compromise and thus corrupts one's religious principles and human dignity. The theological objections to participating in a kafir (disbelieving) system have more resonance in these communities. As one African American imam writes,

TABLE 1.10 ∘ "Muslims Should Participate in the Political Process," by African American Mosques (Percentage Agreeing/Disagreeing with Statement)

	American Muslim Society	Historically Sunni Mosques	Immigrant Mosques
Strongly agree	90%	37%	74%
Somewhat agree	3	22	19
Somewhat disagree	4	17	5
Strongly disagree	3	24	2

Note: N = 409 African American mosques, 114 immigrant mosques, and 295 historically Sunni mosques. Statistically significant at .000.

The political parties in America are "secular" and have no interest in any religious views whatsoever, not to mention the Islamic ones. Their agendas are mainly "unfriendly" to Muslims by admission of their leaders on daily basis on T.V. every day. . . . In politics the rule is very clear, "you scratch my back and I will scratch yours!" The question is how far those "Muslim" leaders are willing to "scratch the backs of the secular agendas" and weaken their faith by engaging in such un-Islamic behavior before they get something out of it?[7]

Most of these African American leaders, however, do not engage in public polemics against participation. The imams of the National Umma, led by Imam Jamil, follow his example in refusing to be involved in politics but not condemning those who do.

In its earlier manifestation as the Nation of Islam, the ASM also shared in the militancy of the 1960s and, like Imam Jamil Al-Amin, helped shape it. But under the leadership of Imam W. Deen Mohammed, the ASM has dropped its anti-American rhetoric. This is one of a few Muslim groups that has appropriated some of America's patriotic symbolism, displaying the U.S. flag and celebrating July 4, for example. Imam Mohammed does not deny the ongoing problems of racism and classism in America, but he now advocates unqualified involvement by Muslims in the American political and social system as the only solution to these problems.

Mosque leaders' Islamic approach also affects their views on political participation (see table 1.11). The majority of mosque leaders, regardless of their approach to interpreting texts, favor political participation. The largest opposition to political participation, however, is found in the mosques that

TABLE 1.11 ∘ "Muslims Should Participate in the Political Process," by Islamic Approach (Percentage Agreeing/Disagreeing with Statement)

	Islamic Approach		
	Contextual	Literal	Madhhab
Strongly agree	79%	60%	46%
Somewhat agree	14	18	38
Somewhat disagree	2	18	8
Strongly disagree	5	4	8

Note: N = 398. Statistically significant at .000.

follow a literal interpretation and those mosques that follow a madhhab—22 percent of literalists and 16 percent of madhhabis oppose political participation, compared to just 7 percent for contextualists.

The three groups, largely immigrant, that oppose political participation are the various Salafi groups, Hizb al-Tahrir, and the Tablighi Jamaat. The Salafi and Tahriri groups object to political involvement on the theory that the American system is a kafir system. Political participation in the system, therefore, is tantamount to supporting it, and God forbids the support of kufr (disbelief) and zulm (oppression). A flyer entitled "Register to Vote . . . Register to Commit Haram!" distributed by Hizb al-Tahrir, states,

> Whether it is in the Muslim World or the West, the systems implemented upon the people now are Kufr systems based in beliefs other that Islam. It is beyond argument that the constitution of the U.S.A. and the laws and systems emanating from it which are being implemented here are not Islamic. The rulers have no other role except to implement these man-made laws i.e. the rulings of kufr. In no uncertain terms Allah forbids that in the Quran. . . . The verses condemn those who rule with anything other than what Allah has revealed regardless of their sincerity, piety, intentions or objectives.[8]

Unlike the African American groups that withdraw from politics in stony silence, the Salafi and Tahriri are vocal in their opposition. Both energetically distribute literature and both will publicly challenge, especially in the mosque, expressions of support for political participation. The influence of their rejectionist views, therefore, extends well beyond the few mosques that they control. The Hizb al-Tahrir is revolutionary in that it envisions the overthrow of current Muslim regimes, but most Salafi groups have no real political agenda. Their priority is the purification of the faith. The Tablighi Jamaat does not argue against political participation but simply ignores the issue, which it sees as irrelevant to its agenda of encouraging Muslims fully to practice Islam.

Resistance to political involvement, like the strong sentiments against America's immorality, is found in only a small minority (11 percent) of mosque leaders—for the most part, African American leaders of HSAAM mosques and mosque leaders who follow a literal interpretation of Islamic texts.

Although mosque leaders and Muslims overwhelmingly support political participation, trepidation and disquiet nonetheless exist. Most mosque leaders are motivated not primarily by a wholehearted commitment to and belief in the American political system (patriotism is not the guiding motivation) but rather by the necessity of protecting Muslim rights and promoting Muslim interests. One of the most respected Muslim thinkers in North America, Jamal Badawi, argues in favor of political participation as a means of bringing benefit and removing harm: "Electing or voting for someone who will do less harm to Muslims obviously would be much better than sitting on the sidelines and just criticizing both and doing nothing about it."[9]

There is also concern that involvement not compromise essential Islamic beliefs and practices. Badawi reflects on this worry: "There is a fear also that you get into a process of gradual concessions after concessions and compromises. Well, to compromise on something in terms of benefit or something which is not very essential might be understandable, but the fear here is to keep pushing, making compromises that really Muslims should draw a line [on]."[10] Kobeisy also indicates that there is an outer limit that cannot be crossed. "We must be cautious not to knowingly or otherwise approve of any behavior unacceptable to Islam or lifestyles such as freedom of adultery, homosexuality, same sex marriages, etc."[11]

Most mosque leaders, therefore, approach the political system not to give reverence to it but to protect their rights and use it to promote policies that reflect their values and interests. The symbols of patriotism, especially the flag, have an honored place in few U.S. mosques. July 4 is a holiday in most Muslim organizations, but little celebration takes place. The tension between Muslims and the American system regarding moral values and policy issues remains real. Especially in the area of foreign policy, Muslims are upset with America's strong support of Israel, war in Iraq, backing of corrupt regimes in the Middle East, and neglect of Kashmir and Chechnya. Muslims also have a pervading sense that politicians are corrupt, which emanates from the disillusionment of the 1960s among African Americans and immigrants' disdain for the autocratic regimes of their homelands. At this point in history, therefore, most mosque leaders in America seem to be seeking a middle ground, rejecting isolation and endorsing political participation while fearing compromise and feeling uneasy about fully legitimating the state. Mosque leaders, in short, want to be insulated in their political involvement from compromising their faith and acquiescing to bad foreign policy.

Although most mosque leaders seek a middle ground regarding legitimation of the state, the Muslim community is in flux, especially after 9/11. Using the paradigm suggested by James Hunter's contribution to this book, immigrant groups in the past have traversed four stages in their relationship to the mainstream society: introduction, recognition, negotiation, and establishment. Introduction is a quiet phase, when the immigrant group is largely invisible. The recognition phase constitutes a time when the religious group enters the periphery of public awareness and starts making public claims that are often met with initial hostility. The negotiation phase is a tumultuous time when the religious group struggles with the larger society for acceptance and both sides consequently reconfigure their boundaries and perceptions of one another. The establishment period is when the religious group is accepted as a full member and partner in American society.

The crucial phase of negotiation, as described by Armand Mauss in his study of Mormon assimilation, comes when the mainstream society attempts to domesticate the minority religious group.[12] Domestication can include the religious group's abandonment of its most threatening characteristics and its acceptance of the underpinning ideas of a civil society in America. For full political participation, mainstream society typically requires the legitimation of the state, including an embrace of patriotic symbolism and rhetoric. The minority group, conversely, desires to see the religious and political establishment modify its boundaries to include the minority group in its vision of the American mainstream. The religious group seeks to maintain its unique identity while claiming a seat at the table. In this phase, the boundaries of both are redrawn.

In the 1990s, Muslims entered this negotiation phase. The formation of national public advocacy groups such as the American Muslim Council (1990), the Council on American-Islamic Relations (1994), the American Muslim Alliance (1994), and the Muslim Public Affairs Council (1988), catalyzed the situation, with these groups fighting discrimination, encouraging Muslim participation in politics, and demanding Muslims' full acceptance into "Abrahamic" America. In this phase, Muslims advanced numerous ideas that argue both for Muslims' acceptance into the mainstream and for Muslim legitimation of the state. And Muslims have taken many actions that embody their commitment to full membership in American society. The overall impression is that the Muslim community is inextricably moving toward drawing the sacred canopy over America and that this movement toward legitimating the state has been accelerated by the 9/11 tragedy.

The most common argument for the inclusion of Muslims in the American mainstream also serves as an important initial step toward legitimizing the United States. The argument is simply that Muslims are in fact Americans, are already acting as full members of this society. Ibrahim Sidicki, a college student, says, "I try to tell them that the overwhelming majority of Muslims living in the United States are Americans and America is now their country."[13] Another student says, "We are part of this country. We feel proud of our American Islamic identity. We want to be part of the mosaic. We don't consider ourselves as belonging to the Middle East or to South Asia. Our roots may be there, but our present and future are here."[14]

Another widespread argument is that "America is the best place to practice Islam."[15] Muslim countries are repressive and corrupt; from this point of view, therefore, America is more "Islamic." A related claim is that America contains much that is good, and Muslims as citizens should celebrate the good and try to change the bad. Javeed Akhter, a Muslim leader in Chicago, says, "There is much good in our country which is good and exemplary and needs to be preserved. However, there is also much which needs to be altered and improved upon."[16]

Two other arguments would give full legitimation to the state. One, championed by Imam W. Deen Mohammed, is that America's founding documents are based on Islam and are, therefore, Islamic documents. Imam Fahim Shuaib, one of the AS M's leading imams, stated that the "real American values are Islamic values." He then read the preamble of the Declaration of Independence and remarked, "This is Islam."[17] Since 9/11, Muslim organizations increasingly are advancing this same claim. The Muslim Public Affairs Council's "Statement on the Role of Muslims in American Citizenry" affirmed, "American Muslims should find no contradiction between Islamic values and the American tradition of liberty and democracy enshrined in the Constitution."[18]

The other argument, propounded by Muslim intellectual Robert Crane, is that Islam is more in line with the Founding Fathers' vision than are its present-day secular interpreters. If Muslims join forces with other like-minded traditionalists, Crane believes, America can be saved from those who would subvert its spiritual foundations: "To be the best Muslim is to be a good American, and to be the best American is to be Islamic. This should be the identity of American Muslims. The destiny of Muslims in America is to work with like-minded traditionalists of America's other religions in a common strategy to bring peace through justice both at home and abroad, because this is the will of God."[19] Such thinking, similar to that of fundamentalist Christians who claim ancestors among the nation's founders while decrying today's politics and culture, would make the Islamic and American identities inseparable.

Many Muslim leaders also argue that Islam is compatible with the civic ideal of pluralism. Mohamed Fathi Osman declares, "The Muslims have the moral and legal principles of pluralism available in their religious sources and heritage."[20]

Pluralism can be defined as "the co-existence with a measure of civic peace of different groups in one society."[21] In other words, pluralism demands mutual tolerance and respect. Muzammil Siddiqi states that pluralism is manifest when four principles are recognized: "The dignity of all human beings. The basic equality of all human beings. Universal human rights. Fundamental freedom of thought, conscience and belief. Islam recognizes these principles and encourages Muslims to struggle for them."[22]

Peter Berger's pluralism does not demand that one relativize one's truth claims. A person in a pluralist society does not have to accede that his or her truth is of equal value as other truths. (Democrats and Republicans certainly do not go that far.) Muslim advocates of political participation are adamant about holding fast to that truth. As Siddiqi says, "Islam does not consider all viewpoints correct or of equal value, but does recognize that differences of opinion can be a sign of Allah's mercy."[23]

Various Muslim groups have demonstrated their commitment to political involvement and their willingness to give a degree of legitimation to the state. Muslim leaders have offered opening prayers in both chambers of the Congress and most state legislatures, and Muslim chaplains have been inducted into all branches of the armed forces. Since the early 1990s, Muslim organizations have conducted major voter registration drives, endorsing political candidates along the way. In the 2000 presidential election, many Muslim leaders and groups endorsed George W. Bush, and U.S. Muslims listened, voting overwhelmingly for the Republican candidate. In 2004, Muslims went the other way, again in overwhelming numbers, casting their votes for John Kerry (and against the Patriot Act and U.S. interventions overseas). The Muslim community is plainly the most politically active of the recent immigrant groups.

The 9/11 terrorist attack gave greater impetus to Muslims who stress political involvement and embrace an American Muslim identity. The revulsion at the hate-filled militancy of al-Qaeda has led some prominent Muslims to call on their coreligionists to drop their politics of the Other. Muqtedar Khan writes in "A Memo to American Muslim Leadership," "Muslims love to live in the U.S. but also love to hate it. . . . As an Indian Muslim, I know for sure that no where on Earth, including India, will I get the same sense of dignity and respect that I have received in the U.S. . . . It is time that we acknowledge that the freedoms we enjoy in the U.S. are more desirable to us than superficial solidarity with the Muslim world."[24] Another prominent Muslim leader, Hamza Yusuf, has announced that he will drop any strident criticism of America and will focus more on a message of love and conciliation. At the 2002 Annual Convention of the Islamic Society of North America, which was attended by thirty thousand Muslims, American flags were prominently displayed on the platform for the first time in the organization's history. During a commemoration of the first anniversary of 9/11 in Toledo, Ohio, a young Muslim girl wearing the hijab (head scarf) sang the national anthem. There is a real possibility that 9/11 will come to be seen as a turning point in the Muslim community, as the proponents of political participation overcome the misgivings of many Muslims and the objections of the vocal minority. Increased scrutiny may spur the community to greater accommodation with the mainstream.

Muslims' involvement in politics and engagement in the noisy process of negotiating their rightful place in America are bringing into being an American Muslim community at home with the patriotic symbols and myths of other Americans. Commitment to political involvement has necessarily entailed both accepting an American identity and engaging in certain public acts of loyalty to American society. Stepping onto the political playing field requires one to play as a loyal U.S. citizen. Such acts of engagement entail crossing the Rubicon of accommodating an American identity and appropriating the ideals of American civic piety. The tension between American society and the Muslim community and the mission to relieve that tension is propelling Muslims to become involved, and that involvement is pushing the Muslim community into the American mainstream. The opportunity to affect change outside the Muslim community is leading to change inside the Muslim community. It seems inevitable, therefore, that mosque leaders will eventually come to embrace fully the American ideals of democracy and to accommodate a form of patriotism colored and defined by Islamic ideals.

Yet a palpable fear of the contamination of pluralism and the slippery slope of compromise abides, making Muslims either cautious regarding or contemptuous of political involvement. The conjunction of both the fear of loss of identity and the impulse to be involved explains the metaphor of insulation— Muslims want to be involved, but they also want to be protected from the possible harmful effects of involvement. The challenge, however, of maintaining one's faith is the same challenge that all believers face. As Berger stated, the challenge is to "hold convictions without either dissolving them in utter relativity or encasing them in the false absolutes of fanaticism. It is a difficult challenge, but it is not an impossible one."[25] The Muslim community seems poised to accept that challenge.

NOTES

1. Peter L. Berger, *The Sacred Canopy: Elements of a Sociological Theory of Religion* (New York: Doubleday, 1967), 32.

2. Peter L. Berger, *A Far Glory: The Quest for Faith in an Age of Credulity* (New York: Free Press, 1992).

3. The MIA study was conducted in conjunction with Hartford Seminary's Faith Communities Today study, which brought together virtually all American denominations and faith groups to devise a common questionnaire and then administer it to leaders of their congregations. The MIA study first identified all the mosques in the United States. Of the 1,209 mosques discovered, 631 were randomly sampled for the study. Telephone interviews were conducted from March to September 2000, with 416 leaders responding (a completion rate of 66 percent). The results have a margin of error of ±5 percent. See Ihsan Bagby, Paul M. Perl, and Bryan T. Froehle, *The Mosque in America: A National Portrait* (Washington, D.C.: Council on American-Islamic Relations, 2001).

4. Ahmad N. Kobeisy, "Interaction between Islamic Communities and Their Non-Muslim Neighbors in Syracuse, USA: A Model for the Nation," in *Islam in America: Images and Challenges*, edited by Phylis Lan Lin (Indianapolis: University of Indianapolis Press, 1998), 76.

5. Michael Paulson, "Muslims Eye Role at U.S. Polls," *Boston Globe*, October 23, 2000, A1.

6. Asad Husain, John Woods, and Javeed Akhter, *Muslims in America: Opportunities and Challenges* (Chicago: International Strategy and Policy Institute, 1996), 81.

7. "Can They Ever Win in Politics?" *Unity/al-Wahda: Newsletter of Masjid Darus Salaam*, November–December 2000, 1.

8. *Register to Vote . . . Register to Commit Haram!* (Walnut, Calif.: Khalifornia, [1999?]). *Haram* means "forbidden" or "prohibited."

9. Jamal Badawi, "Muslim Participation in North American Politics: An Interview

with Jamal Badawi," Radio Islam, September 22, 2000, <http://www.radioislam.com/publicaffairs/publicaffairs.asp>.

10. Ibid.

11. Kobeisy, "Interaction," 77.

12. Armand L. Mauss, *The Angel and the Beehive: The Mormon Struggle with Assimilation* (Urbana: University of Illinois Press, 1994), 4.

13. Richard Wormser, *American Islam* (New York: Walker, 1994), 51.

14. Ibid., 122.

15. Ibid., 54.

16. Husain, Woods, and Akhter, *Muslims in America*, 89.

17. Fahim Shuaib, untitled speech given at conference on Islam in America: Rights and Citizenship in a Post-9/11 World, Berkeley, Calif., September 18, 2002.

18. Muslim Public Affairs Council, "Statement on the Role of Muslims in the American Citizenry," <http://www.mpac.org/NEWS/newsitemdisplay.asp?ID=240&ITEMTYPE=NEWS>.

19. Robert D. Crane, *Shaping the Future: Challenge and Response* (Acton, Mass.: Tapestry, 1997), xix.

20. Mohamed Fathi Osman, *The Children of Adam: American Islamic Perspectives on Pluralism* (Washington, D.C.: Center for Muslim-Christian Understanding, 1996), 42.

21. Berger, *Far Glory*, 37.

22. Muzammil Siddiqi, "Religions Have Unity in Diversity," *Islamic Horizons* 30.5 (September–October 2001): 33.

23. Ibid., 30.

24. Muqtedar Khan, "A Memo to American Muslim Leadership," *Muslim Observer*, October 2001, 21.

25. Berger, *Far Glory*, 46.

2

Progressive Islam in America

The catastrophic events of 9/11 catapulted Muslims and Islam into American public consciousness. Muslims previously entered the spotlight almost always in response to Middle Eastern political events such as the Iranian hostage crisis, the first Gulf war, the rise of the Taliban, and the ongoing Palestine/Israel tragedy. However, the fact that the devastation of 9/11 took place on American soil has resulted in a multiyear gaze at Muslims. This phenomenon is new and has radical consequences for all Muslims, including those with commitments to global justice and gender equality who are the main concern of this essay.

The initial wave of American responses to 9/11 quite naturally focused on the parties responsible for that atrocity. Never before has a U.S. president so immediately and urgently pleaded with all Americans and all Muslims to realize that the "face of terrorism is not the true faith of Islam. That's not what Islam is all about. Islam is peace. These terrorists don't represent peace, they represent evil and war. When we think of Islam, we think of a faith that brings comfort to a billion people around the world."[1] Whatever many Muslims, including this author, may think of the actions that the Bush administration has taken in Afghanistan and Iraq, it has to be acknowledged that the president's remarks in the immediate aftermath of 9/11 were historic and probably helped stem the tide of violence against Muslims in America. These closely watched and often reported remarks represent a direct attempt to engage Islam as a public American religion, and the fact that this intervention took place in the midst of our greatest national crisis in two generations only makes it more significant.

Subsequent months and years have seen attempts to seek out and identify a wider range of Muslim voices, both in the United States and in places such as Iraq, Afghanistan, Israel, and the Palestinian Authority. Foremost among these attempts have been efforts to amplify Muslim voices that represent an alternate vision of Islam to the understanding of those responsible for 9/11. This search for "moderate" and "tolerant" Muslims—I do not find either qualifier helpful[2]—has come from the highest ranks of the U.S. government.[3] Given this vicious attack, many observers have expected these missing Muslims to offer not only a total dismissal of the perspective represented by al-Qaeda but also a wholehearted identification with American national ideals and policies. But this hope has been frustrated as more and more Muslims have sought to occupy that contested space in which one assumes a critical stance vis-à-vis both Muslim extremists and certain U.S. policies. I propose that much of the confusion among casual observers of Islam in America (and many journalists) can be traced to a doomed effort to collapse the distinctions between liberal Islam and progressive Islam, distinctions that are vital for both the American Muslim community and scholars of Islam.

The various understandings of Islam that fall under the "progressive" rubric both continue and depart from the 150-year-old tradition of liberal Islam.[4] Advocates of liberal Islam have generally displayed an uncritical, almost devotional, identification with modernity and have often sidestepped the issues of colonialism and imperialism. Progressive understandings of Islam, conversely, almost uniformly criticize colonialism both in its nineteenth-century manifestations and in its current varieties. Progressive Muslims also advance unapologetically a "multiple critique" with respect to both Islam and modernity. That double engagement, plus an emphasis on concrete social action and transformation, is the defining characteristic of progressive Islam today. Unlike their liberal Muslim forefathers (and they usually were forefathers), progressive Muslims represent a broad coalition of female and male Muslim activists who aim not to develop new and beatific theologies but to effect change in Muslim and non-Muslim societies.

Progressive Muslims adhere to a number of commitments: striving to realize a just and pluralistic society through critically engaging Islam, pursuing social justice, emphasizing gender equality as a human right, affirming religious and ethnic pluralism, and acting via nonviolent resistance.[5] I will come back to a fuller discussion of these broad commitments at the end of this essay.

It would be a mistake to somehow reduce the emergence of progressive Islam to a new "American Islam." Progressive Muslims are found everywhere in the global Muslim umma. When it comes to implementing a progressive understanding of Islam in Muslim communities, groups in Iran, Malaysia, and South Africa lead the United States. Many American Muslim communities —and much of the leadership represented in groups such as the Islamic Circle of North America,[6] the Islamic Society of North America,[7] and the Council on

American-Islamic Relations[8]—are far too uncritical of Salafi and Wahhabi tendencies that progressives oppose.

Wahhabism is by now a well known, puritanical reading of Islam that originated in eighteenth-century Saudi Arabia. Despite their exclusivist ideology and theology, Wahhabis worked closely with the British and since the 1930s have cooperated with American administrations.[9] Not until the discovery of oil in Saudi Arabia did Wahhabism obtain the financial backing necessary to import its evangelistic mission all over the world, including to the United States.

Lesser known is the Salafi movement, an important school of Islamic revivalism. Salafis espouse a "return" to the ways of the first few generations of Muslims, called al-salaf al-saleh (the pious forefathers). Central to their methodology is renewed attention to the Quran and the sunna of the Prophet Muhammad. It is a mistake (though a common one) to describe as Wahhabi American Muslim organizations such as the Islamic Society of North America and the Islamic Council of North America, although it is quite proper to think of them as Salafi groups. Shiite and Sufi interpretations of Islam are largely absent from these organizations, whose conservative approach to gender also reflects a Salafi bent. Many Muslim progressives define themselves in opposition to both Wahhabism and Salafism.

Finally, one other element that sets almost all progressive Muslims apart from mainstream American Muslim organizations has been their profound skepticism toward nationalism in its many forms. As such, they reject the co-optation of this global movement by those who seek to commodify it into an "American Islam" for worldwide export. The progressives' critique of neo-colonialism also represents an effort to avoid their co-optation by the U.S. administration, which has used the language of reforming Islam to justify its invasion of Iraq. ("We need an Islamic reformation," opined Paul Wolfowitz, "and I think there is real hope for one.")[10] For many progressives, this sort of appropriation of the rhetoric of Islamic reform (to say nothing of the pronoun "we") is deeply problematic. Is a reformation of Islam in U.S. interests? What if such a reformation called into question many U.S. policies as well as the wealth and privilege currently enjoyed by so many Americans?

Although progressive Islam is a global movement, one must acknowledge that the North American context has provided fertile ground for its blossoming. Conversations about progressive Islam begin by refusing to admit the absolute distinction between the religious and political domains, and many of the issues that Muslim progressives debate intensely—human rights, state attempts to legislate sexuality and the body, distribution of wealth and resources, democracy—have explicit political ramifications. Many participants in this young movement have found a more hospitable environment in the North America than in Muslim-majority areas. Indeed, a few contributors to a pioneering collection called *Progressive Muslims* (2003), which I edited, have faced harassment and persecution, even bombings, in countries ranging from Malaysia to South Africa. Even the contested world of post-9/11 America and the Patriot Act offers great possibilities for conducting public conversations about matters of religion and politics. In preparing *Progressive Muslims*, participants exchanged some six hundred e-mails and spent countless hours on the phone. It would be hard to imagine those critical conversations taking place freely and openly in many Muslim countries.

One also has to acknowledge the significance of North American educational establishments. Every contributor to that particular conversation has some connection to the North American academy. All have received training in western universities, are currently employed by them, or have published with western presses. Again, one cannot underestimate the importance of financial and institutional support for providing a space in which these conversations can flourish.

The crisis of contemporary Islam is inseparable from the struggle over defining Islam and questions of religious authority. This struggle, of course, has antecedents in other religious and civic traditions in America. At one level, it evokes the "culture wars" model introduced by James Davison Hunter, who talked about the tensions between "orthodox" and "progressive" elements in American religions.[11] The question of authority in Islam is today and has always been contested. Islam has no formal church structure, so religious authority is fluid. However, the lack of a formal structure of authority does not mean that no religious authority exists. Competing groups claim authority for themselves by appealing to religious language and symbols. Our concern here, particularly for the case of American Islam, is examining the basis on which religious authority is claimed and exercised.

Throughout Islamic history, various communities have claimed religious authority. Foremost among them have been the religious scholars ('ulama) and the mystics (Sufis) of Islam. Both groups have representatives in America. Mystics historically have claimed considerable religious authority in Muslim societies.[12] Many North American Muslims, steeped in a modernist, rationalist, and anti-mystical Salafi understanding that in many ways does not reflect the wide historical spectrum of Islamic thought, do not adequately appreciate this point. North America has no shortage of Sufi leaders, of course, and many turuq (Sufi lineages) such as the Mevlevis, Sufi Order International, Ni'matullahi, Naqshbandi, Rifa'i-Ma'rufi, and others have a prominent presence in the wider Muslim and American society here. However, Sufism is a contested category, and many in the Muslim community whose views have been shaped by a Salafi understanding of Islam view Sufis with skepticism.[13] Furthermore, mainstream U.S. Muslim organizations assiduously avoid even mentioning Sufism. Wahhabi-influenced publishing houses based in America have deleted references to mystical understandings of Islam from translations of the Quran (such as the classic work of Abdullah Yusuf Ali). What remains is a situation in which those who are inclined to Sufism turn to their Sufi teachers, while the majority of North American Muslims look elsewhere for leadership.

The majority of the North American Muslim community has turned not to Sufis but to scholars: the 'ulama. To understand the 'ulama, one has to consider both the form of religious knowledge one claims and from whence that religious knowledge is obtained. By and large, no credible institutions of higher Islamic education exist in America.[14] There are, of course, secular American universities in which many have obtained expertise in various aspects of Islamic thought, history, and practice. Yet given the secular nature of these institutions, it is unusual for the wider American Muslim community to receive graduates as members of the traditional 'ulama class (unless these scholars have received parallel training in Muslim madrassas). The American Muslim community may rely on these individuals to act as spokespersons (particularly with the media and to represent Islam at interfaith gatherings), yet many community members view these scholars with skepticism.

The vision of Islam espoused by many North American academics is a more liberal, inclusive, humanistic, and even secular[15] interpretation of Islam, and it is highly skeptical of Islamist political discourse. This skepticism reveals much about the presuppositions of many American Muslims regarding the "purity" of Islamic knowledge and its potential "contamination" by western training. But such a compartmentalized view of knowledge contradicts both medieval philosophical notions and contemporary rigorous interpretations of Islam. A ninth-century philosopher, al-Kindi, stated, "We should not be ashamed to acknowledge truth and to assimilate it from whatever source it comes to us, even if it is brought to us by former generations and foreign peoples. For him who seeks the truth there is nothing of higher value than truth itself; it never cheapens or abases him who reaches for it, but ennobles and honors him."[16] This epistemological pluralism is also echoed in the works of contemporary Muslim philosophers such as well-known Iranian thinker Abd al-Karim Soroush, who states,

> I believe that truths everywhere are compatible; no truth clashes with any other truth. They are all but the inhabitants of the same mansions and stars of the same constellation. One truth in one corner of the world has to be harmonious and compatible with all truths elsewhere, or else it is not a truth. . . . This truthfulness of the world is a blessing indeed, because it instigates constant search and engenders a healthy pluralism. . . . Thus, in my search for the truth, I became oblivious to whether an idea originated in the East, or West, or whether it had ancient or modern origins.[17]

One of the particular contributions of progressive Muslims in the North American context has been to point out the need among Muslims for greater epistemological pluralism—an openness to pursuing wisdom, truth, and beauty in a wide range of religious, philosophical, aesthetic, and scientific discourses as well as to pursuing a fuller spectrum of Islamic sources including but not limited to "Quran and sunna" (the mantra of Salafi Islam).

Yet another source of authority in North American Islam is the imam (prayer leader), often imported from one of the various Muslim countries. All too often, the origin of the imported imam reflects the ethnicity of the community (or at least those with positions of power in it). South Asian Muslims look first to Pakistani imams, Iranians to Iranian Shiite imams, Arab Muslims to Egyptian and Saudi imams, and so forth. A host of problems arise with this approach. First, one has to deal honestly and openly with the fact that traditional madrassa institutions in the Islamic world no longer offer the highest level of critical thought. Whereas these institutions once attracted the community's brightest minds, today they are often a refuge for those who have been unable to achieve admission to more lucrative medicine, engineering, and computer science programs. This is not meant as an indictment of all those who enroll in madrassas, of course, and western media have made far too much recently about madrassas as havens for terrorism. Furthermore, the U.S. has many compassionate and pluralistic imams who for decades have led wonderful interfaith discussions. Still, many graduates of these traditional educational systems are entirely unprepared to deal with American pluralism or to undertake serious interfaith conversations with Jews, Christians, Hindus, and Buddhists. Discussions that pass for "comparative religion" in many parts of the Muslim world are in reality no more than superficial polemics against other traditions.

That leaves American Muslims, particularly those inclined to progressive Islam, in a bind regarding religious authority. The solution for many Muslims has been a more democratic or even Protestant approach whereby any person who undertakes a serious study of Islam has the authority to interpret the tradition. This approach appeals to many American Muslims. It has given many contemporary Muslims in America—scholars such as Amina Wadud[18] and Ebrahim Moosa and writers such as Michael Wolfe,[19] Asma Gull Hasan,[20] and Hamza Yusuf[21]—a voice in rethinking Islam today.

Other, more controversial thinkers have drawn on postcolonialism and postmodernism to resist and indeed undermine appeals to "orthodoxy" and "tradition." In the postcolonial model, which Edward Said has described as placing oneself among the impure, mixed, and heterodox,[22] one begins by pulling the rug out from under the custodians of orthodoxy. If one does not identify as "orthodox," then it is difficult for orthodoxy's guardians to accuse you of heterodoxy. Yet one has to wonder how many ordinary believers will be attracted to such intellectual mischievousness.

None of these approaches lacks problems, of course, and American Muslims need to work out these difficulties. For example, every community needs some structure and some system of authority (even if that authority is diffused among community members). This tendency toward the diffusion of authority in North American Islam was nicely summarized by Hamza Yusuf, who noted that nowadays, "every Tom, Dick, and Abdullah gives fatwas."[23] This decentralization of authority was particularly problematic after 9/11, when American Muslims had to come to terms with the atrocious actions of al-Qaeda terrorists.

It is not an exaggeration to state that 9/11 represents one of the greatest challenges to the status of Muslims in America since the transatlantic slave trade. The instructions to the nineteen terrorists were steeped in the Quran, including what Quranic verses and prayers should be recited at each step of the process.[24] It is easy to make too much of this fact, given that some of the hijackers, including Muhammad Atta, were not particularly observant, as evidenced by their frequenting of bars. Nonetheless, it is clear that, at a minimum, 9/11's masterminds attempted to legitimize their terror by appealing to Islamic symbols and language. Faced with this uncomfortable fact, American Muslims have responded in three ways.

According to the first perspective, the atrocities of 9/11 were not committed by Muslims. They were part of an elaborate plot by the U.S. Central Intelligence Agency or Israel's Mossad to discredit and defame Muslims and pave the way for a brutal attack on Muslim lands.[25] This position of denial was quite popular early on in the Muslim world and spread rapidly throughout the American Muslim community, particularly via the Internet. It represents a goodwilled if naive assumption that no Muslim could be involved in such a hideous act. Yet sticking one's head in the sand will not do here. Muslims committed these actions, and these actions were justified based on a reading (however selective and perverse) of Islam. Sadly, this approach also illustrates how conspiracy theories and anti-Semitism continue to fuel Muslim paranoia.

When the evidence proved that the actions of 9/11 were indeed committed by Muslims, the next approach was to "save Islam" by declaring al-Qaeda beyond the pale.[26] In the face of post-9/11 attacks on Muslims, Arabs, south Asians, and others (even non-Muslims such as Sikhs), this was a reasonable defensive posture. What is ironic here is that supporters of this approach implicitly excommunicated members of their own Muslim community: "These people are not us!" This process of declaring another an infidel is becoming increasingly popular across the Muslim world and is typically thought to fester among fundamentalists. But many self-identifying liberal Muslims in the United States, some of whom have themselves been charged with infidelity (kufr), are now using the same weapon against the al-Qaeda terrorists.

The third option is likely the most difficult for American Muslims, yet in the end it may prove to be the most intellectually and spiritually fruitful: acknowledging that there is a spectrum of interpretations of Islam, including some that attempt to justify violence via Islamic symbols. This situation is not unique to Islam, of course. Both the Reverend Martin Luther King Jr. and the Ku Klux Klan justified themselves on Christian grounds. All the major religious traditions are malleable enough to allow interpreters to justify both violence and nonviolence. It is not my intention to assert that the KKK and King possess equally valid interpretations of Christianity. Most observers would agree that the KKK's hatred and racism go against the teachings of Christ, yet one has to recognize that Klan leaders routinely justify their doctrines by quoting from the Bible. The case of al-Qaeda is no different.

Many scholars of Islam have pointed out that the modus operandi of the al-Qaeda terrorists violated basic foundational principles of sharia (Islamic law).[27] Under sharia, certain guidelines must be followed in undertaking a war. Civilians cannot be targeted. Women, children, the elderly, and those "who would not fight" cannot be targeted. A well-known hadith of the Prophet Muhammad recalls him expressing sadness and grief after finding a woman slain in war. "She was not one who would have fought," he observed, intimating that she should not have been killed.[28] The victims of 9/11 were civilians, including many women. Even if one grants al-Qaeda's claim to be at war with America, such actions violate basic principles of Islamic law.

After acknowledging that the tactics and aims of al-Qaeda violate Islamic principles, one is still faced with the responsibility of contesting the group's discourse and offering viable alternatives. In this approach, one is not simply attributing the events to Mossad or the Central Intelligence Agency, nor is one excommunicating the perpetrators. The only viable progressive response to the tragedy of 9/11 begins when we human beings who are Muslim assume responsibility for the actions of the terrorists. We must acknowledge that they have vented their anger and resentment at a civilian target and that they have sought to justify their actions through Islamic rhetoric. One must then contest that rhetoric by showing how inconsistent it is with Islamic thought and practice.

But rather than remaining at the level of theoretical disputations, progressive Muslims are committed to altering communities and existing social realities. Here there are a number of possibilities. To begin, one can target the Wahhabi ideology of xenophobia and exclusivism responsible for cultivating al-Qaeda's vision.[29] One can then offer an alternate vision that is simultaneously rooted in the foundational sources of Islam and engaged with the ongoing intellectual, aesthetic, political, and social developments of humanity. Then, one can realize that although one may not be able to bring peace and pluralism to the hearts of the Jerry Falwells and Osama Bin Ladens of the world,[30] one can provide alternatives for those who gravitate toward either fundamentalism. Both in the Muslim world and in this country, one can work to provide a higher path for young people's energies, one that brings together rather than divides people. Many observers have noted that poverty and a lack of economic opportunity contribute to the appeal of fundamentalism.[31] The unemployment rate among Palestinians is as high as 48 percent (in Gaza). Many Muslims thus have difficulty finding a sense of purpose for their lives, finding a way to bring honor to their families. It is in this context that some resort to martyrdom through self-sacrifice (suicide bombing), a practice of dubious Islamic merit that nonetheless brings a certain distinction to the families involved. Whereas those of us from the outside see only "terrorists," the families see champions of resistance who bring honor to those around them. The task of progressive Muslims is not merely to engage in disputations about the merits—or lack thereof—of suicide bombing but also to make sure that all parties involved in that terrible struggle—both Palestinians and Israelis —can find some dignity. At least part of that can and must be accomplished through economic development and political change.

But progressive Muslims in this country also have another responsibility. Farid Esack, one of the world's leading voices of progressive Islam, has rightly pointed out that unlike liberal Muslims, progressive Muslims concern themselves with the "non-subjects" of history—those who are marginalized, disempowered, and oppressed. Progressive Muslims in the United States have a responsibility to serve as social critics of American institutions of power, to remain engaged with domestic and social issues, and to push for peace and justice. We are, after all, called to be "witnesses for God in justice."[32] Part of the calling of American Muslims, therefore, is to hold the U.S. government responsible for policies that put strategic interests before human dignity. American progressive Muslims also seek to challenge policies that value the well-being of Americans over that of other human beings.[33]

Many in the Muslim world gravitate toward anti-Americanism for reasons that are well known: the U.S. military presence in more than one hundred countries, American support of undemocratic and antidemocratic regimes, and the unilateral support of Israel in a conflict where Israel already possesses hegemonic power over Palestinians. American progressive Muslims have a moral responsibility to urge other Muslims to realize that even where their cause is just, their tactics and strategies must also be just. King was right: "In the process of gaining our rightful place we must not be guilty of wrongful deeds."[34] At the same time, we have a calling to change American policies domestically and internationally in accordance with the highest standards of peace and justice. This double engagement with both Muslims and Americans is likely to bring discomfort to American Muslims whose survival strategy post-9/11 has been to wrap themselves in the American flag and the rhetoric of patriotism and nationalism. Yet as progressives, we place ourselves with those who follow in King's footsteps, recognizing America as the "dream, a dream as yet unfulfilled,"[35] and working to fulfill it.

Progressive Muslims see themselves as advocates of human beings all over the world who through no fault of their own live in situations of perpetual poverty, pollution, oppression, and marginalization. The plight of these people— mustad'afun, in the Quranic context—is a key concern of progressive Muslims, who take it as their charge to give voice to the voiceless and power to the powerless, to confront powers that disregard the God-given human dignity of the world's *mustadʿafun*. Progressive Muslims draw on the strong tradition of social justice in Islam—from sources as diverse as the Quran and hadith (statements of the Prophet Muhammad) to more recent spokespersons such as Shariati. Quranic verses specifically link fighting in the cause of God (*sabil Allah*) with the cause of *mustadʿafun*. These same verses explicitly identify the oppressed as a broad group of men, women, and children.[36]

The methodological fluidity of progressive Muslims is apparent in their pluralistic epistemology, which freely and openly draws from sources outside of Islam whenever they might serve as useful tools in the global pursuit of justice. These external sources include the liberation theology of Leonardo Boff, Gustavo Gutiérrez, and Rebecca S. Chopp as well as the secular humanism of Edward Said and Noam Chomsky. Progressive Muslims are likely to combine a Quranic call for serving as "witnesses for God in justice" (42:15) with Said's call to speak truth to power.[37]

The question of whether progressive Muslims reflect or initiate larger social processes of transformation is a nonstarter because it is premised on a dichotomy between intellectual pursuit and activism that progressives do not accept. Whereas many (though not all) of the previous generations of liberal Muslims pursued a purely academic approach, progressive Muslims fully realize that the social injustices around them are reflected in, connected to, and justified in terms of intellectual discourse. They are, in this respect, fully indebted to Said. Progressive Muslims are concerned not simply with laying out a fantastic, beatific vision of social justice and peace but also with transforming hearts and societies. A progressive commitment implies a willingness to engage issues of social justice as they unfold on the ground.

Progressive Muslims follow in Boff's footsteps, deeming theology devoid of real commitment to the oppressed "radically irrelevant."[38] Boff recognized that *liberação* (liberation) links together the concepts of *liber* (free) and *ação* (action):[39] There is no liberation without action. Therefore, "vision and activism are both necessary. Activism without vision is doomed from the start. Vision without activism quickly becomes irrelevant."[40]

This informed social activism is visible in many progressive Muslim organizations and projects, ranging from the work of Chandra Muzaffar with the International Movement for a Just World in Malaysia[41] and the efforts of Farid Esack to help HIV-positive Muslims in South Africa[42] to the work of recent Nobel Peace Prize winner Shirin Ebadi[43] with groups such as the Iranian Children's Rights Society.[44]

At the heart of a progressive Muslim interpretation is a simple yet radical idea: every human life, female or male, Muslim or non-Muslim, rich or poor, "northern" or "southern," has exactly the same intrinsic worth. The essential value of human life is God-given and is in no way connected to culture, geography, or privilege. This value derives from the fact that each of us has the breath of God coursing through our being: *"wa nafakhtu fihi min ruhi"* (Quran 15:29 and 38:72). This identification of all human beings with the full human being amounts to nothing short of an Islamic humanism.

An increasing number of those who advocate such a humanistic framework within the Islamic context have self-identified as progressive Muslims. "Progressive" refers here to a relentless striving toward a universal notion of justice in which no single community's prosperity, righteousness, or dignity come at the expense of another's. Progressive Muslims, therefore, conceive of a way of being Muslim that engages and affirms the humanity of all human beings, that actively holds all of us responsible for a fair and just distribution of God-given natural resources, and that seeks to live in harmony with the natural world.

Progressive Muslims insist on a serious engagement with the full spectrum of Islamic thought and practices. There can be no progressive Muslim movement that does not engage the textual and material sources of the Islamic tradition, even if some participants debate which sources matter most and how they ought to be interpreted. Progressives generally hold that it is imperative to work through inherited traditions of thought and practice; Sunni, Shiite, Sufi, juridical, philosophical, theological, mystical, poetical, folk Islam, and oral traditions all must be engaged. Progressives might conclude that certain interpretations now fail to offer sufficient guidance. However, they cannot faithfully claim that position before a serious engagement with the tradition. The way beyond problematic past interpretations of Islam is through them.

Justice lies at the heart of Islamic social ethics. Time and again the Quran talks about providing for the poor, the orphaned, the downtrodden, the wayfarers, the hungry. Progressive Muslims believe that it is time to translate the social ideals in the Quran and Islamic teachings into contemporary terms. Muslims retain a vibrant memory of the Prophet repeatedly talking about a real believer as one whose neighbor does not go to bed hungry. Progressives hold that in today's global village, it is time to think of all of humanity as our neighbor.

Progressive Muslims also believe that the Muslim community as a whole cannot achieve justice unless justice is guaranteed for Muslim women. In short, there can be no progressive interpretation of Islam without gender justice. Gender justice is crucial, indispensable, and essential. As Ebadi has repeatedly stated, it is imperative to conceive of women's rights as human rights.

Progressive Muslims strive for pluralism both inside and outside of the *umma*. They seek to open up a wider spectrum of legitimately Muslim interpretations and practices and follow many paths in pursuing knowledge and truth. In their interactions with other religious and ethnic communities, they seek to transcend arcane notions of "tolerance," striving instead to engage both the commonalities and the differences that they have with those communities.

The term "jihad" has become so misused and misunderstood that one may legitimately ask whether it is redeemable. Part of the problem is that the term is used by both Muslim extremists and western Islamophobes to mean a literal holy war. On the Muslim side, one can point to this public statement (fatwa) signed by Bin Laden: "In compliance with God's order, we issue the following fatwa to all Muslims: The ruling to kill the Americans and their allies—civilians and military—is an individual duty for every Muslim who can do it in any country in which it is possible to do it, in order to liberate the al-Aqsa Mosque and the Holy Mosque [Mecca] from their grip."[45]

Scholars of Islamic law have been quick to point out that this alleged fatwa, especially the call to kill civilians everywhere, violates both the letter and the spirit of Islamic law. This violation must be stressed.[46] At the same time, one must acknowledge that Bin Laden clearly legitimizes his own recourse to violence through the discourse of jihad.

This same sentiment is reflected in western Islamophobia. Many recent books on Islam approach their subject via jihad. Michael Sells, a leading scholar of Islam, has noted that the Islam section of many bookstores should really be renamed the "jihad and terrorism" section, since that subject predominates there. One might add the writings of Christian evangelicals and fundamentalists who are resurrecting centuries-old polemics against Islam in a new guise. These come from prominent preachers, including Jerry Falwell, Pat Robertson, Franklin Graham,[47] and Jerry Vines[48] and even from former U.S. Attorney General John Ashcroft.[49]

In this cauldron of recriminations, is there any possibility of recovering the term "jihad"? Is jihad bound to be a call for blood, for an eternal struggle between Islam and the rest of the world, as Princeton Islamicist Bernard Lewis would have us believe? Progressive Muslims say no, insisting that the root meaning of jihad is not holy war or violence but rather resistance and struggle. From this perspective, jihad reminds us nonviolently to confront injustice and inequality. Here, progressive Muslims are the heirs of both Muslim visionaries such as the great mystic Rumi, who stated, "Washing away blood with blood is impossible, even absurd!,"[50] and recent exemplars of nonviolence such as Gandhi, King, and the Dalai Lama. Their notion of jihad moves them to resist entrenched systems of inequality and injustice through nonviolent conflict. The goal is peace rooted in justice. Or, as the Dalai Lama put it in his Nobel Peace Prize acceptance speech, "Peace, in the sense of the absence of war, is of little value to someone who is dying of hunger or cold. Peace can only last where human rights are respected, where the people are fed, and where individuals and nations are free."[51]

Many progressive Muslims are also inspired by King's efforts to speak for universal justice from inside a faith community. His words about peace provide the clearest example of the progressive Muslim path:

> The leaders of the world today talk eloquently about peace. Every time we drop our bombs in North Vietnam, President Johnson talks eloquently about peace. What is the problem? They are talking about peace as a distant goal, as an end we seek, but one day we must come to see that peace is not merely the distant goal we seek, but that it is a means by which we arrive at that goal.
>
> Now let me say that the next thing we must be concerned about if we are to have peace on earth and good will toward men is the nonviolent affirmation of the sacredness of all human life. Every man is somebody because he is a child of God.[52]

Progressive Muslims are often asked whether their project constitutes an "Islamic reformation." The answer is both yes and no. It is true that the Muslim world has serious economic, social, and political problems that need urgent remedying. Much of the Muslim world is bound to an economic structure in which it provides oil and other natural resources to the global market while remaining dependent on western labor, technological know-how, and staple goods. This economic situation is exacerbated in many parts of the modern Muslim world by human rights violations, crumbling educational systems, and stagnant economies. Most progressive Muslims support the reform of all these institutions.

However, the term "reformation" carries considerably more baggage than that. In speaking of an "Islamic reformation," many people have in mind the Protestant Reformation. This analogy makes many progressive Muslims uneasy. They do not seek a "Protestant" Islam distinct from a "Catholic" Islam. In fact, most insist that they are not looking to split the Muslim community as much as to transform it.

Perhaps the most exciting part of the emerging global Muslim progressivism is that progressives everywhere are seeking one another out, reading each other's work, collaborating with one another's organizations. Much of this cross-pollination is taking place via e-mail and Internet messaging. We are clearly in the initial stages of a movement that has the promise to usher in a paradigm shift in the relationship of Muslims to both Islam and modernity. To the extent that an important part of this unfolding is taking place in the United States, Americans are sure to change and challenge both the future practice of Islam and the "dream as yet unfulfilled" that is America.

NOTES

1. "Bush: U.S. Muslims Should Feel Safe," September 17, 2001, <http://www.cnn.com/2001/US/09/17/gen.bush.muslim.trans/>.

2. I will explain in the discussion of pluralism why the term "tolerance" is inherently problematic. The term "moderate" prompts the question of moderate with respect to what extremes. If on one side moderate is defined against the Islamic terrorism of 9/11, what is on the other side? Total secularism? Alas, moderate Islam seems to be an ill-defined term—a shorthand for Muslims who oppose 9/11 but never oppose the actions of the U.S. government.

3. "Wolfowitz Appeals to Muslim Moderates to Oppose Terrorism," U.S. Department of State, May 3, 2002, <http://usinfo.state.gov/regional/ar/mexico/02050308.htm>.

4. See Charles Kurzman, Liberal Islam: A Sourcebook (New York: Oxford University Press, 1998).

5. For an anthology of progressive Islam, see Omid Safi, ed., Progressive Muslims: On Justice, Gender, and Pluralism (Oxford, Eng.: Oneworld, 2003).

6. <http://www.icna.com>.

7. <http://www.isna.net/>.

8. <http://www.cair-net.org/>.

9. See Hamid Algar, Wahhabism: A Critical Essay (Oneonta, N.Y.: Islamic Publications International, 2002).

10. David Ignatius, "The Read on Wolfowitz," Washington Post, January 16, 2003, <http://www.washingtonpost.com/wp-dyn/articles/A4023-2003Jan16.html>.

11. James Davison Hunter, Culture Wars: The Struggle to Define America (New York: Basic Books, 1991).

12. Vincent J. Cornell, *Realm of the Saint: Power and Authority in Moroccan Sufism* (Austin: University of Texas Press, 1998); Jo-Ann Gross, "Authority and Miraculous Behavior," in *The Legacy of Mediaeval Persian Sufism*, edited by Leonard Lewisohn (London: KNP, 1992), 159–71; Richard Eaton, *The Sufis of Bijapur, 1300–1700* (Princeton: Princeton University Press, 1978).

13. Carl W. Ernst, *Shambhala Guide to Sufism* (Boston: Shambhala, 1997), 199–228.

14. There are educational organizations such as the International Institute of Islamic Thought and the Zaytuna Institute, and efforts have been made to establish a Crescent University outside New York City, but none of these has yet succeeded in answering the call for Islamic higher education.

15. "Secular" is of course a contested term. When I use the word, I am talking about a model of social relations in which the boundaries between religious discourse and political legitimacy are not to be collapsed (as opposed to a model in which the religious is exiled entirely from the public domain).

16. See R. Walzer, "Islamic Philosophy," cited in Seyyed Hossein Nasr, *Three Muslim Sages* (Delmar, N.Y.: Caravan, 1964), 11.

17. See Abdolkarim Soroush, *Reason, Freedom, and Democracy in Islam*, translated and edited by Mahmoud Sadri and Ahmad Sadri (New York: Oxford University Press, 2000), 21.

18. Amina Wadud, *Qur'an and Woman: Rereading the Sacred Text from a Woman's Perspective*, 2nd ed. (New York: Oxford University Press, 1999).

19. See Michael Wolfe, *The Hadj: An American's Pilgrimage to Mecca* (New York: Grove, 1993). Wolfe also produced the PBS program on the Prophet Muhammad. See <http://www.pbs.org/muhammad/>.

20. Asma Gull Hasan, *American Muslims: The New Generation* (New York: Continuum, 2000).

21. For information on Hamza Yusuf's Zaytuna Institute, see <http://www.zaytuna.org/>.

22. Edward Said, *Culture and Imperialism* (New York: Knopf, 1993), xxv.

23. Cited in Laurie Goodstein, "A Nation Challenged: The Role of Religion; Scholars Call Attacks a Distortion of Islam," *New York Times*, September 30, 2001, 1B6.

24. "Translation of Letter Left by Hijackers," <http://ict.org.il/documents/documentdet.cfm?docid=57>.

25. For an insightful BBC commentary on the appeal of conspiracy theories, see <http://news.bbc.co.uk/2/hi/americas/1561199.stm>.

26. For such reactions by Muslim scholars worldwide, see <http://www.unc.edu/~kurzman/terror.htm>. For the responses of the American Muslim community, see <http://groups.colgate.edu/aarislam/response.htm>.

27. See Khaled Abou El Fadl, "Terrorism Is at Odds with Islamic Tradition," <http://www.muslim-lawyers.net/news/index.php3?aktion=show&number=78>.

28. Rudolph Peters, *Jihad in Classical and Modern Islam* (Princeton, N.J.: Wiener, 1996), 33.

29. For a devastating critique, see Algar, *Wahhabism*.

30. I draw this analogy only at the level of Falwell's and Bin Laden's dichotomous worldviews, not in terms of their usage (or nonusage) of violence.

31. Although most al-Qaeda leaders and the 9/11 terrorists came from middle-class backgrounds, Bin Laden is notoriously wealthy.

32. Quran 42:15: "I believe in the scripture which God has sent down, and I am commanded to establish justice among you."

33. This "Americanism" is so deeply embedded in the nation that it is impossible to localize. It characterizes many mainstream news presentations, most notably that of Fox News. In "Skip the Liberal Spin, Report the News Fairly," *New York Daily News*, June 9, 2003 (<http://www.nydailynews.com/news/ideas_opinions/story/90651p-82430c.html>), conservative demagogue Bill O'Reilly criticizes Walter Cronkite's perspective on the Iraq war since "the former CBS News anchorman was coming at it from an internationalist point of view, putting the objective and policies of foreign countries on the same level as those of the U.S.A. In this age of terror, when we are under attack, that attitude just doesn't cut it."

34. Martin Luther King Jr., "I Have a Dream," in *A Testament of Hope: The Essential Writings and Speeches of Martin Luther King, Jr.*, edited by James M. Washington (San Francisco: HarperSanFrancisco, 1991), 218.

35. Martin Luther King Jr., "The American Dream," in ibid., 208.

36. Quran 4:75. This *aya* provides another affirmation that the struggles for gender justice and children's rights are part and parcel of the quest for global justice. Justice remains indivisible.

37. Edward Said died on September 25, 2003. For an archive of tributes by the many progressive Muslims who were influenced by Said, see <http://www.edwardsaid.org>.

38. Leonardo Boff and Clodovis Boff, *Introducing Liberation Theology* (Maryknoll, N.Y.: Orbis, 2001), 9.

39. Ibid., 10.

40. Omid Safi, *"The Times They Are a-Changin'*: A Muslim Quest for Justice, Gender, Equality, and Pluralism," in *Progressive Muslims*, edited by Safi, 6–7.

41. <http://www.just-international.org/>.

42. <http://www.positivemuslims.org.za/>.

43. <http://www.muslimwakeup.com/mainarchive/000242.php>.

44. <http://www.iranianchildren.org/index.html>.

45. <http://www.fas.org/irp/world/para/docs/980223-fatwa.htm>. The Arabic original of the fatwa, published in *al-Quds al-'Arabi*, can be found at <http://www.library.cornell.edu/colldev/mideast/fatw2.htm>.

46. For two exhaustive lists of Muslim scholars condemning Bin Laden, see <http://www.unc.edu/~kurzman/terror.htm> and <http://groups.colgate. edu/aarislam/response.htm>.

47. Franklin Graham, contesting President Bush's characterization of Islam as a religion of peace, stated that Islam is an "evil and wicked religion" (<http://www.cnn.com/2003/ALLPOLITICS/04/18/graham.pentagon/>). After making these remarks, Graham was invited to Good Friday services at the Pentagon on April 18, 2003. Such

juxtapositions of evangelical arrogance with military might rightly arouse Muslims' suspicions of a new crusade.

48. Jerry Vines, former president of the Southern Baptist Convention and a board member of Falwell's Liberty University, stated that the Prophet Muhammad was a "demon-possessed pedophile" (<http://www.washingtonpost.com/ac2/wp-dyn/A14499-2002Jun19?language=printer>).

49. John Ashcroft stated in an interview with Carl Thomas, "Islam is a religion in which God requires you to send your son to die for him. Christianity is a faith in which God sends his son to die for you" (<http://www. beliefnet.com/story/101/story_10140_1.html).

50. Mawlana Jalal al-Din Balkhi Rumi, *Masnavi-yi Ma'navi*, edited by R. A. Nicholson (Tehran: Intisharat-i Nigah, 1371/1992), 532. This passage is found in the third book of the *Masnavi*, line 4726 of the Nicholson Persian edition.

51. Sidney Piburn, comp. and ed., *The Dalai Lama, A Policy of Kindness: An Anthology of Writings by and about the Dalai Lama* (Ithaca, N.Y.: Snow Lion, 1990), 17.

52. Martin Luther King Jr., "A Christmas Sermon on Peace," in *Testament of Hope*, edited by Washington, 255.

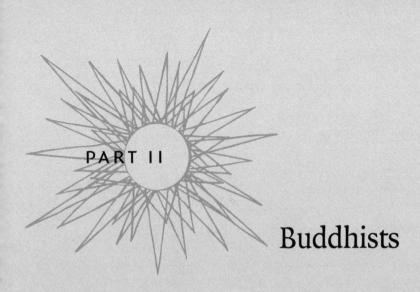

PART II

Buddhists

3

From Pearl Harbor to 9/11

Lessons from the Internment of Japanese American Buddhists

Buddhist priests, classified by the Federal Bureau of Investigation (FBI) as potentially the most dangerous Japanese aliens, were among the first groups arrested by government officials following the bombing of Pearl Harbor on December 7, 1941.[1] Shinobu Matsuura's husband, the Reverend Issei Matsuura, was one such Buddhist priest. He was taken by the FBI in the early hours of the morning and did not know if or when he would see his family again. As she recalled, "February 18, 1942, early morning, still in our night-clothes and huddled by the heater, we listened grimly to the news over the radio. There was a loud rapping on the back door. Three men stood there. They were the FBI. 'We came to arrest Rev. Matsuura,' said one, as they came through the door. . . . I was instructed to pack a change of clothing for my husband. Hurriedly, I put his underwear and toiletries in a bag. Separately, I wrapped his koromo and kesa, seiten and Kanmuryojukyo sutra."[2]

Japanese American Buddhist priests of all denominations, along with Shinto priests, were sent to "alien enemy" camps established by the U.S. Department of Justice in Santa Fe, New Mexico; and Crystal City, Texas. Unlike Japanese American Christian priests and ministers, Buddhist priests were closely associated with Japan and thus with potentially subversive activity. As Bob Kumamoto has noted, "The 'peculiarity' of Eastern languages, religions, customs, and physical appearance had always separated the Japanese from the mainstream of American society. Once considered inferior and insignificant, these ethnic distinctions were now considered by the government as anti-American, potentially subversive and somehow threatening to American security."[3] This perception that Buddhists (in contrast to Christians) were more Japanese than American was held not only by the FBI and the Wartime Relocation Authority (WRA) but also by the public at large, including some members of the Japanese American community. The history of Japanese American

Buddhism during World War II, in fact, centers on this question of identity, both ethnic and religious.

This chapter explores the modes of accommodation and resistance that first-generation Japanese Americans (issei) and their children (nisei and kibei) expressed through their Buddhist identity in the days following Pearl Harbor and in the years of their incarceration in detention camps. The chapter also includes preliminary observations about these processes of religious identity among members of minority religions in America, especially during wartime, by comparing Japanese American Buddhist experiences with the changing landscape for Muslims, Sikhs, and people with ethnic heritages from south Asia and the Middle East after the terrorist incidents of 9/11.

The first Japanese Buddhist priests arrived in Hawaii and the U.S. mainland in the 1890s to minister to the first-generation issei. Most issei were Buddhists who had initially immigrated to Hawaii to work on plantations and to the mainland as contract laborers for railroad, lumber, mining, and cannery companies as well as on farms. In 1900, the Japanese immigrant population had risen to 24,326, most of them transient men. In 1930, however, the Japanese American population had grown to 138,834 and increasingly was composed of families with stable jobs and even small businesses.[4] By the eve of the war, Buddhist temples functioned as both religious and community centers in all areas where Japanese Americans were concentrated, especially in California. Buddhist priests of the Jôdo, Jôdo Shin, Nichiren, Shingon, and Sôtô Zen sects were sent by their respective headquarter temples in Japan to serve as "missionaries" in the United States.

The FBI's targeting of Buddhist priests as potential subversives had little to do with the fact that Buddhist temples, especially those of the Jôdo Shin tradition, had participated in fund-raising campaigns for the Imperial Japanese Army in Manchuria.[5] Japanese American Buddhist ties to Japanese military or intelligence agencies, according to FBI surveillance records, were fairly tenuous. Alan Hynd's "exposé" of the Japanese-German spy network in the years immediately preceding the war, Betrayal from the East: The Inside Story of Japanese Spies in America, could cite only one incident. The FBI apparently suspected the Los Angeles Kôyasan Buddhist Temple of holding spy meetings with members of the Japanese consulate, with Sachiko Furusawa (an adviser to the Temple's Women's Society and wife of a doctor who apparently had ties to German spies), and with other unidentified figures. At one particular meeting, the FBI suspected that the participants had discussed placing detonation devices on American naval ships.[6] In reality, however, the FBI had only unsupported notions that Buddhist priests were more pro-Japan than other members of the Japanese American community; nevertheless, the FBI regarded the priests as "known dangerous Group A suspects," along with employees of the Japanese consulate, fishermen, and influential businessmen.[7] The FBI's decision to target Buddhist priests can be traced primarily to the conflation of Buddhism with state Shinto, which emphasized worship of the emperor as a deity and loyalty to the Japanese imperial empire. Not until the postwar period would Americans see Japanese Buddhism as a distinct tradition.

Newspaper editors and members of Congress accused all Japanese, including Japanese American children, of being loyal to the Japanese government and called for their removal from the West Coast. After their priests were taken away to "enemy alien" camps, the remaining members of Buddhist temples tried their best to continue religious services as well as community affairs. For example, the wives of priests and nonordained temple leaders took on duties that priests previously had performed exclusively.[8]

By February 1942, the U.S. government set in motion the large-scale incarceration of the broader Japanese American community. On February 19, 1942, President Roosevelt issued Executive Order 9066, which ultimately led to the designation of restricted military zones on the West Coast and the subsequent removal of all persons of Japanese ancestry from those areas. In the ensuing months, the atmosphere in the community was one of anxiety, uncertainty, and fear. Immediately following the bombing of Pearl Harbor, the Buddhist Mission of North America (the predecessor of the Jôdo Shin Buddhist Churches of America) sent a notice to its members:

Sirs, REGISTER FOR CIVILIAN DEFENSE—Buddhists! Your loyalty and devotion to the cause of the United States of America in her war against aggressor nations of the Axis, must be translated into action. Do your part unflinchingly in the defense of the STARS AND STRIPES. Acquaint yourself with Air Raid Rules! Mobilize your energies to facilitate America's purpose! Pledge your services unreservedly to the officials and authorities of our country, the UNITED STATES OF AMERICA. With the blessings of Buddha, Rev. K. Kumata (Buddhist Mission of North America).[9]

The major Buddhist organizations tried to provide leadership and convey a strong sense of loyalty to the United States. They urged Japanese Americans to cooperate with the authorities when rumors circulated about forcible removal from the West Coast: "Buddhists with citizenship in America: Remember the spirit of loyalty to your country and filial piety which you have learned through the teachings of the Buddha. . . . Young Buddhists in Prohibited Areas: Cooperate with your local J[apanese] A[merican] C[itizens] L[eague] Chapter in all problems pertaining to the evacuation. With the Blessings of the Buddha, Rev. Kumata (Buddhist Mission of America)."[10]

During this period of war hysteria, some Buddhists converted to Christianity, while others burned Japanese-language books and other personal Japanese cultural artifacts in an attempt to destroy, literally and symbolically, their Japaneseness while simultaneously demonstrating their Americanness.[11] Mary Nagatomi, for example, remembers her parents telling her to go to the wood stove used for the family bath to burn everything in the household with "Made in Japan" on it, including her favorite traditional Japanese doll set. The one item the family members could not bring themselves to burn was a set of Buddhist sutras, which the father buried after wrapping the scriptures in kimono cloth, placing them in a metal rice-cracker box, and using a backhoe to dig a hole for them on the family farm. These sacred texts remain buried somewhere in central California, a silent testimony to the enduring Buddhist identity of one family, testimony that could not be completely obliterated despite the seeming necessity of doing so.[12]

The rush to Christian conversion, ironically, could be part of a Japanese tradition of subsuming religious identity under political or national identity. But conversions were also born of fear of persecution by neighbors and the government, and many converts returned to the Buddhist fold during the camp years.

When stories began to circulate throughout the community that Buddhists would be treated more harshly than Christians, Buddhist leaders sent out a letter:

And contrary to all rumors, those in official positions have assured us that unreasonable persecution shall never be brought against Buddhism or Buddhists. It is with great sorrow then that there have been noted several cases of inferiority complexes, brought about by false tales, wherein Buddhist religious organizations have been disbanded and Buddhists have destroyed or hidden family altars while others have withdrawn from church membership. . . . Buddhists! With true Faith in the Buddha, let us serve our country, the United States of America, in silence. With the Blessings of the Buddha, Rev. Kumata (Buddhist Churches of America).[13]

Buddhists experiencing internal conflict regarding their identity and loyalty soon had to face the reality that they were going to be uprooted from their communities. Japanese Americans in the restricted zones would receive a number at one of the sixty-four Civil Control stations; they then would have between seven and ten days to sell or store their property. They could take only what they could carry by hand to the camps. Without due process of law, more than 110,000 Japanese Americans ultimately were herded to "assembly centers" before being imprisoned at one of ten so-called permanent relocation centers:

> Arise, Arise, all Buddha's soldiers true, and take your stand upon the
> rock of Truth!
> The Holy Law by Lord Buddha taught everyone to endure
> And all who journey by its Light shall reach Nirvana's shore
> In love we stand, by Truth set free, Brothers of Him who found true
> liberty.[14]

Japanese American Buddhists faced a crisis of identity and faith as they endured a harsh journey to the internment camps and the realities of the desert heat, coupled with the knowledge that they were prisoners in their own land. Within the camps, surrounded by barbed wire and armed guards, arose the question of what it means to be simultaneously American and Buddhist. What is an American Buddhist?

Buddhist life in the camps revolved around the barrack "churches," which held religious services and education classes (in some cases in mess halls and recreation buildings), especially on Sundays. According to the Reverend Arthur Takemoto, a young man during the internment period, Buddhist teachings such as those on suffering and patience helped alleviate the pain and confusion that many residents faced: "Understanding the basic tenets of Buddhism orients people to understand the reality of life, that things don't go the way we want them to go. This becomes dukkha, suffering and pain. To be able to accept a situation as it is means we could tolerate it more."[15]

The WRA forced various Buddhist sects to cooperate with each other, which meant that doctrinal differences were often ignored in favor of a shared, transsectarian Buddhism. At times, this process involved finding common ground in areas such as chanting "Namu Butsu" (Homage to the Buddha) instead of the various sects' unique chants: "Namu Amida Butsu" (Jôdo Shin); "Namu Daishi Henjô Kongô" (Shingon); and "Namu Myôhô Renge Kyô" (Nichiren).[16] While this phenomenon represented, as Stephen Prothero has suggested, more of an "ecumenism of circumstance"—reflecting the lack of facilities and government categorization for religious worship rather than a conscious choice—this transsectarianism nevertheless reflects an impulse within Japanese American Buddhism, exemplified by priests such as Yemyô Imamura, toward a form of American Buddhism that transcends Japanese sectarian factionalism.

The Buddhist churches in the camps held annual festivals and services for events such as Obon, Higan, and the Buddha's birthday as well as funerals, memorial services, and weddings for Buddhist families. The traditional ritual life of Japanese Buddhism continued in the camp. Having left behind family Buddhist altars (*butsudan*) enshrining their ancestors, Buddhists resorted to collecting odd pieces of wood in the desert to make altars.[17] The lack of officiants to carry out funerary and memorial services forced Buddhist priests, regardless of sect, to maintain all family necrologies and bestow posthumous names traditionally given to the dead at funerals, two crucial aspects of funerary Buddhism focused on the ancestors in traditional Japanese Buddhism. For example, when a Jôdo Shin priest, Nagatomi Shinjô, conducted the funeral for the father of the Tayama family, Sôtô Zen Buddhists at the Manzanar Camp, he entered the deceased's posthumous name in the family necrology with this note:

Date: 1942, Dec. 24 (deceased)
Dharma Name: SHAKU Saishô'in Hôden; Given Name: Tayama Saki
Age at death: 61
Present address: Death Valley CC; Former address: Los Angeles; Place of
    death: Manzanar
Japanese Place of Origin: Yamaguchi Pref.
Officiant: Nagatomi Shinjô; Head Mourner: Tayama Suguru; Notes:
    Zenshû (Sôtôshû) believer.[18]

The importance of maintaining the Japanese custom of ancestral veneration was so strong that sectarian concerns for each family, while normally crucial for the proper performance of the traditional funeral and the selection of the posthumous name, were set aside in this time of crisis. What mattered was simply to provide funerary rites. In this way, Buddhism not only provided a spiritual refuge for internees but also served the social function of maintaining family and communal cohesion through ancestral and life-cycle rituals and traditional Japanese festivals and ceremonies.

While Buddhism was, in this sense, a repository of Japanese traditions, it was also forced to operate in the context of an Americanization program promoted by the WRA. This program was organized to assimilate the Japanese and allow them to demonstrate loyalty to the United States.[19] According to the *Investigation of Un-American Propaganda Activities in the United States* (1943) prepared by the Subcommittee of the U.S. House of Representatives Special Committee on Un-American Activities, camp administrators should promote recreational activities such as baseball and basketball as well as encourage internees to join groups such as the Boy and Girl Scouts and the YMCA/YWCA.[20] Being Buddhist obviously was not listed as a method of demonstrating loyalty, but Buddhist groups made their own attempts at Americanization.

In May 1944, the name of the largest Buddhist organization in the Topaz Camp was changed from the Buddhist Mission of North America (BMNA) to the Buddhist Churches of America (BCA) to give the organization a more Christian-sounding name. The camp experience, however, only accelerated an assimilation process that had already begun prior to the war.[21] The swastika symbol, often used on Buddhist temple stationery or on temple equipment prior to the internment, disappeared and was replaced almost universally by the dharma wheel. In addition to increased use of English at the barrack churches, new hymnals (the most widely used of which was *A Book of Ceremonies for Use of Buddhists at Gatherings*) were created with the assistance of several Euro-American supporters outside the camps, including American convert Julius Goldwater, to lend the BCA a more Christian (and thus American) format for services. By singing *gathas* as hymns, including Dorothy Hunt's "Onward Buddhist Soldiers" (a section of which was quoted earlier), Buddhists within the camp created a new medium for Americanizing Buddhism. They did so, however, in a way that honored their Buddhist traditions while simultaneously demonstrating loyalty to the United States. The young members of the community, having studied the Buddhist "Junior Catechism," for example, used a Christian medium to maintain Buddhist identity. Many of these elements constitute what might be called the Protestantization of Buddhism, which Prothero has identified as parallel to the process of Americanization.[22]

America was also inscribed into the Buddhist iconographical landscape when members of the Oregon Buddhist Church recarved their temple's main altarpiece, Mount Sumeru (the axis mundi of Buddhist cosmology that lies below a Buddha figure in traditional Jôdo Shin temple altars), to resemble nearby Mount Hood. Here, Buddhists sacralized the American landscape by affirming their home state's symbol as their true home as Oregonians. Such actions function in a way similar to Hindus' identification of the Mississippi

River as the Ganges, a method that, as Vasudha Narayanan argues in her chapter in this volume, makes America "home" both geographically and religiously.

Most importantly, the Young Buddhist Association (YBA) supported the all-nisei 100th/442nd Combat Regiment, in which second-generation Japanese Americans fought in Europe to demonstrate their loyalty to America.[23] As David Yoo has suggested, the nisei "embraced the very markers of racial and religious difference used against them. The faith of their mothers and fathers enabled the second generation to affirm their ancestry and, at the same time, lay claim to their status as Americans. No single definition emerged, but religion offered Nisei Buddhists (also known as Bussei) valuable space to become ethnic Americans."[24] These volunteers were encouraged by many Buddhist priests and the YBAs as well as by army-recognized Buddhist chaplains. (Buddhist chaplains were not allowed in the field in Europe but were permitted in the boot camps before the soldiers were deployed.)

Nevertheless, many Japanese American soldiers had a hard time grappling with the issue of identity, faced as they were with the irony of fighting for a country in the name of freedom while that same country deprived their parents and siblings of the same freedom. One such Buddhist soldier wrote to his parents in broken Japanese the night before leaving boot camp for the European front:

> Dear Mama and Papa. It's me. Tonight, I'm finally being sent to the front. Thank you for loving me all these years. Mama, and Papa too, there's no need to worry. I'll be back soon. I'll rush back to where you are just as soon as I get back. Both of you stay in good health till then, all right? Since everything's set to go, I've got nothing else left to say except good-bye. Take care, Mama and Papa. Good-bye, good-bye. Oh wait, I'd forgotten, there is something else, Mama. That story, you know, the one you used to tell me all the time when I was a kid. The story about the Buddha. I remember that really well, so you can put your mind at ease. The Buddha will always be with me, even when I'm sent to the front. I'm not sad at all because the Buddha will protect me. Mama and Papa, don't worry about me because I remember that story really well. Well, I've got to be off, so you two take care of yourselves. Good-bye.[25]

This letter, given to a Buddhist priest by the parents for safekeeping, reassured them that their son remembered his Buddhist roots and the power of the Buddha to protect believers. The power of the Buddha thus extended ever eastward, across the Pacific from Japan to America, and then east again, across the Atlantic, from America to Europe.

When the war ended and the internees began reintegrating into American society, Buddhist temples such as the Senshin Buddhist Temple in Los Angeles and the San Jose Buddhist Church continued the work of the dharma by serving as hostels for those who could not immediately find housing and jobs. The second-generation nisei of the BCA also organized a Golden Jubilee Festival in 1948 to celebrate the fifty years since the founding of the organization. As Michael Masatsugu has noted, the celebration, which would gather thousands to formalize the changes that had taken place in the camp, emphasized the struggle of issei Buddhist pioneers and the sacrifices of the nisei Buddhist war heroes.[26] Inscribing their forefathers into the landscape of the American West and honoring their brethren who had died in war to prove American loyalty, the organizers managed not only to solidify a new vision of what it meant to be an American Buddhist but also to garner mainstream media attention. *Life* magazine devoted several pages to the jubilee, with photos of two Buddhist priests in front of the Buddhist altar at the San Francisco Buddhist Church, a Bon Odori (a summertime Buddhist dance to placate and honor the spirits of the ancestors) at San Francisco's civic center, and a Caucasian convert cleric, Frank Udale, dressed in his priestly garb.[27]

As Buddhists attempted to find a place in mainstream American society, the English-speaking nisei also worked to gain a place for American Buddhism in the public sphere. They organized two closely related campaigns to remember the lives and sacrifices made by the many nisei servicemen who had served in the 100th/442nd in Europe or as translators and intelligence gatherers in the Pacific Theater's Military Intelligence Service. A war veteran and devout Buddhist, Tad Hirota, led a B for Buddhism campaign to have the army officially recognize Buddhists in the armed services by creating a B designation on dog tags. (During World War II, the military had only three official preferences: P for Protestant, C for Catholic, and H for Hebrew.) Coordinated with endorsements from the Los Angeles County Board of Supervisors and the Republican delegate from the territory of Hawaii, Joseph R. Farrington, Hirota contacted the army's chief chaplain, Major General Luther C. Miller. After some deliberation, a compromise was reached in 1949 that designated X to be used on dog tags for anyone not of the existing three religious preferences. Furthermore, an additional dog tag could be supplied by the soldier's church or temple that would positively identify his religion. The National Young Buddhist Coordinating Council subsequently campaigned for a Buddhist symbol to be placed on the headstones of Buddhist veterans at national cemeteries. After petitions were sent to Secretary of Defense, Louis Johnson, the army agreed late in 1949 to inscribe the "Buddhist emblem" for American soldiers of the Buddhist faith. These two campaigns represent an important legacy of the camps, testing both Japanese American Buddhist loyalty to America and America's loyalty to its Buddhist citizens.

Postwar Japanese American Buddhism was clearly marked by the Buddhism of the camps. Wartime Buddhism functioned both as a repository of Japanese cultural traditions and as a vehicle for becoming American. As Ihsan Bagby suggests in his chapter in this volume, wartime may clarify the stakes involved in articulating to the nation one's religious and ethnic identity as well as accelerate the processes of Americanization. Lacking significant postwar migration from Japan, the Japanese American community, especially in California, has diminished in size as outmarriage and other assimilative factors have increased. With many fourth- and fifth-generation Japanese Americans unable to speak Japanese or uninterested in Buddhist temple life, Buddhist temples have had to find new ways to maintain membership. The paradoxical task of maintaining religious identity through difference—both ethnic (Japanese) and religious (Buddhist)—while simultaneously developing an American identity was sharpened by the wartime incarceration but continues today. The legacy of the camps lives on.

While the long history of the Japanese American Buddhist experience obviously holds lessons for more recent Asian American immigrant Buddhist groups, one wonders if the war and incarceration experience cannot also inform and illuminate the recent unfolding of a "new religious America," as Diana Eck puts it.[28] In particular, one wonders whether the targeting and harassment of Muslim Americans, Arab Americans, and those who may look like those who were responsible for the 9/11 attacks (such as Sikhs and other south Asians) parallels the Japanese American experience following Pearl Harbor.

According to the Council on American-Islamic Relations, which was tracking anti-Muslim incidents long before 9/11, cases of discrimination and attacks have soared since that event.[29] Ethnic and religious profiling at airports and workplaces as well as physical violence (including the shooting of Balbir Singh Sodhi, a Sikh gas station owner in Mesa, Arizona) recall the hate crimes and discrimination faced by Japanese Americans after Pearl Harbor. Just as Japanese American Buddhist temples were vandalized and ancient Buddhist symbols, such as the swastikas (manji) that hung at temple doors, were riddled with shotgun fire by angry white neighbors,[30] one saw an angry mob of three hundred people chanting "U.S.A., U.S.A." and marching on a mosque in Bridgeview, Illinois, right after 9/11. Whether it was the vandalizing of a Muslim bookstore in Alexandria, Virginia, on September 12, or someone shooting into a Dallas-area mosque, the Islamic Center of Irving, Islamic symbols quickly became targets for those caught up in war hysteria. "Visible religion," whether in dress or looks, combined with ethnic profiling has once again proved to be a factor in how American religious pluralism and tolerance are defined.

Just as hundreds of Buddhist priests were picked up by the FBI and hysterical claims were made that Buddhist bells were going to send Morse code messages to the Japanese navy, the post-9/11 period has seen its share of indiscriminate arrests of thousands of young Muslim "enemy aliens" as well as the targeting of Muslim charitable organizations accused of having terrorist links. Many have developed the same kind of loyalty strategies as Japanese Americans did following Pearl Harbor: calls by organizations such as the American Muslim Council to cooperate with the FBI and support the president or drives to donate blood for the victims of the World Trade Center. While the rush to conversion, a strategy followed by some Japanese American Buddhists, is not an option for many Muslims, not only Muslims but also Sikhs and Hindus have sought ways of demonstrating loyalty to America, such as flying American flags or toning down religious or ethnic differences.

Despite these parallels, the differences between Pearl Harbor Buddhists and 9/11 Muslims are striking. Following 9/11, the federal government did not adopt a policy of mass incarceration of Muslims. In the Japanese American case, not only "enemy aliens" but also Japanese Americans citizens—more than 110,000 of them, including babies at orphanages—were imprisoned without trial for the duration of the war as a national security threat. Indeed, President George W. Bush's September 17, 2001, speech at the Islamic Center of Washington, D.C., where he announced his dismay at harassment of Muslims, represented a clear attempt to disentangle American Muslims from the actions of individual terrorists. "Women who cover their heads in this country must feel comfortable going outside their homes. Moms who wear cover must not be intimidated in America," Bush stated. "That's not the America I know. That's not the America I value."[31] While the president's anti-hate-crime message must also be understood in the context of international politics (that is, the imperative that the U.S. "war on terrorism" not be anti-Islamic), his comments set the tone for a government stance against intolerance.[32] Indeed, within days of 9/11, both the House and the Senate passed resolutions condemning bigotry and violence against Arab Americans, American Muslims, and Americans of south Asian origin and calling for the protection of their civil rights and liberties.[33] Such official proclamations of religious tolerance were not forthcoming in 1940s America.

In the sixty years since Pearl Harbor, America has changed dramatically for Japanese Americans. In a June 2000 White House ceremony, President Bill Clinton bestowed the military's highest award, the Medal of Honor, on twenty-two Asian American war veterans. Japanese American veterans of the 442nd Regimental Combat Unit and the 100th Battalion, such as Senator Daniel Inoue (D-Hawaii), were honored for their valor in war. This action clearly signaled that Japanese Americans are no longer seen as foreigners. The ceremony, which also honored veterans posthumously, included the Reverend Shojo Honda, a Buddhist priest from Kyoto who recited Buddhist scriptures for the dead soldiers in front of the president and the army brass. The Buddhist priest, once officially classified as disloyal to his country, can now appear in public as a legitimate religious figure.

Among those in the army hierarchy present at that ceremony was four-star general Eric Shinseki, who had assumed the U.S. Army's top job, becoming chief of staff in 1999. Japanese Americans such as General Shinseki, along with Norman Mineta, who in his capacity as secretary of transportation worked to secure aviation safety after 9/11, have been among the Bush administration's faces in the "war on terrorism." Japanese American and Buddhist occupation of such high-profile public positions demonstrates a significant shift in America's religious, social, and political life. In addition, a traditional Japanese Obon ceremony, an annual event to honor the recently deceased as well as one's ancestors who are believed to revisit the living, was held at Ground Zero. It represented once more an increased Buddhist presence in the American religious imagination. Organized by the Reverend T. Kenjitsu Nakagaki of the New York Buddhist Church and other Buddhist priests, the Hatsu-Bon Memorial Service honored the roughly twenty Japanese and Japanese Americans who died in the 9/11 attack on the World Trade Center.[34]

While the camp experience appears to have accelerated these types of postwar assimilationist tendencies—wanting to belong and to appear loyal—a lingering suspicion of mass incarceration and the denial of civil liberties for Muslim Americans remains strong among Japanese Americans, especially after the FBI brought in five thousand men, primarily of Arab and south Asian descent, for questioning in the domestic "war on terror." Within two and a half weeks of 9/11, two *New York Times* articles, "War on Terrorism Stirs Memory of Internment" and "Recalling Internment and Saying 'Never Again,' " chronicled what many Japanese Americans felt was a special responsibility to guard against ethnic scapegoating.[35] Proclaiming that "we need to do everything that we wish good Americans had done 59 years ago," the executive director of the San Francisco Japanese American Cultural and Community Center, Paul Osaki, was one of many community leaders speaking out against violence and discrimination against Muslim Americans.[36] On September 19, Japanese American leaders coordinated an unprecedented gathering of ethnic and religious leaders, including those from the American-Arab Anti-Discrimination Committee, the American Muslim Council, and the Council on American-Islamic Relations, to meet at the National Japanese American Memorial in Washington, D.C., and call for law enforcement officers and others to adequately address hate violence against religious and ethnic minorities.

Invoking the memory of the World War II incarceration experience, other leaders, such as the executive director of the Japanese American National Museum, Irene Hirano, have also been deeply involved in efforts to reach out to Arab and Muslim Americans, including the construction of a new Arab American national museum. Although the mass incarceration of Arab and Muslim Americans seems unlikely, on July 19, 2002, a member of the U.S. Commission on Civil Rights raised the specter of internment camps for Arab Americans if additional terrorist attacks were to occur on American soil.[37] Despite the religious and political motivations for some Sikh and Hindu organizations to distance themselves from Muslims—itself reminiscent of the attempts by Koreans and Chinese to distance themselves from the Japanese during World War II—Muslim Americans have found allies in many quarters, including among Japanese Americans. The irony here is that the Japanese American Buddhist camp experience, which shaped the impulse to demonstrate loyalty as well as to remain on the outside as a critical voice of injustice in the American project of democracy, has made many Japanese American Buddhists feel excluded from the post-9/11 religiopolitical reality. President George Bush's language of the "Abrahamic faiths" of Judaism, Christianity, and Islam that form the "sacred canopy" of America, coupled with the snubbing of Buddhist representatives at official 9/11 memorial services, has rolled back decades of efforts to root Buddhism more firmly in the American religious landscape.

Many Japanese Americans took on the conflicted identity of being a Japanese American Buddhist in the crucible of war. One wonders if 9/11 will also turn out to be similarly significant for Muslim Americans as they struggle with Americanization and resistance to it in their ethnic and religious identity formation.

NOTES

1. Both Buddhist and Shinto priests were classified in the A (most potentially subversive) "known dangerous" category of the FBI's "ABC list" of aliens targeted for arrest in case of war. See Peter Irons, *Justice at War* (New York: Oxford University Press, 1983), 22.

2. Shinobu Matsuura, *Higan: Compassionate Vow—Selected Writings of Shinobu Matsuura* (Berkeley: Matsuura Family, 1986), 63.

3. Bob Kumamoto, "The Search for Spies: American Counterintelligence and the Japanese American Community, 1931–1942," *Amerasia Journal* 6.2 (Fall 1979): 45–75.

4. For more on the demographics of the early immigrants, see Paul R. Spickard, *Japanese Americans: The Formation and Transformations of an Ethnic Group* (London: Prentice Hall, 1996), 33.

5. See the O-Series: Correspondence, Buddhist Churches of America Archives, San Francisco (hereafter cited as BCA Archives), letters regarding and receipts of the donations collected by Japanese American temples for the Imperial Japanese Army.

6. Alan Hynd, *Betrayal from the East: The Inside Story of Japanese Spies in America* (New York: McBride, 1943), 21, 130–36.

7. For more on the FBI classification lists, see Kumamoto, "Search for Spies," 58.

8. On the "deputation" of Buddhist ministers' wives and others to serve as officiants, see Deborah Malone, "Documents from BCA Archives Vital for Redress Case," *Wheel of Dharma*, May 1997, 3.

9. BCA Archives, Box 1B (Letters—"Register for Civilian Defense," December 12, 1941).

10. BCA Archives, Box 1B (Letters—"Evacuation of Aliens," February 9, 1942).

11. For these phenomena, see Stephen Fujita and David O'Brien, *The Japanese American Experience* (Bloomington: Indiana University Press, 1991), 79.

12. Mary Nagatomi, interview by author, June 5, 2002.

13. BCA Archives, Box 1B (Letters—"Serve in Silence," March 5, 1942).

14. Young Buddhist Association of Butte Camp, ed., *Gathas and Services* (Rivers, Ariz.: YBA, 1944), 9–10.

15. Quoted in Susan Davis, "Mountain of Compassion: Dharma in American Internment Camps," *Tricycle: The Buddhist Review* 2.4 (Summer 1993): 49.

16. Bunyû Fujimura, *Though I Be Crushed* (Los Angeles: Nembutsu, 1995), 95. An exception to this nonsectarian Buddhism occurred in Manzanar Camp, where the main Buddhist church was led by a Jôdo Shin priest while a separate Nichiren Buddhist church existed for believers in that sect.

17. On collecting wood in the desert to make Buddhist altars, see Akemi Kikumura, *Through Harsh Winters: The Life of a Japanese Immigrant Woman* (Novato, Calif.: Chandler and Sharp, 1981), 52–53. Davis has also noted that "in response to the lack of Buddhist articles in some camps, people carved Buddha statues and shrines from scrap wood

and sagebrush found in the desert. At the North Dakota camp, Arthur Yamabe, who later became a minister, once carved a figure of baby Buddha from a carrot" ("Mountain of Compassion," 49).

18. This necrology is held at Zenshûji Temple in Los Angeles.

19. On the Americanization program and religion, see Gary Okihiro, "Religion and Resistance in America's Concentration Camps," *Phylon* 45.3 (Third Quarter 1981): 220–33.

20. For a glimpse into the government's thinking on Americanization, see House of Representatives, Subcommittee of the Special Committee on Un-American Activities, *Investigation of Un-American Propaganda Activities in the United States* (78th Cong., 1st sess., 1943), 21. For the Buddhist basketball team, see "Basketball Title at Hand," *Sangha News* 1.2 (February 13, 1944): 1.

21. In July 1944, the BCA ratified at a Salt Lake City conference a new constitution that adopted English as its primary language. See Kenneth Tanaka, "BCA: The Lotus That Bloomed behind Barbed Wire," *Turning Wheel*, Spring 1993, 41.

22. See Stephen Prothero, "Henry Steel Olcott and 'Protestant Buddhism,' " *Journal of the American Academy of Religion* 63.2 (Summer 1995): 281–302.

23. For YBA activities, see articles from the Rohwer camp's Buddhist newsletter: "YBA Girls Help Red Cross," *Sangha News* 1.2 (February 13, 1944): 1; "Bussei Hostesses Serve Local USO," *Sangha News* 1.4 (March 12, 1944): 1.

24. David Yoo, "Enlightened Identities: Buddhism and Japanese Americans of California, 1924–1941," *Western Historical Quarterly* 27.3 (Autumn 1996): 281. For more on the ethnic and religious identities of second-generation Japanese American Buddhists and Christians, see David Yoo, *Growing up Nisei: Race, Generation, and Culture among Japanese Americans of California, 1924–49* (Urbana: University of Illinois Press, 2000), 38–67.

25. Kihara Jôin, *Arashi No Nakade: Kaisen To Spai Yôgi* (Kyoto: Nagata Bunshôdo, 1985); translation by the author.

26. This section on postwar nisei work on the 1948 Golden Jubilee celebration, the B for Buddhism campaign, and the headstone marker campaign depends heavily on the research of Michael Masatsugu, "Reorienting the Pure Land: Buddhism, Beats, and Japanese Identities in Cold War America, 1945–67" (Ph.D. diss., University of California, Irvine, 2002), chap. 2.

27. See "1948 Buddhist Golden Jubilee Celebration," *Life*, September 1948, 76–77.

28. Diana Eck, *A New Religious America: How a "Christian Country" Has Become the World's Most Religiously Diverse Nation* (San Francisco: HarperSanFrancisco, 2001).

29. See "Bias Incidents against Muslims are Soaring, Islamic Council Says," *New York Times*, May 1, 2002, A22.

30. The Fresno Buddhist Church, for example, was vandalized in this way. I owe this account to Nagatomi, interview.

31. For a transcript of the president's remarks, see <http://www.adc.org/action 2001/17september2001v002.htm>.

32. On the context of Bush's mosque visit, see Dana Milbank and Emily Wax, "Bush Visits Mosque to Forestall Hate Crimes," *Washington Post*, September 18, 2001, A1.

33. House Bill H R 227 was introduced by Representatives David Bonier and Tom Davis; the Senate resolution, S J R 23, was introduced by Senators Orrin Hatch, Tom Harkin, Russ Feingold, and Patrick Leahy.

34. See "N.Y. Buddhist Rite Remembers 9-11 Dead," *Japan Times*, July 18, 2002, 2.

35. William Glaberson, "War on Terrorism Stirs Memory of Internment," *New York Times*, September 24, 2001, A18; Evelyn Nieves, "Recalling Internment and Saying 'Never Again,'" *New York Times*, September 28, 2001, A16.

36. Nieves, "Recalling Internment," A16.

37. Robert E. Pierre, "Fear Permeates Arab Enclave near Detroit, Muslim Americans Say Terror War Targets Them," *International Herald Tribune*, August 6, 2002, 4.

4

Reproducing Vietnam in America

San Jose's Perfect Harmony Temple

On a cold and windy Saturday, April 3, 1999, more than four thousand people paid their final respects to the Venerable Thich Dam Luu (Buddhist name, Thich Dieu Thanh), a Vietnamese American Buddhist nun who had died of cancer at the age of sixty-seven. She had arrived as a refugee from Vietnam in 1980 with nothing but her clothes and her devotion to Buddhism. Ten years later, with money saved from recycling aluminum cans and offered as donations, she had founded Chua Duc Vien (the Perfect Harmony Temple) in San Jose, California. At nine thousand square feet, this is one of the largest Vietnamese American Buddhist temples in the nation and one of the few run by nuns. Monks and nuns from various Buddhist sects had been at Dam Luu's side during the days before her death, and the funeral procession included not only local Buddhists but also the mayor of San Jose, the Venerable Thich Nhat Hanh, and thousands of Buddhists from across the United States and around the world. All paid their respects not only to Luu but also to the vibrant temple community she created and sustained, a community that serves the religious, social, and educational needs of nearby Vietnamese Americans even as it helps them negotiate the difficult process of acculturation.

As Lu and the Perfect Harmony Temple indicate, Vietnamese Buddhism has come to the United States. Understanding its development, however, requires considering in some detail the broader story of Vietnamese immigration. That history is generally divided into two periods, each with several waves. The first period ran from April 1975 through 1977 and included three waves of Vietnamese refugees to the United States.

The first of those waves, involving some ten to fifteen thousand refugees, began at least a week to ten days before the collapse of the South Vietnamese government. The second and probably largest wave included some eighty thousand people who were evacuated by air during the last days of April 1975.

These refugees were relatively well educated, came from urban areas, spoke some English, had some marketable skills, and were moderately westernized. Most members of these two waves were Vietnamese who worked either for the South Vietnamese government or for American businesses or government entities. All were relatively well prepared for American life on the basis of their education, socioeconomic background, and contact with Americans and/or the U.S. government.

The final wave during this initial period involved approximately forty to sixty thousand Vietnamese who left in small boats and ships and commandeered aircraft during the first two weeks of May 1975. They were later picked up by the U.S. Navy or cargo ships standing off the coast of Vietnam and transferred to Subic Bay and Clark Air Force Base in the Philippines and Guam.

The second major period of Vietnamese refugee migration began in 1978 and continues today. Since the fall of South Vietnam in 1975, many Vietnamese have tried to escape the oppression of the Vietnamese communist government. Although the influx continues steadily, the numbers are no longer as large as they once were. A significant characteristic of this period, especially between 1978 to 1980, was the large number of ethnic Chinese who migrated out of Vietnam and Cambodia.

Refugees from this second period have been called boat people because most of them escaped in poorly constructed boats and other homemade vessels. As a consequence of the lack of sophistication of their crafts (which could not long withstand the forces of nature), their scant navigational skills, limited provisions, and attacks by Thai sea pirates, the death rate of these boat people was very high. Verbal testimony from survivors in refugee camps fixes that figure as high as 50 percent, while Bruce Grant and Barry Wain have placed it at 10 to 15 percent.[1] A precise percentage, however, will never be calculated, since there is no way of knowing how many refugees left Vietnam. Owing in equal parts to the chaotic nature of the war and the extreme secrecy employed by those who left Vietnam, the Vietnamese communist government did not keep track of émigrés. Only the survivors have been counted.

The exodus of Vietnamese refugees to the United States was a difficult process. Regardless of when they came, the journey to America left a lasting impression. It was easier for those who were young or were able to leave earlier, when governmental restrictions were not as severe. For others, the journey was more traumatic because of difficult family circumstances or because they were detained by the government and sent to prison. Still, the uncertain and dangerous passage across a vast ocean to an unknown destination made it a difficult journey for all.

The Vietnamese exodus and resettlement in the United States could not have come at a worse time in American history. The Vietnam War divided the nation deeply. Official totals list 57,692 American men and women as having been killed in the war and 2,500 more as missing in action or prisoners of war.[2]

In fact, the American public's general attitude toward Vietnamese refugees at the end of the war was hostility. A May 1975 Gallup Poll showed "54 percent of all Americans opposed to admitting Vietnamese refugees to live in the United States, and only 36 percent in favor (12 percent were undecided)."[3] One common concern was economic self-interest—a fear of having jobs taken away and needing to provide public assistance and welfare to the refugees. During this time, the U.S. economy was in a recession, with an unemployment rate of 8.3 percent.[4] In fact, on April 27, 1975, more than sixty thousand unemployed union members filed into Robert F. Kennedy Stadium in Washington, D.C., to protest the lack of employment opportunities. The May 12, 1975, issue of Newsweek quoted California Congressman Burt Talcott as saying, "Damn it, we have too many Orientals already. If they all gravitate to California, the tax and welfare rolls will get overburdened and we already have our share of illegal aliens." In the same issue, an Arkansas woman said, "They say it's a lot colder here than in Vietnam. . . . With a little luck, maybe all those Vietnamese will take pneumonia and die." Even liberal Democrats such as California Governor Edmund Brown and Senator George McGovern said negative things about Vietnamese refugees. Several studies documented that a substantial number of Americans preferred to exclude the Vietnamese from the United States.[5]

Vietnamese refugees arrived, therefore, in a hostile United States. Most of the hostility was racially and economically based.[6] Still, many Americans extended humanitarian aid and sponsored families from refugee camps, working hard to welcome the newcomers.

When Vietnamese refugees first arrived in April 1975, the U.S. government organized four temporary refugee camps to streamline the refugees' transition into American society or to find third-country sponsors. All the camps were on military bases, which provided the labor and space needed to accommodate large number of refugees. The first to open was Camp Pendleton in southern California, followed by camps at Fort Chaffee in Arkansas, Eglin Air Force Base in Florida, and Indiantown Gap in Pennsylvania.

To minimize the social impact of this large influx of Vietnamese refugees, the U.S. government adopted a refugee dispersion policy that had four purposes: (1) to relocate refugees as quickly as possible so that they could achieve financial independence; (2) to ease the economic impact of a large influx of refugees on any given community; (3) to make it easier to find sponsors; and (4) to prevent the development of an ethnic ghetto.[7] Given the U.S. political and social climate at the time, the factors leading to this policy were primarily political and financial, not social.[8] The policy sought to encourage Vietnamese refugees to assimilate quickly into American society by finding work as soon as possible after leaving refugee camps.

The federal government's Interagency Task Force contracted with nine voluntary agencies to handle the resettlement of the refugees in the United States: United Hebrew Immigration and Assistance Service, the Lutheran Immigration and Refugee Service, the International Rescue Committee, the Church World Service, the American Funds for Czechoslovak Refugees, the U.S. Catholic Conference, the Travelers Aid International Social Service, the Tolstoy Foundation, and the Council for Nationalities Service. Each refugee family chose or was assigned to a resettlement agency.[9] These agencies sought primarily to find sponsors who could fulfill both financial and moral responsibilities as well as to match sponsors and refugees. These responsibilities included providing temporary food, clothing, and shelter; assisting in the search for employment or job training for the head of the household; enrolling children in school; and providing ordinary medical care.[10] In other words, the sponsors would serve as a resource to support refugees until they could become self-supporting. The refugees had four ways in which they could leave these temporary refugee camps and enter American society: (1) by resettling in a third country; (2) by repatriating to Vietnam; (3) by demonstrating proof of financial independence; or (4) by finding a sponsor through the voluntary agencies.[11]

Although the U.S. government encouraged third-country resettlement, this option was rarely used. Very few countries offered such assistance unless the refugees were professionals, had in-country relatives, or could speak the native language.[12] Only a small number of refugees chose to return to Vietnam: "by October 1975, repatriation had been granted to 1,546 refugees by the new government of Vietnam."[13] The majority of these repatriates were military men who had been forced to leave their families behind at the time of their evacuation. Demonstrating financial independence was also difficult. According to Gail Paradise Kelly, "the Task Force required a refugee family to show proof of cash reserves totaling at least $4,000 per household member."[14] Not many could do so. In addition, few refugees reported their financial savings to the authorities because of their understandable fear of governments. Thus, Vietnamese refugees entered American society almost universally through the family sponsorship method.

The sponsors found by voluntary agencies consisted of church congregations, parishes, or affiliates; individual families; corporations; and companies with former Vietnamese employees. In addition, if the refugees had relatives who fulfilled the same requirements, those relatives could also serve as sponsors. Kenneth A. Skinner, however, reports that only fifteen thousand Vietnamese lived in the United States prior to 1975,[15] and most of these individuals were students staying temporarily on visas or wives of U.S. soldiers. In short, because the Vietnamese lacked an established community in the United States, this method was seldom available to the first waves of refugees. However, Vietnamese from the first several waves more frequently used the family sponsorship method to sponsor relatives and friends who entered after 1975.

After living for a time with their sponsors and adjusting to the new environment, many Vietnamese refugees began to relocate throughout the United States. Many reasons led them to leave their original resettlement sites. Family reunification was an important variable, as was the desire to live close to people who were similar to them. Job availability and climate also contributed to this secondary migration. Data from the 2000 U.S. Census indicate that the states most populated with Vietnamese Americans were California, Texas, Louisiana, Virginia, Washington, Pennsylvania, and Florida. In short, the original resettlement pattern and the secondary migration combined to produce Vietnamese American communities throughout the United States. These communities made possible the establishment of religious communities.

The two largest religions in the Vietnamese American population are Roman Catholicism and Buddhism. Approximately 30 percent are Catholics, and Catholicism is especially strong among those who were originally from North Vietnam and those who emigrated in 1975. The rest of the community tends to be Buddhist because of the region's religious history. No matter which religion people claim, however, they also are strongly influenced by the Tam Giao (Three Religions): Confucianism, Daoism, and Buddhism. This does not mean that Vietnamese Americans actively practice these three religions but rather that they incorporate components of these religions (often unwittingly) into their daily lives. They were and are socialized into these values and norms through proverbs, folk sayings, songs, family rituals, and cultural festivals. In other words, the Tam Giao constitute part of being Vietnamese.[16]

Although no agreement exists regarding how Buddhism entered Vietnam (perhaps through China, perhaps through Indian traders), scholars have concluded that Buddhism in Vietnam is ultimately derived from India. Since its introduction, Buddhism has been an important institution in Vietnamese history. It was one of the forces that unified the Vietnamese in their various fights for independence from the Chinese. In recent times, Buddhism acted as a protector of traditional culture when the French seized colonial control in the nineteenth century. During the Vietnam War, Buddhism was again seen as the national conscience when monks and laypersons protested American intervention. One of the conflict's most enduring images is the self-immolation of Buddhist monk Thich Quang Duc in protest of the war. During the course of Vietnamese history, therefore, Buddhists have preserved traditional culture, transmitted Buddhist doctrines and values, and struggled against foreign domination.

One of the advantages enjoyed by Vietnamese Americans is a relatively tolerant U.S. social and political climate. Although Vietnamese refugees have felt tremendous pressure to assimilate economically, there has been, in this post-civil-rights-movement era, far less pressure to assimilate socially and religiously. One major government concern has been to quash public criticisms of too much aid to these refugees, so the refugees have been expected to become self-sufficient very quickly. Moreover, they were allowed to practice their religions without the kind of interference they might have met earlier in American history.

Another advantage for these new immigrants was that Buddhism was no longer a new form of religion in America in the mid-1970s. Many Americans were familiar with at least the religion's basic features.[17] Moreover, the practice of Buddhism in Asian American communities had already been adapted to Christian norms.[18] However, Americans' familiarity with Buddhism varied considerably by region: someone from a California city was far more likely to be familiar with Buddhism than someone from rural Kansas.

The Vietnamese American Buddhist community did not have an established temple or national organization, so no support was available from that source to assist the new arrivals in negotiating the complexities of American life. Vietnamese Catholics, by contrast, could practice their religion more quickly and easily because the United States had an established Catholic

Church; furthermore, the church was one of the voluntary agencies that reset-tled Vietnamese refugees.

The Buddhists also had some advantages, however. Because no community preceded them, they did not have to follow rules, procedures, and policies dictated by a larger group. They could choose where to form temples, in-cluding in some cases in garages and private homes. They also did not have to be involved in the often divisive political struggles of a national religious community.

Although the Venerable Dam Luu passed away on March 26, 1999, her life and legacy, epitomized by Chua Duc Vien and her disciples, demon-strates how a Vietnamese American Buddhist temple has struggled to balance new life in the United States with the traditions of Vietnam. San Jose is no Vietnamese American backwater. In fact, Santa Clara County, where San Jose is located, has the second-largest Vietnamese American population in the United States, with more than 110,000 inhabitants.

According to the Venerable Thich Minh Duc, the Venerable Dam Luu lived an unusual life even before her arrival in northern California.[19] At age sixteen, she had been among the first Buddhist nuns ordained in Vietnam. In her youth, formal education was not a requirement for monastic training. In fact, Buddhist monks and nuns rarely possessed any education, since they basically just followed the instruction of their teachers, reciting the sutras and conduct-ing rituals.[20] Dam Luu's teacher, however, wanted her students to have a deeper understanding of Buddhism and thus encouraged them to become more educated. As a result, Dam Luu was also one of the first nuns in Vietnam to pass the national exam for a high school diploma.

Dam Luu was later assigned to Phuoc Hoa Temple in Saigon (now Ho Chi Minh City), and although she wanted to devote her life to Buddhism, she could not escape the impact of the Vietnam War. At this time, President Ngo Dinh Diem persecuted many Buddhist practitioners for their religious beliefs and their opposition to the war. Alongside others who protested the war and demanded religious freedom, Dam Luu participated in several political dem-onstrations against the government, and in 1963, she was jailed for these activities. Later that year, she was released when Diem was overthrown by a coup d'état.

In 1964, the societal upheaval caused by the war led the United Vietnamese Buddhist Church to recognize the need for members to participate in more secular professional fields. Consequently, Dam Luu was among a handful of people sent abroad to study. She spent five years in Germany, where she received a master's degree in social work. She returned to Vietnam in 1969 to become the director of the newly established Lam Ty Ni orphanage. This orphanage, operated with the help of the local Buddhist community, cared for children who either were victims of the war or could not be cared for by their families for other reasons. It was dissolved after the communist victory in 1975. In 1976, Dam Luu was pressured to make false accusations against a monastic friend. When she refused, the government harassed her. With some help from her lay disciples, she made plans to escape from Vietnam. This exodus was much more difficult than she anticipated: four attempts to leave failed. Finally, in late 1978, disguised as a layperson, she managed to escape via a small fishing boat.[21]

On this escape she saw the desperation of those refugees who fled with her but was troubled by their willingness to blame others for their suffering. While in a refugee camp in Malaysia, she helped others with what little she had. Instead of waxing philosophical, she worked on a practical level to alleviate pain and suffering, providing food and clothing for those who were in need and offering guidance to those who had lost hope. She practiced and taught her religious beliefs without preaching. In short, she continued to live her life as a Buddhist nun.

Dam Luu arrived in the United States in 1980 at age forty-eight and started a new life with less than twenty dollars. Thanh Cat, a monk in East Palo Alto, California, sponsored her resettlement. One of her first acts was to found the Perfect Harmony Temple.

The Perfect Harmony Temple began modestly. With the help of another Buddhist monk, Dam Luu rented a small house on the east side of San Jose and started a "home temple."[22] As with all home temples, the entire house represented a larger temple. She used the living room as the Buddha's hall, and a tent in the backyard served many different functions, including as a dining hall, a lecture hall (for dharma lessons), a school where children learned Vietnamese, and, on occasion, a bedroom for overnight guests. Following Vietnamese practice, Dam Luu received donations from the small Buddhist community immediately surrounding her. These donations, however, were not enough to cover the rent and other expenses, so she had to find other ways to earn money that did not interfere with her religious commitments. After attending to her religious responsibilities at the temple during the day, she used her free time to collect aluminum cans and newspapers to redeem for small change.

Although she did this work quietly and without fanfare, word began to spread about a Buddhist nun who collected recyclables, and Buddhist women and children consequently joined in the effort. Between the late 1980s, when the recycling effort began, and the mid-1990s, Dam Luu saved enough money to start a temple fund. Eventually, with the help of her three thousand disciples plus donations from other Vietnamese American Buddhists in the Bay Area, Dam Luu raised four hundred thousand dollars (about 30 percent of it from recycling) to build a new temple. Construction on the Perfect Harmony Temple began in 1995, and most of it was completed three years later. It features a main hall, dining hall and classrooms, kitchen and eating areas, and sleeping quarters for thirteen resident nuns.

The temple was designed and furnished in the traditional Vietnamese style, with symbols quite different from those in Chinese temples. Dam Luu wanted the temple to reflect the architecture of ancient temples in Vietnam and worked with an architect specifically to assure this fidelity to the tradition. The vast majority of the statues and religious figures were shipped from Vietnam. Although the temple is located in a bustling urban area and faces a busy road, one enters it through a peaceful garden that provides a spiritual respite from metropolitan life.

As the abbess of the home temple, the Venerable Dam Luu observed the challenges faced by Vietnamese refugees as they adjusted to life in America. She noticed that one of the most pressing issues was the generation gap between grandparents, parents, and children. Temple members lamented that the older generation had a difficult time communicating with the younger generation in America. Since children can learn language at a faster rate and are socialized in school, they began to speak English more and more and Vietnamese less and less to their parents and grandparents. Dam Luu addressed this problem by advising older Vietnamese to learn English so that they could develop an understanding of what was happening around them. English literacy, in short, would make their lives easier. She also argued that speaking their children's language would enable better communication. Conversely, she also advocated having children learn their parents' and grandparents' language and began to provide Vietnamese language classes for the younger generation at the temple.

The idea at first encountered some resistance. Parents complained that they were already too busy adjusting to a new life and that these classes would only add to their already busy schedules (which often included multiple jobs). With the help of some volunteers, the temple began to offer free lunches to the students. This was an important incentive for the parents, since it gave them time to complete other errands while the children were at the temple. Language instruction also exposed children to Buddhism, not only through the Sunday school curriculum (which typically concludes with a half hour of Buddhist teachings in stories or songs) but also through participation in annual musicals and skits performed during festivals celebrating, for example, the Buddha's birthday.

Because of the large demand and the lack of classroom facilities, the temple currently offers classes on Sunday mornings (9:00 A.M.–noon) and afternoons (1:00–4:00 P.M.). Each session has roughly fifteen to eighteen classes with about twelve to fifteen students per class. The temple thus serves between three hundred and four hundred students each year. The students pay a small fee (fifty dollars annually) to help defray the costs of course materials. There are about sixty teachers and helpers, all volunteers. Students are assigned to classes according to their Vietnamese language abilities.

The curriculum is designed by the teachers and revised yearly. Before becoming a teacher, each volunteer receives training. Some of the teachers are quite familiar with the curriculum, having gone through it themselves. Students and their families still receive free vegetarian lunches after the morning session. There is no formal recruiting process; most students are the children of temple members. As a matter of fact, the nuns report that many students are turned away each year because the temple cannot accommodate all of the requests from families in the community. Temple leaders and the volunteer teachers constantly struggle to find ways to provide this service to all students, but limits on space and resources prevent the temple from offering additional classes.

In addition to language courses, the temple provides a wide range of other activities. Monday through Saturday, chanting and sutra sessions are offered in the morning from 5:30 to 7:00 and again from 9:00 to 11:00. Afternoon and evening sessions are also held at 3:00–4:00, 5:30–6:30, and 7:00–8:00. On Sunday there is chanting and Buddhist teaching from 10:00 A.M. until noon and from 3:00 until 4:30 in the afternoon. Buddhist classes for adults take place on Mondays from 7:00 to 8:00 P.M. and for young children on Saturdays from 5:00 to 7:00 P.M. Many special events are also celebrated throughout the year, including the Buddha's birthday, the Lunar New Year, the First

Full Moon Festival, the Elder Festival, the Buddha Sakyamuni's birthday, the Avalokitesvara Bodhisattva Celebration, the Ullambana Festival, the Ksiti-garbha Bodhisattva Celebration, the Tenth Full Moon Festival, the Buddha Amitabha's birthday, the End of the Year Festival, and the Mid-Autumn Festival. All of these activities are free and open to the public: everyone, regardless of religion, race, or class, is welcome to attend and participate. Although most participants are Vietnamese Americans, a few non-Vietnamese also participate. The temple holds no celebrations of American festivals (for example, Thanksgiving or Christmas).

The two largest festivals, each attended by hundreds, are the Buddha's birthday and the Lunar New Year. The rituals, chanting, and celebrations take place almost entirely in Vietnamese and involve not only religious but also cultural practice. For example, during the Buddha's birthday celebrated on May 6, 2001, the temple was filled with members and nonmembers alike: all the parking lots were full, and cars were parked throughout the surrounding neighborhood. Several volunteers in front of the temple discouraged people from jaywalking, and signs asked people to use the crosswalks. The San Jose Police Department provided several officers to help with traffic.

The day began very early. By 7:00 A.M., the temple was bustling with people setting up. Parents, grandparents, and children lined up to burn incense in honor of Buddha and their ancestors. The official event began at 10:00 A.M. in the main hall with an hourlong session of chanting and reciting of sutras led by resident nuns. All the nuns and monks were dressed in formal Buddhist attire, while participants wore their best clothes. A dharma talk by the Venerable Thich Minh Duc followed.

Nuns and monks concluded the official service by leaving the temple in a single line. A Su Co, a Buddhist nun, led the procession with a small bell that she rang at regular intervals. The clerics exited through the main hall and then proceeded through the garden to the back of the temple.

The temple later was transformed into a musical celebration of the Buddha's birth. The production was organized, rehearsed, and performed by students and teachers from the Vietnamese language classes. Songs, performances, and short plays depicted the birth of the Buddha and the subsequent joys and celebrations. The musical production alone lasted a little more than an hour, and, with the exception of a ten-minute dharma discussion in English, all of the day's events took place in Vietnamese.

This festival demonstrates Vietnamese Buddhists' desire to maintain as much of their cultural heritage as possible. It remains to be seen, however, how long these Vietnamese Buddhists will be able to hold back the forces of Americanization.

The Perfect Harmony Temple also serves as the first Vietnamese nunnery in the United States. Dam Luu trained between fifteen and twenty nuns. Resident nuns live at the temple year-round, with the exception of several months during the summer when they are sent around the world to learn other Buddhist doctrines and practices. In more recent years, the temple has been training nuns sent by sister temples in Vietnam. After completing their studies, the nuns are expected to return to Vietnam to help develop temples there. The Perfect Harmony Temple also educates monks. Many have become dharma teachers throughout the United States, Europe, and Vietnam.

One other distinguishing mark of this temple has been the abbess's openness to other Buddhist sects and practices. Dam Luu encouraged her students to learn about other Buddhist practices. Tibetan monks have visited and have offered Dharma talks. On many occasions, the temple has also hosted members of other Buddhist sects, and its members have taken part in the annual ecumenical pilgrimage to the Land of Ten Thousand Buddhas in northern California.

One of Dam Luu's other innovations was the creation of her own Vietnamese prayer book. While living in a refugee camp in Malaysia, she noticed that the behaviors of many Vietnamese who claimed to be Buddhists did not reflect the teachings of the Buddha. She wanted to provide people with the opportunity to understand, learn, and practice Buddhist principles. As a result of China's influence on Buddhism, however, Vietnamese prayer books were generally written in ancient Chinese, and most Vietnamese did not understand the meanings of the sutras they were chanting. By changing the prayers from Chinese to Vietnamese, she hoped to offer practitioners a better understanding of the prayers. Furthermore, she wanted these prayer books to include passages applicable to people's daily lives. This change, which mirrors the shift into the vernacular in the Protestant Reformation of the sixteenth century, created some controversy within the temple. Although younger Vietnamese Americans welcomed the shift, many older members were unhappy. They felt Dam Luu was departing too much from their tradition, and some threatened to withhold financial support. But this threat did not deter the abbess from doing what she thought was right, and her idea of chanting Buddhist scriptures in Vietnamese has now gained wide support at many U.S. temples. In fact, many temples now use the chants that Dam Luu and her disciples translated.[23]

One factor underlying the success of the Perfect Harmony Temple is volunteers' tremendous devotion. Countless volunteers run the temple's many activities. For example, a large group of older women prepares free meals for several hundred people after Sunday services. These women also cook vegetarian food that is sold to raise funds for the temple. A cleaning crew composed mostly of young and middle-aged men sets up tables and chairs before meals and washes dishes and pots. An army of mostly young adult male and female teachers volunteers to teach Sunday school. Since San Jose is in the heart of Silicon Valley, some volunteers have the technical skills necessary to record lectures, to videotape important celebrations, to duplicate cassettes and CDs, and to develop and maintain the temple's Web site. A group of middle-aged men nicknamed the Fix-It Crew is responsible for all temple repairs, including donated odds and ends. It seems as if nothing is thrown away; everything possible is recycled. Broken items eventually are fixed or somehow recycled. A nun is responsible for the garden, but she is supported by a group of volunteers who maintain it, tend to the temple's flower arrangements, and grow plants and flowers sold to support the temple's activities.

The life of Dam Luu and the establishment of the Duc Vien Temple provide a good case study for examining the acculturation process of one refugee group to the United States. As a result of the relatively tolerant social, political, and religious climate since their arrival in 1975, Vietnamese American Buddhists were able to build the Perfect Harmony Temple and have used it to preserve and reinforce key Vietnamese cultural traditions. But the temple, while traditional in many respects, does far more than the typical temple in Vietnam, since it takes as one of its key tasks helping its members adjust to life in the United States.

One way the Perfect Harmony Temple differs from a typical temple in Vietnam is by providing Vietnamese language classes to the younger generation. This may be the most important way in which temple leaders are attempting to ensure that their children and grandchildren see the importance not only of Buddhism but also of their Vietnamese heritage. The temple also attempts to address some of the intergenerational conflicts that bedevil all Asian American groups, providing a forum where youth can begin to understand their parents' and grandparents' values and beliefs (even as those parents and grandparents learn English). The language school is tightly integrated into the planning and production of the large festivals held annually at the temple, thereby encouraging young people to participate and giving them a sense of ownership of the temple. With respect to the older generation, by offering religious and social guidance (for example, by translating the prayer book from Chinese to Vietnamese and including some passages addressing struggles in daily life), the temple has also provided a place where members of that generation can continue to practice their traditions and affirm their values even as they adjust to American circumstances. Members of the older generation are particularly active as volunteers and are heavily invested in the temple.

Even inside this fairly traditional temple, Americanization is at work in plain view. Sunday schools are an American tradition, not a Vietnamese one. And trends such as Anglicization and congregationalism, discussed in other chapters in this volume, are also at work here.

NOTES

1. Bruce Grant, *The Boat People: An "Age" Investigation* (London: Penguin, 1979); Barry Wain, *The Refused: The Agony of the Indochina Refugees* (New York: Simon and Schuster, 1981), 70–73.

2. Walter Capps, *The Unfinished War: Vietnam and the American Conscience* (Boston: Beacon, 1982), 1.

3. Thomas Griffith, "The Final Commitment: People," *Time*, May 12, 1975.

4. Gail Paradise Kelly, *From Vietnam to America: A Chronicle of Vietnamese Immigration to the United States* (Boulder, Colo.: Westview, 1977).

5. Angus Deming, "The New Americans," *Newsweek*, May 12, 1975, 32.

6. Sucheng Chan, *Asian Americans: An Interpretive History* (Boston: Twayne, 1991); Alexander Saxton, *The Indispensable Enemy: Labor and the Anti-Chinese Movement in California* (Berkeley: University of California Press, 1971); Sandy Sandmeyer, *The Anti-Chinese Movement in California* (Berkeley: University of California Press, 1973); Ronald Takaki, *Strangers from a Different Shore* (Boston: Little, Brown, 1989).

7. William T. Liu, Maryanne Lamanna, and Alice Murata, *Transition to Nowhere: Vietnamese Refugees in America* (Nashville, Tenn.: Charter House, 1979), 66–68.

8. Kelly, *From Vietnam to America*, 159.

9. Liu, Lamanna, and Murata, *Transition to Nowhere*, 157.

10. Ibid., 157.

11. Kelly, *From Vietnam to America*, 129–36.

12. Ibid., 130.

13. Darrel Montero, *Vietnamese Americans: Patterns of Resettlement and Socioeconomic Adaptation in the United States* (Boulder, Colo.: Westview, 1979), 27.

14. Kelly, *From Vietnam to America*, 129.

15. Kenneth A. Skinner, "Vietnamese in America: Diversity and Adaptation," *California Sociologist* 3.32 (1980): 104.

16. Hien Duc Do, *The Vietnamese Americans* (Westport, Conn.: Greenwood, 1999), 6–9.

17. See Charles S. Prebish and Kenneth K. Tanaka, eds., *The Faces of Buddhism in America* (Berkeley: University of California Press, 1998); Eck, *New Religious America*.

18. Carl Becker, "Japanese Pure Land Buddhism in Christian America," *Buddhist Christian Studies* 10 (1990): 143–56.

19. Thich Minh Duc, "Dam Luu: An Eminent Vietnamese Nun," in *Ky Yen Su Ba Dam Luu* (San Jose: Van Boi, 2000), 139–41.

20. Cong Tu Nguyen and A. W. Barber, "Vietnamese Buddhism in North America: Tradition and Acculturation," in *Faces of Buddhism*, edited by Prebish and Tanaka, 129–46.

21. Minh Duc, "Dam Luu," 141–43.

22. Chloe Breyer, "Religious Liberty in Law and Practice: Vietnamese Home Temples in California and the First Amendment," *Journal of Church and State* 35.2 (Spring 1993): 367–402.

23. Minh Duc, "Dam Luu," 147–48.

5

Tibetan Buddhism in America

Reinforcing the Pluralism of the Sacred Canopy

To understand Tibetan Buddhism in America, we have to consider what Tibetan Buddhism has been at its origination in India and during various periods in Tibet. Only then can we see how Tibet and Tibetan Buddhism came to be perceived in America, how the first Tibetan Buddhists to live in the United States laid the foundations for its American transformations, and how these U.S. forms differ from the Buddhisms of other countries. Then we can evaluate the immense impact of His Holiness the Dalai Lama during more than two decades of visiting and writing in this country, a period during which Tibetan Buddhism became a movement with national and international visibility. Finally, we can survey the present state of Tibetan Buddhism in the United States.

This story has not yet been properly told, since the Tibetan Buddhism described in previous surveys is only a ghost of the real thing. Tibetan Buddhism has often been called Vajrayana Buddhism or Tantric Buddhism. It is thereby distinguished first from the Hinayana or Theravada Buddhism (or, as I prefer to call it, Monastic Buddhism) of Sri Lanka, Burma, Thailand, and Kampuchea and second from the Mahayana (I call it Messianic) Buddhism of China, Korea, Japan, and Vietnam. According to this account, what distinguishes Tibetan Buddhism from other Buddhisms is that Tibetans practice the Buddhist Tantras. They seek Buddhahood in a single life and to do so engage in ritual, magical, yogic, devotional, and contemplative practices that are supposedly unique. These practices revolve around the powerful, charismatic, and authoritative figure of the lama, more or less a guru, which explains why people used to and sometimes still do call Tibetan Buddhism Lamaism. This term seals the idea that Tibetan Buddhism is only Buddhism by proxy—that it amounts in the last analysis to indigenous Tibetan shamanism. This view informs many accounts of the history of Tibetan Buddhism in America, including the most sympathetic and well researched.

This view provides the conceptual foundation of Asian Buddhists' basic attitudes toward Tibetan Buddhism: as a rule, Asians Buddhists do not identify Tibetan Buddhists as fellow Buddhists, preferring to think of them as grisly, yak-meat-eating shamanists who have only the most tenuous link with real Buddhism. This negative attitude helps to explain the lack of interest in the Chinese communist destruction of Tibet or in the efforts of His Holiness the Dalai Lama to combat it. When Asian Buddhists holding these stereotypes meet a Tibetan Buddhist teacher, they always seem pleasantly surprised to encounter living elements of monastic self-restraint, philosophical depth, and contemplative practice with which they can identify. Such personal contacts help to undermine the stereotypes, but those stereotypes remain nonetheless retrenched. The powerful Buddhist institutions of east and south Asia still place a higher priority on relations with the communist Chinese government than they do with their oppressed coreligionists in Tibet or the Tibetan government in exile. The notable exception to this rule has been Japan's Shingon Buddhists, who have interacted generously and respectfully with the Tibetans during their ordeal but have not succeeded in getting the Japanese government to stand up to the Chinese.

A quick look at the evidence will dispel the misperception that Tibetan Buddhism is merely Vajrayana Buddhism, Tantric Buddhism, or Lamaism. Before the 1950 Chinese invasion, the 6 million Tibetans honored and supported between one-tenth and one-fifth of their population—between six hundred thousand and 1.2 million people—as religious renunciants. Tibetan Buddhist mendicant monks and novice nuns (bhikshu/shramaneri) as well as ordained laypersons (upasika/upasiki) took the monastic vows of the Mulasarvastivada Vinaya, a form of Theravada discipline differing only in the most miniscule details from the Vinaya discipline maintained by the monks (there were no ordained nuns in recent centuries) of Sri Lanka, Thailand, Myanmar, and Kampuchea. Thus, before 1950, Tibet was the biggest Theravada or Monastic Buddhist country in the world, since the combined monastic populations of the main Theravada countries or even of all the other Buddhist countries in twentieth-century Asia did not reach such numbers.

But these Tibetan Buddhist Theravada monks and nuns did not just maintain the Vinaya discipline: they also studied and contemplated Mahayana Buddhist sutras. So we are compelled to describe Tibetan Buddhism as a combination of Theravada, or Monastic Buddhism, and Mahayana, or Messianic Buddhism, with the majority of Tibetan Buddhists having only slight knowledge of Tantric Buddhist thought or practices. Most Tibetan Buddhists respected Tantric Buddhist texts, institutions, and teachers as the advanced products of the Mahayana movement, however, so we should not ignore the Tantric element in Tibetan Buddhism.

We cannot speak accurately about Tibetan Buddhism, therefore, as Vajrayana Buddhism or Lamaism even though some nonmonastic Tibetan Buddhists may call themselves by such names. Even these nonmonastics, however, cannot deny that before one can adopt and maintain any Tantric Buddhist vow, one must adopt at least some form of the Theravada layperson's (upasika/ upasiki) vow as well as the Mahayana bodhisattva's vow. Therefore, it is impossible in Tibetan Buddhism to be a Vajrayana Buddhist without also being a Theravada and Mahayana Buddhist.

Even a cursory survey of the history of Indic Buddhism shows that the form of Buddhism practiced in India from the latter half of the first millennium C.E. until the west and central Asian invasions destroyed the key Buddhist monasteries of India corresponds most closely to Tibetan Buddhism. Monastic Buddhist vows were taken and maintained. Mahayana Buddhist texts and doctrines were taught, studied, debated, and contemplated. And some individuals pursued Tantric studies and practices both inside and outside monastery walls. Not everyone did all three of these practices. Much controversy and some divisions existed; it was a pluralistic form of Buddhism. But Indian Buddhist civilization was systematically transplanted into Tibet beginning in the seventh century, complete with huge libraries of Monastic, Messianic, and Tantric texts and traditions of monastic vows, university curricula, communal rituals, esoteric contemplations, and yogas. Over centuries, this civilization gradually enveloped Tibetan culture, taming its violence and transforming it into a shrine for the preservation and elaboration of the multitraditional Buddhism of late classical India.

After that full-blown Indian Buddhism was destroyed in its original sites, a reaction occurred in Sri Lanka, and the Mahayana and Tantric elements of its Buddhism were suppressed, leaving only the monastic traditions supported in the Pali Suttas. As a result, south Asian Buddhists today find it hard to see themselves reflected in Tibetan Buddhism. In east Asia, by contrast, monastic and messianic elements were preserved, but the esoteric elements were mostly overlooked (except by Chinese esoteric Buddhists and Japanese Shingon Buddhists), and Tibetan Buddhism was thought of as aberrant.

Of course, recognizing Tibetan Buddhism as the continuation of the final form of Indic Buddhism does not by itself cleanse the image of Tibetan Buddhism from its distorting aura of corruption. It remains to consider the history of Buddhism in India, to suggest an alternative to the prevailing perception of gradual decadence and decline, again as a result of the misunderstanding of Mahayana devotionalism and Tantric esotericism as popular corruptions of pristine Buddhism:

Indian Buddhism's first five hundred years [were] primarily monastic, solidifying the extra-social society of the Sangha, providing the educationally oriented individual an asylum from all economic, social, political, and religious demands. We see its next five hundred years as incrementally messianic, moving aggressively outward from a solid monastic base in the economy, society, and culture (already changed by five centuries of feedback from the thriving educational community) to tackle the more violent aspects of the ordinary society and teach a social ethic of love and compassion. We see its last five hundred years as culminatively apocalyptic: insisting on a more evolved level of behavior in the developed society, Buddhists moved out aggressively into the marginal areas of society among the lower castes, tribals, and foreign neighbors, such as the Tibetans. They used magical and charismatic means to teach people who could not be approached within the literate conventions of the by now highly refined, urbane, peaceful, civilized, and pluralistic Sanskrit Hindu-Buddhistic society.[1]

In sum, we can see the three vehicles or styles of Buddhism as products of a developing process of gradual improvement of an entire civilization that evolved over many centuries from a militaristic and dynastic culture into a nonviolent nation-state founded on what I have called "inner modernity."[2]

The distinguishing mark of Tibetan Buddhism that emerges in this account is its totalizing transformation of Tibetan civilization into an environment that optimizes the individual's opportunities to become a Buddha. Tibetan Buddhism, in other words, is a monastic, messianic, and apocalyptic tradition that seeks via ethics, religion, science, and technology to turn an entire culture into a theater for enlightenment. This is the same pluralistic civilization we see developing as a counterculture in India over fifteen hundred years, then in Tibet for a thousand years. Finally, inner modernity ensues when, perhaps for the first time in Buddhist history, a counterculture goes mainstream.

Two important, interrelated elements of this mainstreaming of Buddhism in Tibet are (1) the integration of monastic institutions and governmental institutions and (2) the development of the social institution of reincarnation out of the age-old doctrine of rebirth. The former seems at first glance to resemble church/state fusion on the European model until we remember that Buddhist monasticism in both India and Tibet was the cornerstone of social pluralism. The Tibetan expression for this mainstreaming is "coordination of dharma and life in the world [chos srid zung 'brel]," where "dharma" means not just religion but reality and the teaching of enlightenment and "life in the world" means individual existence in culture and society. This expression indicates, therefore, not domination by one religion (defined as dogmatic belief system or creedal institution) over other religions through the coercive powers of a state but rather that the monastic institutions facilitating the teaching and practice of the evolutionary ethic leading to individual enlightenment finally eliminate altogether their age-old rivalries, military institutions, and the militaristic state. In so doing, the monastic institutions absorb the life energies of the entire population into the teaching and practice of enlightenment and regulate the minimal institution of the former state through a bureaucracy that coordinates the shared activities of educated monastic clerks and former warlord nobles. That Buddhism was countercultural in other Asian cultures meant that it was always subordinate to a monarchical state based on military forces obedient to the king, with an entire national culture dedicated to legitimizing that king and army and with the king's support for the countercultural monastic community serving as an important if paradoxical element of his legitimacy. Tibet's historical achievement was thus unprecedented in that it ended the military institution once and for all, allowing the dharmic principle—that evolution and liberation are the overriding aims of living—to seep into all corners of Tibetan life. This society in which Buddhism was mainstream and individual liberation maximally central is thus utterly mislabeled when conflated with an Abrahamic "theocracy," where a monotheistic belief system becomes totally identified with a militaristic monarchy, leading to a totally authoritarian social order with no room for individual liberation.

The key institution that enabled the Tibetans to transform their previous militaristic, imperial order into a nonviolent, dharmic one was the formal recognition of the reincarnation of its most revered exemplars. Beginning in the thirteenth century with the Second Karmapa Lama, Tibetans began to experience the return of beloved leaders as brilliant, gifted children who became recognized a short time after their passing away in a previous body. These children proved their former lives by remembering people, events, possessions, and insights of their former embodiments and then by relearning their former wisdom and behaving compassionately. It all fit, of course, not only with the now matter-of-fact belief in the continuity of lives but also with the semi-esoteric Mahayana understanding of the possibility for advanced bodhisattvas to choose the circumstances of their future lives. From the turn of the fifteenth century, the culture became pervaded by these concrete instantiations of the Tibetan belief in omnipresence of enlightened beings, further confirming the Tibetan sense of the possibility of each individual's attainment of an exalted level of being, limitless in its present and future blissfulness and inexhaustible in its capability to effect the liberation from suffering of others. No wonder Tibetans thought it preferable to delegate political authority to such beings, taking it away from egotistical warlords and turning personal ambitions away from external conquest and toward an inward horizon.

By the end of the inwardly modern period in the 1950s, four or five thousand reincarnate lamas existed, mostly men and mostly monks but including some women and laypersons. Their presence is a clear sign of the totalizing, mainstream presence of Buddhist culture in Tibetan civilization.

Tibetan Buddhism is thus is not just a bunch of Tibetan lamas teaching esoteric Tantric or Vajrayana practices, though this is one manifestation of it. The encounter between Americans and Tibetan Buddhism can only be understood, therefore, as the first western engagement with the full panoply of Indian Buddhist institutions, doctrines, and practices. Before the 1960s, Americans had encountered Buddhism as a world religion through the writings of D. T. Suzuki and Paul Carus's *Buddhist Bible* (1932). They had learned of Zen through the teachings of Zen masters from Japan. They had encountered the religions of Pure Land Buddhism, a Japanese institution organized around faith in the savior-godlike Buddha Amida of the western paradise, and Lotus Sutra Buddhism, another Japanese movement, based on Nichiren Shonin's realization of the importance of the Lotus Sutra revelation by Shakyamuni Buddha. They had encountered a few Buddhist monks who served various Asian ethnic communities in seemingly priestly capacities. Some popular books had appeared, though Vedantic Hinduism and yoga were somewhat better known. Buddhism was thought of as "Eastern mysticism," as "meditation," or as an ethnic Asian religion. A number of recent works have exhaustively chronicled this history.[3]

A key point is that various Buddhisms from various Asian countries entered America by intersecting with various American countercultures, which was natural, since those Buddhisms had never gone beyond countercultural institutional settings in their home countries. Thus, the first Americans to take a personal interest in Buddhism were mystics, poets, philosophers, and sympathetic neighbors of oppressed immigrant communities. Today, to be a convert Buddhist means to adopt countercultural status.

As Tibetan Buddhism first began to become known, it was like something mysterious, perhaps monstrous, perhaps magnificent, heaving into sight on the horizon. The team of Kazi Dawa Samdrup, a Sikkimese schoolteacher, and W. H. Y. Evans-Wentz, a folklorist and yogin, led off with translations of *The Tibetan Book of the Dead* (1927), *The Tibetan Book of the Great Liberation* (1954), and the life of Tibet's great yogi, Milarepa. Each of these works was remarkable, each of interest in its own way, but in the light of our redefinition of Tibetan Buddhism, we can now see that they conveyed to western readers an impression of a different civilization, a civilization that had its own science of mind, its own view of the meaning and purpose of life, that presented a full-scale alternative to the modern, western, materialistic, industrial, postcolonial worldview. It was not just an alien religion, a yoga, a meditation practice, an esoteric cult, something exotic that could be fit neatly into a countercultural niche. It was an entirely new way of looking at life, a way that challenged the "American way." This eruption occurred at a time when World War I had shaken the West's imperial self-confidence, relativistic and quantum physics had shaken scientific absolutism, modern art had shattered the substantiality of the observed object, Freud had shaken the purity and independence of the conscious subject, Marx had challenged the classless sovereignty of the western capitalistic individualism, and Darwin had shattered the plausibility of Creation itself. James Hilton's romantic novel *Shangri-La* and the Frank Capra film of the same name preached on the popular level the image of Tibet as a faraway world that had already resonated among the artistic and literary cognoscenti thanks to Samdrump and Evans-Wentz. The Americans who came to a dawning awareness about this civilizational alternative were either attracted or repelled, longed to escape into it or felt impelled to discredit it. Americans in general tended to think of it as a lost world or lost civilization that had existed everywhere in more Edenic days, akin to Arthurian or Egyptian legends. No one consciously thought of it as a contemporary alternative civilization; rather, it was used as a screen on which to project romantic images of some golden era assumed in the West's past.

During the 1950s, Lama Anagarika Govinda, a German-Bolivian expatriate scholar and spiritual seeker, began to publish the fruits of his research and practice first as a monk in a Sri Lankan Buddhist order and then as a lay lama in the Kagyu order of Tibetan Buddhism. His *Psychological Attitude of Early Buddhist Philosophy* (1961) and especially his *Foundations of Tibetan Mysticism* (1959) presented the first clear and scholarly account of Buddhist scientific psychology and Tibetan contemplative practice. At roughly the same time, Heinrich Harrer's best selling *Seven Years in Tibet* (1953) presented the flavor, beauty, and quirkiness of Tibetan society. French journalist, artist, scholar, and spiritual seeker Alexandra David-Neel provided a colorful and sometimes fanciful information about the mysteries of Tibet, though her harrowing journey in disguise to Lhasa added an air of paranoia to the perception of the Tibetan people, due to her living in fear of discovery by the xenophobic Tibetan, British, and Chinese authorities.

At the same time, the 1950 Chinese invasion of Tibet and Tibet's involvement in the anticommunist struggle of the cold and hot wars began to impinge ever so slightly on the popular mind, though the Tibetan catastrophe was obscured behind the Korean and Vietnamese Wars and global U.S.-Soviet competition. British and American leftist writers during this period, shifting their utopian hopes from the discredited Stalin to the unknown Mao, wrote glowingly of the Chinese revolution and used distorted information from an older layer of anti-Tibetan, Christian missionary writings to add to the Chinese communist propaganda against Tibet, portraying Tibetan Buddhism as a diabolical, oppressive, feudal system of superstitious rituals and bloody sacrifices used to torment simpleminded "serfs." This wave of propaganda went a long way toward forming the negative stereotype about Tibet and its Buddhism that is only now and with great difficulty being dislodged.

To summarize, since Tibetan Buddhism is a matrix containing in some form all the elements of late Indian Buddhism, it presents to the West for the first time a Buddhist civilization in its entirety, an alternative civilization to both Christendom and modern, materialist, secular industrialism. It thus impacts not only religion (as another world religion) but also and perhaps more importantly contemporary psychology and philosophy, presenting alternatives to both. It challenges the sciences, especially in presenting its mind science as a complement to the physical sciences; medicine, by presenting a Buddhist empirical as well as intuitive healing science and art; ethics and governance, by presenting complementary perspectives, especially on individualism, education, altruism, and nonviolence; and aesthetics and art, by contributing an enlightenment-oriented perspective to the enterprise of awakening new visions and insights in creation and performance.

Previous waves of Buddhism from other Asian countries made significant contributions in most of these directions. But in India Buddhism made its most totalistic contributions as a countercultural movement, and in Tibet—and subsequently Mongolia—Buddhism developed from a countercultural movement to a mainstream civilization. The Indo-Tibetan current, therefore, brings the results of that full movement to America and into modern awareness.

The main pioneers who brought Tibetan Buddhism to the United States were the Venerables Geshe Wangyal (1901–83), Deshung Rinpoche (1906?–87), Trungpa Rinpoche (1939–87), Tarthang Tulku (b. 1935), Kalu Rinpoche (1905–89), and Lama Thupten Yeshe (1935–84). They were affiliated with the four main orders of Tibetan Buddhism. Because their stories have been often told, I will not rehearse them in detail here. Still, some discussion is in order.

Geshe Wangyal arrived in 1955 and built a small center in New Jersey; Deshung Rinpoche arrived in 1960 and built a small center in Seattle. Each taught many individuals in secular professions, including academics, through whom they diffused a broader knowledge of Tibet and Tibetan Buddhism to U.S. students. Settling in America when they did (before the post-1965 immigration boom) and coming from the older generation, they kept a low profile, and their centers remained modest. They did not grant Tantric initiations except in the rarest circumstances, and they encouraged the study of the Tibetan language as well as important philosophical texts of the monastic curriculum. They also refrained from ordaining American monks, sending a few of the most determined to Tibetan teachers in India to be evaluated for ordination.

Trungpa Rinpoche was an incarnate lama of the Kagyu order who came to America in 1970 after seven years in Great Britain, where he had built a monastic center in Scotland and developed quite a following. He had abandoned his monastic ordination some time earlier, and in the West he initially adopted a kind of "wild man" approach. This "crazy wisdom," as some of his American followers dubbed it, involved the use of alcohol and psychedelics as well as sexual openness and generally unconventional behavior. Trungpa also worked closely with various Zen masters, notably the Venerable Shunryu Suzuki Roshi of the San Francisco Zen Center. Trungpa incorporated elements of Zen meditation and Japanese aesthetics into his curriculum and attracted many Zen practitioners as students. He wrote inspiring books, which were distributed by Shambhala Publications, which itself grew from a small Berkeley, California, bookstore into a nationally prominent publisher. He attracted a large following and began to open centers, most notably Naropa

University in Boulder, Colorado, the core institution in what quickly grew into an alternative community that survives to this day in Boulder and Halifax, Nova Scotia, called Shambhala International. By the end of the 1970s, Trungpa had become much less wild, and his organizations were becoming more established and conservative in outlook as well as more energetic in preserving Tibetan traditions. Until his premature death in 1987, Trungpa Rinpoche epitomized the totalizing tendency of Tibetan Buddhism to absorb all aspects of the social world, creating not only religious institutions but also educational facilities, communities, businesses, aesthetic styles, and cultural forms in its drive to transform the environment into a support system for individual liberation.

Tarthang Tulku was a reincarnation in the Nyingma order. Like Trungpa, Tarthang had learned something of the wildness of countercultural youth, though his involvement was with traveling hippies in India. He was much more reclusive than Trungpa, however, and settled down in 1969 in Berkeley, California, where he established the Nyingma Meditation Center and Dharma Publications. Through astute business management, Tarthang developed the press and soon raised enough money to purchase a large coastal property in Sonoma County, where he began to build an extraordinary complex of Tibetan buildings, beautiful in their architecture and sumptuous in their appointments. The complex was a shrine to his devotion to the Nyingma order's Guru Padma Sambhava, who brought Shakyamuni Buddha's teachings to Tibet in the eighth century and still lives mystically in Tibetan myth and imagination. In this case, we see the Tibetan Buddhist attempt to create an alternative world, a celestial architecture, and an intentional community.

The Venerable Kalu Rinpoche opened many Kagyu meditation centers throughout the United States. Originally visiting at the invitation of Trungpa's organization, Kalu quickly attracted a strong following of his own as a result of his special ability to teach meditation. Practitioners who learned from him found they made quick progress and naturally became highly devoted to their teacher.

Lama Thupten Yeshe was a member of the Gelukpa order, from Sera Monastic University near Lhasa. He began teaching Americans at the end of the 1960s at a monastery he founded in 1969 in Kopan, Nepal, near the Boudhnath stupa outside of Kathmandu. He soon began traveling around the world, creating with an associate, the reincarnate Lama Zopa Rinpoche (b. 1946), the Foundation for the Preservation of the Mahayana Tradition. In America during the 1970s, Lama Yeshe founded a number of centers, the most important of which was the Vajrapani Retreat center near Santa Cruz, California. He too founded a successful publishing arm, Wisdom Publications, which moved to America from England in the 1980s. Lamas Yeshe and Zopa were the first to ordain American, European, and Australian monks and nuns, and today they constitute the backbone of his worldwide community, though the number of monasteries (as opposed to lay-oriented dharma centers) is relatively small. After he died, Lama Yeshe was recognized as reincarnated in a Spanish family and has been brought up as a reincarnate lama, thus beginning a trend that may prove to be a watershed in the transmission of Tibetan Buddhism in the West.

During the 1970s, as the publications, teachings, and meditation centers grew, the founders of these centers began to invite the heads of their respective orders to tour America, give talks, and meet local dignitaries. During these visits, the training of American followers was put to the test. These followers made donations to the visiting lamas, labored hard to follow traditional Tibetan customs, and carefully attended to the extensive public relations surrounding the visits. The Nyingmapas invited His Holiness Dudjom Rinpoche, the Kagyupas invited His Holiness Karmapa Rinpoche, the Sakyapas invited Sakya Trichen Rinpoche, and the Gelukpas invited the Ganden Tri Rinpoche. When these distinguished lamas came, they met celebrities, senators and members of Congress, church and academic leaders, and the parents of followers.

This founding period was characterized by competition among the various orders and centers within orders, which caused a sort of sectarianism to arise among American followers. In Tibet, orders traditionally had competed for resources and followers, but the competition was clearly always political or economic. There was no sense of sectarian conflict—"Your religion is inferior to mine!"—so Tibetan orders are not properly called sects.

Another important factor in this period was the development of relationships between Tibetan Buddhists and followers of other Buddhist denominations, most importantly Zen and Theravada Buddhism. As mentioned earlier, Trungpa Rinpoche had made initial connections with Zen Buddhist practitioners, and the familiar sitting practice was integrated into most Tibetan Buddhist centers. The Pure Land and Lotus Sutra traditions, mainly still the province of Japanese American Buddhists, had little connection with the burgeoning Tibetan centers.

During this period, Theravada centers underwent major changes since American practitioners of *vipassana* meditation were returning from practicing in India, Thailand, and Burma and began to teach European and African Americans in a culturally neutral way. Joseph Goldstein, Sharon Salzberg, and Jack Kornfield founded the Barre Insight Meditation Center in 1971, and the number of meditators there increased dramatically. This growth paralleled that of Tibetan centers during that decade. Therefore, in addition to competition among Tibetan Buddhist centers, competition existed between Zen, Vipassana, and Tibetan Buddhist groups. Conversely, efforts to bridge gaps were made, with sitting practice serving as the main point of connection. In fact, the Burma-based *vipassana* practice strongly resonated with Tibetan *lhaktong* (critical wisdom practice), and the emphasis on mindfulness was common to both. The Tibetan *zhinay* practice, one-pointed calming of mind, resonated strongly with Japanese Zen, Chinese Ch'an, and Vietnamese Zen. The critical insight dimension of Zen, the cultivation of doubt through focused but critical concentration on a koan puzzle or paradox, also resonated with *vipassana/lhaktong*, and during this time the teaching of American Zen progressed beyond its simplistic beginnings in no-thought meditation to include more study and some Buddhist aesthetics.

Notably absent from this pattern of visits by the heads of different orders was His Holiness the Dalai Lama, who is not the head of the Gelukpa order but the head of the Tibetan "Buddhocratic" government and honorary head of all the orders of Tibetan Buddhism. Geshe Wangyal's followers and other groups tried periodically to invite the Dalai Lama to visit the United States, but the Chinese government sought to block his access to political leaders, seeing him as an embarrassment to them and a threat to their control of Tibet. The Indian government, internally supportive of the Dalai Lama and his community, was reluctant to let him loose on the world, wary of Chinese pressure. And the U.S. government, mindful of the alliances President Richard Nixon and his adviser Henry Kissinger had made with China against Russia, was unwilling to grant the Dalai Lama a visa, fearing that his presence would strain U.S.-China relations. This situation finally changed in 1979, when President Jimmy Carter normalized relations with the People's Republic of China and a politically engaged student of Geshe Wangyal, Joel McCleary, got Carter to agree to a purely religious visit by the Dalai Lama.

In 1979, the Dalai Lama landed in New York, eventually visiting Massachusetts, Virginia, and Washington, D.C. This put Buddhism on the national agenda and prompted some students to found the nation's fourth major Tibetan Buddhist press, Snow Lion Publications of Ithaca, New York. The visit proved to be the first of more than twenty to date, most two or three weeks long. The Dalai Lama's stance during these visits was complicated. He was not visiting as a head of a religious order, since his primary responsibility was to represent the Tibetan people as head of the Tibetan government in exile in Dharamsala, India. So he formally eschewed all missionary aims, accepting invitations to teach Buddhism within Buddhist organizations but insisting in public appearances that his message was "the common human religion of kindness and compassion," which followers of any religion (or no religion at all) could pursue. This stance had the salutary effect of defusing worries inside leading Christian and Jewish organizations that the Dalai Lama might become a pied piper leading away the younger generation. Also, when His Holiness visited Buddhist centers, he always taught with the stated intention of helping practitioners succeed with their personal brand of Buddhism, stating his firm belief in the equal value of all forms of Buddhism (and even all forms of religion) and urging his listeners to make their lives conform increasingly to whatever religious ideals they held. This had the salutary effect of defusing competition and sectarianism among Buddhist groups.

A second complication surrounding the Dalai Lama's activities was the issue of the tragedy of Tibet. During the first visits, in the early 1980s, he talked on a universal and spiritual level, rarely mentioning the travails of his people. His meetings with political figures were private. This time coincided with a series of active negotiations between the Tibetan government in exile and the administration in China of Deng Xiaoping, and observers hoped that Deng would relax Mao Tse-tung's destructive policies and offer a pragmatic new start for the Tibetan people. By the mid-1980s, however, Deng had purged Hu Yaobang, citing as one reason the latter's softness on Tibet. In 1987 and 1988, therefore, the Dalai Lama went to the U.S. Congress and the European Parliament to present his famous Five-Point Peace Plan for Tibet, declaring his wish that it become again a fully demilitarized "zone of ahimsa [nonviolence]" and asking for a withdrawal of Chinese occupation troops, an end to the civilian Chinese population transfer policy intended to colonize Tibet, genuine respect for Tibetans' basic rights and freedoms, the restoration of Tibet's natural environment and protection of wildlife, the cessation of nuclear waste dumping, and the commencement of earnest negotiations between Chinese and Tibetans on the future of Tibet. He presented this plan while declaring his willingness to accept Tibet's formally becoming a part of China if these conditions were granted and guaranteed by international plebiscite. These peaceful overtures won the Dalai Lama the 1989 Nobel Peace Prize, though the Chinese under Deng never engaged in serious negotiations with the Tibetans. The situation has subsequently worsened despite the example set by the dissolution of the Soviet Union. In fact, the vision of the first communist empire falling apart and allowing its captive nations to regain their freedom frightened the Chinese leadership and caused them to intensify their efforts to finish the Tibetan genocide and to assimilate whatever remained into the Chinese motherland.

This political history matters for students of Tibetan Buddhism in America because the emergence of the Tibet cause in public consciousness brought an enormous amount of publicity. In the late 1980s, Tibet House U.S. was founded to preserve Tibetan culture and diffuse knowledge about it, drafting Richard Gere and other celebrities as high-profile supporters of the Tibetan cause and practitioners of Tibetan Buddhism. The International Campaign for Tibet was founded in 1988, and its overtly political agenda quickly won support from the human rights community and from congressional leaders on both the right and the left, even during President George H. W. Bush's strongly pro-China administration. The steadily increasing visibility of Tibet culminated in 1997 with the release of two major motion pictures on Tibet, *Seven Years in Tibet*, starring Brad Pitt, and Martin Scorsese's *Kundun*, written by Melissa Mathison of *ET* fame. These films finally made Tibet a worldwide watchword, and all forms of Buddhism were dragged into the limelight with it. That fall, *Time* ran a cover story on Buddhism in America, with a picture of Pitt (not a Buddhist) wearing a Tibetan jacket. More coverage accompanied the success of the Dalai Lama's book *The Art of Happiness* (1998), which sat for more than ninety-eight weeks on the *New York Times* bestseller list.

In sum, after more than two decades of sustained work, the Dalai Lama placed Buddhism on the map of American culture, with Tibetan Buddhism gaining recognition as the living storehouse of all varieties of Buddhism that flourished in the golden pluralistic phase of Indic Buddhism. Although this rising popularity has alarmed fundamentalists of various persuasions, the Dalai Lama's careful adherence to his political responsibility as leader of the Tibetan people enabled him to avoid being perceived as a guru or cult leader and allowed him to develop a large following yet retain the respect of most U.S. authorities.

But the Dalai Lama is not the only story here. American scholars and translators have produced a mountain of publications, not only from the four big Buddhist presses but also from mainstream presses and newer, smaller upstarts. The result has been an unprecedented wealth of information on Tibet, Tibetan history, Tibetan Buddhism, and Buddhism in general. An enterprising student can now study with considerable sophistication Buddhist ethics, psychology, meditation, philosophy, and history. Naropa University, founded in the 1970s by Trungpa Rinpoche, has persisted, and students now can receive advanced degrees in Buddhist studies as well as Buddhist-inspired training in a variety of humanistic disciplines.

The Internet offers a wealth of information on Tibet—a recent Google search for "Tibetan" came up with nearly 5 million Web sites. When in 1991–92 Tibet House U.S. worked with the Tibetan government in exile to sponsor an International Year of Tibet focusing on Tibetan culture, the list grew to seven thousand different events in thirty-five countries, including more than four thousand in the United States alone. These events ranged from an international exhibition of Tibetan fine art, Wisdom and Compassion: The Sacred Art of Tibet, to a major dog show of Tibetan Lhasa apsos, terriers, and mastiffs.

Under their own natural momentum as well as with encouragement from Tibetan Buddhists, American converts to other Buddhisms in America have become more engaged with the ethical, cultural, and intellectual components of their traditions. Because of an almost myopic focus on meditation maintained in earlier decades, many convert Buddhist groups experienced difficulties in their communities—most notably, ugly blowups caused by misbehaving teachers.

Asian American Buddhist communities have been delighted with the increased visibility of Tibetan Buddhism, which has in turn offered them greater respect. Thus, the much-discussed divide in American Buddhism between Asian American ethnic Buddhists and European and African American convert Buddhists has begun to be bridged. For example, every time the Dalai Lama teaches in any American city, a regional committee of Buddhist groups is formed to invite him for some special event. Such events inevitably cut across the ethnic/convert line.

A new wave of lamas has been rolling across the country, founding still more centers. Most prominent among these have been Sogyal Rinpoche, Penor Rinpoche, and Chagdud Rinpoche of the Nyingmapa order; Lama Zopa Rinpoche and Gelek Rinpoche of the Gelukpa order; Tai Situ Rinpoche and Chetsang Rinpoche of the Kagyupa order; and Sakya Trichen Rinpoche, the head of the Sakyapa order.

Sogyal Rinpoche's Rigpa Foundation has mustered a large international following; his book, The Tibetan Book of Living and Dying (1992) has had a far-reaching impact, selling nearly a million copies worldwide. He has hosted teachings of numerous senior lamas, beginning with the Year of Tibet "Nature of Mind" teachings in New York in 1991. Most of his energies have gone into Europe thus far, but he is beginning to turn his attention to America.

Chagdud Rinpoche has founded centers in California, has trained several prolific translators, and has established a publishing house. Leaving other lamas in charge of his many followers, he has recently "retired" to Brazil, where he is building up another large community.

Penor Rinpoche became the head of the Nyingmapa order with the deaths of Dudjom Rinpoche and Dilgo Kyentse Rinpoche and has taught widely throughout America. He has recognized Americans as reincarnations of Tibetan lamas, most notably Catherine Burroughs, whom he recognized formally as the reincarnation of the Tibetan woman teacher Akhon Lhamo. She founded a large meditation center in Maryland known as Kunzang Palyul Choling and has developed a stable, flourishing community there. Penor Rinpoche also stirred considerable controversy when he recognized screen actor Steven Seagal as the reincarnation of a Tibetan "wild" lama.

Lama Zopa Rinpoche is a reincarnate lama from the Sherpa Tibetan community in Nepal who took over responsibility for the Foundation for the Preservation of the Mahayana Tradition after the death of Lama Thupten Yeshe, building numerous centers in the United States as well as India, Europe, South America, and Australia and continuing to expand Wisdom Publications. Lama Zopa found the reincarnation of Lama Yeshe in a Spanish boy, now named Osal Tenzin, who is being brought up in Nepal and Spain. This recognition was somewhat trendsetting, since Lama Yeshe was not previously a reincarnate, and his apparent choice to be reincarnated in a western body was perceived as innovative. Lama Zopa often invites senior lamas and scholarly *geshes*, including the Dalai Lama, from the Gelukpa order to teach at these centers and has educational, psychological, and prison reform programs.

Gelek Rinpoche founded the Jewel Heart center in Ann Arbor, Michigan, with branches in New York, Cleveland, Chicago, Detroit, and Lincoln, Nebraska. His group is steadily growing and has a number of celebrity followers.

Tai Situ Rinpoche is the most well known surviving member of the Karma Kagyupa regency leadership, charged by H. H. Gyalwa Karmapa Lama to discover his reincarnation and keep the order developing. The Tai Situ presided over considerable expansion of the order during the 1980s, especially the multi-million-dollar construction of a traditional Tibetan monastic temple in Woodstock, New York, called Karma Triyana Dharmachakra. In the 1990s, the Tai Situ rediscovered the Karmapa Lama as a boy from eastern Tibet, though the recognition was marred by a challenge from another regent, the Zhamar Rinpoche, who backed a different boy from Lhasa. After a half a decade of conflict, the Tai Situ's choice, Urgyen Thinley Dorjey, has emerged as the candidate accepted by the majority of Tibetan and western followers of the Karma Kagyupa tradition, although the minority faction shows no signs of giving in. The succession was more or less brought to a head and then settled by the spectacular and dangerous midwinter escape from Tibet of the young Ugyen Tinley Dorjey during the 2000 New Year's celebration.

Chetsang Rinpoche, head of the Drigung Kagyyupa order, has a knack for teaching Americans, since he spent some of his teenage years as an unknown refugee in Texas, where he learned to speak perfect English. During his numerous trips to the United States since the mid-1990s, he has taught many disciples and founded numerous centers, the most important of which is in Washington, D.C. His main building activity, however, has been in India, where he has constructed an impressive complex in Dehra Dun, with a monastery, temple, school, research library, and school of sacred art.

Finally, Sakya Trichen Rinpoche has traveled tirelessly to the West, and the Sakyapas have brought a large group of practitioners into the advanced stages of practice of their trademark Lamdrey "path and fruition" teachings. The Venerable Deshung Rinpoche has been recognized as reincarnated in a Tibetan American boy and is currently being educated in a monastery in Nepal. The Sakyapas are improving a large property in Massachusetts, where they horrified some of their environmentally minded neighbors by re-creating the treeless landscape of southwestern Tibet where the Sakya monastery is located. The site will eventually house a monastery with bountifully re-planted trees.

Many Tibetan centers have built impressive facilities in India as well as America. Among important monasteries in India, the Namgyel monastery, originally in Potala in Tibet and now the Dalai Lama's personal monastery in Dharamsala, has established a thriving institute (loosely affiliated with Cornell University) in Ithaca, New York, where students can study the tradition with authentic teachers. And the Drepung Loseling Monastery, a college of the world's largest monastic university, originally from Lhasa and now still more than four thousand strong in Mundgod in Karnataka in south India, has established an Emory University–affiliated branch in Atlanta. Loseling also has several traveling tour groups of chanting and dancing monks that have performed in more than five hundred cities and towns throughout the United States and Canada, raising awareness of Tibetan Buddhism and the Tibetan cause as well as substantial funds to support monks and build the monastery in India.

Another mark of the most recent period in Tibetan Buddhism in America is the emergence of Euro-American lamas. These practitioners comprise two main types: those from the Nyingmapa and Kagyupa orders who have accomplished the Tibetan three-year retreat and have begun to give teachings and found centers, and those from the Sakyapa and Gelukpa orders who have been monks or nuns for some time, have completed the Geshe degree or other advanced studies, and/or performed shorter or longer retreats on specific practices. Lamas Sara Harding and Surya Das are the most notable examples of the first category (though more than two hundred Americans have graduated from the three-year retreats conducted at the Nyingma retreat centers in France), and Geshes George Dreyfus and Michael Roach are examples of the second.

Various professions—medical, psychological, political, religious, educational, and commercial—are beginning to find uses for elements of Buddhist civilization, either through Tibetan Buddhism or through other Asian Buddhisms now available to them.

In sum, the great event touted by Arnold Toynbee in a speech at Wellesley College toward the end of his career—that is, the full encounter between Buddhism and the West—is now fully under way. But what exactly is this Tibetan Buddhism that has taken root in the United States? Tibetan Buddhism, I have argued, is the totalizing form of Buddhism elaborated in India, with monastic, messianic, and apocalyptic dimensions. While it remained countercultural in India and in almost all other settings throughout Asia, it became mainstream in Tibet, constituting the "sacred canopy" of Tibetan civilization by supplanting the pre-Buddhist Tibetan ethos and sacralizing the lifeworld of Tibet in Buddhist terms. It shared this totalized form with the Mongolian nations and highly influenced the Manchu elite of Ching Dynasty China.

Tibetan Buddhism has come to assume a much larger role in America than the relatively small U.S. Tibetan population would warrant. One reason for this outsized role may be the fact that Buddhism in other Asian countries has remained essentially countercultural. That is, the ideology, ethos, and institutions of Buddhism offered a liberation-seeking elite an alternative from a mainstream royal, militaristic, and theistic culture.

Tibetan Buddhism, in contrast, took over all of Tibet's mainstream ideas, institutions, and ethical traditions, "taming" (in Buddhist parlance) the tribal and national deities and eventually demilitarizing the entire nation, leaving it tragically vulnerable to aggressive neighbors, as the ongoing genocide there has demonstrated. But this history equips Tibetan Buddhism to supply the pluralistic, eclectic American sacred canopy with an ideology, an ethos, and institutions that countercultural forms of Buddhism are not as well suited to supply.

For example, in ideology, Buddhism generally does not accept the existence of a monotheistic Creator deity. Buddhists often will say that they are atheists, a stance that has caused them to die in large numbers at the hands of jihadists and crusaders of various kinds and to be aligned subliminally with communists and secular humanists. However, Tibetan Buddhists reawaken the Buddhist traditions that, far from denying the existence of tribal and national deities (for example, Indra and Brahma) present them as disciples of the Buddha and omnipotent creators. Tibetan Buddhists, in short, are not atheists: they simply do not accept the hegemony of any particular divine being. This stance enables Tibetan Buddhists to get along with Christian mystics, Sufis, Vedantists, and other nonliteralistic theists, finding affinities with believers who affirm that "God is love" and take seriously the prohibition against idolatry.

In issues of ethos, most Buddhist peace activists are accustomed to working, countercultural style, in protest movements. They point to Siddhartha's leaving his throne, his ceding his royal responsibilities and military leadership to the higher ethic of the Buddhist monastic, his teaching of nonviolence, tolerance, dialogue, and reconciliation. Tibetan Buddhists agree wholeheartedly with these principles. However, they also bring forward the complexities that arise in practice and were carefully considered over centuries in Indian Buddhist reflection. For example, the ethics chapter of Asanga's Bodhisattva Stages states that the bodhisattva (a messianically committed Buddhist) should break the general prohibition against killing if it would save more lives in the long run and should revolt when a tyrant is oppressing the people. So the Tibetan Buddhist might be more flexible in understanding the difficulties of a government with the responsibility of rule and the concerns of foreign policy, public health, and population control.

When it comes to institutions, many Buddhists consider general education to be samsaric, concerned with developing mastery of worldly matters and reinforcing the egotistical drives and ambitions of the ignorant being in the world. When people drop out, go to a monastery or retreat center, and learn techniques of contemplative withdrawal, they are on their way to learning what matters for liberation. The monastery and the university, therefore, are considered quite opposed. But Tibetan Buddhists can point to India's great monastic universities of Nalanda, Kanchi, Vikramashila, Vallabhi, and Takshashila and can understand at least the "liberal" elements of mundane education as parallel to if not in ultimate harmony with the aim of enlightenment education. Tibetan Buddhists can also take pride in Tibet's vast monastic establishment— the great universities of Drepung, Sera, Ganden, Tashi Lhunpo, Labrang Tashi Kyil, Dagyab, Kumbum, Sakya, Tsurphu, Minling, and Rebgong. In fact, at one time, sparsely populated Tibet had 6,254 teaching monasteries and monastic universities. Education was the country's key industry.

When it comes to American values such as equality, progress, and pluralism, most Buddhists emphasize the hopelessness of the samsaric world system and the general inadequacy of biological life, stressing their quest for nirvana. Therefore, they tend to tolerate the inequalities of the various caste systems, even reproducing social hierarchies within their *sanghas* (monastic bodies). Tibetan Buddhism allowed the *sangha*'s influence on the originally militaristic and hierarchical Tibetan society to be gradual and cool, rather than sudden and disruptive, but over time Tibetans cultivated a sense of social mobility through the monastic career ladder (even though opportunities were not equal and hierarchies existed within the monastic system). The great turning point in Tibetan social history was the advent in the thirteenth century of the Tulku (reincarnation) system, which enabled the son or (mainly in theory) daughter of the most humble peasant family to be recognized as the reincarnation of a highly developed and respected spiritual teacher and social leader—to be elevated from infancy to a high social position, to be educated by the best tutors in the most sophisticated curriculum, and to assume a role of respect and responsibility (thereby elevating the child's birth relations). This is a kind of Asian analogue of the "log cabin to White House" ideal, effected in this case not through luck and pluck but through the biological cosmology of karmic evolutionary action, reincarnation, and Tantric yoga. In short, at least in its Tibetan form, karmic theory is highly individualistic in effect and strongly supports American egalitarian ideals. The poorest child, we might say, could be the reincarnation of a past president, chief executive officer, spiritual virtuoso, or concert pianist.

As far as an ideal of progress goes—an ideal that is being challenged by conservative Christian notions of an impending apocalypse—most Buddhists adopt the Brahmanical Kaliyuga idea that things are going to the dogs, so it is better to progress individually toward liberation rather than to concern oneself with social progress. The Tibetan Buddhist, however, clings to the Kalachakra Tantra's prophecy of Shambhala, a kind of Armageddonish apocalypse and golden age narrative that sees this world, under the evolutionary aegis of the wonder-working compassion of Shakyamuni Buddha in his Kalachakra (Time Machine) Buddha form, as moving toward a great fulfillment in the near future. So, while the imperative to individual spiritual development remains primary, another dimension sees individual spiritual development as contributing to planetary change that will bring all others into liberation.

Finally, in regard to pluralism, the cornerstone of American civil religion, the greatest threat today comes from fundamentalist movements. Buddhists, by contrast, are in an excellent position to reinforce this ideal. Fundamentalists undertook an effort to use born-again President George W. Bush to break down church-state separation and hand government resources to "faith-based" initiatives, but these efforts stalled when backers realized that it might also be necessary to enrich non-Protestant groups. Ironically, each of the religious institutions seeking funding—many wanting in their own ways to convert others, many intolerant of alternatives—had to reassert some sort of pluralist ideal to prevent the others from gaining advantage. Only the nonliteralist, nonmissionary Buddhists have reasons to sacralize secularity, not just to accept it temporarily as a necessary evil to prevent other religious movements from advancing but to consider it a spiritual necessity, a sacred norm, as evidenced in the edicts of the Emperor Ashoka (c. third century B.C.E.).

If the sacred canopy over America is in fact a communally created patchwork quilt—the pluralistic product of a giant quilting bee of the sacred traditions of immigrant cultures from all over the world—Buddhists must be credited for, among other accomplishments, finding something sacred in it.

APPENDIX
Vehicles or Styles of Buddhism in India

A. Individualistic Style, Monastic Buddhism, dominant ca. 500 B.C.E.–0 C.E.
1. Emphasizes monasticism, as necessary for individual liberation.
2. Socially revolutionary, stressing ethical dualism, though antitheistic.
3. Ideal of monks and nuns is *arhat* (sainthood).
4. Lay community pushed toward tenfold path of good and bad evolutionary action.
5. Reversal of warrior training produces person free of wild egocentric drives.

6. Social result: tamed warrior society with values supporting urban, merchant classes.
7. Spread outside of India, mainly to Sri Lanka, Central Asia, Iran, and West Asia.

B. Universalistic Style, Messianic Buddhism, dominant ca. 0–500 C.E.
1. Incorporating core monasticism, reached out nondually into lay society to transform social ethic through love and compassion.
2. Socially evolutionary: monasteries develop into universities.
3. Ideal of bodhisattva, hero/ine who aims to liberate all beings from suffering and transform universe into Buddhaverse; doctrine of Three Bodies of Buddha: Truth, Beatific, Emanation.
4. Nondualism of nirvana/samsara undergirds nonduality of wisdom and compassion, and of monastic *sangha* and lay society.
5. Conscious adoption of process of evolution, embarking on career of millions of future individual lives to evolve to Buddhahood.
6. Social result: moved society toward a more universalistic orientation, freed popular imagination to envision infinite Buddhaverse.
7. Spread wherever monastic style spread and to China, Mediterranean.

C. Apocalyptic Style, Esoteric, Magical Buddhism, dominant ca. 500–1000 C.E.
1. Monastic universities reach out beyond the literate state into marginal areas. Unpacks furthest implications of messianic style.
2. Ideal of Mahasiddha, female or male Great Adept, the "psychonaut" of Indian inner science, actual perfect Buddha maintaining ordinary human form in history, latent kingship of individual explicated ritually and artistically.
3. Nondualism elucidated to include everything from sexuality to death; wisdom-compassion union becomes wisdom-bliss union; Buddhahood as male-female-sexual-union-orgasmic reality.
4. Apocalyptic insistence on accelerating history and evolution, realization of individual Buddhahood and universal Buddhaverse preferably in this lifetime, through magical, high-tech means.
5. Social result: elevation of women, expansion of culture to marginal low castes, tribals, aliens, permeation of high culture with aesthetic values, loosening of rigidities, living beyond this-worldly identities, unilateral disarmament.
6. Spread everywhere the monastic and messianic styles went, though in subtle streams, reaching Indonesia, Korea, Japan, and Tibet; uniquely kept in total integration with two previous styles in Tibet and later Mongolia.

The first of these five-hundred-year periods, the Monastic Buddhist period, made its main foothold outside of India in Sri Lanka, where it continues today. The second, the Messianic Buddhist period, also spread to Sri Lanka but opened up new territory in Central Asia and China as well. The third, the Apocalyptic Buddhist period, integrated with both monastic and messianic institutions, spread throughout the Buddhist world in small streams but then transplanted itself wholesale into Tibet, especially because of the Islam-driven cultural transformation of Indian Buddhism from the eleventh century forward. After the loss of Buddhist India—the matrix civilization within which the three styles or vehicles were nested—Sri Lanka rejected the apocalyptic and messianic styles and became a bastion of the monastic style alone, East Asia emphasized the monastic and messianic styles, allowing only a trickle of the apocalyptic to survive, while Tibet alone attempted to incorporate all three styles in their originally integrated pattern.

NOTES

1. This quotation paraphrases a chart I made for the introduction to my *Essential Tibetan Buddhism* (San Francisco: HarperSanFrancisco, 1998), 17.

2. For vehicles or styles of Buddhism in India, see the appendix to the chapter.

3. See, e.g., Rick Fields, *How the Swans Came to the Lake: A Narrative History of Buddhism in America* (Boston: Shambhala, 1992); Emma Layman, *Buddhism in America* (Chicago: Nelson-Hall, 1976); Charles S. Prebish and Kenneth K. Tanaka, eds., *The Faces of Buddhism in America* (Berkeley: University of California Press, 1998); Thomas A. Tweed, *The American Encounter with Buddhism, 1844–1912: Victorian Culture and the Limits of Dissent* (Bloomington: Indiana University Press, 1992).

PART III

Hindus
& Sikhs

6

Mr. President, Why Do You Exclude Us from Your Prayers?

Hindus Challenge American Pluralism

The title of this essay is taken from a petition sent by the Hindu International Council against Defamation (HICAD) and several hundred individual Hindus to President George W. Bush following the events of September 11, 2001.[1] It refers to the fact that Bush included Muslim, Christian, and Jewish leaders in his national prayer service on September 16 but excluded Hindus. In the days following 9/11, numerous interfaith services were organized in different parts of the country. These services, formerly Judeo-Christian affairs conducted by Protestant ministers, Catholic priests, and Jewish rabbis, now typically included Muslim clerics, who repeatedly emphasized that they were part of the same tradition as Christians and Jews, saying, "We worship the same God as you do." Almost overnight, America's Judeo-Christian sacred canopy seemed to stretch into an Abrahamic one that included Muslims as well.

The Clinton administration had already recognized the need to include Muslims, "the fastest growing religious group in the U.S.," within the fabric of American religions, but only in the wake of 9/11 did this initiative bear fruit, with the term "Abrahamic" entering public discourse.[2] Hindu Americans, however, viewed this reconfiguration of American religion with alarm, fearing that it would further marginalize nonwestern religions such as Hinduism.

The HICAD petition is a modified version of a post-9/11 letter written to President Bush by an Euro-American Hindu and subsequently posted on a Hindu Internet discussion group. The petition later circulated on several Indian American Internet sites and was widely discussed in laudatory terms. Several Indian American newspapers also carried the letter. (For the full text, see the appendix.)

Three aspects of the petition merit analysis. First and most obviously, the petition calls attention to the fact that Hindus constitute a numerically significant portion of American society. Second, the petition describes U.S. Hindus as model Americans:

> We are a hard working people who contribute to the American society, economy, education and quality of life, in a proportion much larger than our numbers. . . . Non-violence, pluralism, and respect (not just tolerance) of other traditions of worship to the One Almighty God, are integral parts of [Hinduism's] basic tenets. We are a family oriented people, with very low divorce rates. We are frugal, save for our children's education, and support our elders and extended families. Because of these beliefs, Hindu-Americans are called ideal citizens.

Finally, the petition draws attention to the differences between Hinduism and Islam.[3] While the petition does so subtly, the original letter stresses that Bush needs to help educate Americans to the fact that "Hinduism is very, very different from Islam . . . the opposite in fact, in many integral ways." Emphasizing the distinction between Hinduism and Islam becomes prominent in the post-9/11 public statements of many representatives of American Hindus.

For some years, groups of Hindu Americans have challenged the portrayals of Hinduism prevalent in the wider society and have worked to ensure that the religion is recognized as an important contributor to the American religious mosaic. Here, I focus on some of these efforts, particularly the differences between such strategies in the pre-9/11 and immediate post-9/11 periods. Before 9/11, Hinduism's promoters extolled its virtues (antiquity, tolerance, pluralism, and nonviolence) as well as its theological and scientific sophistication. Hinduism's defenders also contested negative American stereotypes of the religion—for example, that it is polytheistic (explaining the petition's reference to "the One Almighty God"), idolatrous, caste ridden, and misogynistic (hence the petition's claim that "Hindus are a family-oriented people with very low divorce rates").

Immediately following 9/11, however, many Hindu spokespersons went on the offensive, publicly attacking Islam, emphasizing the differences between Hinduism and Islam, and taking a strong anti-Pakistani position. These spokespersons also criticized scholars of religion and organizations such as the Academy of American Religion for allegedly being anti-Hindu and pro-Islamic. This anti-Islamic, Hinducentric platform was not just a post-9/11 development. The two faces of American Hinduism that I describe as "genteel multiculturalism" and "militant nationalism" have long coexisted.[4] But in the past, Hindu nationalist attitudes were confined largely to intragroup discussions and presentations, while Hindu American spokespersons publicly projected the kindly visage of genteel multiculturalism. After 9/11, however, anti-Islamic Hindu nationalism emerged publicly for the first time. In addition, many more members of the Hindu American community were galvanized to defend Hinduism and India.

Most adults of Indian origin in the United States today are immigrants who arrived after the passage of the 1965 Immigration and Naturalization Act. The 2000 census found 1,678,765 Asian Indians living in the United States. They were also one of the fastest growing communities in the 1990s, with a growth rate of 106 percent. Key to this explosive growth has been the influx of computer data programmers (on H-1B visas) and their families. Indians have become prominent in the field of information technology and are now important players within the American computer industry. Although their numbers are relatively small, Indian Americans wield disproportionate influence because they are among the country's wealthiest and most educated foreign-born groups.[5]

No official figures exist on the religious distribution of U.S. Indians. According to Indian census figures, Hindus constitute more than 80 percent of the population in India.[6] Hindus likely constitute a much smaller proportion of Indian Americans, since Indian religious minorities, particularly Sikhs and Christians, are present in much larger numbers in the United States. Estimates of the proportion of Indian Americans from a Hindu background range from 45 to 76 percent.[7] While "upper" castes form around 25 percent of the Indian population, given the elite character of the immigration to the United States, most Indian Americans tend to be drawn from this background.

My findings here draw on an eight-year study and book in progress on the new forms, practices, and interpretations of Hinduism in the United States. As part of this research, I studied twelve Hindu organizations representing the five major categories of Hindu organizations in the U.S.: *satsangs* (local worship groups), *bala vihars* (educational associations for children), temples, student organizations, and umbrella groups. In addition to participating in the activities and programs of the organizations, I conducted detailed interviews with leaders and many of the members (more than 120 first- and second-generation Hindu Indian Americans in all). I have also followed the activities of the Hindu Indian community around the country by reading several Indian American newspapers (*India West, India Post, India Journal*) and the international magazine *Hinduism Today*, published in Hawaii. This chapter, however, is based primarily on analysis of discussions posted on four Internet groups as well as articles and discussions on several Web sites and Internet magazines devoted to Indian or Hindu related topics.

Since 2000, the Internet has become a major site of Hindu American activity. Given the educational and occupational profile of Indian Americans, it is not surprising that they have such a large Internet presence. The Internet enables Indian Americans to disseminate information around the world within a matter of minutes and provides a forum for discussion, agenda planning, group mobilization, and the rapid formulation of responses. Through the Internet, even isolated individuals and small groups can be closely networked to provide support for people and issues outside of the mainstream. The four discussion groups I studied consisted of between 150 and 900 members each. Anywhere from five to fifty messages were posted daily. The postings included (1) news items and articles from a variety of sources (newspapers, magazines, other Internet sites, and books); (2) commentary and discussion about current and future events; and (3) reports on actions that individuals and groups had taken or were going to take in support of Hindu and Indian causes (for example, copies of letters sent to newspapers, politicians, and other organizations; speeches given or to be given; and notices of meetings and conferences).

As sociologist R. Stephen Warner points out, immigrants held onto their religious identity and practices even during the assimilationist era of American history, since Americans have traditionally viewed religion as the most acceptable and nonthreatening basis for community formation and expression.[8] In a now classic formulation of the patterns of European immigration to the United States at the turn of the century, Will Herberg writes,

> Of the immigrant who came to this country it was expected that, sooner or later, either in his own person or through his children, he would give up virtually everything he had brought with him from the "old country"—his language, his nationality, his manner of life—and would adopt the ways of his new home. Within broad limits, however, his becoming an American did not involve his abandoning the old religion in favor of some native American substitute. Quite the contrary, not only was he expected to retain his old religion . . . but such was the shape of America that it was largely in and through his religion that he, or rather his children and grandchildren, found an identifiable place in American life.[9]

Writing about contemporary immigrants from India and Pakistan, Raymond Williams makes the same claim: "In the United States, religion is the social category with clearest meaning and acceptance in the host society, so the emphasis on religious affiliation is one of the strategies that allows the immigrant to maintain self identity while simultaneously acquiring community acceptance."[10] The literature on immigrant religion in the United States indicates that religious organizations become the means of maintaining and expressing ethnic identity not just for non-Christians like the Hindus but also for groups such as Chinese Christians, Korean Christians, and Maya Catholics.[11]

Because religion in the United States defines and sustains immigrant ethnic life, religion and religious institutions come to be more important in the immigrant context than in the home country. Thus, Williams indicates, "Immigrants are religious—by all counts more religious than they were before they left home—because religion is one of the important identity markers that helps them preserve individual self-awareness and cohesion in a group."[12]

A multicultural society pressures immigrants to create a public rather than purely private ethnic identity. Because of the importance of religion and ethnicity in defining Americans' personal identities, immigrants frequently must explain the meaning of their beliefs and practices not only to their own children but also to American friends and coworkers. Thus, religious doctrines have to be recast to fit American circumstances. Often, non-Christians find themselves having to legitimize their religion by drawing parallels to Christian concepts and practices. Religious beliefs also have to be simplified and summarized to be presented in "sound bite" versions. In addition, immigrants have the burden of having to confront the negative stereotypes and to correct prevailing misrepresentations of their culture and religion.

Thus, serving as the repository of ethnicity leads to profound transformations in immigrant religions.[13] Immigrant religions experience changes in organization and in interpretation. Because religious institutions generally become the primary ethnic and community centers for immigrants, they increasingly manifest congregationalism and lay leadership.[14] As de facto ethnic institutions, most immigrant religious organizations also develop regional and national associations to unify the group, define members' identities, and represent their interests.[15]

Armand Mauss points out that new religions in the United States have always had to maintain a delicate balancing act between assimilating to established American patterns of religious organization and expression (a strategy of accommodation) and maintaining separateness and distinctiveness (a strategy of resistance).[16] Too much accommodation jeopardizes distinctiveness and risks a complete disappearance. Too much distinctiveness or militancy, however, incurs hostility and repression. According to James Davidson Hunter's essay in this volume, leaders of religious organizations have accomplished this dance between assimilation and resistance through a variety of internal (intragroup) and external negotiations.

After briefly describing the types of internal negotiations taking place within the Hindu American community, this chapter focuses on the external negotiations in which Hindu American leaders have engaged over the past few years. Now that the religious traditions of post-1965 immigrants have become institutionalized, they are increasingly making public claims—demanding recognition and acceptance as *American* religions. Public acceptance of Judaism as an American religion (along with Christianity) after World War II radically transformed the country's religious landscape and with it the self-definition of the American nation. We seem to be at a similarly historic point now. Following 9/11, there have been attempts to refashion America's Judeo-Christian religious identity into a tripartite Abrahamic model inclusive of Muslims as well as Christians and Jews. This attempt is being challenged by groups such as Hindus and Buddhists who argue that it is too narrow and conservative Christians who see it as too broad.[17] While it is too early to gauge the relative success or failure of the Abrahamic model, the public arguments made by critics as well as supporters bear watching.

Religion seems to have become more important for Hindus as a marker of identity in the United States. Many of the Hindu immigrants I interviewed mentioned that they had become more religious in this country. In India, they generally took Hinduism and their identity as Hindus for granted, whereas in the United States they had to think about the meaning of their religion and religious identity for the first time. Other Hindu immigrants claimed that they were not especially religious but nevertheless participated in Hindu organizations for social and cultural reasons and "for the sake of the children."

Unlike many other established religions, Hinduism lacks a founder, a central authority, and a single canonical text or commentary. Consequently, Hinduism in India consists of an extraordinary array of practices, deities, texts, and schools of thought. Some observers even question whether one unitary religion called "Hinduism" exists at all, arguing instead that "what we call 'Hinduism' is a geographically defined group of distinct but related religions."[18] So the nature and character of Hinduism varies greatly by region, caste, and historical period.

For all these reasons as well as the tendency among Hindus to emphasize orthopraxy over orthodoxy, the average Hindu immigrant is often unable to explain to curious Americans the meaning of Hinduism and its central tenets. In the words of Vasudha Narayanan, a Hindu, "We are forced to articulate over and over again what it means to be a Hindu and an Indian to our friends and our children, and one feels ill-equipped for the task. [In India] one was never called upon to explain Deepavali or Sankaranti [festivals], and least of all, 'Hinduism.' "[19] Hindu American organizations seek to fill this need.

Leaders of Hindu American organizations have been trying to recast and reformulate Hinduism to make it a suitable vehicle for Hindu Americans to use for assimilating into multicultural America. These leaders have taken upon themselves the task of simplifying, standardizing, and codifying the religion to make it easier to understand, articulate, and practice. Hindu Web sites summarize the "central beliefs" of Hinduism or the "basic principles of Hindu dharma." Speakers at Hindu student organizations give talks about the "essence of the Gita" (which is generally defined in the United States as the central Hindu text). This process creates a capsulized, intellectual Hinduism that differs substantially from the diversity of ritual practices and caste observances that characterizes everyday Hinduism in India.

Interpretations of Hinduism in the United States explicitly compare and contrast it with Abrahamic religions (the term "Abrahamic" was being used in some Hindu American Internet discussion groups long before 9/11). Many Hindu American leaders are interested in transforming Hinduism into a global, universal religion instead of an ethnic religion tied to India and to the Indian people. In this regard, there have also been attempts to institutionalize conversion practices and ceremonies and to provide support to Western converts.

When I refer to the development of an American Hinduism, I mean the many modifications of Hinduism that have taken shape as Hindu immigrants and their children have developed an ethnic identity and community in the United States. As Mauss points out, some of these modifications represent the outcome of attempts to accommodate to the American environment by making Hinduism more compatible with American culture and society.[20] Others arise out of the struggles of being nonwhite immigrants and religious minorities in the United States and out of trying to resist assimilation by emphasizing the distinctness of Hinduism and Indian culture. The contradiction between these two intertwined strategies is embedded in the emerging American Hinduism. One manifestation of these contradictions can be seen in the two sides of "official" American Hinduism, by which I mean the articulation of Hinduism by spokespersons of Hindu American umbrella organizations.[21] (This I contrast with "popular" Hinduism, or the beliefs and practices of the Hindu masses in the United States.)

Hindu American leaders promote a genteel multiculturalism that emphasizes the tolerance and pluralism of Hinduism and its contributions to American society and to solving global problems. Many leaders, however, simultaneously support a militant Hindu nationalism replete with diatribes against Muslims, Christians, and secular Hindus. Several scholars have argued that Hindu nationalism has more support among Hindus in the United States than in India, since it resonates more in the diaspora, where Hindus are a racial and religious minority.[22] Although the two sides seem very different, they are linked. The same people often promote both facets, albeit in different contexts.

Jews, for example, are used as a model in both cases. In multiculturalist discourse, Jews are emulated as a highly successful group that has integrated into mainstream American society while maintaining its religious and cultural distinctness, close community ties, and connections with the home country. Militant nationalists, in contrast, emphasize a Hindu holocaust (at the hands of the Muslims) and the need for Hindus to have a religious homeland like Israel. Right-wing Hindu nationalist groups have links to extremist Jewish groups, joining together against a common Muslim enemy.[23] The two different self-representations grow out of the contradictions of being part of a professionally successful but racialized minority group in a multicultural society. Both are strategies to obtain recognition and validation within American society, one drawing on a model-minority discourse celebrating the achievements of Hindu culture and Hindu Indian Americans and the other drawing on an oppressed-minority discourse that highlights a history of victimization and the need for recompense and self-determination.[24]

The United States has several types of Hindu umbrella organizations. Some —for example, the Vishwa Hindu Parishad of America (VHPA), the Hindu Swayamsevak Sangh, and the Overseas Friends of the Bharatiya Janata Party— are branches of Hindu organizations based in India. Others, such as the southern-California-based Federation of Hindu Associations and the New Jersey–based Infinity Foundation, are independent, regional, American organizations. These latter organizations sometimes have informal links with the other groups.

In 1970, the VHPA, a branch of the Vishwa Hindu Parishad in India, was founded in New York. It is the oldest Hindu American umbrella organization established in the United States. According to its Web site, the VHPA was founded to support Hindu American families facing the challenges of living in a new country.[25] In 1987, however, the VHPA reached out to students, forming the Hindu Student Council, which regularly organizes campus events open to non-Hindus and showcasing various facets of Hindu life.

At these and other public events, Hindu American leaders characterize Hinduism as the only world religion that is truly tolerant and pluralistic. A verse from the Rig Veda, "Truth is one, sages call it by different names" (1.164.46), is constantly reiterated in support of this claim. According to the Federation of Hindu Associations, Hinduism is the most suitable religion for the twenty-first century because the modern pluralistic world "requires all religions to affirm [the] truth of other traditions to ensure tranquility."[26] Only Hinduism fits the bill. Therefore, the Federation of Hindu Associations takes as its mission the safeguarding of Hinduism "for our children, for the world."[27] Many Hindu American leaders also refer to Hinduism as *sanatana dharma* (eternal faith), reinforcing the point that it is the most ancient and universalistic of all religions.

Hindu umbrella organizations articulate the content and meaning of Hindu American identity. According to the leaders of these groups, they are the proud descendants of the world's oldest living civilization and religion. Hindu Americans are characterized as a group that has maintained the balance between materialism and spirituality, adapting to American life without losing their inner values and cultural integrity. These Hindu organizations also counter negative American images of Hinduism by arguing that it is very sophisticated and scientific. Hindu American publications and Web sites make this point through many examples, such as the Hindu view that the universe is billions of years old and the sophisticated level of ancient Indian knowledge regarding astronomy, mathematics, metallurgy, and physics.

Hindu American leaders explicitly appeal to the "model minority" label, as in the petition to George W. Bush. They attribute the success of Hindu Americans to their religious and cultural heritage, which, the leaders argue, gives Hindu Americans a special aptitude for science and math and makes them adaptable, hardworking, and family oriented. Community spokespersons indicate that these qualities, together with affluence and professional expertise (particularly in the fields of computers, medicine, and engineering), make Hindu Indian Americans a group with an important leadership role to play in twenty-first-century America.

In 1997, the VHPA spawned American Hindus against Defamation

(AHAD), perhaps the first Hindu umbrella group explicitly aimed at American society at large. AHAD seeks aggressively to defend Hinduism against defamation, commercialization, and misuse. According to Ajay Shah, the group's convener, "In seeking the honor of Hindus and demanding they not be ridiculed, . . . we are being good Americans. In our fight for Hindu dignity, we are championing American pluralism."[28] The organization has helped organize several protest campaigns against the use of Hindu deities, icons, and texts by American businesses and the entertainment industry. For example, AHAD and other Hindu organizations launched protest campaigns against the Gap clothing store's Om line of perfume, a CD cover released by Sony Music featuring a distorted image of a Hindu deity, an episode of *The Simpsons* on the Fox network caricaturing the Hindu god Ganesh, a *Xena: Warrior Princess* episode in which Lord Krishna was a character, the use of a verse of the Gita as background music during an orgy scene in the film *Eyes Wide Shut*, and a shoe company and a company making toilet seats that used pictures of Hindu deities on their products. In all of these cases, AHAD persuaded the companies in question to withdraw or modify the offending products. AHAD's success was followed by the formation of several other antidefamation groups around the country, including HICAD, based in New Jersey, which organized the petition drive targeted at George W. Bush.

Other Hindu organizations have focused on the portrayal of Hinduism within academia. This is the central concern of the New Jersey–based Infinity Foundation. In 2000, Infinity founded the Educational Council of Indic Traditions and an associated Internet discussion group. The council seeks to "be involved in the process of conducting independent research to (a) document the contributions by India to world civilization, and to (b) ascertain the degree to which Indic traditions and their contributions are accurately and adequately portrayed in contemporary American society. Preliminary findings indicate that Indic traditions, which include Hinduism, Buddhism, Sikhism and Jainism, have been and continue to be misrepresented, stereotyped, or pigeonholed both in academic institutions and by the mass media."[29] This mission statement made clear that the term "Indic" excluded religions that had been "imported" into India, such as Islam and Christianity. Furthermore, although the term "Indic traditions" was defined to include Buddhism, Sikhism, and Jainism, the foundation has in practice focused largely on Hindu traditions and culture.

One of the Educational Council of Indic Traditions' first activities was to send a letter to the National Endowment for the Humanities, which had funded a project to train high school teachers to teach the Ramayana. The letter protested the inclusion of one lesson (out of a total of around forty) in which the author, anthropologist Susan Wadley, had used a contemporary Dalit (lower caste) song critical of the Ramayana to make the point that caste ideology was contested in India.[30] Describing the Dalit author of the song as an "anti-Hindu activist," the letter argues that many Americans are Hindu and that teachers and scholars therefore have a responsibility to be sensitive about how they represent the religion in a multicultural classroom context:

> This complaint is on behalf of United States citizens and parents of school children. Hinduism and Sikhism are no longer merely about a far away exotic land that Americans have little to do with. We have Hindus and Sikhs right here in our classrooms today, amongst our office co-workers and as our neighbors. It is irresponsible for any multicultural school to introduce a protest song against Hindus and Sikhs that includes hate speech. . . . What does this do to foster mutual respect and understanding among different ethnic and religious communities in America's sensitive tapestry, now represented in classrooms? Should Government funds be used to create such racially and religiously inflammatory teaching materials, denigrating to one's classmates' sensitivities, ironically in the name of multiculturalism? . . . [S]uch bias . . . would lead to a warped understanding of others' history and religions and to unintended consequences, including stereotyping and hatred of minority groups.[31]

Before 9/11, the president of the foundation, Rajiv Malhotra, spoke and wrote publicly about Hinduism's tolerance, pluralism, and dynamism.[32] He emphasized that many Hindu ideas had influenced important Western thinkers (such as Emerson, Thoreau, and Jung). He also noted that Hindu concepts and practices had been incorporated into quantum mechanics, meditation, yoga, and herbal medicine, while lamenting that Hinduism's contributions to these areas have not yet been acknowledged.[33] Malhotra began contracting sympathetic scholars to write papers and books documenting ancient Indian contributions to mathematics, science, technology, philosophy, and psychology as well as organizing conferences to bring together such scholars.

Several other Hindu leaders around the country also spoke against what they felt were fundamental misrepresentations of Hinduism within American society. These efforts focused on three central issues: Hindu conceptions of the divine, the nature of the caste system, and the position of women in Hindu society.

Many American Hindu spokespersons objected to their religion being characterized as "polytheistic" and "idol worshipping." They pointed out that although the Hindu pantheon consists of an array of deities, many Hindus believe that all of these deities are different forms manifested by one Supreme Being. They argued that most Hindus worship a primary deity and that some traditions (such as Vaishnavism) acknowledged the existence only of that primary deity. On this basis, these representatives claimed that Hinduism was in fact a monotheistic religion. Others maintained that essentially western categories such as monotheism and polytheism are inappropriate to describe Hindu notions of the divine. Similarly, most American Hindu leaders found the English term "idol" offensive, since it carried the negative connotation that the worshipper considered the graven image to be divine. They preferred the term "icon" or "image" and argued that these images were intended only to represent the idea of the divine and to provide the worshipper with a tangible mental focus.

Hindu Indian American leaders also maintained that the caste system was never religiously sanctioned by Hinduism and thus was not central to Hindu practice.[34] The absence of immutable birth-based caste groups in the Rig Veda along with Lord Krishna's statement in the Bhagavad Gita, "The four orders of men arose from me, in justice to their natures and their works" (4:13), were often cited in support of the argument that the *varna* system described in Hindu scriptures was based on occupation and individual qualities, not birth. They argued that manuals such as the Laws of Manu that emphasized caste prescriptions and proscriptions were not part of Hindus' *sruti*, or primary scriptural corpus (which is believed to contain revealed wisdom), but were part of the *smriti*, or secondary scriptures (which are not considered divinely ordained).

The position of women within Hinduism was another sensitive issue addressed by Hindu American leaders, who argued that Hinduism gave women and men the same rights and that gender equality and respect for women therefore constituted integral parts of the Hindu tradition. To support their arguments, these leaders pointed to the presence of several powerful goddesses in the Hindu pantheon. Furthermore, these leaders contended that women were held in great esteem in ancient Hindu India. Many of these leaders claimed that the Muslim conquest of India was responsible for the subsequent decline in the status of women.

Other umbrella groups focused on attaining public acknowledgment of Hinduism as an American religion. In September 2000, despite some opposition from conservative Christians, Indian American lobby groups persuaded Congress to allow a Hindu priest to open a session of Congress for the first time (the occasion being an address by Indian prime minister to a joint session), an achievement reported with great pride by Indian American newspapers and Web sites. A second indication of Hindu Americans' recognition by Washington came a month later, when President Bill Clinton issued a proclamation from the White House wishing Indian Americans a happy Diwali (an important Hindu festival). In return for Silicon Valley's contributions to the Democratic Party for the 2000 elections, Indian American computer professionals had requested that the White House officially recognize the festival. The Indian American *India Post* reported that Indian Americans were jubilant when Clinton issued the greeting, since this "is a symbolic gesture that speaks volumes to the fact that Indian culture is accepted as part of America's overall fabric."[35]

As will be discussed later in this chapter, the tolerant and pluralistic tone of the public voice of Hindu Americans changed overnight with the terrorist attacks of September 11, 2001. The militant anti-Islamic, Hinducentric side, previously hidden from public view, suddenly emerged. Many Hindu Indian Americans bombarded their politicians and the media with anti-Pakistani and anti-Islamic propaganda filled with quotations from the Quran and called radio and television talk shows to criticize Islam. (One Internet group even circulated talking points for Hindu Americans to use while calling such shows.) Others spoke up at town meetings to condemn the treatment of minorities in Muslim countries and to challenge Muslim speakers' positive portrayals of Islam. Members of one Internet discussion group shot off letters to the president of the American Academy of Religion, Vasudha Narayanan, demanding that the organization sponsor panels on Islamic fascism and on "Jihad: God as Weapon of Mass Destruction" at the group's upcoming annual meeting. Such gestures, they claimed, would counterbalance the organization's excessive focus on Hindu fascism. Another member of the same group documented Hinduism scholars' alleged contempt for Hinduism and Hindus by compiling a list from the Internet Archives of Religions in South Asia and from the Internet archives of the Society for Hindu-Christian studies. This putative evidence was then sent to the president of the American Academy of Religion as well as to several Internet discussion groups. Some Hindu Americans also sent e-mails and letters to "south Asian" groups to press a point that they had been making all along: India has nothing in common with Islamic countries such as Pakistan and Bangladesh and should therefore not be lumped together with them. Groups such as the Global Organization of Persons of Indian Origin were also criticized for trying to create a pan-Indian platform including both "Indic" and "non-Indic" members.

In the weeks immediately following 9/11, the Infinity Foundation's Malhotra was invited to several universities to speak about the unfolding events from a Hindu perspective. In light of the post-9/11 backlash in the United States, "a lot of Hindus suddenly have started realizing they better stand up and differentiate themselves from Muslims or Arabs," journalist Sarah Wildman quotes Malhotra as saying.[36] In his talks at American University and Princeton University, he took the offensive against Islam, accusing its leaders of "duplicity" for projecting a face of peace and tolerance in the United States while promoting fundamentalism at home. In an American University presentation titled "The Gita's Perspective on the War against Terrorism," he rejected an antiwar stance and argued that the Gita supported "dharmic" or just wars to combat global evil provided that they did not occur merely in self-interest and were carried out ethically, without colluding with evil.[37] Malhotra thus publicly articulated a Hindu argument against U.S. alliances with Pakistan or Saudi Arabia in the fight against the Taliban. He took the opportunity to expound on some of his favorite themes, arguing that the post-9/11 situation should lead the United States to "introspect about its chauvinism towards non-western cultures" more generally. Malhotra also promoted the idea that Indian traditions of debate would allow for "equal self-representation by all major civilizations in the modern discourse" (as opposed to the reigning Eurocentric model).[38]

During a presentation at the annual American Academy of Religion meetings in November 2001 (where he had again been invited as a representative of "practicing Hindus"), Malhotra criticized what he characterized as the "five asymmetries in the dialog of civilizations" and accused American scholars of Hinduism of "denying agency and rights to non-westerners"; of "academic arson," or the "age-old 'plunder while you denigrate the source' process"; and of engaging in "intimidating name-calling to affect censorship," concluding with the demand that Hindus in the diaspora be included as "dialog representatives" in a joint study of the tradition.[39]

Hindu Americans were also more willing to mobilize in support of Indian and Hindu causes in the post-9/11 period. A petition charging CNN with pro-Pakistani and anti-Indian bias (based on allegations in an article by Malhotra published on Sulekha.com) obtained fifty-five thousand signatures. Such an outpouring of support compelled CNN executives to meet in Atlanta with representatives of the Indian community during February 2002.[40] Several Hindu

American groups also mobilized to protest the planned February 2002 screening of two films critical of Hindu nationalism by the New York–based American Museum of Natural History as part of an exhibit titled Meeting God: Elements of Hindu Devotion.[41] A petition (again sponsored by HICAD) sent to museum authorities had an introduction similar to the Bush petition, pointing out that the large number of Hindus living in the United States constitutes a visible and very productive American community. The petition continued,

In the post 9-11 tragedy, we need to develop a greater understanding and appreciation for diversity in our society. We must educate the cosmopolitan population of the greater New York area and the rest of the USA to respect all our neighbors who might be following diverse religions and traditions. . . . The screening of these anti-Hindu movies will be considered by Hindus in the USA and all over the world as an insult to their faith. As an analogy, please consider if it would be appropriate to stage a documentary on Osama bin Laden and the destruction of the World Trade Center in an exhibit on the elements of Islamic devotion; or a documentary on slavery, colonialism, Christian crusades, white supremacy, Holocaust, Auschwitz, or killings of native Americans, in an exhibit on the Elements of Christian Devotion.

The petition concludes, "We the undersigned, being practicing Hindus and a religious minority in the United States, fear that the screening of these anti-Hinduism movies . . . would promote disrespect, bias and hatred against our religion in the general American populace. We, therefore, urge the American museum of Natural History to drop these movies from the exhibition."[42] The showing of the films was initially canceled, allegedly because of the threat of violence. Later, when the films were shown at a different venue, many aggrieved Hindus reportedly turned out. Later in 2002, at the showing of another film critical of Hindu nationalism (this time at Barnard College at Columbia University in New York City), Hindu protesters apparently grew so unruly that the organizers had to be whisked away in a van under police protection.[43]

Although Hindu American spokespersons' genteel multiculturalism and militant nationalism appear to be very different, they are in fact intertwined. Nazli Kibria argues that Asian Americans are a "transgressive" group insofar as their experiences merge those of European "ethnic" immigrants who assimilated into the mainstream and those of racialized minorities whose racial identities have hampered societal integration. She points out, however, that "precisely this transgressive aspect" makes their experience "valuable as a source of clues to the puzzle of new immigrant integration."[44] Similarly, the transgressive nature of the Hindu American experience has, when combined with the unique features of Hindu history, given rise to the two contradictory sides of American Hinduism. As successful ethnics, Hindu Americans embrace a genteel multiculturalism, while their racial and religious marginality pushes them toward militancy and ethnic nationalism.

What explains the turn toward militant mobilization strategies following 9/11? The literature provides two explanations for expatriate nationalism: (1) it is a product of immigrant marginalization; and (2) it is a strategic response to gain resources in multicultural host societies. The public emergence of Hindu nationalism in the post-9/11 period probably has to do with a combination of factors: genuine fears about the further marginalization of Hindus if Muslims were included under the American sacred canopy, resentment and worry about the sudden U.S. rapprochement with Pakistan, and an attempt to exploit the rise of anti-Islamic sentiments in the United States to obtain the recognition and support Hindus had long been seeking.

James Davison Hunter seems to imply that the militancy of new religious groups in the United States is temporary, lasting only until they have been "established" as American religions.[45] This leads to two questions: Will Hinduism be included within the American sacred canopy? If so, will Hindu American militancy then disappear? Only time can provide the answers.

APPENDIX

A Petition from American Hindus to President Bush
Subject: Why do you exclude Hindus from your prayers?

Dear Mr. President,
Last Sunday, during the prayer for the victims of the horrific terrorist attacks, you included Christians, Jews, and Muslims. Many American Hindus lost their lives during these attacks. These citizens of Hindu faith were conspicuously omitted from your prayer services. Hindu Americans feel slighted and wonder: Why do you exclude Hindus from your prayers? Why didn't you ask a Pundit (Hindu priest) to join you, along with the Muslim cleric, the Priest, the Minister, and the Rabbi?

As our national leader, you have repeatedly urged respect for America's pluralistic and multi-cultural traditions. Yet, you have repeatedly excluded Hindu-Americans from your prayers and recognition. There are over 800 Hindu temples in North America, including every major city. All of them had organized prayers to mourn the loss of all those who perished or suffered in the World Trade Center and Pentagon attacks and plane crashes.

Hindus are very much a part of our nation. We are hard working people who contribute to the American society, economy, education and quality of life, in a proportion much larger than our numbers. Hindus are highly visible in this country: in schools, colleges, universities and research institutions; hospitals and healthcare industry; computer, info-tech and telecom industries; banks, law, accounting and investment firms; hotels, motels and restaurants; small businesses, . . . and many other walks of life. And yet, we are omitted from your prayers. Our temples of worship are excluded from your references to the religious traditions practiced in this country. Such conspicuous exclusions can easily be interpreted as a hidden code by the forces of bigotry and extremism. It is unfortunate that some tele-evangelists who thrive on defaming our all-inclusive Hindu faith in their TV and radio broadcasts, have already started their "sly evokings" (as William Safire puts it) by blaming the "pagans" as the cause of these terrorist acts. Please, Mr. President, there must be a Hindu Pundit beside a Protestant minister, a Catholic priest, a Rabbi and a Muslim cleric, when Americans are asked to pray for peace.

Mr. President, Hindus are a peace-loving people. We never threaten violence against our host country. There is no world-wide Hindu network of terrorists. There are almost a billion Hindus living on Earth. They practice the world's oldest religion (over 8,000 years old.)

Non-violence, pluralism, and respect (not just tolerance) of other traditions of worship to the One Almighty God, are integral parts of its basic tenets. We are family oriented people, with very low divorce rates. We are frugal, save for our children's education, and support our elders and extended families. Because of these beliefs, Hindu-Americans are called ideal citizens. American Hindus are highly educated and skilled people, striving to make the US a better place to live for everyone. We deserve inclusion in your public prayers for the nation.

In the aftermath of the heinous terrorist attacks, Hindu-Americans and Hindu places of worship have become the target of xenophobic rage in some parts of North America. This is because many Americans do not know the difference between Hinduism and Islam; they lump them together as foreign religions. Your help in bringing the recognition to Hindus as a peace-loving people who are an integral part of our society, would go a long way in educating Americans about Hinduism. Please help Americans understand these issues by including Hindus in the fold of the President's well wishes and prayers.

In the U.S.A., there are two million people who identify themselves as Hindus, and another 20 million who practice Hindu traditions such as Yoga and Meditation. Lawmakers and officials in Washington do include Hindus when they pray. We urge you to henceforth include Hindus when you list the religiously pluralistic traditions of our country and include Hindu Temples on your list of places of worship in our great nation. God bless America!

NOTES

1. This petition originally appeared at <http://www.hicad.org/bush/htm> but is no longer available. A modified version appears at <http://www.hrk.org/articles/0901/114.html>.

2. See Stephen Prothero, "Love Bombs at Home: A New Holy Trinity Tradition: Judeo-Christian-Islamic," *Wall Street Journal*, December 14, 2001, W21.

3. See the reference to the fact that "there is no world-wide Hindu network of terrorists" as well as the passage that reads, "Many Americans do not know the difference between Hinduism and Islam; they lump them together as foreign religions. Your help in bringing the recognition to Hindus as a peace-loving people who are an integral part of our society, would go a long way in educating Americans about Hinduism."

4. These terms and the general argument are from Arvind Rajagopal, *Politics after Television: Hindu Nationalism and the Reshaping of the Public in India* (Cambridge: Cambridge University Press, 2001), 267.

5. According to the 1990 census, the median family income of Indians in the United States was $49,309, well above that for non-Hispanic whites ($37,630). See Mary Waters and Karl Eschbach, "Immigration and Ethnic and Racial Inequality in the U.S.," in *Majority and Minority: The Dynamics of Race and Ethnicity in American Life*, 6th ed., edited by Norman R. Yetman (Boston: Allyn and Bacon, 1999), 315. The census showed that 43.6 percent of Indians in the United States were employed either as professionals (mostly doctors and engineers) or as managers, and 58.4 percent had at least a bachelor's degree. See Larry Hajime Shinagawa, "The Impact of Immigration on the Demography of Asian Pacific Americans," in *The State of Asian Pacific America: Reframing the Immigration Debate, A Public Policy Report*, edited by Bill Ong Hing and Ronald Lee (Los Angeles: LEAP Asian Pacific American Public Policy Institute and UCLA Asian American Studies Center, 1996), 113, 119.

6. This figure is based on Indian census reports that count Dalits (formerly called Untouchables) and tribals as Hindu. Many members of these groups object to their inclusion within Hinduism.

7. S. K. Hofrenning and B. R. Chiswick, "A Method for Proxying a Respondent's Religious Background: An Application to School Choice Decisions," *Journal of Human Resources* 34.1 (Winter 1999): 193–207; 2002 Britannica Book of the Year and 2000 World Almanac figures obtained from <www.pluralism.org/resources/statistics/tradition.php#Hinduism>.

8. R. Stephen Warner, "Work in Progress toward a New Paradigm for the Sociological Study of Religion in the United States," *American Journal of Sociology* 98.5 (March 1993): 1058.

9. Will Herberg, *Protestant, Catholic, Jew: An Essay in American Religious Sociology*, 2nd ed. (Garden City, N.Y.: Doubleday, 1960), 27–28.

10. Raymond Williams, *Religions of Immigrants from India and Pakistan: New Threads in the American Tapestry* (Cambridge: Cambridge University Press, 1988), 29.

11. For Chinese Christians, see Fenggang Yang, *Chinese Christians in America: Conversion, Assimilation, and Adhesive Identities* (University Park: Pennsylvania State University Press, 1999); for Korean Christians, see Won Moo Hurh and Kwang Chung Kim, "Religious Participation of Korean Immigrants in the United States," *Journal for the Scientific Study of Religion* 29.1 (March 1990): 19–34; for Maya Catholics, see Nancy J. Wellmeier, "Santa Eulalia's People in Exile: Maya Religion, Culture, and Identity in Los Angeles," in *Gatherings in Diaspora: Religious Communities and the New Immigration*, edited

by R. Stephen Warner and Judith Wittner (Philadelphia: Temple University Press, 1998), 97–122.

12. Williams, *Religions of Immigrants*, 11.

13. Fenggang Yang and Helen Rose Ebaugh, "Transformations in New Immigrant Religions and their Global Implications," *American Sociological Review* 66.2 (April 2001): 269–88.

14. Helen Rose Ebaugh and Janet Saltzman Chafetz, eds., *Religion and the New Immigrants: Continuities and Adaptations in Immigrant Congregations* (Walnut Creek, Calif.: AltaMira, 2000); Prema A. Kurien, "Becoming American by Becoming Hindu: Indian Americans Take Their Place at the Multi-Cultural Table," in *Gatherings in Diaspora*, edited by Warner and Wittner, 37–70; R. Stephen Warner, "Work in Progress," and "Immigration and Religious Communities in the United States," in *Gatherings in Diaspora*, edited by Warner and Wittner, 3–34; Yang and Ebaugh, "Transformations."

15. Prema A. Kurien, "Religion, Ethnicity, and Politics: Hindu and Muslim Indian Immigrants in the United States," *Ethnic and Racial Studies* 24.2 (March 2001): 263–93.

16. Armand L. Mauss, *The Angel and the Beehive: The Mormon Struggle with Assimilation* (Urbana: University of Illinois Press, 1994).

17. See Prothero, "Love Bombs."

18. Heinrich von Steitencron, "Hinduism: On the Proper Use of a Deceptive Term," in *Hinduism Reconsidered*, edited by Gunther Sontheimer and Hermann Kulke (New Delhi: Manohar, 1989), 11–28.

19. Vasudha Narayanan, "Creating the South Indian 'Hindu' Experience in the United States," in *A Sacred Thread: Modern Transmission of Hindu Traditions in India and Abroad*, edited by Raymond Brady Williams (Chambersburg, Pa.: Anima, 1992), 147–76.

20. Mauss, *Angel and the Beehive*.

21. See Steven Vertovec, *The Hindu Diaspora: Comparative Patterns* (London: Routledge, 2000).

22. For this argument, see Vinay Lal, "The Politics of History on the Internet: Cyber-Diasporic Hinduism and the North American Hindu Diaspora," *Diaspora* 8.2 (Fall 1999): 137–72; Biju Mathew, "Byte-Sized Nationalism: Mapping the Hindu Right in the United States," *Rethinking Marxism* 12.3 (2000): 108–28; Biju Mathew and Vijay Prashad, "The Protean Forms of Yankee Hindutva," *Ethnic and Racial Studies* 23.3 (May 2000): 516–34.

23. See Dean E. Murphy, "Two Unlikely Allies Come Together in Fight against Muslims," *New York Times*, June 2, 2001, B1; Kurien, "Religion, Ethnicity, and Politics."

24. See Prema A. Kurien, "Multiculturalism, Immigrant Religion, and Diasporic Nationalism: The Development of an American Hinduism," *Social Problems* 51.3 (August 2004): 362–85.

25. See "History of VHPA," <http://www.vhp-america.org/whatvhpa history.htm>.

26. Prithvi Raj Singh, "Discussing Religious Role Models" (letter to the editor), *India Post*, March 14, 1997, A26.

27. Prithvi Raj Singh, interview by author, February 9, 1997.

28. Arthur J. Pais, "A First Line of Defense," <http://www.beliefnet.com/story/57/story_5743.html>.

29. See "Mission Statement," <http://www.infinityfoundation.com/ECITmission frame.htm>.

30. *The Ramayana Project*, chapter 5, unit 25, lesson 2, 335–37, cited in "Complaint against Anti-Rama Song in Secondary Schools," <http://www.infinityfoundation.com/ECITnehletterframe.htm>.

31. See "Complaint against Anti-Rama Song."

32. See, e.g., "The Hindu View of Others," <http://www.NorthJersey.com>.

33. See, e.g., the interview with Rajiv Malhotra on the radio program *Tapestry*, October 22, 2000, <http://www.infinityfoundation.com/ ECITnprinterviewframe.htm>; see also Rajiv Malhotra and David Gray, "Global Renaissance and the Roots of Western Wisdom," *IONS Review*, <http://www.noetic.org/Ion/publications/r56Malhotra.htm>.

34. See, e.g., "Hindu Philosophy Has No Place for Caste System Says FHA," *India Post*, March 17, 1995.

35. V. E. Krishnakumar and L. Prashanth, "Clinton Wishes Indians First Ever Diwali Greetings," *India Post*, November 3, 2000, 22.

36. Sarah Wildman, "All for One," *New Republic*, December 24, 2001, <www.thenew republic.com122401/diarist122401.html>.

37. In the aftermath of 9/11, several Hindu Americans argued that emphasis on *ahimsa* (nonviolence) should be dropped in favor of various examples from the Hindu epics showing the Hindu gods willing to go to war when necessary.

38. The texts of these talks were posted on the Internet discussion group associated with the Infinity Foundation on September 25 and October 4, 2001, and were later combined and archived by HICAD as Rajiv Malhotra, "Lessons from Gita on Fighting Terrorism," <www.hicad.org/gita.htm>. A modified version, "Gita on Fighting Terrorism," was also posted on the Infinity Foundation Web site: <www.infinityfounda tion.com/mandala/s_es/s_es_ malho_gita.htm>.

39. Material for this paragraph was taken from an Internet report on the panel (including the papers presented): John Stratton Hawley, "Defamation/Anti-Defamation: Hindus in Dialogue with the Western Academy," <http://www.web.barnard.columbia.edu/religion/hindu/malhotra_defam ation/html>.

40. Reported at <http://www.infinityfoundation.com/mandala/s_es/s_es_rao-r _govt.htm>.

41. One was on a Dalit critique of the Ramayana, and the other was on a critical look at the Hindu nationalist movement in India.

42. <http://www.petitiononline.com/AMUSEUM.htm> (accessed January 23, 2002; no longer available).

43. This information is based on eyewitness reports by people who attended the film showings.

44. Nazli C. Kibria, *Becoming Asian American: Second-Generation Chinese and Korean American Identities* (Baltimore: Johns Hopkins University Press, 2002), 3.

45. See Hunter, this volume.

7

Sacred Land, Sacred Service

Hindu Adaptations to the American Landscape

Hindus living in India have had the comfort and luxury of having their religion, ethnicity, and culture come together on the south Asian subcontinent. Religious concepts, philosophies, social relationships, and sacred geography are embedded in and articulated through the performing arts. Vegetables, lentils, and spices are connected with notions of orthopraxy. Every religious ritual framed by Brahmanical Sanskrit verses begins with a recitation of the geography of the sacred land in which the observant resides. But what happens when Hindus migrate to a different continent, removed from the sacred territories? How do they see themselves as connected with the new land they call home?

This chapter examines how post-1965 immigrant Hindus are accommodating to the United States in two important ways. The first is by transforming the land, in some cases making places in America sacred by associating them with Hindu geography and mythology. The second is by seizing on a quintessentially American activity—volunteerism—and making it a part of the individual Hindu's duty and the Hindu temple's mission. The American spiritual landscape plainly has been transformed by the addition of Hindu temples to a nation of church spires, synagogue domes, and mosque minarets. But the United States is also changing the Hindu tradition.

For several millennia, Hindus have considered the land of India to be sacred. They think of specific villages, mountains, lakes, and rivers as infused with holiness. In fact, several sacred texts strongly disapprove of living outside this sacred land. Nonetheless, Hindus have been migrating for more than two thousand years, first to southeast Asia and then to other parts of the world. Every migration has entailed negotiations between host cultures and the Hindus' heritage as they struggled to maintain their identity on foreign soil. Hindus' survival and success in any new country depends on their being recognized as part of the new landscape; Hinduism's success and survival have depended on its creative ability to devise out of its large library of stories and memories a continuum of architecture that somehow fits in the new environment while remaining connected with the past. Several thousand years of sacred texts, commentaries, myths, stories, songs, dances, and symbols in Sanskrit as well as various vernacular and elite structures serve as a vast reservoir of resources from which Hindus can draw as they find ways to fit into American communities with different histories and different dreams. For example, in Sanskrit prologues to U.S. Hindu rituals, some Hindus now see America as a continent within the traditional mythical landscape of Hinduism; some Hindus have reinterpreted the American eagle as Garuda, the eagle vehicle of the Hindu god Vishnu; and some Hindus understand working in soup kitchens during the Martin Luther King Jr. weekend as participating in meritorious acts of food giving during the festival of Sankaranti, which falls close to the U.S. public holiday in mid-January.

While temple building has been an immediate imperative for newly settled U.S. Hindus, many Hindu immigrants to Europe set up spiritual shop in warehouses, garages, or the upper floors of shops and only later built more traditional temples. On this basis alone, Hinduism in the United States differs from Hinduism in other places (with the possible exception of Canada). In the United States, citizens are more open and accepting of immigrant customs and traditions. Here it is not considered archaic to go regularly to houses of worship. Religion is not state mandated. And economic institutions will lend money to build temples. So Hindu temples are rising all over the map. Depending on a community's means, these structures range from renovated airport hangars, gymnasiums, and Eastern Orthodox churches to majestic buildings with carved towers resembling eleventh-century south Indian temples. The United States has more Hindu temples than any country except India.

Literally thousands of songs and dances glorify India or speak of the sacrality of Indian land. Do Hindus in America think of themselves as being in exile and away from the holy land? Far from it.

Hindus have made portions of the United States sacred and to some extent contiguous with India in at least four ways: (1) by composing songs and pious Sanskrit prayers extolling the U.S. state in which a particular temple is located; (2) by adapting the classic cosmology of the Puranas to identify America as a specific *dvipa* (island/continent) mentioned in those sacred Sanskrit texts; (3) by physically consecrating the land with waters from a combination of sacred Indian rivers and American rivers; and (4) by literally re-creating in

U.S. locations the physical landscape of certain holy places in India. In addition, Hindus co-opt land or shrines held sacred by Americans, layering motifs and meanings on U.S. sacred spaces.

Many Hindu legal codes speak of parts of the Indian subcontinent as holy ground fit for religious rituals. Indeed, some of these codes say that all of India is holy; ritual actions bear fruit here. The description of the sacrality of the land was confined to the northern part of India, however, when some of the codes of righteousness (*dharma sastras*) were composed around the beginning of the Common Era. Manu says,

> That land, created by the gods, which lies between the two divine rivers Sarasvati and Drishadvati [is] Brahmavarta . . . the tract between those two mountains which extends between the eastern and western oceans, the wise call Aryavarta (the country of the noble ones). . . . The land where the black antelope naturally roams, one must know to be fit for the performance of sacrifices; [this land] is different from the country of the barbarians.[1]

In time, this concept extended beyond the land between the Himalaya and Vindhya Mountains to cover the whole subcontinent. India itself became a divine mother (Bharata Mata).

Now almost every village in India has a story of divine manifestation—a legend of a hierophany. In many parts of India, the name of one's village is part of one's official name. Families periodically trek back to their ancestral villages to worship the family deity; they frequently send money back to hometown temples in acts of mail-order piety.

Still, people from the subcontinent have been migrating to practically every part of the world since the early centuries of the Common Era. They settled and built temples in many places, including the grand monuments of southeast Asia. But immigrants to the United States have had several advantages that their ancestors did not have. At least after 1965, U.S. immigrants enjoyed economic prosperity and with it the luxury of going back regularly to their mother country. They also enjoyed religious freedom, which they exercised first and foremost by building temples and raising their children in Indian religion and culture.

In 1986 the Sri Venkateswara Temple in Penn Hills, Pennsylvania, issued a cassette of popular devotional songs (*bhajans*). In it, the Pittsburgh-area devotees praise Lord Venkateswara (Lord of the Venkata Hills), a manifestation of Lord Vishnu:

America vasa jaya govinda
Penn Hills nilaya radhe govinda
sri guru jaya guru, vithala govinda

[Victory to Govinda who lives in America;
Govinda who with Radha resides in Penn Hills.
Victory to Govinda, Vithala, the sacred Teacher.][2]

This song hails Vishnu as Govinda (one of his many names). Glorifying Vishnu as abiding in a particular place is a way that devotees consecrate that deity in a temple and bring him or her alive. All temples conduct formal ceremonies of vivification with pitchers of sanctified waters, promulgating the sacredness of the land in song and making a particular deity accessible in a particular place. Thus, the deity Venkateswara is believed to be present in Tiru Venkatam in Tirupati, India. But this deity now also abides in local shrines at Penn Hills, Malibu, Chicago, Dayton, and Atlanta, among many others. The devotees in Pittsburgh believe that their lord resides with them, sanctifying the land where they live.

Singing about the deity in a particular location helps mark the sacrality of that spot. Thus, in the Sri Vaishnava tradition—an important faith and one of many Hindu communities—poet-saints who lived between the eighth and tenth centuries C.E. sang in praise of Vishnu in 108 places. They sang about the particular manifestation of Vishnu in a specific town or village and described the surroundings—the tall citadels, the terraced houses and palaces, the expanses of crops, the trees, the sea, and other relevant details of the landscape. These 108 sites are called the "divine places" (divya desa) and are hallowed in the Sri Vaishnava tradition. While other temples are also very prominent, they are not considered among these special 108 because the early poet-saints did not sing about these temples. Singing about a place, therefore, not only articulates its sacrality but makes it holy.

Understanding this context is crucial to any consideration of the popular song declaring "Victory to Govinda who lives in America" and of a more recent poem, "Sri Venkatesha America Vaibhava Stotram" (Praise of the Appearance of Lord Venkatesha in America). The latter is a stately piece of literature composed by Dr. J. Sethuraman, professor of statistics at Florida State University in Tallahassee and an erudite scholar of Sanskrit. Sethuraman's poem glorifies Lord Vishnu in his manifestation as Venkatesha (Venkateswara) in many American towns and states. Most Hindus in south India do not worship generic deities such as Vishnu and Lakshmi; instead, they call these gods affectionately by the particular name by which they are known in a nearby temple. Venkatesha is a well known and popular manifestation of Vishnu, and the temple in Penn Hills is devoted to him. Sethuraman's poem describes the different places in the United States where Venkatesha is enshrined.

"Sri Venkatesha America Vaibhava Stotram" is written in classical Sanskrit, in the style of a traditional *kavya* (poem), replete with exquisite literary devices and ornate verses. It starts off with the idea that Sri Venkatesha (Vishnu), Lakshmi (the goddess of good fortune), and the Earth Goddess have come to America to remove the devotees' miseries. The poem then proceeds, using a time-honored Sanskrit literary strategy, to describe the characteristics of this Lord Venkatesha ("Such a Sri Venkatesha has arrived here."). The Venkatesha who has graced this country, says Sethuraman, is the supreme deity spoken of in the scriptures, the glorious one who is so hard to comprehend and reach. And yet, this majestic, supreme being (*brahman*), to make itself accessible, comes as Venkatesha with Lakshmi and the Goddess Earth to be close to his devotees: "Such a Sri Venkatesha has arrived here—the very Brahman—the one who has to be understood from the Vedas, and one with the brilliance of a thousand rising suns—in whom a large assembly of yogis have placed their minds . . . and are rejoicing day and night."[3] The poet or person who recites this prayer then places his soul at the feet of the Lord and seeks him as a refuge (9–16). The poet then glorifies this manifestation and the many incarnations of Vishnu (17–19). Then comes the "Description of the Grand Tour of Sri Venkatesha in America" (Sri Venkatesha Amerika Vaibhava Sthala Varnanam).

The first place to be glorified, the Sri Venkateswara Temple in Pittsburgh, is the first large temple in America devoted to Venkatesha. It is followed by New York (Flushing) and Boston. In each case, Sethuraman begins the relevant verses with the phrase, "Such a Venkatesha," harking back to the first verse introducing this deity. In a manner reminiscent of the best of the classical Indian poets, he describes the surroundings for every city and state. The first two verses offer a taste of his style, replete with "decorative" Sanskrit embellishments:

Venkatesha, the ocean of nectar of kindness, has come to [the] hill top at the well known city of Pittsburgh, surrounded by the three rivers, Allegheny, Monongahela, and the Ohio, to remove the miseries of the people.

Venkatesha, the ocean of nectar of kindness, has indeed come to the place known as Ashland, Massachusetts (near Boston) which is purified by the waves of the Atlantic ocean, to remove the miseries of the people.[4]

The refrain that this Venkatesha, "an ocean of the nectar of kindness," comes to "remove the miseries" of the people is repeated in the descriptions of twenty-one other places. The list grows when new temples to Venkatesha are added to the American map.

The descriptions are both generic and specific. The cold waves of the Pacific Ocean purify Malibu and San Diego, California; the forests on the banks of the great Mississippi River are near Jackson, Mississippi; and Dayton, Ohio, is purified by the Stillwater, Red, and the Great Miami Rivers. A special touch is added to Venkatesha's manifestation in Houston. This city is now well known among south Indian Hindus in America for its magnificent temple of Meenakshi (the local name of the Goddess Parvati in Madurai, south India). In south India, the popular imagination considers Meenakshi to be the sister of Vishnu. Thus, Sethuraman says that Venkatesha/Vishnu comes to Houston ("in the great state of Texas garlanded by the Rio Grande River") to be near his sister, Sri Meenakshi.

Sethuraman also renders some names in Sanskrit: the Pacific Ocean is called *santyabdi* (24, 25); the Stillwater River is *santambu nadi*, and the Red River is *sindura nadi* (34). Riverdale (near Atlanta) is translated as *nadisu tira* (29), and Bridgewater, New Jersey, is *setunira* (31). These geographic names thus become part of the Hindus' liturgical map. The poem also features several patterns of "ornamentation" that would delight the hearts of Sanskritists. The poem ends with a petition: the poet asks God to grant a calm mind, free of raging desires, to anyone who repeatedly thinks of all these divine residences (New York, Pittsburgh, Boston, and so forth), anyone who contemplates Venkatesha's divine form and praises him with this poem.

This poem makes sacred the towns and states of America where Vishnu has come to reside. India's villages and towns are sacred because the poets have glorified the supreme being who has come to reside there as a god or goddess. Now the same deity resides in America.

At the beginning of all traditional Hindu rituals (weddings, ancestral rites, naming ceremonies, and so on), the officiating priest and his attendants formally declare the coordinates of the land and the time in which the rite takes place. These words are part of the *sankalpa* (declaration of intention) to do the ritual. Such coordinates are in cosmic frameworks; the sacred space is identified with one of the *dvipas* in Puranic cosmology, and the sacred time is parsed in millions of years.

Classic statements of intention identify India as the most fortuitous of land masses—the Jambu Dvipa (Island of Rose-Apple Fruit) located to the south of the mythical Mount Meru, which rises at the center of the universe. Hindu religious texts give a range of between four and thirteen for the number of such islands, which are located like the petals of a lotus flower around Mount Meru. The islands are said to be separated by oceans of water, milk, sugarcane juice, and so forth. The Bhagavata Purana, a text ascribed to the first millennium C.E., identifies seven such islands with the names of various subdivisions. In India, the performer of the ritual further specifies that he or she is in the "division of the world" (*varsha*) called Bhaarata in that "fragment" (*khanda*) of the land named Bharata. The Bhagavata Purana names nine *varshas*, or continents. No serious attempt seems to have been made in the past to identify any other actual continent or land mass with any of these traditional mythical names.

In summary, then, some of the Puranas give details of seven cosmic islands divided into various provinces. The sacred land of India is declared to be in the Island of Rose-Apple Fruit (Jambu Dvipa); the land mass is called Bhaarata (*bharata varsha*), and the country is Bharata (*bharata khanda*). The whole area is considered to be south of the mythical Mount Meru. Thus, Hindus in India begin almost all religious rituals with the intention to perform that rite, which includes the line, "in this Island of Rose-Apple Fruit, in the land of Bharata, in the fragment of land [country] called Bharata, south of Mount Meru [Jambu dvipe Bharata varshe bharata khande, Mero dakshine parsve]."

The rituals in the United States have new parameters and new names. Almost all temples (with the exception of the one in Buffalo, New York) follow the formulaic statement that America is located in the Krauncha (Heron) Island west of Mount Meru. While it is not clear where these phrases were first modified to fit North America, priests' accounts indicate that the change probably happened in the early temples in Pittsburgh and Queens, New York, around 1975. In the ritual intention stated in the Pittsburgh Venkateswara Temple, elaborated in the many temples of America, and repeated in the beginning of every wedding, death, or other ritual, a new cosmology is in place. We are no longer operating on the Rose-Apple Island; we are now in America, the Island of the Heron.

Krauncha is the fifth of the seven land masses in Hindu cosmology. Scholars do not agree on where Krauncha is located: some see it as purely mythical, some as another planet, some as another continent in this world, and others as a spiritual state. Nevertheless, the ritual specialists who composed the groundbreaking rites for the first temples in America came to call their new land Krauncha. According to the Vishnu Purana, a text composed in the first few centuries of the Common Era, all the continents are insular; another text, the Bhagavata Purana (composed 100–600 C.E.), says that the Krauncha *dvipa* is surrounded by an ocean of milk and that it is free from fear because it is guarded by the god Varuna.[5]

There is some variation in the identification of both the continent and its subdivisions. In general, two versions prevail: Pittsburgh, Atlanta, and some others identify this land as the golden continent (*hiranyaka varsha*), and the temple is in the part called "the sacred place of cattle-herds" (*go tirtha khanda*). The word *tirtha* in Sanskrit indicates a holy place, a place of pilgrimage; use of the term for the American subcontinent asserts its sacrality.[6]

In the second version, used in Chicago, Jacksonville, and other places, America is described as the "delightful, pleasant" part (*ramanaka khanda*) of the "delightful" continent (*ramanaka varsha*), still in the island of Krauncha. Combinations of the two statements are seen in various parts of the United States, with minor variations. The second version also mentions the "sacred" rivers in the United States.

A declaration of intention in Tallahassee, Florida, began,

> In this island of Krauncha, in the delightful continent, in the sacred province of the cows that is west of the Mississippi River, in the sacred land [*punya kshetra*] called Tallahassee . . .[7]

In Jacksonville, Florida, by contrast, a fuller version of the declaration of intention was used:

> In the Krauncha island,
> in the golden continent,
> in the pleasant land that is west of Mount Meru,
> in North America,
> where there are rivers like the Mississippi, Kansas, Alabama, Illini
>   [Illinois], Ohio, Hudson, St. John, etc., teeming with various forms
>   of life in them,
> surrounded by mountains like the Rockies and the McKinley,
> in the midst of the great oceans like the Prashanta [literally, "peaceful,"
>   here referring to the Pacific] and the Atlantic,
> in the city of [Jacksonville],
> in the presence of all the divine beings, Brahmans et al.
> I am performing [this ritual].[8]

Several variations on this theme exist, but in all these formulaic salutations, worshipers place themselves in a land both pleasant and part of Puranic geography. It is a bold move. It is not that America is some offshore colony to Bharata or India: instead, America is identified as a specific part of the Sanskrit textual cosmology, and this recognition is fitted seamlessly into the rituals.

One way American places can be brought under the sacred canopy of Hindu cosmology is by the mixing of sacred waters. In *Walden*, in a passage penned at the end of a winter spent with the Hindu holy book the Bhagavad Gita, Henry David Thoreau reports seeing workers cutting the ice on Walden Pond into large chunks for export to India:

> In the morning I bathe my intellect in the stupendous and cosmogonal philosophy of the Bhagavat Geeta, since whose composition years of the gods have elapsed, and in comparison with which our modern world and its literature seem puny and trivial. . . . I lay down the book and go to my well for water, and lo! there I meet the servant of the Brahman . . . come to draw water for his master, and our buckets as it were grate together in the same well. The pure Walden water is mingled with the sacred water of the Ganges.[9]

Thoreau could scarcely have imagined that within 150 years of his meditations, the waters of the Ganges (referred to henceforth by the Indian name "Ganga") would be brought to Massachusetts to a temple of the Goddess Lakshmi in Ashland (not far from Walden Pond) and to dozens of other U.S. temples, then mingled with the waters of local rivers to make those spaces sacred.

Hindus think of rivers as liquid purifiers, capable of spiritually cleansing all who bathe in them. But why should they be mingled with the waters of the Mississippi and the Suwanee?

On the simplest level, there is a powerful notion of contagion—the idea that the sacrality attached to the Ganga and other rivers will physically attach itself to whatever rivers it touches. In fact, this is what many Hindus attending the rituals will tell you. The waters of the Ganga are, as it were, contagiously purifying. That is why, when a person dies, sacred water is sprinkled on the body and even poured into the mouth. This is why the impure ashes of the cremated are immersed in sacred rivers.

When water is not physically present, it is possible to project the presence of sacred rivers spiritually into the local waters. In a prayer that is often used to consecrate the waters to be used in a religious ritual or even daily before bathing, the Ganga is invoked by its popular names—Nandini, Bhagirathi, Jahnavi. The river goddess is requested to come and abide in the waters one will be using. Thus, in Hindu weddings in Gainesville, Florida; in temple consecrations in Houston or Chicago; or before bathing in India, the Ganga is ritually invoked even when there is no water present. And India's other rivers are petitioned to come in spirit and reside in that water. All of India's rivers— the Ganga, the Yamuna, the Godavari, the mythical Sarasvati, the Narmada, the Sindhu (Indus), and the Kaveri—are said to pool in the ritual jar wherever the rite takes place.

But there is more going on here than just spiritually or physically inviting holy Indian rivers into local liquid. It is simply not the case that the water of the Suwanee is a passive holder for the sacred energy of Indian water. As noted earlier, during the intention to perform any ritual, the names of American rivers—the Mississippi, the Hudson, the Suwanee, and so on—are mentioned. And they would not appear in this litany if they were not already sacred in some intrinsic way. Rivers nourish crops and feed human beings—they are "mothers." And while the biological mother from India is special, one learns to revere one's adoptive mother too. In this way, American rivers become part of the sacred geography of Hinduism's mother.

Finally, one may meditate on the patterns of a pilgrimage described in Sanskrit texts and done regularly in India, a ritual with some bearing on the mingling of sacred waters. In a practice described in a medieval text, the Adhyatma Ramayana (a version of the Ramayana epic), pilgrims go to the seaside town of Rameswaram, located near the subcontinent's southern tip and sacred to the gods Rama and Shiva. The pilgrims bathe in the Bay of Bengal, take sand from the beach, and carry it to either the city of Kasi (Banaras) or Prayag (Allahabad). The Ganga flows through Kasi; in Prayag, there is an auspicious confluence of the Ganga, the Yamuna, and the (mythical) Sarasvati, which is said to flow underground. The pilgrims dissolve the sands from Rameswaram in a holy river in northern India. Then they carry some water from these northern rivers back to the southern town of Rameswaram and use it to bathe the image of Shiva there. Physical elements from two distant parts of India are thus united in the ritual of pilgrimage. Therefore, in U.S. rituals used to consecrate the land by mingling waters from two continents, devotees are adapting rituals that go back to the Puranas.

Hindus from many philosophical communities believe that the supreme being makes itself accessible through incarnations on earth. But landscapes can be incarnated, too, and can take on new forms. Some American temples now try either to recognize resemblances between an American landscape and distinctive sacred spots in India or to re-create such similarities. The earliest attempt to recognize a geographical similarity came with the building of the Venkateswara Temple in Pittsburgh, which, as this 1986 statement indicates, many devotees likened to India's Prayag, another site where three rivers join together:

> Pittsburgh, endowed with hills and a multitude of trees as well as the confluence of the three rivers, namely, the Allegheny, the Monongahela, and the sub-terranean river (brought up via the 60 foot high fountain at downtown) to form the Ohio river is indeed a perfect choice for building the first and most authentic temple to house Lord Venkateswara. The ever-growing crowds that have been coming to the city with the thriveni Sangama of the three rivers to worship at the Temple with the three vimanas reassure our belief that the venerable Gods chose this place and the emerald green hillock to reside in.[10]

To understand temple building in the United States, it may be helpful to recall a Hindu tendency that Kees Bolle calls "topographical religiosity." Bolle's comments in "Speaking of a Place" are particularly relevant: "Naturally, some of the temples are more famous than others; one might say that they are more tangibly the real residence of God. But unless one understands the primacy of the place, the nature of the sacred in most of Hinduism remains incomprehensible, and the plurality and variety of gods continues to form an unsolvable puzzle. God is universal because he is there."[11] In being "there" at Penn Hills, Pennsylvania, and Poughkeepsie, New York, this universal God becomes particular, this land, holy.

There are now at least two Kasis (Banarases) in the United States: the Western Kasi Shiva Temple (Paschima Kasi Viswanatha Temple) in Flint, Michigan, and the Kashi Ashram (hermitage) in Sebastian, Florida. But some of the most intriguing attempts to re-create the landscape—to make it mirror an Indian site—have come in Barsana Dham, near Austin, Texas, and in the Iraivan Temple in Kauai, Hawaii.

In Hawaii, not only are the names reminiscent of India (the Path of the Nayanmars, San Marga Path, Rishi Valley, Rudraksha Forest, and so forth), but in each environment "pilgrims enjoy groves of plumeria, konrai forest hibiscus, fragrant vines, lilikoi, native Hawaiian species, ferns, bubbling waterfalls, ponds and more."[12] Thus, the physical environment of India meshes with the local Hawaiian land to create a unique milieu.

Barsana Dham has been made to resemble Barsana in northern India, said to be the hometown of Radha, the beloved of Lord Krishna. At Barsana Dham, all the important landmarks of Braj, the area in northern India where Krishna and Radha lived, have been re-created: "This beautiful 230-acre property is a representation of the holy land of Braj in India where Shree Radha Rani and Shree Krishn appeared 5,000 years ago. Areas of Barsana Dham have been developed to be places for devotional inspiration and meditation. All the important places of Braj like Govardhan, Radha Kund, Prem Sarovar, Shyam Kuti, Man Mandir and Mor Kuti, etc. are represented in Barsana Dham where the natural stream named Kalindi represents the Yamuna river of Vrindaban."[13]

Thanks to these similarities, Barsana in Texas is, according to its champions, fated to become a key pilgrimage site for those who cannot go to India: "Barsana Dham will be a place of pilgrimage for millions of Indians living in the Western world. There are thousands of people who desire to go to Braj, the birth place of their beloved Lord Shree Krishn, but they cannot go for the lack of time or for any other reason. They all can easily come to Barsana Dham and have the same spiritual feelings as though they were in Braj in India."[14] In a parallel situation in Hawaii, Dr. Sambamurthi Sivachariya, who came from a large temple in Madras, India, to preside as chief priest for two days of ceremonies, said, "I am too old to go on pilgrimage to the holy sites in the Indian Himalayan mountains, where, according to Hinduism, God Himself resides and gives His grace to pilgrims. That was a life-long dream of mine. But now that I have come to the most beautiful place in the world, Kauai, to this sacred land, I feel my dream has been fulfilled. I have come to the home of God."[15]

One of the smallest public Hindu shrines in this country is in the register of tourist attractions in the Hawaiian island of Oahu. This little place of worship, now run by Hindus from India, is a small street-side shrine in Wiahiawa dedicated to Viswanatha (a form of Shiva). Local devotees translate Viswanatha as "Lord of the Universe," and the organization that initially oversaw it was called the Lord of the Universe Society (LOTUS). The shrine contains two conical stones regarded as "healing stones" in traditional Hawaiian religion but revered by Hindus as a manifestation of Shiva. Hindus believe that the main stone here is a linga (a manifestation of Shiva); in indigenous religion, that stone embodies the Hawaiian priest-healer god Lono. According to another local myth, this stone represents two sisters from Kauai who were turned into rocks. Regular Hindu worship at this shrine, located not far from Pearl Harbor, is conducted on the third Sunday of every month. Hindus plainly have co-opted the Hawaiian deity. As one south Indian there told me, "Lord Shiva has manifested himself here."

On the Hawaiian island of Kauai, an existing Hindu temple is gradually being replaced by a larger one being carved in India and transported overseas in segments. This stone temple, which devotees say will last for 1,001 years, is designed by Sri Ganapati Sthapati, an important sculptor and architect of temples from India. The current temple on the site was built in 1970 by Swami Sivaya Subramuniyaswami, who was born in America and initiated in Sri Lanka. Gurudeva ("the divine or respected teacher"), as he is popularly known, says that in 1975 Shiva appeared to him in three visions, inspiring him to locate the temple there: "I saw Lord Siva walking in the meadow near the Wailua River. . . . His face was looking into mine. Then He was seated upon a great stone. I was seated on His left side. . . . An inner voice proclaimed, 'This is the place where the world will come to pray.' "[16] This vision has only reaffirmed, in Hindu terms, the indigenous holiness of the site, which lies at the foot of Mount Waialeale near the sacred Wailua River. The ancient Hawaiians are said to have called it Pihanakalani, "where heaven touches Earth." In fact, one of the ancient Hawaiian temples allegedly was located here. The ritual to lay the foundation incorporated rites from Hindu and local Hawaiian traditions: "A series of fire ceremonies were performed over a 48-hour period to purify the site and to invoke the blessings of God, gods and the local Hawaiian and Hindu guardian spirits. On the first day, April 4th, specially invited local guests joined the proceedings at the usually cloistered monastery. They included the Honorable Maryanne Kusaka, Mayor of Kauai, Hawaiian priestess Leimomi Mo'okini Lum, . . . former Kauai mayor Joanne Yukimura."[17]

While it seems both natural and practical to honor Hawaiian traditions in the consecration of a Hindu temple in Hawaii, this is not an interfaith or syncretic temple, of which there are many in America. In fact, it is not even a pan-Hindu temple. Most American temples (there are a few exceptions) are home to multiple deities. The Kauai temple, however, is unambiguously sectarian. Dedicated to the god Shiva, it has a large dancing Shiva in the middle. Toward the front is a nonanthropomorphic form of Shiva, the linga, a conical piece of crystal rock. In 1987, a rare six-sided quartz crystal Shiva linga was said to have been discovered and brought to Kauai from Arkansas. It is significant that this crystal is American born. But while the manifestation of

Shiva as this crystal lingam is American and the land is American territory, the temple itself will be carved in India. The ritual landscape will be reaffirmed in terms of Puranic geography, and consecrating waters will come from both India and America.

Is the American land holy? It is important to note that there was no concerted Hindu effort, no grand strategy by religious leaders, and no commission to discuss this question in the wave of the post-1965 immigration. The Hindus who settled here and the priests who came from India worked with traditional cultural tropes, ritually consecrating and praising the land they were inhabiting, formally glorying it in song.

Hindus have drawn several other homologies to show how this land is sacred and to make it so. The American eagle, for example, has been compared to Vishnu's mount, Garuda. In fact, many Hindus find this an obvious comparison. In an e-mail posted on December 31, 2000, on a listserv run by members of the Hindu Sri Vaishnava community, a writer wished the moderator a happy new year in English and Tamil. "America now seems to be the place of Sri Maha Vishnu," he wrote. "This is a land with devotion to God; this is a land of tranquility [amarikkai in Tamil, a pun] Is not their national bird [the] eagle—Garudan? May your spiritual work continue to spread our sampradaya [tradition]. May Sri Maalolaa [another name of Vishnu] bless you all with long life, excellent health and prosperity."[18]

While it has largely been post-1965 Hindus who have sacralized the land while building their temples, attempts to mimic the Indian landscape in their new country can be seen as early as 1905 in California. Hindu temples—at least those founded by immigrants from southern India—ordinarily resemble in some respect the medieval temples of south India. But the first Hindu temple in this country imitated not only temple towers from the Indian state of Bengal but also Muslim and European architectural tropes. It also explicitly incorporated American symbols. And a pamphlet issued at the consecration pointed out these features in case the reader missed the symbolism.

One of the teachers in the Vedanta Society (the leading American Hindu group during the first quarter of the twentieth century), Swami Trigunatita, oversaw the construction of what he called "the First Hindu Temple in the Whole Western World."[19] Sister Gargi, his biographer, notes, "To Swami Trigunatita the first Hindu temple in the whole Western world would be a vital piece of India planted on American soil. The Temple represented the influx of India's great spiritual wisdom into the culture of the West—there to grow and flourish."[20] But although he pronounced this structure a Hindu temple, he said that it was for Americans. "In actual fact, the Temple was not in any sense Hindu," Sister Gargi notes—"not in organization, activities, membership, architecture, or decor."[21]

The temple's five towers resemble onion domes and call to mind the Kremlin's bulbous towers. Swami Trigunatita, however, specifically designed the architecture to resemble various cultural forms. As a Vedanta Society pamphlet notes, "The Temple may be considered as a combination of a Hindu temple, a Christian church, a Mahommedan mosque, a Hindu math or monastery and an American shrine."[22] So the tower over the main entrance to the auditorium was supposed to look like the bell tower of a church as well as resemble the Taj Mahal. The first tower from the west was an exact miniature of a temple in Benares, except it had a weathervane on top. The second tower was like the Shiva shrine in the Kali temple in Dakshineswar (Calcutta). This tower has three symbols on top, representing the three Hindu spiritual paths, as well as a crescent—a "Turkish or Mahomedan emblem"—at the bottom.[23] The crescent was also said to be sacred to a group of Vaishnavas (Vishnu followers) who believed that it expressed ideas of softness, love, and affection associated with the moon—in short, the path of devotion. The second symbol looks like the sun, which is needed to grow and work and thus depicts the path of karma. The third symbol on this tower is a trident, representing the scepter of Neptune and Shiva. A symbol for the destruction of ignorance, it represents the path of knowledge. The northeast corner—traditionally the most important in any Hindu building—has a tower that resembles the Hindu god Shiva. The tower on the southeast corner was said to resemble European castles and to stand for "the great strength of character and spiritual culture."[24]

The rampant symbolizing did not stop there, however. The building also integrates elements from Indian yogic practice. The canopy over the mosaic and marble entrance represents the thousand-petaled lotus, which certain schools of Indian thought believe lies in the brain. In yogic anatomy, a subtle passage called the *sushumna* is said to go up the spinal cord to this lotus. On either side are two auxiliary passages, known as the *ida* and *pingala*. The tubular lights on both sides of the canopy represents these two passages.

Moving from the yogic to the patriotic, at the head of the canopy—the one that represented the thousand-petaled lotus on the crest of the *sushumna* tube —was an eagle. As the explanatory pamphlet put it, because the structure was America's first Hindu temple, "honor and appreciation have been shown by carrying in the architectural art of the temple, the Sushumna—the main channel of spiritual illumination—up to an American eagle."[25] Lest this patriotism be lost on anyone, under the wings of this eagle were painted American flags. Even the colors of the American flag were said to be echo sentiments sacred to the Hindu—red was the color of Brahma (a minor Hindu creator deity), white of Shiva, and blue of Lord Vishnu. Further, red was the color of *rajas* (passion), white of *sattva* (purity), and blue of *tamas* (inertia).[26]

Boldly and with considerable creative synergy, Swami Trigunatita designed this building in the first few years of the twentieth century. We see in this process an important trend: the ability of creative Hindu thinkers to harmonize diverse thoughts and material forms, variant cultures and religions, and disparate philosophical and patriotic traditions. In fact, one would be hard-pressed to find a better example of this kind of syncretic creativity than this pioneering temple.

Members at this first temple reached out to their fellow Americans through talks on Vedanta—its nondualistic philosophy, meditations, and yogas. The post-1965 immigrant community has discovered different ways to reach out to its neighbors. One key strategy is engaged Hinduism.

The western model of interreligious dialogue is heavily slanted toward the Protestant preoccupation with beliefs. Hindus, by contrast, have typically focused their piety on ritual action, particularly in the sphere of dharma. Dharma means "duty"—doing what is right. When combined with another key concept, that of detached action, dharma yields one of the major emphases of the Hindu tradition. The Bhagavad Gita speaks of the importance of doing one's duty without expectation of reward or punishment.

In this sphere of righteous and detached action, U.S. Hindu institutions are finding common ground with volunteer organizations around the United States. Many American temples, including the Hindu Temple of Atlanta, conduct regular blood drives. This may not seem unusual, except that in the Hindu ritual context, the shedding of blood is highly polluting. Nonetheless, blood drives—almost entirely unknown in India—take place regularly in U.S. Hindu temples, typically in downstairs halls and often in conjunction with the American Red Cross. The Hindu temple in Tampa encourages not just blood donations but also organ donations. Its temple magazine speaks about donating organs as doing one's dharma.

The context in which this social engagement takes place is, of course, significant. Many of the trustees, founders, and major donors to U.S. temples are physicians with an acute awareness of the importance of blood and organ donations. Through their encouragement, these drives have become quite prominent in many temples. Physicians also help organize regular temple-based health fairs. Major health care companies set up booths and health screening stalls and sometimes pay the temple a modest fee for that privilege.

Even more striking are the efforts of Hindu temple participants to work alongside people of other faiths to help the less fortunate. In November 1998, volunteers from the Kalamazoo, Michigan, temple worked at the Gospel Mission to provide food for the homeless during Thanksgiving time. Under the headline "Thanksgiving Dinner for the Homeless," the newsletter reports that under the temple's auspices, "on Nov, 15, 1998, a dinner for 110 homeless people was prepared and served at the Gospel Mission's kitchen and dining facilities. It was coordinated by the SHAKTI committee."[27] Shakti, in Sanskrit, is power and energy, frequently conceptualized as a goddess. While Hindus laud the donation of food (Sanskrit, *anna dana*), only a few temples in India do it and then only under specific ritual conditions. For example, this kind of donation also traditionally occurs in memory of one's ancestors.

Temples with more volunteers, such as the Hindu Temple of Atlanta, now have volunteer programs in the soup kitchens of the Atlanta Union Mission and other evangelical churches. The mission has no connection with the Hindu tradition except perhaps one that happened felicitously and by chance —it is known by its acronym, AUM, which is the traditional spelling for the sacred sound of "om" in India. On its Web site, the AUM describes itself as "a non-denominational Christian ministry that brings Christ's healing power to any person in crisis through programs of rescue and recovery."[28]

The mission is explicitly evangelical, yet members of the Hindu temple work there in common cause. Ravi Sarma, the former chair of the temple's Community Services Committee, observes,

Four years ago, we started a holiday food drive and Toys for Tots program to participate in the needs of the community. Last year, Seshu Sarma started a semiannual blood drive for the local chapter of the American Red Cross. This year, we sponsored two days of meals served at the Atlanta Union Mission, which provides food and shelter to local homeless and indigent population. We chose January 15 and 16 to commemorate Martin Luther King's birthday as well as Sankranthi. Community members provided funds in memory of loved ones who passed away (as *anna dana*). Our volunteers also provide staffing for the soup kitchen one weekend a month as part of our ongoing work with the AUM.

We also support the Atlanta Community Food Bank by collecting nonperishable canned food and money. In 1998, we provided 890 pounds of food. (The local Swaminarayan Temple provided 1,800 pounds of food.) We were the top two religious institutes in their holiday food drive. I am in the process of putting together a summer internship program with temple youth to provide help with the food bank's assembly line, where they sort out donated items and get them ready for distribution. . . .

We consider this *seva* [community service], and our motto is, "Serving with devotion, the volunteers of the Hindu Temple of Atlanta." Our hope is that our community realizes the value of and need for service.[29]

The dates the Atlanta temple chooses for its cooperative ventures with the AUM are noteworthy. One such period was January 15–17, 1999, which coincided with both the Hindu festival of Pongal and Martin Luther King Jr.'s birthday. The south Indian festival of Pongal, or Makara Sankaranti, ordinarily observed at the winter solstice, is a time of thanksgiving; it is also an especially meritorious time to make donations.

So why do the Hindu temples cooperate with evangelical groups such as the Gospel Mission in Kalamazoo and the AUM? It might be simpler for them to associate with mainline Protestant churches or even secular institutions. One very pragmatic reason is that Hindu temples lack the financial or human resources to mount these operations on their own and find it easier to plug into existing organizations.

The other reasons are more interesting. First, evangelical churches have a history of running outreach programs in these communities. They have already identified basic needs and are meeting them. Second, these are not the kinds of religious institutions that would in the ordinary course of events engage in conversation with Hindus. Some temples seek such institutions out for precisely this reason. With evangelicals, there is no push for interreligious dialogue, though the ad hoc conversations that happen in the course of volunteer activities may bring these people together and foster better understanding. One Hindu told me that mainline Protestants focus too much on dialogue and that meetings with them often achieve nothing more than making the participants feel good about themselves. In soup kitchens, real work gets done.

Based on the need issue, the Hindu temple of Atlanta also takes the time to volunteer for children who have at least one parent afflicted with AIDS. A December 27, 1998, e-mail bulletin from the temple says, "The Community Services (Humanitarian Activities) Committee of the Hindu Temple of Atlanta is pleased to inform that the 1998 Holiday Food and Toys Drive has been successfully completed. Nearly $600 dollars worth of new toys were gift wrapped and delivered to AID Atlanta, for children with AIDS or children of parents with AIDS. Several hundred pounds of canned food and a check are being presented to the Atlanta area Community Food Bank."[30] According to Sarma, "We hope to continue that activity. . . . Our plans include: working in shelters for women and children in some of the counties of Atlanta. Since Atlanta is very big now, we want to provide volunteer help in several areas in the metro area, near where people live."[31] This *seva* is karma yoga, or action without expectation of reward; this is engaged Hinduism; this is American volunteer activity. In calling it *seva* or connecting it with the act of *anna dana*, we have an American activity explained through a traditional Hindu idiom.

Many narratives describe Hindus transforming, transmitting, and jettisoning traditions from India in the American landscape. Certain deities—village goddesses, for example—are not brought to the United States, and the phenomenon of Hindu goddesses possessing devotees is not common here, as it is in India. Performing arts serve as effective ways of transmitting religion and culture. In a wide assortment of areas, we see the transformation of existing customs as well as the development of new ones. Thus, Hindu temples have now introduced new worship services to mark graduation exercises in school; newsletters announce that, on Mother's Day weekend, the Goddess Lakshmi will be worshipped in the Ganesha Temple in Nashville. By introducing these new customs, Hindus are participating in American civic life, reiterating their Indian American status.

But Hindus are also transforming Hinduism and America with a their new understanding of the American landscape. Hinduism, as a religion, is closely tied to land in the Indian subcontinent and is very territorial. The immigrants ordinarily view Puranic cosmology and Hindu stories in a nonliteral sense, yet it is ceremonially necessary to locate oneself in the correct part of the universe at the right moment of time. To transform and in some way acknowledge the American land—the land that the Native Americans held sacred, the land on which the early Christians built their churches—as sacred is a bold, innovative, and perhaps necessary act of being Hindu on foreign soil. It is a form of internal negotiation within Hinduism to adapt to a new environment. It is an Americanization of the Hindu tradition. Landscape patterns of traditional sites are recognized in the American geography; the familiar holy spots are re-created. From such acts of whimsical recognition, some people move into a state of awe at a divine teleology. Manu, in the first century C.E., said that the holy territory in India was the land where the black antelope freely roamed.

The Hindus in America have traded it for the land where the deer and the antelope play.

But there is also external negotiation—that is, with the Gospel Mission, evangelical churches, and the like. One can think of several kinds of external negotiations: between individuals, between civic institutions and individuals, between religious institutions and individuals, between religious institutions and civic institutions, and between religious institutions and other religious institutions. When members of the Hindu Temple of Atlanta work with the town authorities to have a statue of Mahatma Gandhi erected at the Martin Luther King Jr. Center, when they collect blood for the Red Cross, we have external negotiations between a religious (Hindu) institution and a civic one. However, when the Kalamazoo temple works alongside members of a Gospel Mission soup kitchen or the Hindu Temple of Atlanta collaborates with the Atlanta Union Mission, we have members of one Hindu institution negotiating their space in America with members of an external religious institution. Members of both institutions are negotiating their connection with the other in the simple act of serving food for the homeless; members of both religions are changed through this interaction.

In the late seventh century, Parsis—that is, Zoroastrians from Persia—came to India for refuge and wanted to remain in the new country. They petitioned a local ruler for permission to stay. Worried about a drain on his resources, the ruler replied with a symbolic action. He sent his chief minister to the head of the Parsis with no verbal message. The chief minister was to show the potential immigrants a glass of milk, filled to the brim. This would indicate that there was no more room in the country. It was all filled up.

The head of the Parsi delegation got the message. Silently, he took the glass of milk, stirred in a spoonful of sugar and sent it back to the king, asking him to taste it. The Parsis, he alleged by this action, would not take up much room but instead would add flavor to the land and its people. The king smiled and allotted the land to the fledgling immigrant community. And indeed, over the centuries the Parsis have added to India's intellectual, cultural, and political strengths. So too, say the Hindus who tell and retell this story, will every new immigrant, every new religious and ethnic group that gets the privilege of calling America home.

NOTES

1. Law of Manu, 2:17–23; adapted from *The Laws of Manu*, translated by Georg Buhler (New Delhi: Motilal Banarsidass, 1975).

2. Transcript of devotional song from *Bhajans at Sri Venkateswara Temple*, Sri Venkateswara Temple, 1986.

3. J. Sethuraman, "Sri Venkatesha America Vaibhava Stotram," 8; all translations by Sethuraman.

4. Ibid., 20, 22.

5. *Vishnu Purana*, translated by H. H. Wilson (Calcutta: Punthi Pustak, 1961), 2:2; *Bhagavata Purana*, translated by Ganesh Vasudeo Tagare (Delhi: Motilal Banarsidass, 1978), 20, 18–19.

6. Diana L. Eck, *Banaras: City of Light* (New York: Knopf, 1982), 34–36.

7. Recited by Sethuraman during a ritual in Tallahassee, Florida, July 1999.

8. Sri Nathamuni, Jacksonville Temple, personal communication, September 1999.

9. Henry David Thoreau, *Walden and Other Writings*, edited by Joseph Wood Krutch (New York: Bantam, 1981), 324–25.

10. "Kavachas for the Deities," Sri Venkateswara Temple, Penn Hills, 1986.

11. Kees Bolle, "Speaking of a Place," in *Myths and Symbols: Essays in Honor of Mircea Eliade*, edited by J. M. Kitagawa and C. M. Long (Chicago: University of Chicago Press, 1969), 128–29.

12. See <http://www.himalayanacademy.com/hawaii/iraivan/iraivan_temple.htm l>.

13. <http://www.barsanadham.org>.

14. Ibid.

15. "San Marga Foundation Stones" (press release), April 9, 1995, quoted at <http:// www.hindunet.org/alt_hindu/1995_Apr_1/msg00001.html>.

16. "Mystical Master," *Hinduism Today*, April–June 2002, <http://www.hinduism today.com/archives/2002/4-6/26-33_mystical_master.shtml>.

17. "San Marga Foundation Stones." According to this press release, "It was Leimomi's ancestor, Kuamo'o Mo'okini, who founded this very temple in 480 C.E."

18. Letter from Sri Anbil Ramaswami, forwarding a letter from Sri K. Devanathan Swami, posted on the Yahoo listserve SriRangaSri, December 30, 2000, <http:// groups.yahoo.com/group/SriRangaSri/message/26>.

19. Marie Louise Burke, *Swami Trigunatita: His Life and Work* (San Francisco: Vedanta Society of Northern California, 1997), 175.

20. Ibid., 170.

21. Ibid., 169.

22. Ibid., 198, 368.

23. Ibid., 198.

24. Ibid., 203.

25. Ibid., 369.

26. Ibid.

27. *Kalamazoo (Michigan) Indo-American Cultural Center and Temple Newsletter*, December 1998, 2.

28. <http:www.aumcares.org/AboutUs.htm>.

29. Ravi Sarma, conversation with author, November 1999.

30. Hindu Temple of Atlanta, e-mail to members, December 27, 1998.

31. Ravi Sarma, personal communication, November 1999.

8

Making Home Abroad
Sikhs in the United States

Beginning with the first wave of Sikh migration to the United States in 1900, the Sikh tradition has become part of the American religious landscape. While Sikh men, women, and children have adapted their traditions to this new land, American society has only slowly come to accept their presence. The most recent and most explicit recognition of the Sikh community manifests in the respects paid to Sikhs by President George W. Bush on the birth anniversary of Guru Nanak (1469–1539), the founder of the community, on November 7, 2003.[1]

Unfortunately, the press concerning Sikh beliefs and practices has not always been positive. In light of the attacks of September 11, 2001, and given the similarities in appearance between Sikh males who mark their faith with distinctive dress (turbans and beards) and al-Qaeda leaders, the U.S. media took pains to explain why Sikhs look the way they do and thereby to protect them from bigotry and hatred. But happier stories have also been heard, including a greater acceptance of religious diversity, as evidenced by a 2003 New York Times editorial endorsement of "the scarf of a Muslim woman, the skullcap of an observant Jew and the turban of a Sikh" as exercises in "freedom of conscience."[2]

This chapter begins with a brief introduction to basic Sikh religious beliefs and history. It then traces Sikh immigration to the United States, analyzes the current composition of the Sikh community, and examines Sikh negotiations with American culture by focusing on the establishment in the United States of a key Sikh institution, the gurdwara (house of the guru, or Sikh temple). A brief concluding section argues that the Sikh community's interactions with American society, both historically and currently, have not only introduced a new faith to American society but also helped the evolution of the Sikh tradition. This creative interaction has forged a tradition of Sikhism that may have lasting implications for the future of the Sikh community both in its homeland in the Punjab in northwest India and in other areas around the globe.

There are currently some 23 million Sikhs—17 million in the Punjab, 4 million in other parts of south Asia, and 2 million in southeast Asia, east Africa, Europe, and North America.[3] Their history starts with Guru Nanak, who founded the community in the central Punjab in the 1520s. His writings emphasize the unity of God (Vahiguru, the Great Sovereign), who runs the world with the twin principles of justice and grace. Guru Nanak believed in a life oriented around the values of personal purity, charity, hard work, service, and social and gender equality. Liberation, understood as attaining a place of honor in the divine court, is presented as a collective responsibility. The heart of Sikh piety comprises congregational prayer in which men, women, and children gather together and sing praises (kirtan) of the divine.

After Guru Nanak's death, a line of nine continuous successors provided leadership. As the fledgling group expanded and its influence grew in the central Punjab, problems with the ruling Mughal administration arose. Guru Arjan (1581–1606) and Guru Tegh Bahadur (1666–75), the fifth and the ninth Sikh gurus, respectively, were executed as political threats. With the office of the personal guru under constant attack, Guru Gobind Singh (1675–1708), the tenth guru, declared in the late 1690s the Sikh community to be the Khalsa (the pure). Sikhs now understood themselves to be a special people accountable only to God.

In addition to values promulgated in early Sikh history, the use by men of external symbols such as kes (unshorn hair), kanga (comb), kirpan (sword), karha (steel bracelet used to protect the wrist), and kaccha (breeches worn by warriors) became the markers of loyalty to the Khalsa. While the unshorn hair and comb were rooted in Sikh belief in keeping the body in its pristine form, the sword, steel bracelet, and breeches represented Sikh readiness to confront injustice. Guru Gobind Singh's declaration of the Khalsa was thus both religious and strategic, as it ultimately prepared the way for the discontinuation of the personal authority of the living guru, provided the community with a visible identity, and established a well-defined political agenda of establishing Sikh sovereignty, the Khalsa Raj, by supplanting the unjust Mughal Empire.

Guru Gobind Singh also elevated the Sikh scriptural text to the status of the Guru Granth (the guru in book form). As the repository of revelation, the Guru Granth serves as the ultimate source of Sikh belief and practice. Punjabi, the language of the text, and Gurmukhi, its script, are deemed sacred, and the Sikh community as a whole, collectively referred to as the Guru

Panth, has the authority to interpret its text. The tradition thus does not require ritual specialists to provide religious instruction; instead, a handful of Sikhs can establish and run a congregation. This development allows Sikhs to reconstitute authority wherever the Guru Granth is present, making the tradition transportable.

Sikhs believe in divine immanence, so they consider the whole world to be sacred. But the *gurdwara* and other places of worship (*dharmsals*) have long been regarded as particularly sacred. When the Guru Granth replaced the personal guru, its text was displayed in all places of worship, turning them into *gurdwaras*. The Darbar Sahib (honorable court) in the town of Amritsar, India, emerged as the center of Sikh sacred geography and the focal point of Sikh pilgrimage.

Sikh insistence on the fundamental purity of creation and individuals on the one hand and charity, service, and philanthropy on the other manifested in the practice of *langar* (sharing of food), an institution that the Sikhs borrowed from the Sufis and turned into a key *gurdwara* and community activity.[4] Finally, the Nishan Sahib, a triangular saffron flag, marked the sovereignty of the *gurdwara*. While the traditional *gurdwara* building is an architectural design of domes, arches, and open space, its three essential elements—the Guru Granth, the *langar*, and the Nishan Sahib—are easily transported to new contexts.

The Sikhs' belief in the sacrality of all creation has had major ramifications for Sikh migration outside the Punjab.[5] In fact, the tendency to emigrate in search of new opportunities has been pronounced since the inception of the Sikh community. Apart from the travels of the Sikh gurus, Sikh traders began to move to major centers of commerce in south and central Asia toward the end of the sixteenth century. A larger wave of emigration began with the British arrival in the Punjab in the mid–nineteenth century. During this period, Sikhs joined the British Army in large numbers and traveled to the far reaches of the British Empire. Throughout the twentieth century the Sikhs had opportunities for emigration, and at present they constitute the largest single group to have moved out of the subcontinent.

After Guru Gobind Singh's declaration of the community as the Khalsa, the Sikh tradition became largely nonproselytizing, and Sikh numbers consequently have remained small. At the peak of Sikh political power in the Punjab during the early nineteenth century, they numbered less than 5 percent of a local population that comprised Muslims (48 percent), Hindus (45 percent), and a much smaller group of Jains. Yet this historical experience as a minority group among much larger religious communities has provided the Sikhs with survival techniques and has helped shape their expectations in the new lands and societies to which they later migrated.

Finally, the Sikh experience of working closely with the British (1849–1947) resulted in their introduction to print culture and western systems of administration, education, and justice. The Sikhs were open to incorporating modern ideas while maintaining their religious heritage. The Guru Granth was first printed in 1865, and the Khalsa College, intended to prepare Sikh students in the sciences and English literature while keeping them immersed in Sikh heritage, was established in 1892. In the early 1920s, the Sikhs worked with the British to create the Shiromani Gurdwara Prabandhak Committee (Supreme Gurdwara Management Committee), an elected body in which both Sikh men and women voted and whose primary responsibility was managing historic *gurdwaras*. The Sikhs were thus already exposed to modern western institutions before their arrival in the United States at the beginning of the twentieth century.

The earliest reference to the landing of the Sikhs on the West Coast appears in the April 6, 1899, *San Francisco Chronicle*. Effectively navigating their way through racial and legal discrimination (the Alien Land Law of 1913, the Asiatic Barred Zone Act of 1917, and the Oriental Exclusion Act of 1924), Sikhs continued to immigrate to the United States, and their numbers reached around seven thousand by the 1920s. The early community was overwhelmingly male and came by and large from the rural Punjab. Amazed by California's open and fertile land, they became farmers and worked hard to establish themselves quickly. A 1920 report listed eighty-five thousand acres in the Sacramento and San Joaquin Valleys and thirty thousand acres in the Imperial Valley under Sikhs' control.[6]

This first phase of settlement was followed by a 1924 U.S. government ban on Asian immigration, which resulted in a significant decrease in the immigrant Sikh community. While some Sikhs stayed on and found ways around legal restrictions on landowning, some chose to go back to the Punjab, and by the mid-1940s only about 1,500 Sikhs remained in the United States. With the passage in 1946 of the Luce-Celler Act, which opened the door to Indian immigration and naturalization, the Sikh community began to grow once again, increasing over the next twenty years to about 6,000 members. The current phase of expansion began with the 1965 immigration liberalization, and the Sikh community now comprises approximately 250,000 persons— about 100,000 on each coast and the remainder in the Midwest.

The oldest segment of today's Sikh community consists of descendants of the early immigrants who, prompted by a sense of adventure and the pursuit of the American dream, came from small landowning families in the Punjab. They worked as laborers, used local resources such as banks, bought land, and began to farm. Many of them married Mexican women, and their descendents are settled on the West Coast.[7]

Another segment came in pursuit of higher education beginning in the 1910s. While some of these immigrants returned to India, others stayed on after completing their studies, with many of these garnering white-collar jobs. Even when they had the opportunity to work in the states in which they went to school, many moved to the West Coast to be nearer to other Sikhs.[8] They worked closely with Sikh leadership in the middle decades of the twentieth century, and, though some married Caucasian women, they continued to play an important role in Sikh community life.

The most prominent segment of the Sikh community consists of men and women who came to the United States after 1965. This group includes professionals with advanced degrees obtained in the Punjab in medicine, engineering, and other fields. From both rural and urban backgrounds, they arrived in large cities, reoriented themselves to American work demands, and relocated wherever jobs in their areas of expertise were available.

More recent arrivals include families who have come to the United States as a result of political persecution. These are divided into two groups. The first comprises those who fled political persecution in east Africa. Their ancestors had arrived in Kenya and Uganda at the turn of the twentieth century to work in the British-run railway system. Political upheavals in these countries during the 1970s forced these families to leave their homes.[9] In addition, a number of Sikh traders who had lived in Afghanistan for several centuries left when war broke out there in the late 1970s. Members of both groups arrived in the United States with considerable business experience and quickly put down roots in large urban centers such as New York City. The second group came directly from the Punjab. During the 1980s, the Indian government's use of force to bring the political situation there under control prompted large-scale flight of rural Sikh youths (most of them college graduates) to western countries. After gaining legal residence essentially as political refugees, these men brought their wives and children over and settled down during the mid-1990s.

The Sikh community in the United States also includes a small group of Euro-Americans who converted to Sikhism beginning in the 1970s. They took up the Sikh path under the spiritual guidance of Harbhajan Singh Yogi, a Punjabi Sikh who had arrived in the United States in 1968.[10] They constitute a small but visible segment of the community and are sometimes called American Sikhs, an epithet now increasingly used by all Sikhs living in the United States. This is a rare case of a non-Punjabi group joining the Sikh community.

How did the early Sikh immigrants respond to arrival in the United States? They interpreted their migration generously—as "taking the Sikh beliefs" to the farthest corners of the divinely created world and as a major opportunity in Sikh history.[11] California's natural beauty fascinated the Sikhs, and they had no inclination to interpret it in metaphors of either conflict (dar-ul harb) that must be brought under control or impurity that must be sanctified (as was the case with some Muslims and Hindus, respectively).[12]

The Sikhs seemed confident that their belief in one God, the possession of a sacred book, and a life oriented around human equality, congregational worship, and social responsibility placed them closer than other Indians to the world of the Christian West. The Articles of Incorporation of the Pacific Coast Khalsa Diwan Society, the first U.S. Sikh organization, created in 1912 in Stockton, California, open with an assertion of Sikh belief in the "Fatherhood of God and Brotherhood of Man" and may have been crafted to explain Sikhism to Americans. The British provided the Sikhs with respectful treatment that seemingly reinforced the perception that Sikhs' Aryan roots related them racially to Europeans.

Once in the United States, the Sikhs did not see themselves as travelers interested in making money to send home, a perception often associated with new immigrants. Instead, they wanted to put down new roots in new soil. Following or circumventing the law as needed, they began to buy or lease agricultural land. It should come as no surprise that some Sikhs considered joining the U.S. Army, continuing a long and honorable tradition of fighting for their country.

Incidents of racial violence caught the Sikhs unawares, but they defused these situations—from Bellingham, Washington, in 1907 to Marysville, California, in 1915—largely by retreat.[13] Unable at first to understand the cause of this discrimination, the Sikhs made sense of their mistreatment by tying it to the fact that they were subjects of a British colony. Some Sikhs even decided to return to India to fight for its freedom.[14] By the early 1920s, however, this movement fizzled, and the Sikhs began to focus their energies on their American lives. They benefited from new attitudes regarding race and civil rights and by and large have not nursed any major complaints regarding their overall treatment in the United States.

In its century-long history, the American Sikh community has worked the

U.S. political and legal system with a reasonable degree of success. The community has remained small, but individual Sikhs have taken to the courts when necessary. In the 1920s, Bhagat Singh Thind, a veteran of the U.S. Army, fought for citizenship (*United States v. Bhagat Singh Thind*, 1923) all the way to the Supreme Court. In the 1940s, Jagjit Singh worked closely with Congressman Henry Luce, paving the way for the Luce-Celler Act, which opened citizenship rights to U.S. Sikhs and arranged for a quota of immigration for their relatives from India.[15] With the newly acquired citizenship, Dalip Singh Saund, a Sikh from Imperial Valley, California, made it to Capitol Hill as a three-term member of Congress between 1957 and 1963.[16] He was the only south Asian to achieve that honor until Bobby Jindal was elected to represent Louisiana's First Congressional District in 2004.

Tensions between local norms and the Sikh insistence on wearing religious symbols has surfaced repeatedly. The turban was deemed to clash with the civil norms of removing hats at restaurants. It was also said to be unsafe as a replacement for hard hats at construction sites. And Sikhs with turbans are not currently permitted to join the U.S. Army. The *kirpan*, or ceremonial sword, has been interpreted to be a weapon not permissible in schools, courts, and during air travel. Some fast food chains do not allow their Sikh workers to wear the steel bracelet, or *karha*, on the grounds that it is a health hazard. It has been difficult to transplant these Sikh symbols onto American soil.[17]

While Sikhs have arrived in the United States eager to fit in, wanting to settle down and be productive citizens, their religious symbols have clashed regularly with U.S. norms. Sikhs, however, have shown an openness to adapt religious symbols to local realities. For example, in light of post-9/11 restrictions on air travel, Pashaura Singh, a leading scholar of Sikhism in North America, has argued that a "mini sword" hanging on a chain is an appropriate substitute for the traditional *kirpan*. Not every Sikh agrees with this arrangement, but it is a significant adjustment and falls in line with the adaptations the minority Sikh community has made throughout its history.[18] Still, Sikhs' adjustments do not seem to reach far enough to satisfy all concerned.

An examination of the history of the *gurdwara* in the United States sheds important light on the nature of the Sikh community's attempt to integrate into American society while simultaneously maintaining a religious identity. This complex is manifested on the exteriors of *gurdwara* buildings and includes the architecture and activities of its essential components—the congregation hall with the Guru Granth at its head, the *langar*, and the Nishan Sahib hoisted in its precinct.

Ad hoc arrangements for congregational worship were made as soon as the Sikhs began to arrive in the United States, and discussions regarding the establishment of an actual *gurdwara* started in 1907. The Pacific Coast Khalsa Diwan was incorporated as a nonprofit organization under California law on May 27, 1912. That same year, the first U.S. *gurdwara* was built in Stockton, California.[19] That place of worship remained the nucleus of the U.S. Sikh community during the first half of the twentieth century. Thanks to increased immigration after 1965, the United States now has more than two hundred Sikh societies, half of which have built *gurdwaras*.[20]

The title "Sikh Temple" was inscribed in large letters on the front of the Stockton *gurdwara*, but no effort was made to introduce external features associated with traditional *gurdwara* architecture. Faithfulness to the California landscape was considered in line with the Sikh spirit. After all, the traditional *gurdwara* architecture did not mandate any orientation toward a particular direction, as in the case of a mosque, nor did it follow elaborate beliefs for selection, sanctification, architectural design, and the establishment of an icon, as in a Hindu temple. Because the *gurdwara* is the house of the Guru Granth, California *gurdwaras* are often designed to be impressive versions of surrounding residences.

After 1965, rising demand for new *gurdwaras* was met by remodeling churches and large houses and by creating new buildings specifically for this purpose. The largest *gurdwara* on the East Coast, located in Richmond Hill, New York, was originally a Methodist church.[21] After its purchase in 1972, no effort was made to change its exterior. Until its destruction by a fire in 2001, stained-glass windows depicting Gospel scenes continued to enliven the sacred space inside the building.

In the case of new buildings, Sikhs have consciously incorporated the latest innovations in U.S. architecture. The most creative such effort is a *gurdwara* in Palatine, Illinois. Amarjit Singh Sidhu, a student of famed architect Louis Kahn at the University of Pennsylvania, designed this building on a thirteen-acre lot. Built ten feet above ground, the *gurdwara* blends with its surroundings; a landscaped earth berm on the street side physically connects it to the neighborhood.[22] Sidhu also believes that his design blends Sikh beliefs with Kahn's emphasis on "keeping things what they want to be," as in the case of the structure's interior (discussed later in the essay).

Some tendency exists to introduce traditional *gurdwara* styles into the designs of new buildings. The features often associated with *gurdwara* architecture include a dome at the center, arches at the doors and windows, and a congregational hall with doors opening in all four directions. In El Sobrante, California, Sikhs bought a hilltop lot, and construction of a *gurdwara* started in the late 1970s. Though some of those involved in the effort wanted to incorporate traditional Sikh designs, no attempt was made to bring builders from the Punjab. Instead, Ajit Singh Randhawa, a University of California at Berkeley–trained architect, and J. P. Singh, an engineer educated at the same school, created the final design. A set of domes and curved arches provide the building's exterior with a distinctly Sikh look, but the circumstances of the site necessitated the repositioning of the central dome and limited the doors in the congregation hall to three.[23]

While significant adaptations appear in American *gurdwaras'* exteriors, the tradition of hoisting the Nishan Sahib, the Sikh flag, as an insignia of charity, justice, and divine victory (*degh tegh fateh*) is strictly followed. The fact that it is a symbol of Sikh religiopolitical sovereignty and therefore may be in conflict with the strictly religious and social mission of these U.S. societies posed a problem from the start. With the passage of time, two solutions arose. First, the Nishan Sahib was increasingly interpreted in purely religious terms, shorn of all political connotations. Second, while that flag alone adorns the *gurdwara* precinct, in public Sikh processions an American flag invariably accompanies it. The two flags together represent the Sikhs as both a religious community and a part of the American nation.

The buildings' interiors largely maintain the traditional layout of Sikh sacred space. At Stockton, the top floor is allocated to congregational worship. Close to the wall facing the entrance, a small stage stands with four pillars at its corners and the text of the Guru Granth placed on a raised platform at its center. As tradition dictates, the Guru Granth is enclosed in the regalia of a canopy, a throne, and silken robes. In a traditional *gurdwara* setting, the Guru Granth is placed more toward the center of the hall, which provides the congregation a feeling of closeness and enables people to circumambulate the text, but this arrangement wastes space behind the sacred text. So Stockton Sikhs chose to create more seating by moving the text closer to the wall.

All members of the congregation take off their shoes before entering the presence of the Guru Granth. Men sit on one side of the carpeted floor and women on the other. Sikhs married to local women often sit with their wives, which would not be regarded as an anomaly even in the Punjab, given the doctrinal emphasis on gender equality. The worship service is held in Punjabi, and in both content and form the devotional practices largely follow what these Sikhs knew in the Punjab.[24] The new placement of the Guru Granth, however, is now followed in most U.S. *gurdwaras*.

The Palatine *gurdwara* offers an interesting example of traditional Sikh elements interpreted in contemporary architectural idioms. The structure has is a square congregation hall with the Guru Granth placed closer to the center, as is traditional. Four sets of concrete columns hold exposed wood tresses, which structurally frame the roof; four skylights, placed where the columns meet, focus on the Guru Granth underneath. The traditional four doors are repositioned at the corners of the building, where they also serve as mandated fire exits. Other than the supporting columns, the entire four sides of the square, beginning two feet above the sitting level, are made of glass.

Sidhu argues that U.S. *gurdwaras* should incorporate local norms while evoking the timeless Sikh spirit. For him, the exposed concrete columns and the rugged wood planks framing the ceiling represent the Sikh emphasis on honesty and truthfulness. The natural light falling on the Guru Granth and the audience's close visual contact with the landscape blend Sikh devotional experience with nature, a theme that often appears in Guru Nanak's writings.

The Stockton *gurdwara* is useful for a discussion of the *langar*. The traditional Sikh doctrine of social equality via the sharing of food, charity, service, and philanthropy continued to shape the *langar*, but its external forms underwent important changes. Food was served on a table placed next to the kitchen, and the devotees helped themselves (buffet style) to their meals, eating at dining tables instead of sitting, as Punjabis traditionally do, on the floor.

In one corner of the Stockton *gurdwara*'s ground floor, which is allocated for the *langar*, a place was created for people to sit and chat, and stacks of books were placed in another corner. This collection included books and periodicals published in the Punjab as well as basic volumes on American history, law, and English grammar. Office space and restrooms were also added on this floor. Not all *gurdwaras* built after 1965 follow the tradition of eating *langar* on chairs and tables, but they typically add amenities such as offices, classrooms, libraries, rooms where senior citizens can meet, residences for custodians and visitors, and parking lots, none of which figure in traditional *gurdwara* design.

The rituals and ceremonies enacted inside American *gurdwaras* show many local impacts. For example, in a traditional Sikh setting, parents are responsible for selecting their children's marriage partners, and an elaborate system of social differentiation has shaped this matchmaking process. Following American cultural norms, however, many young Sikhs have rejected arranged marriages. Furthermore, young Sikh women have shown an inclination to walk alongside the groom while circumambulating the Guru Granth. (Traditionally, the bride followed the groom.) Punjabi cultural resistance to this change may exist, but Sikh doctrine does not oppose this practice. Because there is no Sikh priestly class, anyone can perform the wedding ceremony, and Sikh women have begun to do just that. Not surprisingly, the American work schedule dictates that weekends matter at the *gurdwara*. Sunday is a busy day, and marriages normally take place on Saturdays.

Sikh mortuary rites have also changed under American pressures. In keeping with tradition, many Sikh families continue to take the cremated remains of the deceased to Kiratpur in the Punjab, but the rituals associated with the bathing of the body, putting it on the pyre, and cremating it have all been modified to conform to the norms and requirements of U.S. funeral homes. Given work demands, there is no provision for the traditional practice of several days of public mourning.

The American setting has also greatly expanded the list of Sikh festivals. To the birth and the death anniversaries of the gurus and the declaration of the Khalsa, a new year celebration has been formally appended. A prayer is offered at midnight, and the congregation is welcomed into the year ahead. After the 9/11 tragedy, a special reading of the Guru Granth was performed at several *gurdwaras*, along with a prayer for the peace of humanity. Celebrations of Thanksgiving and Christmas also take place in many Sikh homes.

Except for the consumption of tobacco, Sikhs have few food-related taboos. There is no doctrinal restriction against eating meat. However, Sikhs follow the Indian cultural practice of slaughtering animals with a single stroke and not eating beef. Sikh literature bans eating meat where the animal is slaughtered the Islamic way (*halal*)—that is, slowly bled to death. Though the general avoidance of eating beef continues in the United States, few Sikhs insist on distinguishing among the different methods of slaughter practiced in the United States. The ban on tobacco, however, is maintained.

Coming from a tradition that recognizes separate seats for religion (the Darbar Sahib) and politics (the Akal Takhat) in Amritsar, Sikhs have little difficulty understanding the constitutionally mandated church/state split in the United States. Sikh leaders have taken pains to ensure that *gurdwaras* are managed in accordance with the law and that political activity supporting the freedom of India in the first half of the twentieth century and Sikh efforts to help create a sovereign state of Khalistan in the 1980s were kept separate from the *gurdwara* activities and accounts.

In early 1910s, the Guru Nanak Dev Hostel arose in Berkeley as a place where Sikh and other Indian students at the University of California could live free of charge. To help these students further, Sikh philanthropists established the Guru Gobind Singh Educational Scholarship and placed it under the stewardship of two professors at the school. These efforts sought to prepare Sikh students to play the role of Sikh ambassadors to American educational institutions. The Stockton *gurdwara* also made donations to the Stockton Community Chest and contributed fifty dollars annually to the local hospital beginning in the mid-1930s. Sikhs were proud and gratified when some Americans stopped by to partake in *langar*.

Recent decades have seen the expansion of these efforts to reach out to mainstream Americans. Sikh leaders at the Richmond Hill *gurdwara* often invite local political figures to visit, and the dignitaries who have accepted these invitations have included senators, members of Congress, New York's governor, and several New York City mayors. The *gurdwara* leaders encourage Sikhs to participate in fund-raising dinners for both Democratic and Republican candidates and argue that Sikh visibility at these public functions is important.

The teaching of Sikhism and the Punjabi language in leading American universities is another way to manifest a Sikh presence in the United States. The Richmond Hill *gurdwara* sponsored a Sikh studies program at Columbia University from 1988 to 1999. Sikhs elsewhere have backed programs at the University of Michigan at Ann Arbor (1992–), the University of California at Santa Barbara (1999–), and Hofstra University on Long Island (2001–). Conferences on Sikhism held at these universities have resulted in new studies and interpretations. They have also helped to disseminate information about the Sikh tradition among American students and through them to society at large.[25] Sikh-initiated programs at the Museum of Asian Art in San Francisco and the Smithsonian Institution in Washington, D.C., have had similar effects.

Other outreach efforts include Sikh Day parades, which are now organized in many U.S. cities. The Richmond Hill *gurdwara* helped to start the Vaisakhi parade in New York in 1988.[26] This is now an annual event, with more than twenty thousand Sikhs gathering in Times Square and parading down to Madison Square Park with more than thirty floats representing different facets of Sikh life and history. Over the years, the parade has become Americanized.

In 1988, for example, several women sought a place among the five leaders at the head of the parade but were denied. More recently, however, women have received these prime spots.

In addition to increasing visibility, such parades offer opportunities for Sikh leaders to work with city administrators. And these events provide opportunities for Sikhs to educate other Americans about Sikhism. Floats representing important facets of the Sikh tradition, embellished with American symbols, manifest the Sikh belief in being a good citizen of one's country. Sikhs also enjoy explaining to American passers-by the significance of *langar*, inviting them to share food.

Gurdwaras are also involved in interfaith activities. The Sikhs use these occasions to present their beliefs and practice. The *gurdwara* at Palatine, for example, played an enthusiastic part in the 1993 Parliament of World Religions convened in Chicago. Sikh leaders nationwide also work with other groups to address mutual social concerns such as discrimination, racially motivated violence, and hate crimes. The Richmond Hill *gurdwara* holds blood and food drives.

All of these activities have helped Sikhs attain recognition in their new home. Sikh leaders used their political ties to brief President George W. Bush on September 26, 2001, about their post-9/11 concerns. In California, the courts have recognized Punjabi as one of the languages for which interpreters will be provided. Classes in Punjabi are available at high schools in Queens, New York; and Fresno and Yuba City, California. In April 2001, the Civil Rights Division of the U.S. Department of Justice circulated a Punjabi version of a statement regarding federal protection against discrimination based on national origin. A wide array of governmental and nongovernmental institutions is thus beginning to take notice of the Sikh presence in the country.

A broad consensus currently exists among Sikhs worldwide that the United States is the best country in which Sikhs can make their homes. Many Afghani, east African, and even Punjabi refugees know how harsh life can be in those places, and they are grateful to have arrived here. Sikhs also believe that American society is far more open and respectful of diversity than is Australia, Great Britain, or Canada, and they encourage Sikhs living in these countries to come to the United States, which Sikhs, like many immigrants before them, continue to regard as a land of unique opportunities.

The Indian government's squelching of Sikh political aspirations and violent crushing of the Sikh secessionist effort to create an independent Khalistan (Land of the Khalsa) has resulted in profound alienation of the Sikhs from the government. The 1984 killing of several thousand Sikhs by a Hindu mob after the assassination of Indian Prime Minister Indira Gandhi by her Sikh bodyguards eroded any identification U.S. Sikhs may have had with the Indian nation. Unlike other immigrant Hindu groups, Sikhs plainly do not see India as a second home.

Moreover, the Punjab is thoroughly immersed in corruption. Contemporary Punjabi Sikh leaders have shown little willingness to address the problems confronting the broader Sikh community, preferring to expend their energies on parochial, even personal, squabbles. This situation makes it impossible for American Sikhs to consider relocating to the Punjab. The "myth of return" often associated with first-generation immigrants is nonexistent among U.S. Sikhs today.

These international circumstances have solidified Sikh identification with the United States. The American flag often appears on Sikhs' cars and houses, and the shirts worn by young Sikhs in parades often boast, "Proud to be American." In the past decade, Sikhs have attempted to win election to school boards and city councils, and a Sikh candidate ran in California's 2003 gubernatorial election. Sikhs enjoy basking in the glory of being part of the world's only superpower.

Sikhs born and brought up in the United States are taking a more proactive stand in asserting Sikh identity than did their parents. In 1996, a group of young Sikh graduate students at American universities created the Sikh Mediawatch and Resource Task Force (SMART). This apolitical Washington, D.C.–based Sikh advocacy group began as a cyberspace organization with the primary objective of providing mainstream American media with accurate information on various aspects of Sikhism. In recent years, the group has expanded its range of activities to include working with civic, governmental, and law-enforcement associations as well as informing Sikh Americans about their constitutional rights. This step in the direction of advocacy marks a new level of confidence within the American Sikh community.[27]

Representations of Sikhism are in flux. In this new land, new questions regarding Sikh beliefs and practices have been asked and are being answered. While U.S.-based Sikh architects are creating new *gurdwara* designs, American scholars have offered postmodern and feminist interpretations of Sikh history. Sikh migration to the Unites States has thus resulted in a reinterpretation of Sikh ideas.

For example, since its inception, the Sikh community has been associated with the land of the Punjab. The gurus sang about the beauty of the land and the sanctity of the town of Amritsar in contradistinction to the decadence of the Mughal center at Lahore. Because the gurus' lives unfolded there, the Punjab is sacred land for the Sikhs. During the eighteenth century, Sikh blood was spilled in the creation of the Khalsa Raj, further sanctifying the land. Within the thinking of the U.S. Sikh community, a new distinction has recently emerged between the sacred land (the Punjab), where one may go for pilgrimage when the time and money permit, and the homeland (the United States). Furthermore, places in the homeland itself are acquiring their own history and traditions; the Stockton *gurdwara* will be a century old in 2012.

Other reinterpretations concern the issue of religious authority. In the late 1920s, a debate regarding the Stockton congregation's relationship with the Shiromani Gurdwara Prabandhak Committee broke out. Some members of the Stockton congregation argued that Sikh doctrine supported the autonomy of each congregation, while others thought that the Stockton *gurdwara* represented a satellite community beholden to Amritsar. In 1931, the purchase deed of the *gurdwara* was deposited in the committee's offices, but a few years later, authorities in Amritsar returned the document, asserting the independence of the Stockton *gurdwara*.[28]

American Sikhs continue to debate issues of polity. A consensus seems to be emerging around the view that the Shiromani Gurdwara Prabandhak Committee represents the symbolic authority to be consulted on doctrinal details, but the final decision in day-to-day affairs should ultimately lie with local *gurdwaras*. One issue is clear: no authority in Amritsar can dictate terms to U.S. Sikhs.

Since their community's founding, Sikhs have been proud of the fact that their literature is written in Punjabi and the Gurmukhi script. Sikhs historically have insisted on understanding these sacred writings in their original form even while conceding that the contents of those sacred texts must be translated into local languages and individual circumstances. With increasing numbers of Sikhs born in the United States, however, the insistence that religion must proceed in the vernacular has had radically new implications. Sikhs are beginning to accept the Guru Granth transliterated in Roman script or even in English translation in place of or in addition to the original text. A new edition of the Guru Granth with the original text in Gurmukhi, its Roman transliteration, and translation in English was created in the early 1990s and is now in use within the U.S. Sikh community.[29]

Relatively little resistance to replacing Punjabi cultural norms with American ones has arisen, and it is not unimaginable that vegetarian burgers and other local food items will eventually replace the Punjabi meal served in the *langar*. There is also an increasing awareness that American soil may well be more fertile than the Punjab for the flourishing of the Sikh doctrine of social and gender equality.[30]

These challenges are not unique to U.S. Sikhs, of course. All Sikh communities that have settled outside the Punjab confront similar challenges. The composition of Sikh society—which includes those trained at American universities, professionals trained in the Punjab, and the highly educated children of immigrants—makes for a formidable group grappling with these issues. Furthermore, the intellectual and cultural ferment experienced in the United States is far more intense than that of any other country, making it a more conducive setting for resolving these problems.

Finally, the Sikh community in the United States includes some of the richest individuals in the world. Some American Sikhs entertain Sikh political and religious leaders from the Punjab during their visits to the United States and send money for communitarian causes there, ensuring that their voices are heard in the Punjab and their version of Sikhism is taken seriously there. For example, in 1996, Sikh women from the United States demanded that they be allowed to participate in the ritual washing of the floor of the Darbar Sahib in Amritsar. This has traditionally been a male privilege, but their wishes were granted.[31]

U.S. Sikhs have been forced unexpectedly into a historic role. Time alone will tell the nature of the imprint they will leave in the evolution of the Sikh tradition.

NOTES

I am grateful to Ami Shah and Gurdit Singh for their helpful comments on earlier drafts of this paper.

1. The following was the text of the president's recent letter:

The White House
Washington
November 7, 2003

I send greetings to those celebrating the 534th anniversary of the birth of Guru Nanak. As the founder of Sikhism, Guru Nanak taught the ideas of interfaith acceptance and meditation. Through their dedication to service, humility, family, and equality, Sikhs enrich communities across America and worldwide. This celebration helps Sikhs pass on values and customs to future generations.

As Americans, we cherish our freedom to worship freely, and we remain committed to welcoming individuals of all religions. By working together, we help advance peace and mutual understanding around the world and build a future of promise and compassion for all.

Laura joins me in sending our best wishes for a memorable celebration. George W. Bush.

2. "Muslims in European Schools," *New York Times*, October 8, 2003, A30; see also Laurie Goodstein, "At Camps, Young U.S. Sikhs Cling to Heritage," *New York Times*, July 18, 1998, A1.

3. For more details, see my *Sikhism* (Upper Saddle River, N.J.: Prentice Hall, 2004); W. H. McLeod, *Sikhism* (New York: Penguin, 1997); J. S. Grewal, *The Sikhs of the Punjab* (New York: Cambridge University Press, 1990).

4. The Sikh belief in sharing food completely rejects the notions of purity and impurity around which the Hindu caste hierarchy is constructed.

5. Whereas many Hindu communities have traditionally believed that travel entailed a loss of caste identity, the Sikhs have had no reluctance to travel to new lands.

6. Excellent studies of Sikh migration include Joan M. Jensen, *Passage from India: Asian Indian Immigrants in North America* (New Haven: Yale University Press, 1988); Bruce La Brack, *The Sikhs of Northern California, 1904–1975* (New York: AMS Press, 1988).

7. For an important study of Sikh Mexican families, see Karen Isaksen Leonard, *Making Ethnic Choices: California's Punjabi Mexican Americans* (Philadelphia: Temple University Press, 1992).

8. Concerning this period, see D. S. Saund, *The Congressman from India* (New York: Dutton, 1960).

9. P. Bhachu, *Twice Migrants: East African Sikh Settlers in Britain* (New York: Tavistock, 1985).

10. S. K. Khalsa, *The History of the Sikh Dharma of the Western Hemisphere* (Espanola, N.M.: Sikh Dharma, 1995).

11. Teja Singh, *Raj Jogi Sant Attar Singh* (Barhu Sahib: Kalagidhar Trust, 1996).

12. For Hindu and Muslim attitudes, see Narayanan, this volume; Bagby, this volume.

13. "Bellingham, Washington's Anti-Hindu Riot," *Journal of the West* 12.1 (January 1973): 163; "White Residents Have No Love for Hindus," *Marysville (California) Evening Democrat*, July 7, 1915.

14. See M. Juergensmeyer and N. G. Barrier, eds., *Sikh Studies* (Berkeley, Calif.: Graduate Theological Union, 1979), 179–90.

15. Robert Shaplen, "Profiles: One Man Lobby," *New Yorker*, March 24, 1951, 33–55.

16. Saund, *Congressman from India*.

17. Details of these cases appear at <http://www.sikhcoalition.org/LegalCenter. asp>.

18. Pashaura Singh has taken this stand in several court cases and confirmed this position in a telephone conversation with the author on November 13, 2003. In the middle decades of the twentieth century, Kapur Singh, another major scholar of Sikhism, took the same position regarding adjustments in the use of the kirpan. See his *Parasaraprasna* (Amritsar: Guru Nanak Dev University, 1989), 108. Sikhs traditionally carried a sword with a thirty-six-inch blade; to conform to the British Arms Act of 1912, the size was reduced to nine inches.

19. The community bought a large lot for thirty-four hundred dollars, and a new two-story building cost around twenty thousand dollars. See Anne Louise Wood, "East Indians in California, 1900–1947" (master's thesis, University of Wisconsin, 1966). This excellent piece of research was based on firsthand accounts of the people involved and the society's records.

20. For these societies, see <http://www.pluralism.org./directory/index.php>.

21. I am grateful to Harpreet Singh Toor, the president of the Richmond Hill gurdwara, for providing a copy of the purchase deed.

22. I am grateful to Amarjit Singh Sidhu for a detailed discussion of this subject.

23. I am grateful to J. P. Singh for his help regarding the history of this gurdwara.

24. During the 1930s, it was suggested that chairs be brought into the congregational hall. Sikh scholars in Amritsar, recalling prior debates regarding how Sikhs should respond to the forces of modernity, posed no objection to this action as of April 25, 1935. But this did not resolve the debate among Stockton Sikhs. Not until 1946 were chairs were finally moved into the congregation hall, beginning a new way of worship. Respect for the Guru Granth was obviously maintained, but its formal details were interpreted in more Christian terms; keeping shoes on and sitting on chairs while praying in the presence of the Guru Granth became the norm. After 1965, when new immigrants came from the Punjab, this practice was discontinued.

25. This method of outreach to the American public has not gone entirely smoothly. Debates about university programs are ongoing, and many questions have been raised about the value of examining Sikh beliefs via such disciplines as history and anthropology. These tensions erupted in a controversy around doctoral work completed at the University of Toronto by Pashaura Singh, who was called before the Akal Takhat to justify his research results and was forced to perform religious penance (Indian Express, June 28, 1994).

26. "Spare Times," New York Times, April 24, 1988, E40.

27. For more information, see <http://www.sikhmediawatch.org/>.

28. In a significant development, the Sikh community in England has recently designated the Akal Takhat and the Shiromani Gurdwara Prabandhak Committee to inherit all gurdwara properties worth over £25 million in case the Sikhs are ousted from that country ("UK Gurdwaras to Form Council," Chandigarh [India] Tribune, November 4, 2003, <http://www.tribuneindia.com/2003/20031104/punjab1.htm>).

29. See P. S. Chahil, Sri Guru Granth Sahib (New Delhi: Crescent, 1995).

30. Whereas Punjabi Sikhs are trying to draw boundaries between Sikh beliefs and Punjabi culture (to leave the cultural dimension behind), Euro-American Sikhs prefer to tie together religion and culture. They have built a school in Amritsar, where they feel that Sikh children can be best educated.

31. Another example of this influence can be seen in the advocacy of Ganga Singh Dhillon, a Sikh leader based in Washington, D.C., area, which resulted in the Pakistan government's decision to create a gurdwara committee to oversee the buildings and properties in Pakistan. This major development could have significant implications for the Sikh community living in the diaspora.

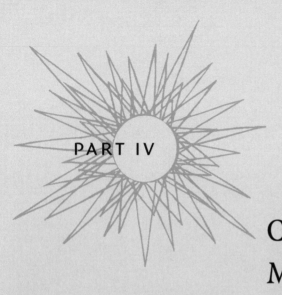

PART IV

Church,
Mosque,
Temple,
& State

9

From Alleged Buddhists to Unreasonable Hindus

First Amendment Jurisprudence after 1965

       After the passage of the 1965 Immigration Act, religious diversity in the United States began to expand beyond the scope of Protestant-Catholic-Jew and the occasional new religious movement to include adherents from Islam, Hinduism, Buddhism, Sikhism, and other religious traditions. This chapter investigates how this new religious immigration has changed and challenged First Amendment jurisprudence. How are the courts responding to this new religious diversity and, in particular, to the claims of adherents of Asian religious traditions? What impact are Asian religions having, in practical or theoretical terms, on First Amendment jurisprudence?

To answer these questions, we first sketch some of the broad changes in First Amendment jurisprudence in the post-1965 period. We then review cases in this period wherein adherents of Islam, Buddhism, Hinduism, or Sikhism have made Free Exercise or Establishment Clause claims. We assess the kinds of actors most prominent in these cases as well as the venues and areas of public life where religious free exercise and establishment appear most pressing for Asian religious actors. We then address how the judiciary's explicit and tacit definitions of religion influence these decisions. Cases involving First Amendment issues regularly require judges to analyze the "religiousness" of certain symbols or acts to a "reasonable observer," the "centrality" of a practice to a religious adherent, or the "sincerity" of an adherent in his or her "belief." Given these well-documented requirements, we show how Asian religions have presented new challenges to the judiciary's operative definitions of religion, particularly those that rely on tacitly Protestant notions of the scope and impact of religion in American public life.

As legal scholar Kent Greenawalt notes, it is easy to summarize the U.S. Supreme Court's pre-1960s views on free exercise, given that the Court did not say very much.[1] *Reynolds v. United States* (1879) established a distinction between belief (or conscience) and action, finding that the Free Exercise Clause protected religious belief in polygamy but not actually living in polygamous marriages. This belief/action distinction was not successfully challenged until 1940 when, in *Cantwell v. Connecticut*, the Supreme Court ruled that distributing religious literature was protected religious activity and thus was not subject to the same restrictions as nonreligious solicitation. Further shifts away from the belief/action distinction came in the 1960s as the Warren Court expanded both the scope of protected religious action and the legal definition of "religious." In *Sherbert v. Verner* (1963), the Supreme Court established a test that placed a burden on the government to demonstrate a "compelling interest" when enforcing generally applicable laws that infringe on individuals' religious practices. In this case, it determined that a Seventh-Day Adventist who was fired for refusing to work on Saturday (her Sabbath) could receive unemployment benefits.[2]

A few years after *Sherbert*, the Court ruled in *United States v. Seeger* (1965) that its definition of religion would not require belief in a Supreme Being, effectively determining that "religion" included many personally held matters of conscience.[3] Asian religions played an important role in this broadening definition, as the Court felt compelled to recognize both the legitimacy of nontheistic religions (for example, Buddhism) and the unconstitutionality of defining religion in such a way that required theistic beliefs.

These Free Exercise decisions (and the increasing separation of church and state developing in Establishment Clause decisions) made clear the judiciary's view of itself as an active protector of minority religions, a position that Justice Robert Jackson had earlier stated was the Court's fundamental purpose: "The very purpose of a Bill of Rights was to withdraw certain subjects from the vicissitudes of political controversy, to place them beyond the reach of majorities and officials and to establish them as legal principles to be applied by the courts. One's right to life, liberty, and property, to free speech, a free press, freedom of worship and assembly, and other fundamental rights may not be submitted to vote; they depend on the outcome of no elections."[4] This view did not pass unnoticed; the number of Free Exercise cases expanded notably into the early 1990s. Between 1963 and 1990, the Supreme Court heard and decided 17 Free Exercise cases (compared to 12 in the preceding forty years) and declined to hear numerous others. The growth of Free Exercise cases was more apparent in the federal appellate courts, which decided 22 cases between 1963 and 1970, 62 between 1971 and 1980, and 110 between 1981 and 1990.[5] Such cases continued to mount even after it became clear that the courts usually did not rule in favor of expanding American citizens' Free Exercise rights.[6]

Some judges expressed disapproval of these trends in Free Exercise juris-prudence, especially as these changes threatened to overburden the courts with claims. In his dissent to a 1969 appellate court decision that Muslim prisoners were entitled to one pork-free meal daily, Judge Edward Tamm stated, "The court having opened this Pandora's Box must not hereafter com-plain about hornets."[7] In ensuing years, Tamm's statement would prove to be prophetic, particularly in predicting how some justices on the Supreme Court would view Free Exercise claims.

The door that *Sherbert* and *Seeger* opened for Free Exercise claims closed abruptly when, in *Employment Division v. Smith* (1990), the Supreme Court held that drug counselors fired for ingesting peyote in a religious service were lawfully denied unemployment benefits. Writing for the majority, Justice An-tonin Scalia rejected the *Sherbert* balancing test, arguing that the government need not demonstrate a "compelling interest" for generally applicable laws to be constitutional. Such laws, he claimed, should not be subject to the vicissi-tudes of individual conscience, lest the country devolve into anarchy and lawlessness. Recognizing the burden that this decision placed on religious minorities, Scalia nevertheless considered it the lesser of evils: "It may fairly be said that leaving accommodation to the political process will place at a relative disadvantage those religious practices that are not widely engaged in; but that unavoidable consequence of democratic government must be pre-ferred to a system in which each conscience is a law unto itself or in which judges weigh the social importance of all laws against the centrality of all reli-gious beliefs."[8] Many lawyers, legal scholars, pundits, and religious groups strenuously objected to *Employment Division*'s insensitivity to religious mi-norities. In her partially concurring opinion, Justice Sandra Day O'Connor dismissed Scalia's references to anarchy and lawlessness as a "parade of horribles" that represented more a rhetorical scare tactic than anything else. Nonetheless, in the years leading up to the 1990 *Employment Division* decision, the number of free exercise cases brought to the court had jumped, as had the range of religious actors making those claims. And, as Nancy Rosenblum suggests, "The combination of religious pluralism and government activism spurred Justice Scalia . . . to take a strong stand against what he portrayed as an avalanche of religious opt-outs from civic obligations . . . into ungoverna-bility."[9] Scalia makes it clear that he expects the courts to have little further role in adjudicating requests from actors seeking exemptions from general laws. Responding to O'Connor's complaints in a footnote, Scalia replied, "It is a parade of horribles because it is horrible to contemplate that federal judges will regularly balance against the importance of general laws the significance of religious practice."[10] As he would have it, the courts—and American society—would not be undone by religious diversity.

The public controversy following *Employment Division* exposed the difficulties involved in balancing Americans' collective conviction that the judicial branch is charged with protecting religious minorities against the courts' increasing resistance to enforcing those protections. Many legal scholars, pundits, and religious leaders were outraged by the decision, and public outcry led to the passage in 1993 of the Religious Freedom Restoration Act (RFRA), which essentially wrote the *Sherbert* test into federal law.[11] The Supreme Court struck down the RFRA in *Boerne v. Flores* (1997) on the ground that Congress had overextended its powers to enact federal laws (by dictating how to interpret them).[12] Since 1997, many state legislatures have passed "baby-RFRAS" that require state courts to adopt "compelling interest" tests.

While *Employment Division* severely curtailed the prospects of those seeking federal protection for religious actions, the Rehnquist Court's Establishment Clause rulings effectively weakened the "wall of separation" set in place during the Warren Court. Legal scholar Ira Lupu notes that *Employment Division* "invited a new and wider scope of permissive accommodation by the political branches, and hinted that courts might tolerate such activity more than prior establishment clause opinions would otherwise suggest."[13] Others have noted that the court has used Establishment rather than Free Exercise cases to fine-tune the line "between impermissible state action and permissible collective private action" in public life, arguing that this shift could potentially benefit all religious actors.[14]

The Rehnquist Court favored less separation of church and state in its establishment rulings. While the Warren Court's decisions sharply limited publicly funded displays of religion and religious activities, the Rehnquist Court loosened up on such displays. The move toward what Justice Stephen Breyer calls an "equal opportunity" approach to religious establishment contrasts with earlier "neutrality" approaches. "Equal opportunity" means, for example, that public schools must allow Bible study clubs to meet in public school buildings after hours if the schools also allow nonreligious groups to meet and that public universities cannot deny funds to student-run religious groups if funds are provided to nonreligious groups. In *Zelman v. Simmons-Harris* (2002), the Supreme Court upheld an Ohio school voucher law that allows students to use public funds to attend private schools, including religious schools. Such judgments demonstrate the majority's opinion that the government should not actively restrict government funding of an enterprise merely because it is religious; if the state funds other private activities of a similar kind, it can likewise support religious ones.[15]

Sociologist Phillip Hammond argues that Chief Justice William Rehnquist and those who join him in these decisions have been "less bothered than some others on the Court by the vestiges of 'establishment' left over from a time when governments did indeed sponsor or endorse religion, often unwittingly."[16] That indeed appears to be the case. One possible consequence of a weakened "wall of separation" is the development of a tacit religious establishment or civil religion. As Thomas Curry argues, "The very argument that the government can be nondiscriminatory in its sponsorship of religion is a violation of the First Amendment in that it advances the belief that government can know what is evenhanded in religious matters."[17]

If the past is any guide, there is reason to consider whether recent Establishment Clause rulings might be used to such an end. As Philip Hamburger documents in *Separation of Church and State*, Jefferson's metaphoric wall first entered the Supreme Court's lexicon in the twentieth century. Justice Hugo Black, a one-time Klansman committed to maintaining Protestant hegemony against a rising tide of Catholics and other immigrants, introduced the metaphor in *Everson v. Board of Education* (1947).[18]

While historical precedent suggests that "equal opportunity" models may veer toward endorsement of some religions over others, recent decisions may lead to other unintended consequences. Equal opportunity does not prima facie exclude school vouchers being sent to Islamic, Hindu, Jewish, or any religious primary schools. In other words, recent equal opportunity decisions can be read in such a way to encourage minority religious groups to vie for such resources.

This prospect worries some judges and scholars. While Hammond and Curry express concern that equal opportunity will support the establishment of one position, others, including Breyer, worry that equal opportunity will lead to increased religious and sectarian strife. In his dissent in *Zelman v. Simmons-Harris*, Justice Breyer asked how the equal opportunity principle would work in a nation of "Catholics, Jews, Muslims, Buddhists, Hindus, and Sikhs." This trend, he argued, would require the courts to play a more active role in religious matters. "Just how is the State to resolve the resulting controversies without provoking legitimate fears of the kinds of religious favoritism that, in so religiously diverse a Nation, threaten social dissension?"[19] Therefore, although the equal opportunity interpretation holds out the possibility of magnifying the public voice of religious minorities (and tempering some of the effects of *Employment Division*), it has not yet presented the rules and tests needed to keep public religious conflict at a minimum.

This cursory survey of the past forty years of First Amendment jurisprudence underlines a substantial shift in the Supreme Court's interpretations of the appropriate space of religion in public life during the period of the new religious immigration. The Warren Court, cognizant of the variety of religions present in American life, expanded the lists of constitutionally protected religious actions. It also insisted on greater separation between government and religion, effectively excluding many public displays of religious symbols and government funding of religious activities. In short, it acted on the vision that religion was a private matter of individual conscience. In contrast, the Rehnquist Court curtailed federal judicial protection of religious exercise and reinterpreted the Establishment Clause to allow for equal opportunity for religious groups in public life. The Rehnquist Court rejected the view that religion should be relegated to individual expression alone and was more willing than the prior Court to sacrifice the activities of religious minorities to the greater good of a well-functioning society.

We now ask what role Hindus, Muslims, Sikhs, and Buddhists have played in these shifts and assess how these groups have fared during this period. Do religious actors who bring complaints based on Free Exercise issues to the courts fare well? Who are these actors? What arenas or public issues seem most important to them, and why?

Post-1965 Asian immigration came during an era of judicial expansion of religious protections. This expansion placed new religious immigrants in a different relation to American society than that experienced by nineteenth-century Catholics and Jews. Even if Asian immigrants faced religious discrimination in daily life, the courts were a potentially powerful avenue for redress.

The shift toward increased judicial protection for religious minorities was prompted largely by claims made by sectarian Christians and Jews; in general, cases involving Asian religions have differed little from those involving such groups. Nonetheless, over the past forty years, Muslims, Hindus, Buddhists, and Sikhs have exercised their First Amendment rights by bringing grievances to federal courts. Most such cases that have reached the appellate level concern one of three venues: prisons, public schools, or municipal zoning. Here we survey these venues, the individuals or groups who bring cases to court, and the success or failure of their claims. Most of these cases deal with Free Exercise rather than Establishment issues, a pattern that mirrors larger trends, where religious actors are three times more likely to bring Free Exercise cases than Establishment cases to court.[20] We concentrate on U.S. Supreme Court and federal appellate court opinions between 1963 and 2000.

Of all Asian religions, Islam has had the greatest presence in the courts. According to John Wybraniec and Roger Finke's 2001 statistics, more than 4 percent of all court cases on religion between 1981 and 1996 (including more than 7 percent of all Free Exercise cases) were brought by Muslims, even though during this period only about 0.5 percent of the U.S. population was Muslim.[21] Almost all of these cases were brought by inmates, many of whom converted (or became actively religious) during incarceration, and many of whom are African American.[22] Far fewer cases were brought by immigrant or second-generation Muslims or, for that matter, by Buddhists, Hindus, or Sikhs. (In fact, Wybraniec and Finke do not include any of those groups as independently significant in their survey of more than twenty-one hundred cases.)

Until the late 1990s, most First Amendment cases involving Asian religions were brought by Euro-American converts rather than by immigrants or their children.[23] Several factors may account for this. Compared with their immigrant coreligionists, "twice-born" converts generally have less difficulty in establishing legal residency in the United States and likely have more access to the social and economic resources required to press such claims. Converts also may be more likely to see themselves as religious minorities with rights and the courts as a place where those rights might be protected.

Converts have also figured in many of the most prominent cases dealing with Asian religions. These cases have not always put the best face on Asian religions: when Timothy Leary's lawyers argued that smoking marijuana was an integral part of his experience as a Hindu, the circuit court analyzed the role of marijuana in Hindu religious doctrine (or lack thereof) and found for the United States.[24] Judges still cite this case when seeking ballast against those who mount frivolous religious claims to justify criminal acts. Other cases brought by converts to Asian religions (or Asian-influenced "new religious movements") stretched the limits of "real" religion (as opposed to cultlike activity).

Still, the U.S. Supreme Court took seriously the self-identity of Cassius Clay (Muhammad Ali) as a Muslim and included a lengthy discussion of the meaning of "jihad" in its per curiam report. After determining that it is indeed possible for a practicing Muslim to be a conscientious objector much in the same sense that a Catholic would be, the court overturned Ali's criminal conviction for draft dodging and remanded the case of his conscientious objector status to the appellate court. Likewise, the Supreme Court determined in *Cruz v. Beto* (1972) that a Buddhist convert was impermissibly denied the right to exercise his religion. The Court found that a man's unconventional beliefs should not exclude him from practicing his religion: "If Cruz was a Buddhist and if he was denied a reasonable opportunity of pursuing his faith comparable to the opportunity afforded to fellow prisoners who adhere to conventional religious precepts, then there was palpable discrimination by the State against the Buddhist religion, established 600 B.C., long before the Christian era." The court continued, "Opportunities must be afforded to all prisoners to exercise the religious freedom guaranteed by the First and Fourteenth Amendments without fear of penalty."[25]

Despite these decisions, many judges evince lingering doubts as to the sincerity of religious converts, particularly those who converted while in prison. Because the courts have determined that religion is a matter of individual conviction, many of these cases turn on the issue of a petitioner's sincerity. In his dissent to *Cruz v. Beto*, Rehnquist called into doubt Cruz's sincerity, noting that if courts could construe "every inmate's complaint under the liberal rule" that protects religious free exercise, they would be without "the latitude necessary to process this ever-increasing species of complaint." He closed by urging courts to resist hearing First Amendment cases from inmates such as Cruz who have "nothing to lose from a complaint stating facts that he is ultimately unable to prove."[26]

Free Exercise cases also require judges to determine the centrality of a religious practice to the believer's faith, another issue that takes on a particular cast within the prison system. Prisoners retain constitutional rights despite their status as criminals or accused criminals. At least theoretically, their rights to exercise religion freely cannot be abridged; prison authorities cannot establish religion in the prison or discriminate among religions in prison policy. In practice, however, prison authorities have wide latitude to restrict religious practice; the courts generally permit restrictions as long as authorities can show a governmental interest in doing so. So although prisoners bring a high proportion of cases, they seldom succeed.

One factor is the matter of the centrality of a religious practice. Whereas mainstream western religions have few daily constraints that are not already absorbed into or accommodated by American culture, Asian religions often appear to demand special requirements—clothing, hairstyles, diet, holidays, and sexual modesty concerns—that do not fit the majority's cultural frame.

Some of these differences are more easily accommodated than others. Prison authorities understand that Muslims, like Christians, worship communally, so they permit Friday j'umma (although not always to the satisfaction of Muslim prisoners). They also allow visits from local imams, who bear functional similarities to Christian clergy.

Such accommodations, however, do not necessarily offer a Zen Buddhist convict his full measure of religious freedom. Buddhist meetings do not require a spiritual leader, so some prison authorities have refused to allow them, citing policies that require an outside minister. Religiously based dietary codes create other challenges, as they require officials (and judges) to determine whether fasting for Ramadan, for example, is a practice central to Islam. The accommodation cases are legion: Muslims ask to be able to follow the commandment to give alms; Sikhs refuse to cut their hair or take off their turbans; Muslim converts demand that they be addressed by new Muslim names. In the mid-1990s, a Sikh prisoner complained that being assigned to share a cell with a smoker forced him to break a religious law against smoking tobacco; the prison authorities and the courts refused to accommodate him.[27]

One conceptual roadblock to accepting practices as central is a Protestant heritage that sees practices as peripheral to the central religious concerns of belief and speech. Judges have seen such "externals" as theologically and legally less important than the beliefs that supposedly prompted them. Likewise, while most American judges have little difficulty recognizing the centrality of the Eucharist or even the rituals of foot washing or laying on of hands, jurists run into difficulties with Asian religious rituals. Judicial determinations of centrality are further complicated by the fact that practices essential to one believer may not be central to another. (Not all Sikh men wear turbans.)

To summarize, most Free Exercise claims made to date by adherents of Islam or Asian religions have come from converts or convicts. It is hard to imagine that this fact has not negatively impacted courts' views of Asian religions. Converts may be deemed overzealous and their claims overdrawn. Convicts (as Rehnquist made clear) may be deemed prevaricators who use religion as an excuse for special treatment. In either case, the centrality of any religious practice and the sincerity of the practitioner may be called into question.

Although Asian religious immigrants have rarely pressed Free Exercise claims, the cases they have brought have gravitated toward two key issues: zoning and religious expression in public schools. In the courts, Asian religious actors press for rights that are often (though not always) given without question to Christians and Jews. Such claims expose the inequities of religious protections afforded by U.S. jurisprudence.

Very few laws in the United States have explicitly prohibited religious free exercise; those that have (such as a city ordinance that explicitly outlawed animal sacrifice) have usually been dispatched as unconstitutional.[28] More often, religious free exercise collides with generally applicable rules. Cases of solicitation by Hare Krishnas (discussed later in the chapter) provide one example: solicitation ordinances meant to apply to Fuller Brush salespeople and Greenpeace fund-raisers also apply to religious groups that go door to door. And, at least until 1990, judges needed to decide whether these general ordinances placed a substantial burden on religious exercise.

Zoning for worship buildings has become a particular point of concern for Asian religious groups, especially as local ordinances have been used from time to time to restrict these groups from meeting. In 1984, the Islamic Center of Mississippi successfully argued before the Fifth Circuit Court of Appeals that the city of Starkville, Mississippi, unconstitutionally limited its members' free exercise by enforcing zoning laws in a discriminatory fashion. Starkville's officials had repeatedly denied the group's requests to rezone buildings on the market for worship and, when the center finally purchased a house on the edge of a university campus, threatened the group with further sanctions unless it held its worship services elsewhere. The city's argument that it was not required to guarantee meeting space for religious groups within its limits was dismissed by the appellate court as "reminiscent of Anatole France's comment on the majestic equality of the law that forbids all men, the rich as well as the poor, to sleep under bridges, to beg in the streets, and to steal bread." Noting the meager financial resources of the (mostly) student group, the court stated,

> Laws that make churches, synagogues, and mosques accessible only to those affluent enough to travel by private automobile obviously burden the exercise of religion by the poor. . . . And a city may not escape the constitutional protection afforded against its actions by protesting that those who seek an activity it forbids may find it elsewhere. By making a mosque relatively inaccessible within the city limits to Muslims who lack automobile transportation, the City burdens their exercise of their religion.[29]

The Islamic Center won its case after demonstrating that a "loud" charismatic Christian congregation that met next door had not encountered any opposition from city officials.

Traffic congestion, noise, and other inconveniences brought about by congregational meetings often arise in religious zoning cases, where municipalities (often legitimately) question the impact of religious groups on residents' quality of life. While zoning has in some cases plainly been used to discriminate against groups, in other cases the discrimination is not as clear cut. For example, in *Four-Three-Oh v. BAPS* (2001), the Third Circuit Court of Appeals decided on a case of a Hindu congregation (BAPS) that wished to purchase a building previously used as a nightclub in North Bergen, New Jersey. The local zoning board ruled that to use the building as a temple, the group had to hire off-duty police officers to manage traffic and to enforce the legal maximum number of attendees. When the local police force stated that it could not supply off-duty officers and the zoning board refused to withdraw its requirements, the Hindu group went to court seeking rezoning. Both the district court and court of appeals found the zoning requirements to be "arbitrary and unreasonable."[30]

Neither party made religion or free exercise part of its argument. Nevertheless, the court apparently considered First Amendment issues in making its decision, as the dissenting judge stated that the majority had failed to judge the case on its merits (that is, whether too many cars would clog the highway and whether a private voluntary group would be able to enforce rules limiting the number of participants). As BAPS had not made religious free exercise an issue, he argued, neither should the court. He "would view this case quite differently if there were any suggestion that the [zoning board] harbored any bias towards BAPS or its members," he wrote, "but I am aware of no such evidence."[31] This dissent implies that the majority assumed that religious discrimination was at play in this case.

The public school system is another avenue through which Asian religions have appealed to the courts. Every child in the United States is required to attend school of some kind; student bodies consequently are religiously diverse. We should not be surprised, therefore, to find Hindu students challenging the largely beef-based federal lunch program or Muslim students asking for the freedom to perform required prayers (even though no such cases have as yet arisen). Nevertheless, students' constitutional rights, like those of prisoners, may be restricted by school authorities in the interests of safety, security, discipline, or efficiency.

Such a case recently arose in California's public schools when two Sikh boys wished to wear *kirpans* (small yet fully functional daggers) to school. While school policy forbade knives for safety reasons, the Cheema boys and their families argued that Sikhism required that they wear the kirpan at all times. Any proposed "compromises" (including riveting the dagger in its ceremonial sheath, dulling the edge, making it smaller, or replacing it with a symbolic medallion) invalidated the religious requirement that the dagger must be functional and the wearer able to draw it. Faced with this impasse, the appeals court found in a divided decision that the boys should be able to wear their kirpans sewn into the sheaths and hidden under their outer clothing. The dissenting judge argued that this decision put all other students at risk. It was impossible to trust an eight-year-old boy, no matter how religious, with a knife, he said, pointing to how "experts" had agreed that a Sikh must use the kirpan if he or "innocents" were threatened.[32]

Religious diversity in public schools heightens governmental interest in preserving an appearance of nonendorsement and nonestablishment of religion. Though children are occasionally believed to have some semi-independent religious rights (as the Cheema case shows), they are more often cast as uniquely sensitive and impressionable and thus liable to perceive religious activities as being endorsed by school authorities. As a result, cases concerning the regulation of the religious practices of teachers (and consequently their free exercise in the classroom) have arisen.

Alima Delores Reardon, a longtime substitute teacher in the Philadelphia public schools, began in 1982 to dress in traditional Muslim garb, including a veil that covered her head. In 1984, a principal sent her home to change her clothing, stating that Pennsylvania's garb statute prohibited her from teaching in religious dress. The statute specifically stated that it was not legal for teachers to wear "any dress, mark, emblem or insignia indicating the fact that such teacher is a member or adherent of any religious order, sect or denomination."[33] Reardon refused and subsequently lost her job.

Reardon filed a complaint with the Equal Employment Opportunity Commission, and the Justice Department took up her case, arguing that the statute conflicted with civil rights law and that the school district had failed to "accommodate individuals who wear or who seek to wear garb or dress that is an aspect of religious observance." The commonwealth of Pennsylvania argued that the statute helped maintain the religious neutrality in the public schools. The district court ruled that the school district was in error but did not find the garb statute discriminatory.

Both the school district and the Justice Department appealed, and the Third Circuit Court of Appeals found for Pennsylvania, affirming the lower court's ruling in favor of the commonwealth's law and reversing the lower court's ruling against the school district. It is in the commonwealth's interest, the opinion stated, to maintain "religious neutrality in the public school system, and accordingly [to] conclude that it would impose an undue hardship to require the Commonwealth to accommodate Ms. Reardon and others similarly situated."[34]

This opinion draws heavily on a similar case brought before the Oregon state court in 1986 by a convert to Sikhism. Janet Cooper, who had taught in public schools for twelve years, started to dress in all white, with her hair in a turban. Like Reardon, she was dismissed from her teaching duties for violating her state's religious garb law. While Cooper won a short-lived victory in the Oregon Court of Appeals, the Oregon Supreme Court reversed the decision, arguing that statutes prohibiting religious dress were "narrowly tailored to the compelling state interest in preserving the appearance of religious neutrality in public schools."[35]

Both cases focus on state garb laws that specifically target public school-teachers who dress in a distinctively religious manner. The states in both cases effectively argued that while such laws limit teachers' free exercise of religion, the state's overriding interest in religious disestablishment makes such limits permissible. Where young and fertile minds are involved, teachers do not have the right to present their students with a constant reminder of religious beliefs.

Several other issues arise in these cases. First, while the schools are to remain religiously neutral, the judges do not suggest that they become religiously arid. Drawing on the opinion in *Cooper*, the Third Circuit opinion noted that Oregon's (and Pennsylvania's) garb laws do not prohibit teachers from wearing "ambiguous" religious symbols such as a cross or a "Star of David" on a necklace or charm bracelet. Likewise, a teacher may dress in religious garb "on her way to or from a seasonal ceremony." Teachers are prohibited only from dressing in a way that "may leave a conscious or unconscious impression among young people and their parents that the school endorses the particular religious commitment of the person whom it has assigned the public role of teacher."[36] Teachers who cultivate less "obvious" or less "daily" expressions of religion need not hide them from their students.

Toward the end of its opinion on the Philadelphia case involving Alima Reardon, the appellate court mentioned the Establishment issues that arose obliquely in the case. Lawyers representing the Justice Department on Reardon's behalf had argued that the origins of the garb statute were not neutral but rather intentionally discriminatory. In 1894, a year before the garb statute's passage, Pennsylvania's Supreme Court held that there was no constitutional barrier to keeping Catholic nuns or priests from teaching in public schools. The state legislature circumvented this judicial ruling by passing the garb statute.

The appellate court acknowledged the law's anti-Catholic history but stated that past motivations had no bearing on the fact that the garb statute's current purpose was to maintain the appearance of neutrality in the public schools. The opinion stated that "where [a] statute bans religious attire and is being enforced by the Commonwealth in a non-discriminatory manner with respect to the Muslim teachers as well as Catholics, we conclude that it is irrelevant whether a portion of those who voted for the statute in 1895 were motivated by the desire to bar Catholic habit from the classroom."[37]

The Third Circuit Court of Appeals gave the garb rule a second life, thanks to twentieth-century Establishment notions of religious neutrality. That this statute will discriminate against Sikhs and Muslims (and presumably some Hindus) but not against other religious groups (including, ironically, most Catholic orders) is lost on the court. The statute's "second life" thus may well mirror its discriminatory first; as Philip Hamburger has argued, the nineteenth-century concept of a "wall of separation" originally excluded an increasingly vocal religious minority from public life, including public schools.[38] Regardless of what we make of this decision, this statute continues to effectively exclude from public schools teachers of some minority faiths.

As many have observed, U.S. courts have often interpreted "religion" in Protestant ways. So we might imagine that Asian religious actors would successfully challenge this bias under the Establishment Clause. But this has not yet come to pass. Few Asian religious actors have directly drawn on the Establishment Clause to challenge the Protestant assumptions undergirding American public life. Indeed, many Asian immigrants may well find the tacitly Protestant aspects of public life more welcoming than alienating. Hindus, Muslims, and Sikhs eager to win a place at the political table might find doing so difficult if secular humanism exiles religion from public life. Ironically, recent Establishment Clause cases based on equal opportunity for the public expression of religion may well fit with some new immigrant religious groups' perceptions of how they will be included in a religiously plural public sphere.

Some exceptions bear mentioning, however. Chief among these is *Chaudhuri v. Tennessee* (1997), in which a Hindu professor sued the public university that employed him for establishing religion first through prayers and later through a moment of silence at university functions.[39] Dr. Dilip Chaudhuri argued that the prayers—"nonsectarian" according to the Tennessee State University administration—were actually Christian, given that they were monotheistic and referred to "our Heavenly Father." When the university responded to Chaudhuri by instituting a moment of silence rather than a prayer at football games and college events, members of the audience "spontaneously" recited the Lord's Prayer—evidence that many participants considered the activity a Christian one.

The Sixth Circuit Court of Appeals determined that the "prayers did, to be sure, evoke a monotheistic tradition not shared by Hindus such as Dr. Chaudhuri." However, quoting from *Marsh v. Chambers* (1983), the court stated that "the content of the prayer is not of concern to judges where, as here, there is no indication that the prayer opportunity has been exploited to proselytize or advance any one, or to disparage any other, faith or belief."[40] In other words, the court found that although the prayers evoked a particular tradition, they were not advancing that tradition. "No reasonable observer could conclude that TSU, merely by requesting a moment of silence at its functions, places its stamp of approval on any particular religion or religion in general."[41]

In coming to its decision that a monotheistic prayer did not advance any particular faith, the Sixth Circuit relied on a "reasonable observer" test used in many similar cases to determine whether a particular symbol or act is religious. But who is a reasonable observer? By definition, the reasonable observer is not a real person—and certainly not a person of any particular religion—but rather an abstraction of a person who is not completely ignorant of the meaning and history of a symbol or act.[42] But the Sixth Circuit clearly envisioned its reasonable observer as someone similar to the Christian students and faculty of Tennessee State, comfortable with a fairly high level of accommodation between religion and government, expecting religious "solemnization" of public events, and sufficiently Christian to view a prayer to "our Heavenly Father" as nonsectarian.

Some judges see grave problems in relying on this abstract and unreal "reasonable observer." Justice William Brennan dissented bitterly to its use in *Allegheny v. ACLU* (1989), arguing that the "reasonable observer" test allows for only one reasonable position. Concerning this case, in which the Court decided that the public display of a crèche and a menorah on state property was nonreligious and thus constitutional, he states, "I shudder to think that the only 'reasonable observer' is one who shares the particular views on perspective, spacing, and accent expressed in [the majority] opinion, thus making analysis under the Establishment Clause look more like an exam in Art 101 than an inquiry into constitutional law."[43] And although Chaudhuri lost his case, a partial dissent to the opinion recognized the shortcomings of the majority position. Circuit Judge Nathaniel Jones reminded his peers that they must be "vigilant to guard against quantifying the humiliation visited upon one who follows a non-Christian religion or tradition within a nation that maintains a strong Christian tradition. . . . The majority has applied a litmus test that will certainly confuse future officials and policy makers confronted with the increasingly diverse religious orientation of the American public."[44]

Chaudhuri's supposedly unreasonable perspective is a religious perspective. Chaudhuri made his claims as a Hindu, arguing that even a moment of silence is an establishment of the majority Christian tradition. This is particularly true when the case history shows that the authorities embraced a moment of silence only after retreating first to nonsectarian prayer and that the moment of silence was intended to preserve the community's tradition of solemnizing public events with prayer. The audience's recitation of the Lord's Prayer during the "moment of silence" (and the loud applause that accompanied it) shows that the majority wanted its own traditions to prevail, regardless of Chaudhuri's discomfort as a religious minority. While the judges suggest that the prayers to "our Heavenly Father" are civic and not sectarian, a Hindu (apparently unreasonably) sees otherwise.[45] But majority religions are not the only faiths that might be established in public space.

In *Brooks v. Oak Ridge* (2000), Tennessee resident David Brooks argued that the display of a "Friendship Bell" in a public park in Oak Park unconstitutionally endorsed Buddhism.[46] The Sixth Circuit Court of Appeals acknowledged that the bell was cast in Japan, dedicated by Japanese monks, and inscribed with religious symbols. It also noted that bells of a similar sort were used by Buddhists in Japan for religious purposes. Using the "reasonable observer" test, however, the court nevertheless determined that "although the religious aspects of the bell and its casting ceremony remain troubling, on balance we believe that the reasonable observer would determine that the City of Oak Ridge intended to endorse peace and friendship with Japan, not the Buddhist religion, by adopting and displaying the Friendship Bell."[47] In short, Brooks's view of these symbols as primarily religious was "unreasonable."

In a similar case, *Altman v. Bedford* (2001), a group of Roman Catholic parents charged that the Westchester, New York, public schools were endorsing —and inculcating—Asian religions, paganism, and witchcraft. They cited, among other things, a teacher's lessons on India, in which she read her class a "folktale" about the Hindu deity Ganesh ("How Ganesh Got an Elephant

Head") and had them craft small Ganesh sculptures as a project. The school had also hired a yoga teacher (called the Yoga Guy) who dressed in distinctively Sikh clothing to teach part of its physical education curriculum. The court ruled in favor of the school district, referring to the "reasonable observer" in its decision. The Sikh teacher did not teach yoga as a spiritual discipline, it determined, and reading the Ganesh story was an exercise in cultural contact and therefore was not impermissibly religious. The court did find, however, that having the children make Ganesh "idols," as the Catholic parents put it, violated the Establishment Clause, but this part of the decision was reversed on appeal because of a legal technicality.[48]

The "reasonable observer" concept can in theory be applied to each case de novo, since it is, aside from reasonableness, contentless. But every "reasonable observer" conjured up by the courts has specific characteristics. She has some knowledge of the history of symbols. She reads civic and cultural meaning into symbols but rarely religious import. In *Brooks*, this reasonable observer saw the bell as a sign of cultural interchange, not religious proselytization. In *Altman*, she read stories about Ganesh culturally rather than religiously. Similarly, in *Chaudhuri*, the courts focus on the civic rather than the religious aspects of a moment of silence. In other words, the "reasonable observer," whether protecting traditional Christian norms or denying that municipalities are endorsing Asian religions, tends to remove rites, activities, and symbols from a religious to a secular context. The courts appear to be rather consistently rejecting citizens' arguments that religious symbols are, in fact, religious.[49]

The key question here, of course, is what religion is and what it is not. The courts' definitions of religion plainly influence their decisions. Judges understandably do not wish to play theologians, so they work hard to appear detached and objective, yet those who rule on Free Exercise and Establishment cases necessarily operate, either consciously or unconsciously, with particular definitions of religion. And such definitions matter.[50]

Scholars of religion are quick to remind legal scholars that there is no such thing as generic "religion," only particular "religions." Accordingly, personal or mainstream assumptions always have the potential unwittingly to leak into legal judgments. This problem has been duly noted by legal scholars, many of whom now concede that the court's operative definitions have a de facto Protestant character.[51] (Whether this fact "establishes" Protestantism is of course another question.) These operative definitions of religion have several properties. First, they privilege individual conscience over collective religious authority. Second, they presume that the core of religion is belief or conscience, from which action follows. Third, they presume that religion is primarily private.

These notions are widely and deeply embedded in our implicitly Protestant political culture, notably in our conception of human rights, which are typically understood to protect individuals rather than groups. J. S. Mill and other liberals argued that "liberty of conscience" was particularly worth protecting, and so they pressed for the maintenance of a vast, unregulated "private sphere" wherein individuals could pursue their independent religious, ideological, and aesthetic goals (as long as they did not harm society).[52] The goal of the First Amendment, Martha Nussbaum states, is to promote "a regime in which each citizen's liberty of conscience is preserved inviolate, despite the pressures that corporate bodies of various types, whether religious or secular, may bring to bear."[53] The courts' language of rights, therefore, neatly dovetails with Protestant definitions of religion that give conscience and individual self-determination a central place. This intersection might be inevitable. "Even were it true that focusing on individual claimants has some slight effect on encouraging individuality in religion, the law has little choice," Kent Greenawalt argues. "Free exercise rights are mainly individual; legal rules should not insist that members see things according to prevailing views within a denomination."[54] Greenawalt nevertheless fails sufficiently to address the impact of these definitions on religious minority groups. As the courts link religious conviction to the right to choose a religion, they simultaneously provide less latitude to those whose religious convictions are based not on individual choice but on a duty to moral communities that precedes such choices.[55]

The courts' definitions of religion started to expand in the 1960s, partly in response to the growing presence of Asian religious actors (nontheistic Buddhists in particular). The court relied largely on academic definitions of religion and in some cases on academic experts who provided "unbiased" views of the essentials of particular religions. (For example, in *Cheema v. Thompson*, Columbia University Professor Gurinder Singh Mann testified about the kirpan and the religious obligations of Sikhs.) Nevertheless, courts generally use such testimony to arrive at a correct interpretation of a specific religion within the operative definitions already employed. For example, in the ISKCON cases detailed later in this chapter, experts testified about whether *sankirtan*, a tradition of soliciting funds as a form of proselytizing, is central to the religion but did not call into question the standard of centrality itself.

The judiciary did not explicitly take up the burden of defining religion until the 1960s, when the courts determined in *Torcaso v. Watkins* (1961) and again in *Welsh v. United States* (1970) that they could not discriminate against religions that did not believe in a Supreme Being or a God.[56] After the courts saw that not all "world religions" (for example, Daoism and some forms of Buddhism) or home-grown religions (such as Ethical Culture) were theistic, the old substantive definitions came under fire. Not wanting to appear to privilege some forms of religion over others, the courts sought alternatives to those substantive definitions. More specifically, the courts began to draw on functional definitions of religion, which emphasize religions' role in believers' lives. Many courts drew heavily on the work of the Protestant theologian Paul Tillich, whose definition of religion as a matter of "ultimate concern" quickly replaced the older content-based definition of religion as belief in a Supreme Being.

This "ultimate concern" perspective reinforced the psychological dimension (inspired by the work of William James) already embedded in the courts' content-based definitions. Ultimate concern was construed as an allegiance to what people "really care about" and act on, regardless of temporal or earthly consequences.[57] In other words, ultimate concern definitions continued to focus on the beliefs and concerns of individuals.[58] But the courts could now entertain arguments from individuals expressing sincere beliefs, even if those beliefs contradicted their religion's orthodoxy. For example, although not all Muslims or Catholics are conscientious objectors, those who claimed to be so (qua Muslims or Catholics) could still be viewed as acting on religious convictions. This emphasis on personal conviction, while congruent with notions of individual liberty, placed an even greater burden on the courts to ascertain an individual's sincerity. And, as we have seen, determining sincerity is not a straightforward task.

Both substantive and functional definitions of religion can exclude groups and theologies that many consider religious. Not all religions emphasize conviction as Protestantism does. So Greenawalt and others have proposed an analogical approach that escapes some of the underlying theological assumptions embedded in functional definitions. An analogical definition draws on Wittgenstein's notion of family resemblance and determines the "religiousness" of the object in question based on its resemblance to a number of elements found in other clear-cut cases of religion. Some appellate courts have used analogical definitions to make decisions in gray areas, where the religiousness of an entire ideology or system is in question. Analogical principles in theory short-circuit the bias that exists in other definitions and seem especially suited to cases involving Islam, Hinduism, Buddhism, and other Asian religious "families." To date, however, applications of analogical thinking have relied on those "families" (Protestant, Catholic, and Jewish) closer to home.

The impact of these various definitions of religion is most obvious in cases where courts must determine whether a group is religious or merely ideological (for example, cases involving Scientology or MOVE), but they also influence decisions about Islam, Buddhism, and Hinduism.[59] That is, even though the courts have no difficulty determining that Muslims are religious, judges still draw on particular definitions of religion and religious practice to interpret whether a Muslim's particular practice is central or essential and whether she is sincere in claiming constitutional protections.

The consequences of one's choice of definitions become clear when we compare two cases argued before different appellate courts in the early 1980s. Both turn on a similar issue: whether the Hare Krishnas' practice of *sankirtan* is a constitutionally protected religious activity. As we will see, the courts continue to use definitions of religion that reinforce commonplace American boundaries between religious and nonreligious activity. These boundaries are not always appropriate, however, when dealing with Asian religions, Native American faiths, or even sectarian Christian and Jewish groups.[60] By rarely taking Asian religions on their own terms, court decisions limit free exercise along the boundaries implicit in their definitions.

In *ISKCON v. Barber* (1981), the Fifth Circuit Court of Appeals determined that *sankirtan* conducted at a state fair is a protected religious activity and allowed the Hare Krishnas to solicit funds and evangelize there. In *ISKCON v. Houston* (1982), the Second Court of Appeals ruled that *sankirtan* is not a protected religious activity insofar as it involves solicitation of funds and determined that Hare Krishnas must register with the city before they make their rounds of local residences. While these circuit courts of appeals agree that the International Society for Krishna Consciousness (ISKCON) is a religion, they disagree about how religious the practice of *sankirtan* is. This disagreement hangs in large measure on their operating definitions of religion.

ISKCON v. Barber concerns whether ISKCON members can practice *sankirtan* at the New York State Fair. This fair, the judges note, has for years allowed "religious, fraternal, and political groups" to participate but has also (by long-standing unwritten rule) prohibited these groups from soliciting funds. The State Fair formalized this solicitation rule in 1978, only after sankirtan became an issue. The change, the group argued, unconstitutionally restricted the Hare Krishnas' free exercise of religion.

The Second Circuit Court of Appeals began its ruling by stating that ISKCON is a religion and then proceeded to determine the place of sankirtan within it. The ruling drew on the language of centrality and sincerity of practice and discussed the history of the ISKCON tradition. Without noting individual sources, the opinion referred at several points to "experts" in south Asian religions and Hinduism who had testified for and against ISKCON. The court laid out at some length its reasons for considering ISKCON a religion, no doubt as a result of contemporary charges that ISKCON was a cult: "Krishna Consciousness is an outgrowth of the Chaitanya movement of Bengal, which derives from the Bhakti tradition. . . . Lord Chaitanya made the chanting of the Hare Krishna mantra central to sankirtan. He opened up the process of spiritual liberation to the masses by bringing into his movement people who were outside the standard Hindu community and the caste system and proclaimed that one day his name will be chanted in every town and village of the world." The opinion then discussed the introduction of ISKCON to the United States and described the differences in sankirtan practice in the United States and India. By situating Krishna Consciousness within a long tradition and positioning sankirtan as part and parcel of the religion, the court brought the practice inside the circle of centrality. This finding, in turn, defined sankirtan as a constitutionally protected religious activity, exempt from the fair's general restrictions against soliciting money.

The majority also commented on why it reversed the lower court's ruling, which found in favor of the state after determining that sankirtan fell under the heading of "commercial speech." Here the appeals court relied on a "functional, phenomenological investigation of an individual's 'religion'" that drew explicitly on Tillich's definition of religion as "ultimate concern."[61] The opinion stated that such a concern "is more than intellectual when a believer would categorically 'disregard elementary self-interest in preference to transgressing its tenets.'" Sankirtan is therefore not some secular thing that Hare Krishnas do simply to make money; it emerges from the "literature and doctrine" of the movement. Sankirtan is protected, in short, because it has been a central Hare Krishna practice for some time and because those who perform it do so sincerely.

While this case's decision represents a victory for free exercise, the decision was written in light of a plainly Protestant view of religion, where issues of ultimate concern help to establish the sincerity of religious claims and the centrality of a given practice. The court also allowed itself a few parting words about its distaste for those who use religion to further less tasteful ends: "We do not condone the odious tactics of swindling and harassment hidden beneath a veneer of religion. But when we are asked to sacrifice legitimate First Amendment rights at the altar of law enforcement, we are given pause. The unpopular traditions, practices, and doctrines of alien religions need not receive our approval or support, but must be tolerated if our freedoms are to be preserved."[62]

The outcome of *ISKCON v. Houston* was quite different. In this case, Hare Krishnas argued that they should not be restricted by a Houston ordinance that required those who ask for money by going door to door to register with the city and to wear or possess a permit. The city argued that the ordinance was religiously neutral and had never been used to restrict or censor anyone who wished to go door to door but merely placed on public record those groups who were doing so. ISKCON argued that solicitation of funds was a religious practice rather than a commercial activity and that the ordinance unfairly burdened its practitioners' ability to practice a fundamental religious obligation.

Here, as in *Barber*, the court found it necessary to explain why ISKCON is a religion. Rather than appealing to history, however, the *Houston* decision employed an analogical approach. ISKCON is a religion, it found, because "Krishna followers have a temple in Houston, ordained priests, are guided by their construction of the Bhagavad-gita, a sacred Hindu text as important in the Buddhist [sic] religions as the Bible is to Christians and Jews and, as far as the record goes, are members of an institutionalized religion on the same institutional level as many other religions."[63] While the judge had some difficulty in differentiating between Hinduism and Buddhism, both are religions, just like Christianity and Judaism. Each has sacred scripture. Each has religious authorities (priests) and a temple. The opinion then discussed *sankirtan*, defining it in terms of its purpose: spreading religious beliefs, financially supporting the group, and attracting new members. In reaching its decision, the appeals court then extended its analogical definition to ISKCON's practice: "Krishna devotees have complete freedom to exercise their religion by distributing their literature and otherwise spreading the society's religious beliefs. They also have complete freedom of speech to express their views and to proselytize by persuasion. The third element, solicitation of funds, is a different matter; it is circumscribed by the requirements of the ordinance."[64]

In this case, an analogical definition of religion includes proselytizing but excludes what the judge sees as economic activity. In short, while spreading the word or handing out literature are recognizable religious practices, asking strangers for money is not.[65] Hare Krishnas apparently can engage in a "religious practice" only insofar as it seems analogous to practices of mainstream religious groups. Here we see the limitations of the analogical method at work: in the contemporary United States, the mainstream religions from which judges draw their analogies do not send priests or monks out to beg for food in the streets or ask lay adherents to solicit strangers for charity. Thus, despite the acknowledgment that Krishnas "ritualize" solicitation (a point argued in *Heffron v. ISKCON*), *sankirtan* remains an economic rather than a religious activity in the eyes of this court.

Although these two court decisions are not identical, both turn on the degree to which *sankirtan* is viewed as a religious practice. Both turn, in other words, on the courts' definitions of "religion," which compel judges to evaluate religious action by drawing on Christian norms such as religious individualism and the primacy of religious conscience.

The period of new religious immigration has coincided with notable growth in Free Exercise cases. Growing recognition of the United States as a nation of religions has played a role in the jurisprudential turn that the Supreme Court has taken in recent decades. The courts have responded to the presence of Asian religious actors in varied ways: by expanding definitions of religion to include nontheistic varieties, by drawing on the ideal of religious pluralism to call for stricter separation of church and state, and by limiting free exercise lest a nest of hornets or a "parade of horribles" overtake American society.

The courts' views of religious diversity depend in part on the cases they hear. Thus, it is important to reiterate that most cases to date dealing with Asian religions and Islam heard by the federal courts involve European and African American converts and prison inmates. These classes of claimants arguably face more of an uphill battle in establishing the sincerity of their religious practices than do nonconverts and nonconvicts. All Asian religious claimants, however, encounter the additional burden of educating judges who are largely unfamiliar with Asian religions and therefore operate with implicitly Christian distinctions between the sacred and the profane. Asian religious actors, in short, begin at a distinct disadvantage. At the same time, cases such as *Four-Three-Oh v. BAPS* suggest that some federal judges are willing to take religious discrimination into account even in cases that do not seem on the face to be about religion.

One consequence of the presence of Asian religious actors in the courts is their ability to expose the Christian principles that work by stealth in courts' operating definitions. In the cases involving *sankirtan*, neither functional nor analogical definitions of religion preclude the court from favoring some religions over others. Functional definitions emphasize the psychological over the practical elements of religions and accrue to the favor of religions that define themselves as springing from individual conviction (rather than duty to a community, family tradition, or religious authority). Analogical definitions tend to exclude from protection actions and activities that are historically viewed in the United States as political or economic rather than religious. Free exercise is restricted in either case but even more so for those who must first instruct judges as to which practices are central to the faith and for those whose claims of sincerity are framed in terms other than personal conviction.

Ongoing changes in Establishment Clause interpretation present a somewhat different picture. The recent stress on "equal opportunity" or "evenhandedness" rather than "separation" reminds us that the United States has never attained true separation of church and state (a fact reinforced by public outcry over the Ninth Circuit Court of Appeals' 2002 decision that the Pledge of Allegiance's "under God" language constitutes an unconstitutional endorsement of religion).[66] Whether this shift toward an equal opportunity interpretation will expand the spaces where adherents to Asian religions can act religiously remains to be seen and must be viewed in light of other recent developments, including the courts' reliance on a "reasonable observer" in its Establishment Clause rulings. Unlike the Catholic parents in Westchester, Brooks in Oak Ridge, or Chaudhuri at Tennessee State, the courts continue to posit a "reasonable observer" for whom the religious symbols and ideas of both majority and minority can coexist but only insofar as religious symbols serve as mnemonic devices to remind Americans of both our diverse cultural origins and the political state that supersedes them all. To this reasonable observer (and the judges and justices who use this fiction in their decisions), the challenges presented by a nation of religions do not seem insurmountable. These recent decisions are certainly reshaping the contexts in which all religious actors can act in public life. Whether they are adequate to the task of anticipating and shaping the challenges of a nation wherein religion's power remains more than a cultural marker remains to be seen.

NOTES

1. Kent Greenawalt, "Religion as a Concept in Constitutional Law," *California Law Review* 72.5 (September 1984): 753.

2. *Reynolds v. United States*, 98 U.S. 145 (1898); *Cantwell v. State of Connecticut*, 310 U.S. 296 (1940); *Sherbert v. Verner*, 374 U.S. 398 (1963).

3. Greenawalt, "Religion as a Concept"; Philip E. Hammond, *With Liberty for All* (Louisville, Ky.: Westminster John Knox, 1998); *United States v. Seeger*, 380 U.S. 163 (1965).

4. *West Virginia State Bd. of Ed. v. Barnette*, 319 U.S. 624, 638 (1943).

5. We compiled this data by searching the legal case archives in Lexis-Nexis. We located Free Exercise cases heard at the Supreme Court and Federal Appeals Court levels from 1963 to 1999 through keyword searches (e.g., "free exercise" and "religion"). We coded as relevant all cases in which Free Exercise constituted the primary legal issue, excluding all cases where the decision was determined by the courts not to be publishable.

6. John Ryan, "Smith and the Religious Freedom Restoration Act: An Iconoclastic Assessment," *Virginia Law Review* 78 (September 1992): 1407. Even after *Sherbert*, the courts rarely ruled in favor of expanding Free Exercise. Only four of the seventeen cases to reach the Supreme Court between 1963 and 1990 won, and almost three-quarters of all Free Exercise cases to reach federal appellate courts between 1963 and 1994 lost. A recent study finds that at all court levels, Free Exercise cases made by mainline Protestants are almost twice as likely to succeed than those brought by Muslims or members of "new religious" groups. Native Americans and sectarian Christians are also less likely to win cases. See John Wybraniec and Roger Finke, "Religious Regulation and the Courts: The Judiciary's Changing Role in Protecting Minority Religions from Majoritarian Rule," *Journal for the Scientific Study of Religion* 40.3 (September 2001): 427–44.

7. *Barnett v. Rodgers*, 410 F. 2nd 995, 1004 (1969).

8. *Employment Division v. Smith*, 494 U.S. 872, 890 (1990).

9. Nancy Rosenblum, "Introduction: Pluralism, Integralism, and Political Theories of Religious Accommodation," in *Obligations of Citizenship and Demands of Faith*, edited by Nancy Rosenblum (Princeton: Princeton University Press, 2000), 13.

10. *Employment Division v. Smith*, 891.

11. See, e.g., Stephen Carter, *The Culture of Disbelief* (New York: Basic Books, 1993); Michael McConnell, "Free Exercise Revisionism and the Smith Decision," *University of Chicago Law Review* 57 (Fall 1990): 1109–53.

12. *City of Boerne v. Flores*, 521 U.S. 507 (1997).

13. Ira Lupu, "The Trouble with Accommodation," *George Washington Law Review* 60.3 (March 1992): 754.

14. Noah Feldman, "From Liberty to Equality: The Transformation of the Establishment Clause," *California Law Review* 90.3 (May 2002): 673.

15. *Rosenberger v. University of Virginia*, 115 S. Ct. 2510 (1995); *Lamb's Chapel v. Center Moriches School District*, 508 U.S. 384 (1993); *Zobrest v. Catalina Foothills School District*, 509 U.S. 1 (1993); *Zelman v. Simmons-Harris*, 122 S. Ct. 2460 (2002).

16. Phillip E. Hammond, "American Church/State Jurisprudence from the Warren Court to the Rehnquist Court," *Journal for the Scientific Study of Religion* 40.3 (September 2001): 463.

17. Thomas J. Curry, *Farewell to Christendom: The Future of Church and State in America* (New York: Oxford University Press, 2001), 59.

18. Philip Hamburger, *Separation of Church and State* (Cambridge: Harvard University Press, 2002); *Everson v. Board of Education*, 330 U.S. 1 (1947).

19. *Zelman v. Simmons-Harris*, 2505.

20. Wybraniec and Finke, "Religious Regulation and the Courts."

21. Tom Smith places the number of Muslims in the United States roughly between 1.4 and 1.9 million, making the number closer to 0.67 percent of the population ("Religious Diversity in America: The Emergence of Muslims, Buddhists, Hindus, and Others," *Journal for the Scientific Study of Religion* 41.3 [September 2002]: 577–85).

22. Although more research is required to verify this, it also appears that many cases in the 1970s were brought by inmates identified with the Nation of Islam and that in recent years a larger proportion are identified (if at all) as "Orthodox" Muslims.

23. The scholarly debate over how to best categorize Asian religions' "immigrant" and "convert" groups continues. For a history of this debate, see Martin Baumann, "Protective Amulets and Awareness Techniques, or How to Make Sense of Buddhism in the West," in *Westward Dharma: Buddhism beyond Asia*, edited by Martin Baumann and Charles S. Prebish (Berkeley: University of California Press, 2002), 51–65; Charles S. Prebish, *Luminous Passage: The Practice and Study of Buddhism in America* (Berkeley: University of California Press, 1999), 57–63.

24. *Leary v. United States*, 383 F. 2nd 851 (1967).

25. *Clay v. United States*, 403 U.S. 698 (1971); *Cruz v. Beto*, 92 S. Ct. 1079, 1081 (1972).

26. *Cruz v. Beto*, 1084.

27. On the Zen Buddhist prisoner unable to practice congregational chanting, see *Spies v. Voinovich*, 173 F. 3rd 398 (1999). Numerous cases deal with prisoners and Ramadan fasting, and they are frequently brought by segregated or solitary confinement prisoners rather than prisoners at large (for whom prisons attempt to schedule Ramadan meals). A typical example is *Akeem Abdul Makin v. Colorado Dept. of Corrections*, 183 F. 3rd 1205 (1999). On the Sikh forced to room with a smoker, see *Grote v. Ramirez*, 1998 U.S. App. LEXIS 34239. On the objections of Sikhs and Muslims to beard and hair-length regulations, see *Silvey v. Schriro*, 117 F. 3rd 1423 (1997). Cases of prisoners unable to use Muslim or religious names are also many; see, e.g., *Matthews v. Morales*, 23 F. 3rd 118 (1994).

28. *Church of the Lukumi Babalu Aye v. City of Hialeah*, 508 U.S. 520 (1993).

29. *Islamic Center v. Starkville*, 840 F. 2nd 293, 299 (1988). Internal citations omitted.

30. *Four-Three-Oh v. BAPS*, 256 F. 3rd 107, 111 (2001).

31. Ibid., 119.

32. *Cheema v. Thompson*, 67 F. 3rd 883 (1995). For an excellent treatment of this case, see Vinay Lal, "Sikh Kirpans in California Schools: The Social Construction of Symbols, the Cultural Politics of Identity, and the Limits of Multiculturalism," in *New Spiritual Homes: Religion and Asian Americans*, edited by David K. Yoo (Honolulu: University of Hawaii Press, 1999), 87–133.

33. *United States v. Board of Education*, 911 F. 2nd 882, 885 (1990). See also Kathleen Moore, "The Hijab and Religious Liberty: Anti-Discrimination Law and Muslim Women in the United States," in *Muslims on the Americanization Path?*, edited by Yvonne Yazbeck Haddad and John L. Esposito (New York: Oxford University Press, 2000), 105–27.

34. *United States v. Board of Education*, 894.

35. Cited in ibid., 888.

36. Ibid., 890.

37. Ibid., 894.

38. Hamburger, *Separation of Church and State*.

39. *Chaudhuri v. Tennessee*, 130 F. 3rd 232 (1997), cert. denied.

40. *Marsh v. Chambers*, 463 U.S. 783 (1983).

41. *Chaudhuri v. Tennessee*.

42. Justice O'Connor wrote in a concurring opinion to *Allegheny v. ACLU*, 492 U.S. 573 (1989), in which the court ruled that a crèche display in a county courthouse violated the Establishment Clause but that a similar display with a menorah did not, "Under the endorsement test, the 'history and ubiquity' of a practice is relevant not because it creates an 'artificial exception' from that test. On the contrary, the 'history and ubiquity' of a practice is relevant because it provides part of the context in which a reasonable observer evaluates whether a challenged governmental practice conveys a message of endorsement of religion. It is the combination of the longstanding existence of practices such as opening legislative sessions with legislative prayers or opening Court sessions with 'God save the United States and this honorable Court,' as well as their nonsectarian nature, that leads me to the conclusion that those particular practices, despite their religious roots, do not convey a message of endorsement of particular religious beliefs" (630).

43. Ibid., 643.

44. *Chaudhuri v. Tennessee*, 241.

45. Ibid., 241 n.2.

46. *Brooks v. Oak Ridge*, 222 F. 3rd 259 (2000), cert. denied, February 2001.

47. Ibid., 266.

48. *Altman v. Bedford Cent. Sch. Dist*, 245 F. 3rd 49 (2001), cert. denied, October 1, 2001. Yoga and meditation classes in schools are a frequent target of such lawsuits. Since these activities can be taught as either religious disciplines or stress-reducing (or weight-reducing) activities, and since they are frequently taught by "New Age" or Asian religious practitioners, some parents feel that their children's rights are violated when they are taught in public schools. At least one such complaint—where students were directed to perform *puja* (a form of Hindu worship) and learn mantras from their yoga teacher—seems to be valid. See *Malnak v. Yogi*, 592 F. 2nd 197 (1979).

49. One possibility is that it will lend ballast to the claims of conservatives that secular humanism is an established religion. Putative evidence for such establishment is located in court decisions and government policies that refuse to view religious symbols as inherently religious. See Graham Walker, "Illusory Pluralism, Inexorable Establishment," in *Obligations of Citizenship*, edited by Rosenblum, 111–36.

50. Kent Greenawalt, "Five Questions about Religion Judges Are Afraid to Ask," in *Obligations of Citizenship*, edited by Rosenblum, 197.

51. See, e.g., Catharine Cookson's discussion of the four models of religion used by courts in Free Exercise cases, derived almost exclusively from Christian (especially Protestant) theology in *Regulating Religion: The Courts and Free Exercise* (New York: Oxford University Press, 2001); Winnifred Sullivan's close reading of the "narrow" Protestant-

inflected conceptions of religion in Establishment decisions in *Paying the Words Extra: Religious Discourse in the Supreme Court of the United States* (Cambridge: Harvard Center for the Study of World Religions, 1994); Michael J. Sandel's related argument that the courts often incorrectly view religion as a "choice" rather than a "duty" in "Freedom of Conscience or Freedom of Choice?" in *Articles of Faith, Articles of Peace: The Religious Liberty Clauses and the American Public Philosophy*, edited by James Davison Hunter and Os Guinness (Washington, D.C.: Brookings Institution, 1990), 74–92.

52. See, e.g., J. S. Mill, *On Liberty* (Indianapolis: Hackett, 1978), esp. 53–57, 82–83, 87–91.

53. Martha C. Nussbaum, "Religion and Women's Equality," in *Obligations of Citizenship*, edited by Rosenblum, 348.

54. Greenawalt, "Five Questions," 227.

55. Sandel, "Freedom of Conscience." Sandel places a finer point on it when he argues that "what is denied" to the liberal, unencumbered chooser "is the possibility of membership in any community bound by moral ties antecedent to choice; he cannot belong to any community where the self itself could be at stake" (76).

56. *Torcaso v. Watkins*, 367 U.S. 488 (1961); *Welsh v. United States*, 398 U.S. 333 (1970).

57. Jesse Choper, "Note: Toward a Constitutional Definition of Religion," *Harvard Law Review* 91.5 (March 1978): 1056; Greenawalt, "Religion as a Concept."

58. William James, *Varieties of Religious Experience* (New York: Penguin, 1982).

59. *Africa v. Pennsylvania*, 662 F. 2nd 1025 (1981); *Hernandez v. Commissioner*, 490 S. Ct. 680 (1989).

60. Winnifred Sullivan states, "Whereas, as Durkheim and others observed, it is in the nature of the human religious imagination to distinguish between the sacred and the profane, legislating on the basis of that perception is extremely difficult because of the shifting and fertile nature of religion. The structural possibilities of the coexistence of a secular state and of human religion in a situation of radical pluralism—plural religious and legal traditions, plural experience of those readings—are not obvious" (*Paying the Words Extra*, 44–45).

61. *ISKCON v. Barber*, 650 F. 2nd 430, 439 (1982), cert. denied.

62. Ibid., 447.

63. *ISKCON v. Houston*, 689 F. 2nd 541, 553 (1982).

64. Ibid., 545.

65. Compare *Heffron v. ISKCON*, 452 U.S. 640 (1981).

66. *Elk Grove v. Newdow*, 542 U.S. 1 (2004).

10

Agonistic Federalism

The Alabama Ten Commandments Controversy

The controversy over the installation (and subsequent removal) of a 2.5-ton granite monument of the Ten Commandments in the rotunda of the Alabama State Judicial Building has elicited arguments from around the country and across the political spectrum. Much of the public discussion on this issue is distinguished by its loudness, stridency, and sharp partisanship. Substantive political issues have received short shrift amid a plethora of emotional calls to arms. In this chapter, I set out these substantive political issues and propose a remedy not simply to the Alabama Ten Commandments monument controversy but to the larger issue of public recognition of shared values in a pluralistic society.

The United States has from the beginning enjoyed a rich tradition of religious diversity. Increasingly, however, traditional liberal interpretations of the First Amendment's religion clauses have proven inadequate for the task of resolving issues regarding public recognition of moral and religious values.[1] This inadequacy stems from the traditional liberal bifurcation between public secularity and private religiosity. That is, the logic of the traditional liberal reading of the First Amendment's religion clauses produces a public square naked of religion. Such an approach lacks the capacity to address shared values through political channels: traditional liberalism evades the problem of recognition by promoting a policy of equal exclusion.

Many traditional liberals argue that perfectly valid reasons exist for a public square shorn of religiosity. Foremost is the First Amendment to the U.S. Constitution, which by this view expressly prohibits public recognition of the kind epitomized by the Ten Commandments monument. The Alabama monument does not exactly establish religion but does endorse it, and the perception of endorsement is sufficient for the monument to founder on the shoals of First Amendment jurisprudence.[2] Without these constitutional protections, traditional liberals protest, religious majorities would overwhelm and dominate religious minorities. Religious freedom would atrophy.

Traditional liberals often cite the fact of religious diversity as a warrant for maintaining a "high and impregnable" wall separating church and state.[3] Constitutional protections for religious freedom differ from ordinary law precisely because they are not open to the vicissitudes of political compromise. Constitutional rights, in other words, are those freedoms that have been removed entirely from the give-and-take of politics. Hence it is the constitutional duty of the federal courts to guard against all instances of establishment, of endorsement, and of interference with an individual's free exercise of religion by governments of all stripes—federal, state, and local. In the words of religious studies scholar Diana L. Eck, the "one vital area of America's new pluralism is the courts."[4] Indeed, many traditional liberals (as well as their conservative opponents) see the courts—not a deliberative body such as the legislature—as the central political institution.[5] (One could say that the American culture wars consist largely of conflicts waged through the courts over which rights and liberties are to be removed from political deliberation.)

Traditional liberals claim that the flourishing of religious diversity depends on the courts' ability to maintain a stout wall of separation. In practice, this wall separates an increasingly abstract, universal concept of religious freedom from all particular vestiges of lived religion. The wall can be viewed as a metaphor for the liberal state itself, a neutral, disinterested framework of universal political institutions. Many critics of traditional liberalism (most notably John Gray) have observed that a fundamental contradiction lies at the heart of this project. The deep diversity of American public life is cited as a warrant for purging the concept of religious freedom of all traces of religion itself, lest the concept be compromised by implicitly favoring one religion or one set of religions. But this concept is not itself neutral or disinterested: it is robustly secular. While secular is clearly synonymous with nonreligious, it is not at all reducible to neutral disinterest. This point can be stated differently: the traditional liberal concept of religious freedom is comprehensive in the same way that an explicitly Christian or Buddhist concept of religious freedom might be. It advances a substantive conception of the good; it is part and parcel of a comprehensive way of life.

The attempt to isolate a theoretical principle or right of religious freedom is part of the larger traditional liberal project: to specify once and for all a set of basic rights and liberties that are to be removed entirely from the political process. In carrying out this program, traditional liberals are advancing their own comprehensive conception of the good. They do so, however, under the guise of neutrality or disinterestedness. Here we come to the contradiction. Traditional liberals claim neutral disinterest for their conception of the good by arguing that no comprehensive conception of the good enjoys special authority, a claim endorsed by the fact of deep diversity. But this argument deprives the traditional liberal good of any claim to special authority. There is no warrant, in other words, for liberal government to promote or otherwise privilege liberal goods. That liberal government persists in doing so under the fiction of neutral disinterest can be attributed with charity to conceptual confusion. (Lacking charity, we might attribute it to cynicism and disingenuousness.)

The task of liberal government, according to these critics, is not the advancement of liberalism as a comprehensive good (and especially not under the fiction of disinterest) but promotion of a modus vivendi among people holding different, often conflicting, beliefs and values. This calls for a new style of politics that has been dubbed agonistic liberalism.[6] Political theorists describe agonistic politics as the ongoing clash of pluralities, a permanent contest among political actors lacking final settlement and punctuated only intermittently by brief periods of placid commonality. Sheldon S. Wolin describes this new style of politics: "Politics refers to the legitimized and public contestation, primarily by organized and unequal social powers, over access to the resources available to the public authorities of the collectivity. Politics is continuous, ceaseless, and endless."[7] Pluralism, Bonnie Honig argues, requires affirmation of "the inescapability of conflict and the ineradicability of resistance to the political and moral projects of ordering subjects, institutions, and values. . . . It is to give up on the dream of a place called home, a place free of power, conflict, and struggle."[8] Agonistic liberalism, in short, seeks to combine the advantages of commodious living with a provisional civil peace among rival and conflicting ways of life.

Agonistic-style politics, however, is often subjected to two criticisms. First, there is the persistent concern that diversity is in fact so diverse as to be divisive—that there exists a tipping point beyond which diversity crumbles into ungovernability. Second, the question is raised regarding the limit at which so-called competitive politics ceases to be fair and just and instead becomes "instances of fascism, xenophobic nationalism, and right-wing populism."[9] Benjamin Barber argues that these concerns are misplaced: "Democracy is self-correcting: its insufficiencies are corrected democratically rather than by the imposition of externalities on the democratic process. The process is dynamic because it is self-transforming: educative."[10] Seyla Benhabib builds on this argument by listing some of the self-correcting mechanisms of democracy: "the institutions of the Bill of Rights, constitutionalism, the interplay of the highest court of the land with the elected representatives of the people, processes of constitutional review, and the like."[11] Agonistic liberalism can thus be distinguished from closely related persuasions such as participatory democracy. While the latter remains vulnerable to certain excesses, such as majority tyranny (Barber's democratic sanguinity to the contrary), the former combines a greater role for democratic engagement with self-correcting mechanisms of the kind given by Benhabib. The result is the Tocquevillian ideal of moderate democracy.[12]

In this chapter, the Alabama Ten Commandments monument controversy serves as a case study in the application of agonistic-style politics to issues of public religious recognition. This approach is not entirely theoretical. A recent U.S. Supreme Court decision has opened the possibility for resolving issues of constitutionality relating to the public expression of shared religious values politically, through democratic processes, rather than leaving these controversial issues exclusively to the adjudication of the federal judiciary. This case, *Employment Division v. Smith* (1990), makes what I call a "federal opening" in the First Amendment religion clauses: the Court reserves the prerogative to enforce infractions of the religion clauses by federal as well as state governments but leaves open the possibility of positive recognition of shared religious values by state governments.[13] In other words, *Smith* makes possible agonistic religious accommodation—within carefully prescribed limits—by states. To demonstrate the applicability of *Smith* to the Alabama Ten Commandments monument, we must make two determinations. First, we must ascertain that the monument fits through the federal opening established by *Smith*. We will attempt to do so by developing a fictitious "Smith test." Second, we will evaluate the outcome of applying the Smithian federal opening to the Alabama monument controversy. What are the benefits of such an application? What are the possible complications or unintended consequences? We shall address these questions at the end of this essay.

Employment Division v. Smith involved two Native American counselors employed by a private drug rehabilitation center who were fired because they ingested peyote for sacramental purposes during a religious ceremony. The state of Oregon denied their application for unemployment compensation under a state law denying unemployment benefits to anyone discharged for "misconduct." The respondents in turn claimed that their First Amendment right to free exercise effectively voided Oregon's controlled substance law.

The relevant constitutional issue in *Smith* concerns whether the possible violation of First Amendment rights (in this case, free exercise) is sufficient to nullify generally applicable state law. Put differently, is the state of Oregon bound by the First Amendment to accommodate minority religious practices by allowing exceptions to otherwise generally applicable state law? Precedent for court action of this kind was established in *Sherbert v. Verner* (1963), when the Warren Court developed a "balancing test" for evaluating instances where government interest in enforcing general applicable laws conflicted with an individual's right to the free exercise of religion.[14] The Court ruled in *Sherbert* that the burden of proof fell on the government to show its compelling interest, finding that a Seventh-Day Adventist who was fired for refusing to work on Saturday (the day set aside by her faith for worship) was nevertheless eligible for unemployment benefits.

Critics denounced the *Sherbert* test then and later as an open-ended invitation for individuals to pick and choose which laws of the land to obey. A latter-day critic, Supreme Court Justice Antonin Scalia, writes in *Smith*,

> The government's ability to enforce generally applicable prohibitions of socially harmful conduct, like its ability to carry out other aspects of public policy, "cannot depend on measuring the effects of a governmental action on a religious objector's spiritual development." To make an individual's obligation to obey such a law contingent upon the law's coincidence with his religious beliefs, except where the State's interest is "compelling"—permitting him, by virtue of his beliefs, "to become a law unto himself"—contradicts both constitutional tradition and common sense.[15]

Scalia argues against interpreting the Free Exercise Clause as a categorical exemption for sincere believers of all stripes from generally applicable criminal law. He does so by distinguishing between government infringement on First Amendment freedoms and public recognition of those freedoms. Oregon's controlled substance law, because it is generally applicable, does not qualify as government infringement on First Amendment freedoms.

This is not to say, however, that the plaintiffs' argument (that the sacramental use of peyote should be evaluated differently from the recreational use of marijuana or crack cocaine) is rejected outright. Rather, Scalia argues that the enforcement of negative prohibitions against government encroachment is the constitutionally mandated responsibility of the Court. But political recognition of First Amendment freedoms, such as providing an exemption for the sacramental use of peyote, should be left to the democratic process. The people of the state of Oregon, not the U.S. Supreme Court, determine whether the sacramental use of peyote should be allowed as an exemption to state drug laws. (He cites Arizona, Colorado, and New Mexico as examples of states that have made similar exemptions.) Scalia thus concludes, "It may fairly be said that leaving accommodation to the political process will place at a relative disadvantage those religious practices that are not widely engaged in; but that unavoidable consequence of democratic government must be preferred to a system in which each conscience is a law unto itself or in which judges weigh the social importance of all laws against the centrality of all religious beliefs."[16]

In essence, the Court's decision federalizes *Sherbert* in part by leaving positive recognition of the freedoms enshrined in the Bill of Rights to the democratic process while preserving the federal judiciary's prerogative to enforce infractions of those freedoms by states as well as the federal government. Scalia's argument effectively divides jurisdiction of the religion clauses between the federal and state governments. Limiting the role of the federal judiciary to adjudication of possible First Amendment violations creates an opening for public recognition of shared religious values. Such recognition might take the form of granting exemptions, as the state of Arizona does, for example, in permitting the sacramental use of peyote. Other examples of public recognition include beginning legislative sessions with prayer (as the state of Nebraska does), invoking the "favor and guidance of Almighty God" (as found in the preamble to the Alabama State Constitution), and the widespread practice by state and federal elected officials of appending the phrase "so help me God" to their oaths of office.[17]

The relevant question for our interest here, of course, is whether the Alabama Ten Commandments monument could be considered an example of political recognition of the kind singled out in the *Smith* decision. We can make this determination by reference to a fictitious *Smith* test consisting of four criteria. First, public recognition must derive from the democratic political process rather than the court. Second, democratic recognition must be in accordance with some constitutional standard for religious freedom. In the kinds of cases addressed by the *Smith* tests, the relevant constitutional standard would be provided in nearly all cases by a particular state's constitution. Without any constitutional standard, of course, "religious freedom" would become a license for any democratic majority to impose its will without restriction. Third, recognition must be nonobligatory. It must either be cost-free (such as an exemption for the sacramental use of peyote) or paid for out of the largesse of private donors. Furthermore, it must not incur any coercive obligations, such as mandatory observance or affirmation. Fourth, public recognition must be nonsectarian. It should not be so narrowly construed as to recognize only a specific religious body, mode of worship, or religious doctrine.

Consider now the history of the Alabama Ten Commandments controversy.[18] By all accounts, the chief protagonist was Roy S. Moore, who was elected chief justice of the Alabama Supreme Court in November 2000 with 55 percent of the vote. Much of his campaign literature called him the "Ten Commandments Judge," referring to the hand-carved wooden plaque of the Ten Commandments he had displayed in his courtroom during his tenure as a circuit judge. And one of his oft-repeated campaign promises was to display the Ten Commandments in the Alabama Supreme Court.[19] Moore delivered on this promise on the night of July 31, 2001, when he supervised the installation of a 2.5-ton monument (referred to locally as "Roy's Rock") in the rotunda of the Alabama Judicial Building, which houses the Alabama Supreme Court, the Courts of Criminal and Civil Appeals, the state law library, and the Alabama Administrative Office of Courts. Moore did so without any prior approval by or knowledge of the Alabama Supreme Court's other eight justices. He was not under any obligation to include his colleagues on the bench in his decision, however, for under Alabama law the office of the chief justice is vested with final authority regarding what decorations may be placed in the rotunda.

In late October 2001, two lawsuits were filed in federal court against the chief justice.[20] The lawsuits were consolidated, and the trial commenced on October 15, 2002. On November 18, 2002, Judge Myron H. Thompson ruled that the Ten Commandments monument violated the Establishment Clause and gave Moore thirty days to remove the monument.[21] Moore refused. On December 19, therefore, the district court issued an injunction ordering him to remove the monument by January 3, 2003. The chief justice then filed a notice of appeal, requesting that the court stay or suspend the injunction while the case was pending on appeal. This request was granted on December 23.

The Eleventh Circuit of the U.S. Court of Appeals affirmed the district court's ruling on July 1, 2003.[22] On August 5, the District Court lifted the suspension of the December 19 injunction and ordered Moore to remove the monument no later than August 20. Moore then requested on August 15 that the district court stay its August 5 injunction. This request was declined on August 18, setting up a final confrontation between the chief justice and Judge Thompson. On August 20, the final day of the injunction, Moore filed a motion to recall and stay the mandate with the U.S. Supreme Court, which denied the application the same day. The following day, Moore's eight colleagues on the Alabama Supreme Court voted unanimously to reverse the administrative decision of the chief justice with respect to the district court's injunction and ordered the building manager to have the monument removed "as soon as practicable."[23] Moore announced on August 22 that he would not attempt to block removal of the monument.

On the same day, Stephen R. Glassroth and Melinda Maddox, two of the plaintiffs who filed the original suit against the monument, entered a formal compliant with the state's judicial board.[24] They charged Moore with failure "to respect and comply with the law," failure "to comply with an existing and binding court order directed at him," failure "to observe high standards of conduct," and failure "to avoid impropriety and the appearance of impropriety in his activities." Moore was at that time suspended without pay. His case went before the state's nine-member Court of the Judiciary, which voted unanimously on November 13, 2003, to remove Moore from the bench. As for the Ten Commandments monument, workers removed it from the rotunda and placed it in a storage room at the Judiciary Building on August 27.

With regard to the first Smith test—that public recognition must derive from the political process—the evidence in this case is mixed. In his trial defense, Moore argued that he acted within the constitutional limits of his office. The office of chief justice is responsible for the administration of the state court system, including any and all decorations placed in the rotunda of the Alabama Judicial Building. Moore had argued that the decision to install the monument was administrative and thus was not open to the political process or court review. The Court of Appeals rejected this argument, noting that "if we adopted his position, the Chief Justice would be free to adorn the walls of the Alabama's Supreme Court's courtroom with sectarian religious murals and have decidedly religious quotations painted above the bench. Every government building could be topped with a cross, or a menorah, or a statue of Buddha, depending upon the views of the officials with authority over the premises."[25]

No one, presumably not even the chief justice, would argue that the monument is only decorative. To do so obscures the popular warrant for Moore's actions. His decision to install a monument to the Ten Commandments was not arbitrary. Moore campaigned on a pledge to do so. In fact, owing to the administrative responsibilities held by the office of chief justice, such a campaign promise would likely not be construed by the electorate as mere rhetorical grandstanding. Moore was not elected to erect a Latin cross or a menorah. He was elected on his promise to display the Ten Commandments. The people of Alabama endorsed that promise in electing the Ten Commandments Judge by majority vote. Hence, we can say that the decision to recognize the moral values of the people of Alabama by the installation of a monument to the Ten Commandments originated democratically, with the people of Alabama, even if the details of that decision were left to the discretion of the official elected to carry out that decision. The first of the four fictitious Smith tests has been met.

The need for the second test—for democratic recognition to be bound by some constitutional standard—speaks to concerns about Moore's use of the discretionary powers of his office. What if, we might ask, Moore campaigned on the promise to install a Latin cross on the roof of the Judiciary Building and the people of Alabama elected him by an overwhelming margin? If Moore's discretionary power allows equally for a monument to the Ten Commandments, a Latin cross, or a menorah, and if he was popularly elected on a campaign promise to install a Latin cross or a menorah, would he be able to do so? The answer is no. Even if political recognition is left to state governments, they are bound nevertheless by their state constitutions. Section 3 of the Alabama State Constitution, subtitled "Religious Freedom," reads,

> That no religion shall be established by law; that no preference shall be given by law to any religious sect, society, denomination or mode of worship; that no one shall be compelled by law to attend any place of worship; nor to pay any tithes, taxes, or other rate for building or repairing any place of worship, or for maintaining any minister or ministry; that no religious test shall be required as a qualification to any office or public trust under this state; and that the civil rights, privileges, and capacities of any citizen shall not be in any manner affected by his religious principles.

Thus, we can say provisionally that the Ten Commandments monument meets the requirements of the second Smith test insofar as it is not simply an act of the majority. What remains to be seen, of course, is whether the monument violates the standards provided by section 3 of the Alabama State Constitution.

This question requires that we first clarify the distinction between establishment and endorsement or preference. We shall return to this question following our discussion of the third and fourth *Smith* tests.

The third *Smith* test requires that public recognition not impose financial or any other coercive obligations on citizens, such as mandatory observance and/or affirmation. This in effect reaffirms the long-standing constitutional prohibition against establishment. To take the sacramental use of peyote as an example, a state might grant an exemption to existing state drug laws, but in doing so it incurs no obligation to furnish worshipers with peyote, to provide a place where sacramental use might take place, to maintain a spiritual leader of some kind, and so forth. Likewise, the Ten Commandments monument itself was paid for by the chief justice. Coral Ridge Ministries, an evangelical Christian organization with which Moore had enjoyed a long-standing relationship, defrayed the costs of the monument's installation. The presence of the monument in the rotunda did not obligate anyone, for example, to stop beside it and silently reflect or pray, even though it quickly became an area where employees and visitors to the Judicial Building chose to pursue these activities. The Ten Commandments monument, to echo Thomas Jefferson, neither picked anyone's pocket nor broke anyone's leg. If narrowly construed in this way, the monument passes the third of the four *Smith* tests.

With regard to the fourth *Smith* test (that is, public recognition must be nonsectarian), the monument would appear to pass as well, since the Ten Commandments embraces a plurality of religious traditions.[26] Hence, the monument would seem not to establish, endorse, or otherwise favor any particular religious sect.

Or does it? Both federal court decisions ruled that the Ten Commandments monument indeed violated the First Amendment's Establishment Clause. Both decisions appealed to the ideal of religious pluralism, citing the "history and tradition of religious diversity" in America, as warrant for the First Amendment's religion clauses.[27] Judge Thompson, in his decision for the District Court, emphasized that "the First Amendment does not elevate one religion above all others, but rather it places all religions on par with one another, and even recognizes the equality of religion and non-religion."[28] It does so by the mechanism of separation. The idea of separation was given its imprimatur by Justice Hugo Black in *Everson v. Board of Education* (1947):

> Neither a state nor the Federal Government can set up a church. Neither can pass laws which aid one religion, aid all religions, or prefer one reli-

gion over another. Neither can force nor influence a person to go to or to remain away from church against his will or force him to profess a belief or disbelief in any religion. No person can be punished for entertaining or professing religious beliefs or disbeliefs, for church attendance or non-attendance. No tax in any amount, large or small, can be levied to support any religious activities or institutions, whatever they may be called, or whatever from they may adopt to teach or practice religion. Neither a state nor the Federal Government can, openly or secretly, participate in the affairs of any religious organizations or groups or vice versa.[29]

The idea of separation ultimately bedevils nearly all contemporary interpretations of the religion clauses of the First Amendment.[30] Separation, in this view, is the legal practice of religious freedom.

There remains a certain opacity shrouding the contemporary idea of separation. Much of it, as noted earlier, can be attributed to the universal presumptions of traditional liberalism. Separation erects an impregnable wall that partitions an abstract, universal religious freedom from all particular instances of actual religion. Religious freedom, in other words, is uncontaminated by anything religious. Yet this leaves religious freedom without a clearly delimited object ("religion"). Such was not always the case. At the time of the passage of the Bill of Rights, the definition of "religion" provided by James Madison in his well-known "Memorial and Remonstrance against Religious Assessment"—"the duty we owe our Creator and the manner of discharging it"—commonly served as the constitutional standard for religion.[31] As late as 1931, this definition was affirmed by Chief Justice Charles E. Hughes in his dissent in *United States v. McIntosh*, where he defined religion as "belief in a relation to God involving duties superior to those arising from any human relation."[32] But, following *Everson*, the Court increasingly emptied "religion" of qualities and characteristics. *Torcaso v. Watkins* (1961) served to evacuate the Court's earlier definition of religion. In this decision, the Court discarded belief in the existence of God as a viable characteristic of religion.[33]

With the paucity of definitional criteria, the court began developing tests to detect the presence of religion. One of the first is provided in *United States v. Seeger* (1965), where the Court developed the test of "sincerity": "A sincere and meaningful belief which occupies in the life of its possessor a place parallel to that filled by the God of those admittedly qualifying comes within the statutory definition."[34] The most influential test, however, is found in *Lemon v. Kurtzman* (1971). Chief Justice Warren Burger, writing for the majority, broadly interprets the prohibition against establishment, arguing that "a given law might not establish a state religion but nevertheless be one 'respecting' that end in the sense of being a step that could lead to such establishment and hence offend the First Amendment."[35] Lacking "precisely stated constitutional prohibitions," the court must test possible violations with regard to three tests: "First, the statute must have a secular legislative purpose; second, its principal or primary effect must be one that neither advances nor inhibits religion; finally, the statute must not foster 'an excessive government entanglement with religion.' "[36] In effect, the Burger Court redefines "establishment" to include not only actual violations but also all actions that might possibly lead toward establishment.[37]

Judge Thompson, writing for the Circuit Court, argues that the Ten Commandments monument fails as an example of public recognition because, viewed alone or in the context of its history, placement, and location, the primary effect of the monument is the endorsement of religion—in other words, violation of the first and second prongs of the Lemon test. The plaintiffs contended that Chief Justice Moore's installation of the Ten Commandments monument deprived them of their rights of religious freedom (that is, Moore abridged religious freedom by the putative endorsement contained in the act of installing the monument), and thus they sought to rectify this injury by means of the monument's removal. Hence, according to the decision reached by the federal courts, the Alabama Ten Commandments monument fails as an example of public recognition of moral values because it endorses religion and thus violates the Establishment Clause. Since we had earlier reached the tentative conclusion that the monument in fact succeeded as an example of public recognition according to the fictitious Smith test, we should be able to account for the court's decision in terms of the Smith test. If we are unable to do so, then we must conclude that either the court's decision is correct and our application of the Smith test is flawed (for example, based on faulty legal reasoning) or the Smith test itself as we have developed it here is insufficient and thus should be revised or discarded.

Consider again the third Smith test (public recognition must not impose financial or any other coercive obligation on citizens, such as mandatory observance and/or affirmation). The monument, as noted earlier, did not incur any positive obligations. No government funds were used for its construction or installation. Employees and visitors to the Judicial Building were free to stop at the monument and silently reflect or pray. They were equally free to ignore the monument and walk on by.

But the three plaintiffs did not argue that the monument imposed direct or positive obligations. All testified that they found the monument "offensive," they felt like "outsiders" because of the monument, and their "use and enjoyment" of the rotunda had significantly decreased because of the monument.[38] (Two of the three plaintiffs—all three are attorneys who for professional reasons regularly use the Judicial Building—testified that they had changed their behavior because of the monument, deliberately avoiding the rotunda when possible because of the monument's presence.) In other words, the three plaintiffs testified that the monument evoked unpleasant subjective attitudes —feelings of being offended, being excluded, and being uncomfortable while in the rotunda—that could be objectively discerned in their behavior (for example, physical avoidance of the rotunda, purchase of books and other resources to avoid using the library, and so forth).

These subjective attitudes suffered by the plaintiffs we can understand in terms of a negative coercive obligation. Had the state, in the figure of the chief justice, not installed the monument, the three plaintiffs would have been spared feelings of offense, exclusion, and discomfort arising from the monument's presence. One could even say that a negative coercive obligation (in the language of the third Smith test) represents a perceived endorsement of religion, and thus our earlier provisional conclusion that the monument passed as an example of public recognition should be revised in light of this new subjective criterion. The question that we must now address is whether the perception of a negative coercive obligation suffices for the purpose of finding the monument unconstitutional.

There are two problems with answering this question affirmatively. First, one of the long-standing criticisms of the Lemon test is that the standard of "endorsement" is premised on the court's ability to discern subjective attitudes. As Courtney Bender and Jennifer Snow note in their chapter in this book, the court often does so by means of the "reasonable observer" standard, asking whether a reasonable observer would perceive a given government action as endorsing religion. Criteria for a reasonable observer have been the focus of sharp judicial dispute. For example, Justice Sandra Day O'Connor describes the "reasonable observer" as someone "aware of the history and context of the community and forum in which the religious display appears," while Justice John Paul Stevens holds the reasonable observer to be any reasonable person without necessarily possessing any knowledge of the community where the disputed practice occurs.[39]

In a sharp dissenting opinion, Scalia derides both constructions of the reasonable observer's perception of endorsement. In *Lamb's Chapel v. Union Free School District*, the Court had analyzed endorsement in terms of "what would be thought by 'the community'—not by outsiders or [uninformed] individual members of the community [who] might leap to the erroneous conclusion of state endorsement."[40] Scalia's remark represents an advance on the endorsement test: the community, rather than outsiders or the uninformed, constitutes the standard for calibrating endorsement. This approach, however, does not address what is most problematic about any endorsement test: its reliance on subjective attitudes (especially as they take the place of "precisely stated constitutional prohibitions"), be they individual or communal, and the presumption that the court is competent to discern them.[41] This shortcoming becomes problematic when genuine issues of constitutionality become enmeshed in the idiosyncratic attitudes of those who might—out of malice, ignorance, or deliberate provocation—misconstrue particular public displays, utterances, or actions. The court, in other words, while it can detect instances of perceived endorsement, lacks any certain means of evaluating those perceptions for accuracy and genuineness.

Second, we recall the second *Smith* test (that is, public recognition is not simply decided by majority rule but is bound by some constitutional standard, and this standard is generally though not always provided by a particular state's constitution). In the case of the Ten Commandments monument, the relevant constitutional standard would be section 3 of the Alabama State Constitution, not the First Amendment's religion clauses.[42] The protections afforded religious freedom in section 3 generally mirror those provided in the First Amendment. The prohibitions described in section 3, however, are more detailed than in the First Amendment. "Establishment," for example, is unequivocally prohibited in both. Unlike the First Amendment, however, section 3 also addresses explicitly the idea of "preference" or "endorsement." Endorsement of "any religious sect, society, denomination, or mode of worship" is prohibited. This is an important distinction. Unlike the *Lemon* test, which extends endorsement to the perception of religion in general, section 3 limits endorsement to those acts of government extending official preference to particular religious bodies. Put differently, the *Lemon* test excludes certain ideas merely because they are religious; it is an ideological test. Section 3 allows for official recognition of religious ideas as long as those ideas are not the exclusive province of any one religious body. So, section 3 would clearly prohibit the display of a Latin cross or a menorah in the rotunda of the state Judicial Building because both are unambiguous symbols of particular religious traditions. But the Ten Commandments monument would not be prohibited under section 3 because, as already noted, the Ten Commandments are embraced by a plurality of religious traditions.

Therefore, the Ten Commandments monument passes the Smith tests as a constitutional example of public recognition. It does so in large part as a consequence of the fact that section 3 of the Alabama State Constitution, with its precisely stated prohibitions against endorsement, provides a clearer constitutional standard than the First Amendment's Establishment Clause and the imprecise guidelines for endorsement provided by the Lemon tests. The Ten Commandments monument, in other words, fits through the federal opening made by Smith.

Now we are in a position to consider the possible advantages and disadvantages of such an application. The principal disadvantage of this proposal is that it increases the risk that religious majorities might dominate religious minorities by appropriating the instruments of government to recognize publicly the majorities' symbols, values, and way of life. Religious minorities, furthermore, risk being placed at a "relative disadvantage" with regard to recognition of their symbols, beliefs, and ways of life (to quote Scalia), owing to their small numbers. Application of the Smith test, therefore, might inflame political passions by tilting the playing field in favor of religious majorities. Such a proposal would be unfair; indeed, insofar as it would putatively increase rather than decrease inequality, it can be said to lead outside of the American political tradition altogether.[43]

Some participants in the Ten Commandments monument controversy no doubt encouraged such dark predictions. Although a majority of Alabama's voters supported the Ten Commandments Judge, many supporters were undoubtedly discomforted by the covert midnight installation of the monument and the highly visible role played by Coral Ridge Ministries. Moore, furthermore, seemed to go out of his way to antagonize potential allies. In 2001, for example, he rejected out of hand a request by black lawmakers to place a monument to Martin Luther King Jr. in the rotunda. In his reply to State Representative Alvin Holmes, Moore wrote, "The placement of a speech of any man alongside the revealed law of God would tend in consequence to diminish the very purpose of the Ten Commandments monument."[44] He alienated more supporters during his trial when he claimed complete authority for his decision to install the monument by virtue of the powers of his office, reminding more than one observer of former Alabama Governor George Wallace's defiant attempt to resist federal desegregation orders in

1963.[45] Moore, intentionally or not, succeeded in making the controversy personal: the political and constitutional merits of public recognition of shared religious and moral values were subordinated to the Christian witness and professional martyrdom of Roy S. Moore. Yet the political psychology of the chief justice is ultimately incidental to this investigation. Even if Moore was a bad man acting for the wrong reasons, that does not necessarily mean that his actions did not warrant a fair hearing.

There are three possible advantages offered by a Smith-mediated resolution to this controversy. The first is that it restores what could be called a federal proportion to the First Amendment religion clauses. Rather than imposing a one-size-fits-all interpretation for all cases, recourse to state constitutions allows for a plurality of solutions. Issues regarding public recognition of shared religious and moral values would be decided differently in, for example, Alabama and California. Not only would schemes of public recognition possibly differ, but the actual content of those shared values might differ too. The second advantage is a practical correlation of the first. An agonistic federalist settlement would release to some degree the political pressures characteristic of culture conflict. Controversies of this kind would be opened —and would remain open—to the political process. Furthermore, the actions of one state would not impose coercive obligations on any other state. Agonistic politics, paradoxically, might ultimately moderate the political process by lowering the stakes of cultural conflict.

The third advantage is that constitutional protections would be detached from the universalizing tendencies of traditional liberalism. As noted at the beginning of this essay, pluralism is often cited as a warrant for traditional liberal institutions and practices. Yet pluralism does not stop at the courtroom door; pluralism deprives traditional liberalism of any special authority it might presume for itself. There is no compelling necessity, in other words, to argue in terms of a universal principle of religious freedom and an impregnable wall of separation. Traditional liberals should not delude themselves into thinking that they have solved the intractable problems engendered by the Protestant Reformation. Rather, they should aim more modestly at a modus vivendi among people holding different beliefs and values. Such a provisional settlement would be dynamic and open to future revision. Its lack of finality, however, should not be taken as a defect but as a strength. That there is ultimately no satisfactory Archimedean point whence all human beliefs and values can be leveled (and thus dealt with once and for all) is not a consequence of political inequality (and thus exasperated by the democratic process) but in all possibility is intrinsic to the human condition itself and therefore beyond the reach of political remedy.[46]

NOTES

1. By "traditional liberal," I mean someone who takes J. S. Mill as a distinguished forebear, John Rawls as a near contemporary, and Louis Hartz's *The Liberal Tradition in America* (New York: Harcourt, Brace, 1955) as "our" story. The rank and file of the American Civil Liberties Union, for example, is composed largely of traditional liberals.

2. The distinction between "establishment" and "endorsement" will be expounded later in the chapter.

3. Supreme Court Justice Hugo Black described the wall separating church and state as "high and impregnable" in *Everson v. Board of Education* (330 U.S. 1 [1947]). This influential Supreme Court decision enshrined in constitutional law Thomas Jefferson's metaphor of a wall separating church and state. Indeed, much First Amendment jurisprudence since *Everson* can be read as a long-running effort to clarify the terms of this separation. See Jo Renée Formicola and Hubert Morken, eds., *Everson Revisited: Religion, Education, and Law at the Crossroads* (Lanham, Md.: Rowman and Littlefield, 1997).

4. Diana L. Eck, *A New Religious America: How a "Christian Country" Has Become the World's Most Religiously Diverse Nation* (San Francisco: HarperSanFrancisco, 2001), 321.

5. For this reason (among others), John Gray sees traditional liberalism as a "species of anti-political legalism" (*Two Faces of Liberalism* [New York: New Press, 2000], 16).

6. For a superb introduction to agonistic liberalism, see John Gray, "Agonistic Liberalism" and "From Post-Liberalism to Pluralism," in Gray, *Enlightenment's Wake* (London: Routledge, 1995), 64–86, 131–43; John Gray, "Rawls's Anti-Political Liberalism," in Gray, *Endgames: Questions in Late Modern Political Thought* (Cambridge: Polity, 1997), 51–54; John Gray, "Postscript," in Gray, *Mill on Liberty: A Defence*, 2nd ed. (London: Routledge, 1996), 130–58; John Gray, *Isaiah Berlin* (Princeton: Princeton University Press, 1996); John Gray, "Berlin's Agonistic Liberalism" and "What Is Dead and What Is Living in Liberalism," in Gray, *Post-Liberalism: Studies in Political Thought* (London: Routledge, 1993), 64–69, 283–328; Gray, *Two Faces of Liberalism*.

7. Sheldon S. Wolin, "Fugitive Democracy," in *Democracy and Difference: Contesting the Boundaries of the Political*, edited by Seyla Benhabib (Princeton: Princeton University Press, 1996), 31.

8. Bonnie Honig, "Difference, Dilemmas, and the Politics of Home," in *Democracy and Difference*, edited by Benhabib, 258.

9. Seyla Benhabib, "The Democratic Moment and the Problem of Difference," in *Democracy and Difference*, edited by Benhabib, 8. Benhabib's examples are complemented in Richard J. Ellis, *The Dark Side of the Left: Illiberal Egalitarianism in America* (Lawrence: University Press of Kansas, 1998).

10. Benjamin R. Barber, "Foundationalism and Democracy," in *Democracy and Difference*, edited by Benhabib, 354.

11. Benhabib, "Democratic Moment," 9.

12. For discussion of this ideal, see Pierre Manent, *Tocqueville and the Nature of Democracy*, translated by John Waggoner (Lanham, Md.: Rowman and Littlefield, 1996).

13. *Employment Division v. Smith*, 494 U.S. 872 (1990).

14. *Sherbert v. Verner*, 374 U.S. 398 (1963).

15. *Employment Division v. Smith*, 885. Internal citations omitted.

16. Ibid., 890. The *Smith* decision was extremely controversial. In response to a barrage of criticism from traditional liberals and their conservative opponents alike, Congress passed the Religious Freedom Restoration Act (RFRA) in 1993. The RFRA putatively restored the balancing test articulated in *Sherbert*, which places the burden of proof on government to prove a compelling interest in cases where generally applicable laws infringe on the free exercise of religion. The Supreme Court, however, struck down RFRA in 1997 as an unconstitutional attempt to legislate the legal precedent set by *Sherbert*. In passing the RFRA, Congress had justified its actions by appealing to section 5 of the Fourteenth Amendment, which gives Congress the right to enforce through "appropriate legislation" the fundamental rights and liberties protected by that amendment. In striking down the RFRA in *Boerne v. Flores* (117 S. Ct. 2157 [1997]), the Court did not deny this constitutional role of Congress with regard to the Fourteenth Amendment; it found, however, that the "RFRA is so out of proportion to a supposed remedial or preventive object that it cannot be understood as responsive to, or designed to prevent, unconstitutional behavior" (2169). That is, rather than preventing unconstitutional activity, the RFRA was seen as an unwarranted, unconstitutional legislative attempt to make a "substantial change in constitutional protections" (2169), something that can be accomplished only by the amendment process.

17. See, for example, article 2, section 7, of the Constitution of Virginia: "All officers elected or appointed under or pursuant to this Constitution shall, before they enter on the performance of their public duties, severally take and subscribe the following oath or affirmation: 'I do solemnly swear (or affirm) that I will support the Constitution of the United States and the Constitution of the Commonwealth of Virginia, and that I will faithfully and impartially discharge all the duties incumbent upon me as [title of office], according to the best of my ability (so help me God).'" This practice harkens back to George Washington's first inauguration, where he added "so help me God" to his oath of office. Presidents and other elected officials have since followed Washington's example.

18. My account of the Alabama Ten Commandments controversy is indebted to Tom Baxter and Juanita Poe, "Ten Commandments Furor," *Atlanta Journal and Constitution*, August 23, 2003, 8A; Steve Benen, "Monumental Mistake," *Church and State* 54.11 (December 2001): 8–12; Steven Lubet, "Rule of Law," *Lynchburg (Virginia) News and Advance*, August 31, 2003, E1; Charlotte Moore, "Ten Commandments Furor: Q & A with John Witte Jr., Director of the Law and Religion Program at Emory University," *Atlanta Journal and Constitution*, August 23, 2003, 8A; Marvin Olasky, "Push Has Come to Shove," *World Magazine* 18.33 (August 30, 2003): 1; Bill Rankin and Juanita Poe, "Commandments Justice Outvoted," *Atlanta Journal and Constitution*, August 22, 2003, 1A; Jim Ringel, "Ten Commandments Symbol Passes Test," *Legal Intelligencer* 228 (June 4,

2003): 4; Manuel Roig-Franzia, "Alabama Judge Relents on Monument," *Washington Post*, August 24, 2003, A6; Manuel Roig-Franzia, "Two Tablets May Renew a High Court Headache," *Washington Post*, August 31, 2003, A3; Saul Singer, "Who's Afraid of the Ten Commandments?" *Jerusalem Post*, July 4, 2003, 8A.

19. In 1995, Moore began displaying a wooden plaque of the Ten Commandments and inviting clergy into his courtroom to lead prayer before trials. In March 1995, the ACLU of Alabama filed a lawsuit against Moore, which was later dismissed for lack of standing. The state of Alabama brought a second suit in April 1995 seeking a declaratory judgment that Moore's display of the Ten Commandments was constitutional. This suit was dismissed by the Alabama Supreme Court as "nonjusticiable," or incapable of being decided by legal principles.

20. The first was *Johnson v. Hobson*; the second was *Glassroth v. Moore*. "Hobson" in the first case refers to Rich Hobson, the administrative director of courts for the state of Alabama. He is second in the administrative hierarchy of the Alabama court system, answerable only to Chief Justice Moore, who was listed as co-defendant.

21. *Glassroth v. Moore*, 229 F. Supp. 2nd 1290 (M.D. Ala. 2002).

22. *Glassroth v. Moore*, 335 F. 3rd 1282 (11th Cir. 2003).

23. See "In the Matter of Compliance with Writ of Injunction of the United States District Court for the Middle District of Alabama," August 21, 2003, 7, <http://news.corporate.findlaw.com/hdocs/docs/religion/glsrthmre82103alsc.pdf>.

24. For the text of the complaint, see "Judicial Inquiry Commission of the State of Alabama" at 11, 13, In the Matter of Roy S. Moore (Ala. Ct. Judiciary Aug. 22, 2003) (No. 33), <http://www.judicial.state.al.us/documents/complaint.pdf>.

25. *Glassroth v. Moore*, 335 F. 3rd 1282, 1309 (11th Cir. 2003). A statue of the Buddha is not sectarian (at least if by sectarian one means confined to only one sect), as the Buddha is revered by Buddhists as well as by certain Hindu sects.

26. This plurality comprises Christianity, Judaism, and Islam. As an example of the latter, the Alabama House passed in March 2003 an amendment (which would have to be approved by voters in a statewide referendum) to allow the posting of the Ten Commandments in public school classrooms across the state. In the floor debate, Representative Yusuf Salaam, a Democrat from Selma and a Muslim, supported displaying the Ten Commandments, declaring that they "were revealed to Moses by the followers of Judaism. The Islamic faith does not have a problem with the Ten Commandments" (Bob Johnson, "House Passes Amendment to Allow Ten Commandments in Schools," Associated Press State and Local Wire, March 11, 2003).

27. The phrase "history and tradition of religious diversity" repeats the formulation given in the Supreme Court decision *Allegheny v. ACLU* (492 U.S. 573, 589 [1989]), which contended that the Bill of Rights was appended to the Constitution "precisely because of the religious diversity that is our national heritage."

28. *Glassroth v. Moore*, 229 F. Supp. 2d 1290, 1343 (M.D. Ala. 2002).

29. *Everson v. Board of Education*, 11.

30. Much First Amendment jurisprudence regarding religion seeks to clarify the terms of separation. Two broad interpretive models developed in *Everson's* wake: neutrality (sometimes called strict separation) and accommodation. According to the

former, government must be held strictly to the standard of neutrality with respect to all public expressions of religion. According to the latter, the Constitution only prohibits bestowing official favor or privilege upon a particular church or sect in such a way that would compromise free exercise by believers of other faiths. From this second perspective, legal rulings on religion should strive for accommodation, or equal opportunity, rather than neutrality. "Accommodation" refers specifically to the position of Justice William Rehnquist in his dissent in *Wallace v. Jaffree* (472 U.S. 38 [1985]): "The Establishment Clause did not require government neutrality between religion and irreligion nor did it prohibit the Federal Government from providing nondiscriminatory aid to religion. There is simply no historical foundation for the proposition that the Framers intended to build the 'wall of separation' that was constitutionalized in *Everson*" (106).

31. James Madison, "Memorial and Remonstrance against Religious Assessment," in *The Papers of James Madison*, edited by Robert A. Rutland and William M. E. Rachal (Chicago: University of Chicago Press, 1973), 8:299. This commonly accepted definition was officially affirmed in *Davis v. Beason* (133 U.S. 333 [1890]): religion consists in "one's views of his relations to his Creator, and to the obligations they impose of reverence for his being and character, and of obedience to his will" (342).

32. *United States v. McIntosh*, 283 U.S. 605, 633–34 (1931).

33. *Torcaso v. Watkins*, 367 U.S. 488, 495 (1961).

34. *United States v. Seeger*, 380 U.S. 163, 176 (1965).

35. *Lemon v. Kurtzman*, 403 U.S. 602, 612 (1971).

36. Ibid., 612–13. The tests developed in *Lemon* were crafted in light of *Walz v. Tax Commission* (397 U.S. 664 [1970]), which held that the Establishment Clause, broadly interpreted, prohibited three discrete categories of action: "sponsorship, financial support, and active involvement of the sovereign in religious activity" (668).

37. The idea of "possible establishment" was clarified in terms of "endorsement." The Supreme Court has defined "endorsement" in terms of "conveying or attempting to convey a message that religion or a particular religious belief is favored or preferred" (*Wallace v. Jaffree*, 70).

38. *Glassroth v. Moore*, 229 F. Supp. 2d 1290, 1304 (M.D. Ala. 2002).

39. *Capital Square Review and Advisory Board v. Pinette*, 515 U.S. 753, 779–80, 800 (1995); *Lamb's Chapel v. Union Free School District*, 508 U.S. 384 (1993).

40. *Capital Square Review and Advisory Board v. Pinette*, 765.

41. *Lemon v. Kurtzman*, 612. By making the subjective attitude of the community prior to that of outsiders or the uninformed, Scalia has only relocated rather than resolved the fundamental problem of the endorsement test.

42. Finally we cash in the promissory note left earlier in this essay to consider whether the monument violates the standards provided by section 3 of the Alabama State Constitution.

43. Many traditional liberals hold that equality—first pronounced by Thomas Jefferson in the Declaration of Independence ("We hold these truths to be self-evident, that all men are created equal") and brought to fruition by Abraham Lincoln—is the core American principle. For Lincoln, who called equality an "apple of gold" and the

Constitution a "picture of silver" (*The Collected Works of Abraham Lincoln*, edited by Roy P. Basler [New Brunswick, N.J.: Rutgers University Press, 1953], 4:169), the great purpose of American government was to extend to all persons the practical benefits of this principle. In other words, Lincoln held unabashedly to the political faith that government must and should advance a comprehensive conception of the good, and he did so without reliance on the fiction of disinterested neutrality. This interpretation of Lincoln is not exclusive to traditional liberals. Some conservative critics make a similar argument. See, e.g., Harry V. Jaffa: "Equality as a Conservative Principle," in Jaffa, *How to Think about the American Revolution* (Durham, N.C.: Carolina Academic Press, 1978), 13–48; Harry V. Jaffa, *A New Birth of Freedom: Abraham Lincoln and the Coming of the Civil War* (Lanham, Md.: Rowman and Littlefield, 2000).

44. Stan Bailey, "Moore Says No to King Monument; Chief Justice Plans to Install a Plaque at Own Expense," *Birmingham News*, September 28, 2001.

45. Baxter and Poe, "Ten Commandments Furor," 8A.

46. This assertion should be taken in the spirit of Isaiah Berlin's conclusion to his celebrated essay "Two Concepts of Liberty": "To demand [an ideal of freedom lacking eternal validity] is perhaps a deep and incurable metaphysical need; but to allow it to determine one's practice is a symptom of an equally deep, and more dangerous, moral and political immaturity" (*Four Essays on Liberty* [New York: Oxford University Press, 1969], 172). This position does not entail relativism. See Adam B. Seligman, *Modest Claims: Dialogues and Essays on Tolerance and Tradition* (Notre Dame, Ind.: University of Notre Dame Press, 2004).

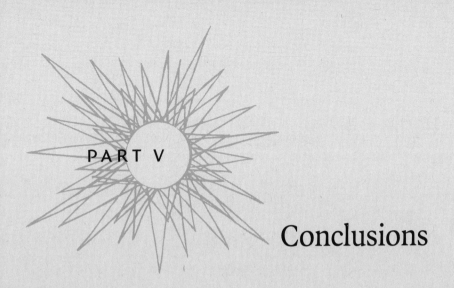

PART V

Conclusions

The De-Europeanization of American Christianity

Christianity is not the property of Europeans: it is a world religion. I learned this lesson unforgettably in 1994 when the fellows of the New Ethnic and Immigrant Congregations Project (NEICP) convened in Chicago for a six-week seminar on ethnographic methods in congregational study that led off the project.[1] I made a point of apologizing to the fellows for the Eurocentrism of the syllabus of readings, one heavily focused on studies of Christian churches. I explained that sociological ethnographies of religious communities to date had been produced primarily in the United States. Part of the goal of the NEICP, I said, was to extend that literature beyond its Eurocentric base. Sheba George, an Indian-born, American-raised sociologist from Berkeley, objected to my phrasing this apology in terms of "Eurocentrism," letting me know that her ancestors had probably been Christian far longer than mine. Legend holds that Christianity came to her Indian homeland of Kerala in the first century C.E., and history confirms that it has been there for at least sixteen hundred years; much of northern Europe, where my grandfather came from, was not Christianized until a thousand or even (as in the case of Lithuania) six hundred years ago.[2] The Keralites are one of many indigenous Christian communities all over the world. Even where non-European Christianity stems historically from European or North American missions (as in Mexico, the Philippines, and sub-Saharan Africa), many indigenous populations have long since taken over the missions and made them their own. But even today, a college religion course with proportionate attention paid to Christian communities is unlikely to earn its students "diversity" or "world culture" degree credit. With a mixture of arrogance and exasperation, white Americans still tend to claim Christianity as their property, even when many of them wish they could disown it.

A shorter version of this essay appeared earlier as R. Stephen Warner, "Coming to America," *Christian Century* 121.3 (February 10, 2004): 20–23. Copyright 2004 Christian Century. Reprinted by permission. Subscriptions: $49/yr. from P.O. Box 378, Mt. Morris, IL 61054; 1-800-208-4097.

One consequence of the new, post-1965 immigration will surely be that white Americans will come to see that Christianity is neither theirs nor their European ancestors' alone.[3] New immigrants of myriad races and national origins are now practicing their Christianities on these shores.[4]

I will develop this argument in four parts, beginning with (1) a sketch of the religious demography of post-1965 immigrants before (2) describing a few Christian communities established by these immigrants in the United States. I will then (3) explicate dynamic processes endemic to these communities that portend change over the next several decades before (4) concluding by considering what these facts about Christians of non-European origin might mean for American public life.

Despite being overwhelmingly (about 85 percent) non-European, at least two-thirds of post-1965 immigrants are Christian.[5] There are several reasons why such is the case. Many new immigrants come from historically Christian countries, such as Mexico, the Dominican Republic, Jamaica, Haiti, Guatemala, El Salvador, and the Philippines. More new immigrants come from Mexico than from any other country (it is the largest sending country), and Mexico's population is overwhelmingly Christian. To take an Asian example, according to the 1990 census, the population of the Philippine Republic was 83 percent Catholic, 5.5 percent Protestant, and 4.5 percent Muslim, with the remainder affiliated with Buddhist and indigenous Christian movements.[6] Filipinos are the second-largest Asian-origin group (after Chinese) in the United States. Few countries where religions other than Christianity predominate are among the top sending countries (a few exceptions are Taiwan, India, and Pakistan).

Many immigrants come disproportionately from Christian segments of religiously mixed countries—for example, Korea, Vietnam, India, Lebanon, Jordan, and Palestine. Although these are not majority-Christian countries, those who leave them for the United States are either mostly Christian (in the cases of Korea and Vietnam) or disproportionately Christian (in the cases of India and the Levant). The population of India, for example, is about 2 percent Christian, but 10 percent of Indians in America likely are Christian.[7] Similarly, Muslims are overrepresented among Indian immigrants, while Hindus are underrepresented. The general principle is that migration is not random with respect to religion.[8]

Some immigrants come from countries with rapidly growing Christian movements—for example, such sub-Saharan African countries as Nigeria, Ghana, and Congo. As the world's South turns Christian, many immigrants from these regions bring with them the enthusiastic faith of new converts.[9] Thus, America's cities have many new African Protestant congregations, and other African immigrants worship in Episcopal congregations.[10]

Most of those Europeans and white North Americans who are numbered among the new immigrants (for example, Poles, Irish, British, and Canadians) are Christian, although they range from the more pious (Poles) to the less (British). Many immigrants from the former Soviet Union are Jewish, and even more claim no religion. But Soviet-origin immigrants to the United States who are Jewish may be outnumbered by those who are Orthodox Christians.[11]

Many of those who come with no religious identity (for example, from officially atheistic states like China and the former Soviet Union) convert to Christianity soon after coming to the United States. It has been estimated that about one-third of Chinese in America are Christian, and many have become so very recently.[12]

Immigration is also biased in favor of Christians through the marriage provisions of U.S. immigration policy. Those who enter the United States on visas set aside for spouses of U.S. citizens are likely to be religiously similar to their sponsors; U.S. women in particular seem to be biased toward Catholic immigrant husbands.[13]

For these and other reasons, when one multiplies individuals' religious identities by the numbers of immigrants coming from the various countries, we would expect the product to yield very large numbers of Christians among post-1965 immigrants in the United States. The trouble is that hard data are scarce, which is one reason why claims about the size of minority religious groups vary so widely. U.S. government agencies, including the Census Bureau and the Immigration and Naturalization Service, may not collect data on individuals' religion. Academic and commercial social surveys that do a good job of predicting the presidential vote every four years do not work well for estimating numbers of people who constitute, as most immigrant groups do, small proportions of the overall population. A pilot study for a planned New Immigrant Survey (NIS-P) was conducted, however, by Guillermina Jasso and her associates between October 1996 and February 1998 on a probability sample of 976 legal immigrants who were admitted in the summer of 1996.[14] The NIS-P yielded the most reliable quantitative estimates we have on the religious identities possessed by new immigrants upon arrival (see table 11.1).[15] According to the NIS-P, almost two-thirds (64.7 percent) of the sample claimed a Catholic (41.9 percent), Protestant (18.6 percent), or Eastern Orthodox (4.2 percent) "religious preference." This figure compares to the 76.5

TABLE 11.1 ∘ Distribution of Religious Preference of U.S. Adults:
New Immigrant Survey—Pilot (NIS-P) and American Religious Identification
Survey (ARIS)

Religious Preference	Immigrants (NIS-P)	U.S. Population (ARIS)
Jewish	2.6	1.3
Christian Catholic	41.9	24.5
Christian Orthodox	4.2	0.3
Christian Protestant	18.6	51.7[a]
Muslim	8.0	0.5
Buddhist	4.04	0.5
Hindu	3.4	0.4
Other	1.4	1.0
No religion	15.0	14.1
No response	1.2	5.4
Total	100.0	100.0

Sources: Guillermina Jasso, Douglas S. Massey, Mark R. Rosenzweig, and James P. Smith,
"Exploring the Religious Preferences of Recent Immigrants to the United States: Evidence from
the New Immigrant Survey Pilot," in Religion and Immigration: Christian, Jewish, and Muslim
Experiences in the United States, edited by Yvonne Yazbeck Haddad, Jane I. Smith, and John L.
Esposito (Walnut Creek, Calif.: AltaMira, 2003), 217–53; Barry A. Kosmin, Egon Meyer, and
Ariela Keysar, American Religious Identification Survey (New York: Graduate Center of the City
University of New York, 2001).

Note: Percentages are for adults eighteen and older and are based on weighted data. NIS-P data
come from a probability sample of all immigrants legally admitted in July and August 1996
(N = 976). ARIS data come from a random-digit dialed telephone survey of households in the
contiguous forty-eight states conducted between February and June 2001 (N = 50,281).
[a]ARIS "Protestants" include Mormons and Jehovah's Witnesses.

percent of the American population that professed a Christian religious identity in the 2001 American Religious Identification Survey (ARIS), a very large
scale random telephone survey of the adult American population in the contiguous forty-eight states.

For several reasons, the relatively high portion (64.7 percent) of Christians
among new immigrants is a conservative figure. The NIS-P survey excluded
illegal immigrants (many of whom are from Mexico and are very likely to be
Christian); furthermore, the completion rate was biased toward those whose
phone numbers could be determined, which also probably excluded many
poor legal immigrants, those from the Western Hemisphere again likely constituting a Christian population. The data also indicate that substantial num-

bers of Muslim, Buddhist, Hindu, and Jewish immigrants are coming to the United States, in each case in much greater proportions than those of their cobelievers already here. The new immigration is definitely changing the U.S. religious profile. Yet if we count the three branches of Christianity as a single "religious family," the second-largest religious family, at 15 percent of the total, is those who claim no religion.[16] Given that the survey queried legal immigrants over eighteen years of age and not their children, and given that immigrants tend to be younger than the population they are joining and more likely still to be in their reproductive years, the survey undoubtedly understates the long-term effect of immigration on the U.S. religious demography. Thus, there can be no doubt that the new immigration is greatly diversifying the religious profile of the United States, with greatly increased numbers of non-Christians and those with no religion. But among Christians, this immigration is significantly increasing the relative presence of Catholics and Eastern Orthodox at the expense of Protestants.

There is every reason, then, to believe that the great majority of new immigrants are Christian. They are not only augmenting the numbers of their cobelievers in the United States but also greatly increasing the internal ethnic and racial diversity of American Christians.

Probably the most self-conscious and certainly the best-documented new immigrant Christian community is Korean American Protestants. Their story is in many ways remarkable.[17] Due to a very rapid process of evangelization spanning the twentieth century, South Korea now has about as many Christians as Buddhists (each with one-quarter of the population). Because of selective migration (from the younger, more highly educated, and urban sectors of the Korean population), half of these emigrants are Christian. And because the Korean immigrant church is the center of Korean American community life, half of the non-Christian immigrants become church members as they settle in the United States. As a result, approximately 75 percent of Korean immigrants here are Christian. Korean American Christians have founded more than three thousand congregations, in which they tend to be highly involved, attending regularly and contributing generously. Already well educated in Korea, they have nurtured a critical mass of religious studies scholars so that there is a large and growing literature by Korean Americans on the Korean American church.

Because the most successful turn-of-the-century evangelists in Korea were Presbyterians and Methodists, many Korean American churches retain such affiliations. They are thereby one of the few sources of growth in otherwise declining mainline Protestant denominations. However, because Korean Americans tend to be more conservative than white Presbyterians and Methodists, many of their churches are affiliated with ethnic judicatories in white denominations, ethnic Korean denominations, and conservative American denominations such as the Presbyterian Church in America and the Southern Baptist Convention. A minority among Korean American Christians, accounting for some 10–15 percent, are Catholics, who attend ethnic parishes dedicated to such Korean martyrs as St. Andrew Kim and St. Paul Chung or designated centers within mixed-ethnic parishes.

Whether Protestant or Catholic, Korean immigrant churches are not, by and large, neighborhood churches. Korean Americans are one of the many Asian immigrant religious groups who travel relatively long distances to get to their places of worship. There is also remarkable membership turnover in Korean Protestant churches, caused, in the judgment of some researchers, by competition for status, leading to schisms and the founding of new churches.

The largest but probably one of the most diffuse and least defined of the new immigrant religious communities is certainly that of Mexican-origin Catholics.[18] With the high and rising rate of migration, many millions of Mexican immigrant Catholics live all over the United States, refilling pews in both urban parishes left empty by upwardly mobile, now-suburban Catholics and midwestern small-town parishes whose young people have left for the cities. Mexico itself is a regionally, culturally, and socially diverse country, and Mexican Americans are correspondingly diverse.[19] A few are descended from families who became part of the United States by conquest a century and half ago, and others are third-, fourth-, and fifth-generation descendants of late-nineteenth- and early-twentieth-century immigrants, religious refugees from the Cristero rebellion against the anticlerical postrevolutionary government of the 1920s, and guest workers of the 1942–64 *bracero* program. One thrust of the Chicano movement of the 1960s was itself an anticlerical protest against neglect on the part of the institutional church, but over the past thirty years, the size of the immigrant flow has brought to the United States a vastly larger number of first-generation immigrants and their children for whom U.S. history is less salient and Mexican-origin Catholic identities more so.

Today, Mexican Americans are, of all Hispanics/Latinos, the group most likely to retain their Catholic heritage; about three-quarters identify as Catholic, according to the national survey conducted for HCAPL. In contrast to Korean American Protestants, Mexican American Catholics tend to attend nearby neighborhood churches and in that respect are good American Catholics.[20] Because of residential segregation and the Catholic parish system as well as the strenuous efforts of the U.S. Catholic Church to accommodate their presence and rectify decades of neglect and abuse of Hispanics, Mexican-origin Catholics are likely to congregate for Spanish-language masses, often in churches that make special symbolic provision for their presence (for example, with images of the Virgin of Guadalupe) and sometimes in de facto or de jure national parishes.[21]

Without many of their own clergy, either from Mexico or from the Mexican American community, Mexican American Catholics are likely to be served, more or less sensitively, by Spanish-speaking Anglo priests and for that among other reasons have yet to coalesce into the huge, cohesive bloc that is one potential of their presence.[22] Yet their religiosity is distinctive, and their growing presence in parishes of Irish, German, Polish, and other European provenance seems to be steering American Catholicism away from its previously dominant asceticism and more recent post–Vatican II tendencies to Protestantization and religious individualism. Their religiosity seems to be more sacramental and devotional than that of Anglo-Catholics: they are more likely to go for private confession, make stations of the cross, say the rosary, ask the priest's blessing on their households, and have home altars featuring images of Jesus, Mary, and the saints, mementoes of the deceased, candles, and religious jewelry.[23] Heirs to traditions that enshrine mixtures of late medieval European and pre-Columbian Meso-American elements, they are comfortable holding onto what Anglo-Americans tend to experience as symbolic opposites (for example, individual and community or the material and the spiritual), and they resist top-down efforts to "purify" religion of popular culture and practices.[24] Especially because of immigration from Mexico, the future of the U.S. Catholic Church lies increasingly with Hispanics.

The largest Asian Christian community, that of Filipino Catholics, is one of the least visible and least studied but, at least at an individual level, is among the most religiously devout.[25] They are the largest because of the size (second to Chinese among Asian-origin groups) and long duration (since the 1910s) of immigration from the Philippines, which, as has been noted, is overwhelmingly and robustly Catholic. (Something of a Catholic counterreformation took place in the Philippines after the American conquest in 1898.) Filipino Catholics are relatively invisible because they adhere to the parish system and because Filipino Americans tend not to be residentially concentrated. Filipino parishes are thus rarer than Filipinos' numbers would warrant, and Filipino Catholics often represent small minorities in their mixed ethnic parishes.

(Many Filipino Catholics gather periodically at regional centers and private homes for saints' days and hometown festivals, however.) They are least studied in part because of antipathy to religion among many postcolonial scholars of Filipino origin. Filipinos are among the most active Catholic laypeople because their high educational and occupational levels endow them with cultural capital and their religious conservatism gives them an impetus to become "reverse missionaries" involved in movements such as Cursillo, Opus Dei, and Couples for Christ.

Two additional, mostly conservative, forces within American Catholicism are enclaves of refugees concentrated in places known as Little Saigon and Little Havana.[26] As different as these communities are (the former is sometimes characterized as "Confucianized Christianity," and the latter mixes Afro-Caribbean elements at the popular level), their leadership tends to be nationalistic and anticommunist. Many of the Vietnamese who left for the United States after 1975 were in fact twice refugees from communism, having left North Vietnam after the 1954 Vietminh victory over the French. The first refugees from Saigon were followed by those less elite and less piously Catholic, which is also the case for Cubans (the anti-Castro elite having been followed twenty years later by Marielitos). Nonetheless, Vietnamese Catholics manifest high levels of vocations to the priesthood, and Cuban Catholics have taken up the Cursillo movement. Both communities have a strong Catholic self-consciousness, and because of their spatial concentration, both are visible, not least to the politicians who represent those districts.

At the other end of the social ladder from the first wave of anti-Castro Cubans are lower-class Cubans, Dominicans, Haitians, and (although they are not technically immigrants) Puerto Ricans. Many immigrants from the Caribbean are Protestant, but most are Catholic, and they are contributing Afrocentric practices, including Vodou and Santeria, to the U.S. religious mix. While some of these practices, such as outdoor processions, are highly visible, others, such as all-night domestic devotions, are much less so.[27] Despite the protestations of purists on both sides—indigenists and "pure" Catholics— an intimate overlap exists between popular Catholicism and such practices.[28] For example, one of the largest annual Catholic festivals in Cuban Miami is the December 17 festival of San Lázaro, the "man with the crutches," who is an ambiguously Christianized version of the Yoruba *orisha* Bábalu Ayé.[29] Many of those who partake in such hugely popular rites think of them as genuinely Catholic, a notion of which some church authorities are understandably reluctant to disabuse them.[30] To take an example from the other side, Vodou rituals often begin with lengthy recitations of the Our Father and the Hail Mary (in Kreyol, led by a Vodou priest), the people taking charge, as it were, of the religion.[31]

One of the more widely heralded "discoveries" of the past decade on the part of observers of U.S. religion was that not all Hispanics are Catholic. That millions are in fact Protestant began to dawn on the American consciousness ten years ago thanks to thousands of Spanish-language storefront churches dotting American cities, newspaper features about them, and survey research. According to the HCAPL-sponsored survey, Protestants account for 23 percent of the 37 million American Hispanics, so the United States has more Latino Protestants than Jews or Muslims.[32] Most of these Hispanic Protestants identify with evangelicalism and Pentecostalism and with Mormons and Jehovah's Witnesses rather than with mainline Protestant churches. Thus, Latino Protestantism represents another rapidly growing theologically conservative presence.

Reliable data on this trend are hard to come by, a problem for religious statistics generally but exacerbated for a population that is not comfortable answering surveys in English. For example, the General Social Surveys, the source of the richest, most reliable religion data for the majority of the American population, is by definition a survey of the noninstitutionalized adult English-speaking U.S. population. Nonetheless, some statements can be made with confidence:

- Many Hispanic Protestants immigrate as Protestants. For example, in the NIS-P data, Mexico is not only the largest single sending country for Catholic immigrants but also the largest single source of Protestant immigrants. Thus, it is a mistake to conclude that the millions of Hispanic Protestants are defectors from the American Catholic Church.
- Hispanic Protestants are less attached to the neighborhoods of their residence than are Hispanic Catholics, because Hispanic Protestantism tends to organize congregationally rather than by parish.[33] For example, in Washington, D.C., the parishes of Salvadoran Catholics tend to link them to the local and panethnic community, whereas the more homogeneous congregations of Salvadoran Protestants link them to coreligionists in the home country and elsewhere in the United States.[34]
- Proportionately more U.S. Hispanics of Puerto Rican and Cuban origin than Mexican Americans are Protestant. Indeed, as many as one-third of Puerto Ricans, either on the island or on the mainland, are Protestant.

Other things being equal, the more Mexican a city's Latino population is, the more likely its Latinos are to be Catholic.

◦ To say that Hispanic Protestants tend to be theologically conservative is not to say that they are politically conservative. Tending to vote for Democratic candidates, they are likely to consider themselves political independents. Moreover, for all the theological differences between Catholicism and Protestantism, millions of adherents of both confessions affirm cross-cutting born-again and charismatic identities.[35]

Protestants come to the United States from all over the world. In metropolitan Chicago, for example, I have visited Jamaican, Nigerian, Ghanaian, Congolese, Liberian, Puerto Rican, pan-Hispanic, Korean, Chinese, pan-Asian, and Indian Protestant congregations, some of which met in their own facilities, some of which share quarters with white American mainline Protestant congregations. Many west African and Jamaican immigrants are Anglicans, but an increasing percentage of Protestant immigrants from Africa, the Caribbean, Latin America (for example, Guatemala), Asia (for example, the Philippines), and eastern Europe (for example, Ukraine) have their roots in indigenous evangelical and Pentecostal churches.[36]

Some 4 percent of the NIS-P respondents identified with Christian Orthodoxy, two-thirds of them from such bastions of Eastern Orthodoxy as the former Soviet Union, Yugoslavia, and Romania. But others came from the original heartland of Orthodoxy in countries of the Middle East, including Turkey, Lebanon, and Ethiopia. Given the accepted pattern of ethnic particularism within Orthodoxy, it is not surprising that the United States today has not only Greek, Russian, Romanian, and Serbian Orthodox churches but also Albanian, Arab, Assyrian, and Indian Orthodox congregations.[37]

The immigrant impact on the U.S. religious profile, however, does not end with the religions they bring with them. Specific processes of change extend, mitigate, and refract immigrants' religious presence.

As the children of immigrants (the second generation) grow up, their religious identities may change. They may revert to a faith more in keeping with the national/ethnic identity associated with the home country, they may adopt a version of their parents' religion that they feel is more in keeping with their new circumstances, they may follow more closely in their parents' religious footsteps, and, of course, they may abandon their parents' religion altogether. Once again, the religious lives of Korean Americans have been most thoroughly analyzed, and the literature discusses all four of these possibilities.

Because the net rate of immigration from Korea dropped precipitously at the end of the 1980s (from more than thirty thousand per year to a third of that number), fresh cultural input from Korea has greatly diminished, the first generation is aging, and an ambiguously Americanized second generation is emerging. A large demographic bulge is now moving through Korean American society, a distinct second generation whose religious proclivities illustrate the options of generational succession.[38] The members of the second generation prefer English, and many of them identify more as Christian than as Korean.[39] In such respects, their religiosity differs significantly from that of their parents. However, members of the founding generation have many years ahead of them, and great resistance to the use of English in Korean immigrant church services exists. As a consequence, some observers have sensed the onset of a second-generation "silent exodus." Others see in the reported disaffection of youth a long-delayed recognition of the dubious legitimacy of Christianity for an Asian culture.[40] But surveys show that second-generation Korean Americans have problems with the immigrant church, not with their Christian faith, and there is a growing literature on the English-language worship services (ELWs) they have founded, whether as freestanding churches or as parallel congregations.[41] Like their parents' churches, these ELWs are predominantly if not exclusively Korean; unlike the parents' churches, the worship is informal and contemporary. Those ELWs that remain part of immigrant congregations—often called the "youth department" or the "English congregation" of a Korean immigrant church—may presage the future of such churches as the first generation slowly gives way to the second.[42]

Other immigrant Christian communities may languish as they negotiate viable identities in the United States. For example, Indian Christians suffer an identity crisis between their more numerous Hindu coethnics and pervasive evangelical Protestants, both of which appeal to college-bound youth.[43] At the same time, the male elders of the community, suffering significant loss of status in the migration process and finding in the church a close-at-hand answer to their status needs, seem loath to cede much cultural room to their children's generation.[44] In response, the children may well assimilate to other segments of the population, joining predominantly white churches or converting to other religions. Either way, the immigrant religious tradition itself may slowly go dormant, as happened with the Buddhism and Daoism of nineteenth-century Chinese on the West Coast and the Islam of many turn-of-the-century Lebanese immigrants.[45]

If a religious community may lose adherents by defection (a failure of cultural reproduction), it may also augment its numbers by natural reproduction. Fertility is in decline worldwide, and the fertility of Asian immigrants and Asian Americans in particular tends not to differ greatly from that of white Americans, with that of African Americans being somewhat higher. But the fertility of Hispanic women is higher still.[46] Bringing children into the world does not automatically add to the rolls of religious institutions, yet because of the Hispanic component of the new immigration, differential fertility is another factor that seems likely to at least maintain if not increase the Christian share of the population.

In the past four decades, the U.S. Christian community has lost members by conversion to Islam (especially African Americans) and to Buddhism (especially European Americans) but has gained by the conversion to Christianity of others, especially Chinese.[47] Most Chinese who immigrate to the United States (the majority of immigrants from China and a sizable proportion from Taiwan) bring no religious identification with them, but the least stable religious identification in the United States is "none."[48] In other words, proportionately more of those who grow up in America without a religious identification later affirm one than those who grow up with a religious identification and later affirm none. In a society where some religious identification characterizes the vast majority of the population, many Chinese become Christian as they settle in the United States.[49] In converting to Christianity, these new immigrants—who are often of high professional status—do not wish to turn their backs on their Chinese identification, so they practice a form of "adhesive assimilation."[50] Their churches are internally diverse (with Chinese members speaking several languages), and some have a history of serving generations of Christians. These churches are typically nondenominational conservative Protestant (preaching respect for family and elders), and they are constrained to be indubitably Chinese.[51] Thus, although Chinese Christianity is largely made in America, it does not represent assimilation in the sense of conformity with Anglos.

Some Asian American (as well as Latin American and African) immigrants, and especially their children, gravitate toward panethnic ELWs and congregations. On the West Coast in particular, pan-Asian churches have a growing presence.[52] Some are new, and some are formerly monoethnic Japanese or Chinese churches reconfigured to be pan-Asian as the founders die off and their offspring lose interest in their parents' religion. It is an emerging issue in the literature whether such churches are governed primarily by an "ethnic" or a "racial" logic.[53] In other words, are members brought together more by their common cultural experience as upwardly mobile children of immigrants or by their common racial experience as outsiders in America? Russell Jeung, for one, shows that among West Coast pan-Asian congregations, those under evangelical Protestant auspices adopt the ethnic approach, while mainline Protestants adopt the racial one.

Adhesive assimilation (maintaining old-country identities in the process of adding host county ones) and panethnicity (joining with others who share an often disesteemed status in the host country) are two processes representing amendments to classic assimilation. That theory came under intense criticism beginning in the 1960s for both its ethnocentrism and its misrepresentations of American realities. Previous generations of immigrants had not simply melted into the American population, nor should they have done so. In particular, classic assimilation was seen as the ideology of what came to be called Anglo-conformity, a false promise of acceptance on the part of American society of those groups who led their lives according to the dominant model (false because it denied the reality of American racial and ethnic exclusion). Assimilation theory was decidedly out of fashion for a whole generation of social scientists. Over the past decade, however, the recognition has emerged that post-1965 immigrants—especially their children—are indeed assimilating to America but not necessarily to the dominant (Anglo) model. Recognizing that the receiving society is itself racially and economically segmented, the new theory of "segmented assimilation" both conceptualizes diverse assimilation trajectories and explains why those who assimilate to one of the available American models may do worse in America than those who adhere to select old-country ways. For example, the children of black West Indians who avoid becoming African American are likely to get better jobs, and children of immigrants from Mexico may do better in school if they stay closer to their parents than to their peers.[54] In today's multicultural society, religion may play a role in protecting members of the second generation from deleterious influences of the host society to the extent that they remain at least partly aloof.

The academic success of certain Vietnamese Catholic youth in New Orleans provides the best documented example of this phenomenon.[55] To the extent that they do well in school (as is the case with many but by no means all second-generation Vietnamese youth), they may be said to be on the road to assimilation. But Min Zhou and Carl L. Bankston III show that these Vietnamese youth succeed in school partly by virtue of involvement in religion (specifically, in this case, Catholicism). Religious participation seems to link them to their parents and their parents' values, thereby differentiating them from the peer culture of inner-city youth that would otherwise undermine their academic orientation. Thus, they succeed in school. According to this line of reasoning, insofar as second-generation Vietnamese are represented in higher reaches of American society in years to come, it will likely be those Vietnamese who are most Catholic and least Americanized.

The theory of segmented assimilation assumes that incorporation into one or another stratum of American culture is inevitable, with the key question being which racial, ethnic and/or social class "segment" of American society the group will assimilate to. Especially for groups who for racial, cultural, or other reasons have ready at hand a "proximal host" that is underprivileged in American society (as, for example, Jamaicans are often taken to be African Americans and Guatemalans taken for Chicanos), parents may use whatever resources they have to distinguish their children from those whom parents fear will become their children's peers.[56] Parents with the resources to live in the suburbs, to send their children to private (often religious) schools, and/or to create cultural capital through religious institutions may have some chance of defeating the powerful processes of racialization in American society. If their efforts succeed, historians may look back on our time and say that whereas religiously grounded ethnicity was the fate of the 1880–1920 immigrant working class, something their children could not escape, it was the privilege of the 1965–2000 immigrant middle class, something for which the parents had to strive. In post-1965 America, ethnic religion, including unfamiliar forms of Christianity, may become more a help than a hindrance to success.

The point of this essay is not to celebrate Christianity, to claim that immigration has had few effects on American religions, and least of all to deny that substantial numbers of Muslims, Buddhists, Hindus, and Sikhs are now among America's believers. There is no question that immigration is greatly diversifying the American religious order (see table 11.1). The argument of this chapter is not religiously triumphalist. It is empirical—an insistence that we must face the facts as they are and not as we wish they might be—and theoretical. Religion in the United States is not now (if indeed it was ever) a monolithic overarching symbol system under which a pluralistic society carried on its business.[57] If indeed the country was unified for three-quarters of a century under a "civil religion" in which Abraham Lincoln played the part of messiah, confessional religion in America is and has long been constitutively pluralistic.[58] Today's increasingly diverse religious institutions—Christian, Jewish, Muslim, Buddhist, Hindu, and other—largely serve the interests of their constituents (and indirectly of society) in "(sub)cultural reproduction," but such trends do not portend a process of Balkanization.[59]

Because of the new immigration, American religious pluralism extends not only to denominational and ethnic diversity within American Christianity and to non-Christian alternatives but especially to increasing racial diversity within Christianity. Thus, when Americans think of Christians, they will decreasingly be able to think simply of whites and the captive Africans they Christianized. They will also think of Asian students conducting Bible studies and witnessing for Christ on college campuses nationwide. They will think about Mexicans observing Holy Week with open-air passion plays known as Via Crucis and observing Christmas with the pageant known as Posada, about Haitian Catholics marching through the streets of New York to honor the Virgin Mary in July, and about Cuban Catholics gathering outdoors by the thousands to celebrate the feast of Our Lady of Charity in early September.[60] "Catholic" will no longer be a code for "Irish, Polish, and Italian" but will have to include "Mexican, Filipino, and Vietnamese." When Americans think of Asians, they will not just think of exotic religious Others but also of believers who thump the Bible and ask you if you are saved. Race and religion are increasingly decoupling.[61]

One consequence of such decoupling should be an increased appreciation of the salience of both religion and race as axes of social differentiation so that, for example, African American Christians are seen as Christians, not only as blacks, and Asians as racial, not only religious, Others. This trend may even have the salutary effect of causing European American Christians to reflect on the cultural oddity of figures in their own religious penumbra, such as St. Nick and the Easter Bunny. Insofar as this means that significant axes of division are juxtaposed instead of superimposed, the decoupling of religion and race should be conducive to civility.

Within the American religious order, the new immigrants undoubtedly strengthen the Catholic Church, certainly in numbers of parishioners if not yet in monetary donations or vocations to the priesthood. The hierarchy's increasingly assertive claim to speak for the society is made more credible by the palpable diversity and size of its constituency. As low-wage immigrants, especially Hispanics, come to constitute a greater percentage of Catholics, the church's "preferential option for the poor" will seem less a matter of the noblesse oblige that characterized liberal Protestant outreach in the middle of the twentieth century than a return to an older constituency-driven ethical stance.[62] New immigrants are also strengthening religiously conservative tendencies in both Catholicism and Protestantism: biblicism and supernatural-ism (especially among Asian and Hispanic Protestants), sacramentalism, mysticism, and devotionalism (among Asian and Hispanic Catholics, some of whom are bringing back religious artifacts and practices that Vatican II re-formers tossed out). Across the religious spectrum (including Hindus and Muslims as well as Christians), new immigrants tend to be conservative on many of the social issues that get wrapped up with religion, especially ques-tions of sex and gender. (If the Democrats and Republicans knew how conser-vative new immigrants tend to be on these issues, they might switch sides on their relative openness to immigration.) Americans of color are not an auto-matic constituency of the Democratic Party.

As a case in point, Adventist sociologists of religion speak of the "brown-ing of Adventism," where Asian, African, Caribbean, and South American converts to the American sectarian movement known as Seventh-Day Adven-tism immigrate to the United States in sufficient numbers to have a notable impact on the parent body.[63] Adventists of color are now "returning" to the United States and increasing the numbers of such sectarian groups, both uncoupling them from presumptive whiteness and slowing down their rate of accommodation to the culture. Among other things, the "browning of Adven-tism" means that the Seventh-Day Adventist church will remain a sect for the near future.

Yet, for at least two reasons, it is unlikely that the new immigrants, espe-cially the Christians among them, will line up with the American right to exacerbate the so-called culture wars. First, a plurality of them, a near major-ity, are Catholics, and Catholics tend to sit astride the left-right divide in American politics, taking conservative stances on sex and personal morality but more liberal stances on social issues such as income distribution and minority rights. In Los Angeles, organizers from such Catholic networks as the Industrial Areas Foundation help dampen the otherwise deep-seated con-servatism of immigrant Latino Catholics.[64] The findings that are emerging from the project on the Hispanic Church and American Public Life point to a consistent pattern: conservatism on theology and personal morality, liberal-ism on social welfare, growing independence in party identification, and continuing Democratic leanings when it comes time to vote.[65]

Second, insofar as they experience racial discrimination—which most do, even after they have become acculturated—non-European immigrant Chris-tians will have less in common with a Religious Right that is perceived to be a movement of whites.[66] That is one lesson we can learn from the experience of African Americans, whose moral conservatism does not bring them into alignment with the Republican Party. To be sure, some Asians have aligned themselves with the Republicans, and it is possible in the future that American politics as well as American religion will become decoupled from race. But we have not yet come to that point. Race is likely to be a factor in American politics well after the current "culture wars" have become a distant memory.

NOTES

1. Funded by the Lilly Endowment and the Pew Charitable Trusts and headquartered at the University of Illinois at Chicago (U I C), the three-year N E I C P provided research training and support to graduate students and postdoctoral students studying immigrant religious communities. Twelve N E I C P fellows participated in a six-week workshop on sociological field methods and sociology of religion under the direction of Stephen Warner and Judith Wittner at U I C in the summer of 1994. Warner visited their research sites with them during the 1994–95 academic year, and the group reconvened in July 1995 for a one-week writing workshop in Port Antonio, Jamaica. Fellows then presented their research at the Association for the Sociology of Religion Conference in New York in August 1996, and the conference papers were revised by the authors and edited by Warner and Wittner under the title *Gatherings in Diaspora* (Philadelphia: Temple University Press, 1998).

2. See Raymond Brady Williams, *Christian Pluralism in the United States: The Indian Immigrant Experience* (Cambridge: Cambridge University Press, 1996).

3. "The rapidity with which Asians have become Christian and Latinos have become Protestant forces us to reconsider our notions of Christianity as a 'Western' tradition that has encountered the mysterious East and triumphed over it. It is equally true that Christian traditions have been internationalized, thanks in large measure to impulses originating on the Pacific Rim. Pentecostalism, perhaps our best claim to an originally internationalist religious movement, began with revivals in Los Angeles" (Laurie Maffly-Kipp, "Eastward Ho!: American Religion from the Perspective of the Pacific Rim," in *Retelling U.S. Religious History*, edited by Thomas A. Tweed [Berkeley: University of California Press, 1997], 146).

4. Thus, this essay might have been titled, "The De-Whitening of American Christianity," and the first line might have read, "Christianity is not a white person's religion."

5. This fact is obscured in the influential writings of Diana Eck, where Christian immigrants are all but neglected in discussions on religion and post-1965 immigration. See Diana L. Eck, *A New Religious America: How a "Christian Country" Has Become the World's Most Religiously Diverse Nation* (San Francisco: HarperSanFrancisco, 2001), 45.

6. Steffi San Buenaventura, "Filipino Religion at Home and Abroad: Historical Roots and Immigrant Transformation," in *Religions in Asian America: Building Faith Communities*, edited by Pyong Gap Min and Jung Ha Kim (Walnut Creek, Calif.: Alta-Mira, 2002), 144.

7. Williams, *Christian Pluralism*.

8. R. Stephen Warner, "Religion and the New (Post-1965) Immigrants: Some Principles Drawn from Field Research," *American Studies* 41.2–3 (Summer–Fall 2000): 267–86.

9. See Philip Jenkins, *The New Christendom: The Coming of Global Christianity* (New York: Oxford University Press, 2002); Toby Lester, "Oh, Gods!," *Atlantic Monthly*, February 2002, 37–45.

10. See, e.g., William David Stevens, " 'Taking the World': Evangelism and Assimilation among Ghanian Pentecostals in Chicago" (Ph.D. diss., Northwestern University, 2003).

11. Guillermina Jasso, Douglas S. Massey, Mark R. Rosenzweig, and James P. Smith, "Exploring the Religious Preferences of Recent Immigrants to the United States: Evidence from the New Immigrant Survey Pilot," in *Religion and Immigration: Christian, Jewish, and Muslim Experiences in the United States*, edited by Yvonne Yazbeck Haddad, Jane I. Smith, and John L. Esposito (Walnut Creek, Calif.: AltaMira, 2003), 217–53.

12. Fenggang Yang, *Chinese Christians in America: Conversion, Assimilation, Adhesive Identities* (University Park: Pennsylvania State University Press, 1999).

13. Guillermina Jasso, Douglas S. Massey, Mark R. Rosenzweig, and James P. Smith, "Family, Schooling, Religiosity, and Mobility among New Legal Immigrants to the United States: Evidence from the New Immigrant Survey Pilot," in *Immigration Today: Pastoral and Research Challenges*, edited by Lydio F. Tomasi and Mary G. Powers (Staten Island, N.Y.: Center for Migration Studies, 2000), 52–81.

14. For this study's findings, see Jasso et al., "Exploring the Religious Preferences."

15. Jasso et al., "Family, Schooling, Religiosity, and Mobility," incorrectly assigned an additional 13.6 percent of the sample to the Other religion category. Most of these were self-identified Christians (primarily evangelical Protestants who do not answer to the Protestant label) or Eastern Orthodox Christians who are neither Catholic nor Protestant.

16. See Wade Clark Roof and William McKinney, *American Mainline Religion: Its Changing Shape and Future* (New Brunswick, N.J.: Rutgers University Press, 1987).

17. For further discussion, see Ho-Youn Kwon, Kwang Chung Kim, and R. Stephen Warner, eds., *Korean Americans and Their Religions: Pilgrims and Missionaries from a Different Shore* (New York: New York University Press, 2001).

18. My discussion of Hispanic/Latino religious communities, Protestant and Catholic, is based on many sources, including unpublished conference presentations and my unpublished field notes. The most important of the conferences is the Hispanic Church in American Public Life (HCAPL), held in Washington, D.C., May 3–4, 2002. See Gastón Espinosa, Virgilio Elizondo, and Jesse Miranda, "Hispanic Churches in American Public Life: Summary of Findings" (interim report), Notre Dame University Institute for Latino Studies, 2003; Gastón Espinosa, "Demographic Shifts in Latino Religions," *Social Compass* 51.3 (September 2004): 303–20. HCAPL was a three-year study (1999–2002) funded by the Pew Charitable Trusts and co-sponsored by the Alianza de Ministerios Evangélicos Nacionales (AMEN), a Protestant association, and the Mexican American Cultural Center (MACC), a Catholic research and teaching institution. HCAPL thus from the start represented a Protestant-Catholic collabora-

tion. The codirectors were AMEN founder Dr. Jesse Miranda and MACC founder Dr. Virgilio Elizondo. The project manager was Dr. Gastón Espinosa, a historian of religion and visiting researcher at the University of California at Santa Barbara. The national survey was conducted by telephone on four different probability samples intended to ensure representation of urban, rural, Protestant, and Puerto Rican Hispanics.

19. "The term *Mexican American* is not the only self-designation used by people of Mexican heritage born and/or living in the United States. Since the 1960s, some U.S. residents of Mexican descent have rejected the term as assimilationist and instead called themselves *Chicanas* and *Chicanos*, usually as a means of expressing a strong ethnic consciousness and orientation toward social struggle and justice. Many recent Mexican arrivals call themselves *Mexicanos* or simply Mexicans, while some native-born Texas of Mexican heritage call themselves Tejanos. Still others identify themselves as *mestizos* to accentuate their mixed descent from Native American and Spanish ancestors" (Timothy Matovina and Gary Riebe-Estrella, *Horizons of the Sacred: Mexican Traditions in U.S. Catholicism* [Ithaca: Cornell University Press, 2002], 153).

20. See Helen Rose Ebaugh and Janet Saltzman Chafetz, eds., *Religion and the New Immigrants: Continuities and Adaptations in Immigrant Congregations* (Walnut Creek, Calif.: AltaMira, 2000); Janise D. Hurtig, "Hispanic Immigrant Churches and the Construction of Ethnicity," in *Public Religion and Urban Transformation: Faith in the City*, edited by Lowell W. Livezey (New York: New York University Press, 2000), 29–55.

21. Alan Figueroa Deck, "The Challenge of Evangelical/Pentecostal Christianity to Hispanic Catholicism," in *Hispanic Catholics in the U.S.: Issues and Concerns*, edited by Jay P. Dolan and Alan Figueroa Deck (Notre Dame, Ind.: University of Notre Dame Press, 1994), 409–39.

22. Virgilio Elizondo, a Catholic priest native to the west-side barrio of San Antonio, Texas, is a notable exception to the generalization about a lack of indigenous leaders. The concept of *mestizaje*, on which he has been working for more than twenty years, is one of the most promising developments in Catholic theology. See Virgilio Elizondo, *Galilean Journey: The Mexican American Promise* (Maryknoll, N.Y.: Orbis, 1983); Matovina and Riebe-Estrella, *Horizons*; R. Stephen Warner, "Elizondo's Pastoral Theology in Action: An Inductive Appreciation," in *Beyond Borders: Writings of Virgilio Elizondo and Friends*, edited by Timothy Matovina (Maryknoll, N.Y.: Orbis, 2000), 47–57.

23. Dean R. Hoge, William D. Dinges, Mary Johnson, S. N. D. de N., and Juan L. Gonzales Jr., *Young Adult Catholics: Religion in the Culture of Choice* (Notre Dame, Ind.: Notre Dame University Press, 2001); Milagros Peña and Lisa M. Frehill, "Latina Religious Practice: Analyzing Cultural Dimensions in Measures of Religiosity," *Journal for the Scientific Study of Religion* 37.4 (December 1998): 620–35. Although some Mexican Americans have left the Catholic Church for Pentecostal and evangelical Protestantism, it should not be assumed that they do so in reaction to the perceived inhospitality of the U.S. Catholic Church, which, in many dioceses is trying hard to welcome them, partly to counter Protestant competition. For further discussion, see Deck, "Challenge of Evangelical/Pentecostal Christianity." Many Hispanic Protestants, including some Mexican immigrants, bring their Protestantism with them. According to the NIS-P

(Jasso et al., "Exploring the Religious Preferences"), Mexico is the top sending country not only for Catholics but also for Protestants: 15.5 percent of the summer 1996 legal immigrants in the survey who came from Mexico were Protestant; 77.8 percent were Catholic.

24. See Matovina and Riebe-Estrella, *Horizons*, esp. Robert S. Goizueta, "The Symbolic World of Mexican American Religion," 119–38.

25. Pyong Gap Min, "Introduction," in *Religions in Asian America*, edited by Min and Kim, 1–14; San Buenaventura, "Filipino Religion at Home and Abroad," 143–83; Joaquin L. Gonzales, "Christianity Returns to America," report from the Religion and Immigration Project, University of San Francisco, [2001].

26. Min Zhou, Carl L. Bankston III, and Rebecca Y. Kim, "Rebuilding Spiritual Lives in the New Land: Religious Practices among Southeast Asian Refugees in the United States," in *Religions in Asian America*, edited by Min and Kim, 37–70; Kathleen Sullivan, "St. Catherine's Catholic Church: One Church, Parallel Congregations," in *Religion and the New Immigrants*, edited by Ebaugh and Chafetz, 255–89; Thomas A. Tweed, *Our Lady of the Exile: Diaspora Religion at a Cuban Catholic Shrine in Miami* (New York: Oxford University Press, 1997).

27. "Since the upper socioeconomic levels were overrepresented in the early wave of the migration from socialist Cuba, the incidence of Afro-Cuban religious practices among Cuban Americans was not as evident in Miami prior to 1965. As the successive waves of migrants became increasingly more representative of the Cuban population, Afro-Cuban religious practices became more evident in Miami. The Mariel boatlift was especially important in increasing in Miami the number of practitioners and believers in the various Afro-Cuban cults" (Lisandro Pérez, "Cuban Catholics in the United States," in *Puerto Rican and Cuban Catholics in the U.S., 1900–1965*, edited by Jay P. Dolan and Jaime R. Vidal [Notre Dame, Ind.: University of Notre Dame Press, 1994], 207).

28. Elizabeth McAlister, "The Madonna of 115th Street Revisited: Vodou and Haitian Catholicism in the Age of Transnationalism," in *Gatherings in Diaspora*, ed. Warner and Wittner, 123–60; Elizabeth McAlister, *Rara!: Vodou, Power, and Performance in Haiti and the Diaspora* (Berkeley: University of California Press, 2001).

29. Tweed, *Our Lady of the Exile*, 50. It would be a mistake to regard the Catholicism in Vodou and Santeria as a mere veneer overlaid on a deeper African base or vice versa. Both the Catholic and the African expressions are robust. "In Africa, Bábalu-Ayé is a most dreaded *orisha* since he controls infectious diseases. . . . In Cuba, he is identified with Saint Lazarus, 'the man with the crutches,' a merciful and suffering leper. Saint Lazarus has greatly influenced the personality and character of Bábalu-Ayé. Thus, in Cuba, this *orisha* is perceived as a pious, merciful, and miraculous healer who is inclined to forgiveness and goodness and is most loved instead of dreaded" (Mercedes Cros Sandoval, "Afro-Cuban Religion in Perspective," in *Enigmatic Powers: Syncretism With African and Indigenous Peoples' Religion Among Latinos*, edited by Anthony M. Stevens-Arroyo and Andres I. Pérez y Mena [New York: City University of New York, Bildner Center, 1995], 87–88). Because surveys of American religion tend to offer their respondents mutually exclusive choices of "religious preference" (i.e., "are you Protestant, Catholic, Jewish, or something else?") and because "Catholic" is typically offered as

one of the legitimate choices, it is a safe assumption that U.S. survey data underestimate the number of practitioners of Santeria, Vodou, and the like. But because these practices overlap so intimately with folk Catholicism, such survey data do not necessarily overestimate the number of self-identified Catholics.

30. Author's field notes, Hialeah, Florida, March 1, 2002.

31. Author's field notes, Brooklyn, New York, September 17–18, 1994.

32. Espinosa, Elizondo, and Miranda, "Hispanic Churches," 14–16.

33. For Hispanic Catholics, see Hurtig, "Hispanic Immigrant Churches"; for Hispanic Protestants, see R. Stephen Warner, "The Place of the Congregation in the American Religious Configuration," in *New Perspectives in the Study of Congregations*, edited by James P. Wind and James W. Lewis (Chicago: University of Chicago Press, 1994), 54–99.

34. Cecilia Menjivar, "Religious Institutions and Transnationalism: A Case Study of Catholics and Evangelical Salvadoran Immigrants," *International Journal of Politics, Culture, and Society* 12.4 (June 1999): 589–612.

35. See Espinosa, Elizondo, and Miranda, "Hispanic Churches."

36. See Jenkins, *New Christendom*; Lester, "Oh, Gods!"; Stevens, " 'Taking the World.' "

37. For Indian Orthodox churches, see Sheba M. George, "Caroling with the Keralites: The Negotiation of Gendered Space in an Indian Immigrant Church," in *Gatherings in Diaspora*, edited by Warner and Wittner, 265–94.

38. R. Stephen Warner, "The Korean Immigrant Church as Case and Model," in *Korean Americans and their Religions*, edited by Kwon, Kim, and Warner, 25–52; Jung Ha Kim, "Cartography of Korean American Protestant Faith Communities in the United States," in *Religions in Asian America*, edited by Min and Kim, 185–213.

39. Jeanette Yep, Peter Cha, Susan Cho Van Riesen, Greg Jao, and Paul Tokunaga, *Following Jesus without Dishonoring Your Parents: Asian American Discipleship* (Downers Grove, Ill.: InterVarsity Press, 1998).

40. See Karen Chai, "Competing for the Second Generation: English-Language Ministry in a Korean Protestant Church," in *Gatherings in Diaspora*, ed. Warner and Wittner, 295–331; see also Pyong Gap Min, "Immigrants' Religion and Ethnicity: A Comparison of Hindu Indian and Korean Christian Immigrants in the United States," *Bulletin of the Royal Institute for Inter-Faith Studies* 2.1 (Spring 2000): 122–40.

41. For survey results, see Young Pai, Deloras Pemberton, and John Worley, *Findings on Korean-American Early Adolescents and Adolescents* (Kansas City: University of Missouri School of Education, 1987); for discussion, see Peter Cha, "The Role of a Korean-American Church in the Construction of Ethnic Identities among Second-Generation Korean Americans" (Ph.D. diss., Northwestern University, 2002); Chai, "Competing for the Second Generation"; Soyoung Park, "The Intersection of Religion, Race, Gender, and Ethnicity in the Identity Formation of Korean American Evangelical Women," in *Korean Americans and Their Religions*, edited by Kwon, Kim, and Warner, 193–207.

42. Robert D. Groette, "The Transformation of a First-Generation Church into a Bilingual Second-Generation Church," in *Korean Americans and Their Religions*, edited by Kwon, Kim, and Warner, 125–40; Warner, "Korean Immigrant Church."

43. Prema Kurien, "Christian by Birth or Rebirth? Generation and Difference in an Indian American Christian Church," in *Asian American Religions: Borders and Boundaries*, edited by Tony Carnes and Fenggang Yang (New York: New York University Press, 2003), 160–81; Min, "Immigrants' Religion and Ethnicity."

44. George, "Caroling with the Keralites."

45. For discussion of the decline of Buddhism and Daoism among nineteenth-century Chinese immigrants, see Fenggang Yang, "Tenacious Unity in a Contentious Community: Cultural and Religious Dynamics in a Chinese Christian Church," in *Religions in Asian America*, edited by Min and Kim, 71–98.

46. Georges Sabagh and Mehdi Bozorgmehr, "Population Change: Immigration and Ethnic Transformation," in *Ethnic Los Angeles*, edited by Roger Waldinger and Mehdi Bozorgmehr (New York: Sage Foundation, 1996), 79–107.

47. Yang, "Tenacious Unity"; Yang, *Chinese Christians*; Yang, "Religious Diversity."

48. Jasso et al., "Exploring the Religious Preferences"; on "none" being the least stable religious identification, see R. Stephen Warner, "Work in Progress toward a New Paradigm for the Sociological Study of Religion in the United States," *American Journal of Sociology* 98.5 (March 1993): 1077.

49. See Yang, *Chinese Christians*, for further discussion. Other Chinese, especially Taiwanese with residual Buddhist identification, turn assertively toward Buddhism under pressure from coethnic Christian proselytizers. For more, see Carolyn Chen, "Getting Saved in America: Taiwanese Immigrants Converting to Evangelical Christianity and Buddhism" (Ph.D. diss., University of California at Berkeley, 2002), esp. 87–137.

50. Kwai Hang Ng, "Seeking the Christian Tutelage: Agency and Culture in Chinese Immigrants' Conversion to Christianity," *Sociology of Religion* 63.2 (Summer 2002): 195–214.

51. Fenggang Yang and Helen Rose Ebaugh, "Religion and Ethnicity among New Immigrants: The Impact of Majority/Minority Status in Home and Host Countries," *Journal for the Scientific Study of Religion* 40.3 (September 2001): 367–78; Ng, "Seeking the Christian Tutelage."

52. Russell Jeung, "Asian American Pan-Ethnic Formation and Congregational Culture," in *Religions in Asian America*, edited by Min and Kim, 215–43. Pyong Gap Min ("A Literature Review with a Focus on Major Themes," in *Religions in Asian America*, edited by Min and Kim, 15–36, esp. 23–24) has rightly pointed out that such communities, while often called "pan Asian," are really pan–east Asian, bringing together, as they do, Chinese, Koreans, and Japanese but not south Asians.

53. For different perspectives on this issue, see Groette, "Transformation"; Jeung, "Asian American Pan-Ethnic Formation"; Jung Ha Kim, "Cartography of Korean American Protestant Faith Communities"; Min, "Literature Review"; Park, "Intersection."

54. Mary C. Waters, *Black Identities: West Indian Immigrant Dreams and American Realities* (Cambridge: Harvard University Press, 1999); Marcelo M. Suárez-Orozco and Carola E. Suárez-Orozco, "The Culture Patterning of Achievement Motivation: A Comparison of Mexican, Mexican Immigrant, Mexican American, and Non-Latino White Students," in *California's Immigrant Children: Theory, Research, and Implications for Educational Policy*, ed-

ited by Rubén G. Rumbaut and Wayne A. Cornelius (San Diego: University of California, San Diego Center for U.S.-Mexican Studies, 1995), 161–90.

55. Min Zhou and Carl L. Bankston III, *Growing up American: How Vietnamese Children Adapt to Life in the United States* (New York: Sage Foundation, 1998).

56. David Mittelberg and Mary C. Waters, "The Process of Ethnogenesis among Haitian and Israeli Immigrants in the United States," *Ethnic and Racial Studies* 15.3 (July 1992): 412–35.

57. R. Stephen Warner, "Changes in the Civic Role of Religion," in *Diversity and Its Discontents: Cultural Conflict and Common Ground in Contemporary American Society*, edited by Neil J. Smelser and Jeffrey C. Alexander (Princeton: Princeton University Press, 1999), 229–43.

58. Robert N. Bellah, "Civil Religion in America," *Daedalus* 96 (Winter 1967): 1–21; Warner, "Work in Progress."

59. Warner, "Changes in the Civic Role."

60. For Mexican Catholics, see Hurtig, "Hispanic Immigrant Churches"; Warner, "Elizondo's Pastoral Theology." For Haitian Catholics, see McAlister, "Madonna of 115th Street." For Cuban Catholics, see Tweed, *Our Lady of the Exile*, 125–33.

61. See Kwang Chung Kim, R. Stephen Warner, and Ho-Youn Kwon, "Korean American Religion in International Perspective," in *Korean Americans and Their Religions*, edited by Kwon, Kim, and Warner, 3–24; David Cho, "On Campus, Spiritual Groups Witness a Cultural Conversion," *Washington Post*, May 4, 2003, C1.

62. Compare Joseph P. Fitzpatrick, "Hispanic Parishes Where Something Seems to Be Going Right," in *Strangers and Aliens No Longer, Part I: The Hispanic Presence in the Church of the United States*, edited by Eugene F. Hemrick (Washington, D.C.: U.S. Catholic Conference, 1992), 1–21.

63. Edwin Hernández, "The Browning of Adventism," *Spectrum* 25 (December 1995): 29–50; Ronald Lawson, "From American Church to Immigrant Church: The Changing Face of Seventh-Day Adventism in Metropolitan New York," *Sociology of Religion* 59.4 (Winter 1998): 329–51.

64. See, for example, Donald Miller, "The Role of Religion for New Immigrants in Los Angeles: A Report from the Religion and New Immigrants in Los Angeles Project," lecture presented at Loyola University of Chicago, February 21, 2002.

65. Espinosa, Elizondo, and Miranda, "Hispanic Churches."

66. In other words, in many cases the first generation can attribute the discriminatory treatment they receive to their poor English and their unfamiliarity with American manners. Members of the second generation are more sensitive to racism.

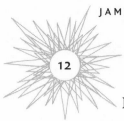

Religious Pluralism and Civil Society

The vitality of political institutions presupposes cultural understandings and social practices within which those institutions make sense and have legitimacy. In the American case, the realm of civic culture on which democracy depends rested from the beginning on a unique combination of Reformed Protestantism, Lockean individualism, and neoclassical republicanism. The political culture of American democracy at its founding was neither radically secular, as some have argued, nor radically religious, as others have claimed; rather, it represented a unique combination of moral traditions and ideas in a tense but workable equilibrium. What is so striking, in retrospect, is the contingency of these cultural factors and their relationship to each other. Democracy has long been called an "experiment," but we now have some understanding of just how fragile it was at the time of the founding of the new republic.

We are, at the same time, acutely aware of how fragile that experiment remains. As Adam Seligman observes in his brilliant study, *The Idea of Civil Society* (1992), those cultural conditions that made civil society so vital are no longer in place, and the social institutions that reinforced them have long disappeared. The sources of this disintegration are varied and complex—the growth and transformation of capitalism, the expansion and secularization of the state, the marginalization of religious institutions from public life, and so on. Yet the disintegration also results partly from successive waves of immigration and the expansion of religiocultural diversity that came with them. Through immigration and religious diversity, our public culture has evolved and been reconfigured by multiple traditions and competing ideals. It continues to do so today. What is the social and political significance of this widening diversity? What challenges does it portend?

© 2006 James Davison Hunter and David Franz

The Expansion of Religious Pluralism in America

One way that the history of America can be told is through the story of expanding religious diversity. Start with the colonists, mainly from Great Britain, whose culture was dominated by the particularly Puritan mandate to build a "city upon a hill" in the New World. Insular and homogeneous by any definition, that culture recognized little if any distinction between the community faith and the political order. The covenant of Reformed Christianity defined the boundaries and agenda of each. As the population grew through the thirteen colonies, this mandate was diffused and reconfigured in terms that were more broadly Anglo-Saxon and Protestant. This represented a subtle shift from our twenty-first-century perspective, but at the time it was deeply felt and the changes challenged profoundly the colonists' collective self-understanding. Through the early years of the new republic, the number of Catholics remained miniscule (in the nation's first census in 1790, Catholics made up less than 1 percent of the population). Their numbers expanded greatly, particularly between the 1830s and 1850s, with the great migrations from Ireland and Germany. In time, their presence forced an enlargement in the nation's collective identity: Americans came to see themselves as properly and more generically Christian and to see that view as strongly compatible with republicanism. Similarly, the presence of Jews in America was insignificant until the 1880s, but as their numbers grew and presence stabilized, the American national identity absorbed this community too, into an ideal and heritage that by the middle of the twentieth century had plainly become Judeo-Christian. To be sure, the influx of new immigrants from around the world after 1965 increased the numbers and diversity of people within the larger Judeo-Christian framework (most notably through the immigration of Latin American and Asian Christians), yet the number of immigrants rooted in Buddhism, Hinduism, and Islam has reached a new and critical mass. This too represents an expansion of American religious and cultural diversity in ways that are novel. In turn, this development has come to challenge inherited understandings of America's collective identity and civic culture.

To recite this history quickly without consideration of the rich and complex historical detail of lived experience is to suggest that the expansion of diversity in America has been, by and large, linear, gradual, and harmonious. In reality, of course, it has been none of these things. Every surge of expansion challenged the stability of public culture. Accordingly, tension, conflict, and even violence ensued as rising groups challenged an existing social, religious, and political establishment that often excluded them from public life and from membership and participation in collective life. Though hard to imagine now, Episcopalians', Baptists', and Congregationalists' hostility toward each other was both oppressive to individuals and disruptive to the social order. As the number of Catholics increased, their marginality was reinforced through institutional, physical, and symbolic coercion. Not merely were innumerable small groups such as the Know-Nothing Society bent on purging the country of "Popery, Jesuitism, and Catholicism"; the sentiment was deeply embedded within the entire society's economic, educational, and status structures. Only after more than a century of hostility and the realization that Catholics were not going away did the attitude toward Catholics change to one of grudging inclusion. The experience of the Mormons partially overlaps that of Catholics: Mormons, too, received a reception that was anything but warm and hospitable. Rejection, denunciation, exclusion, and even murder forced their westward migration. The same of course can be said of the Jewish immigration: anti-Semitism was part and parcel of the Jewish experience in America from the beginning. While anti-Semitism has diminished dramatically in the past thirty years, its remnants remain aggressive and intractable. And so it is that the murder of a Sikh who was mistaken for a Muslim soon after September 11 is part of a long-standing historical pattern of violence directed at members of minority immigrant religions in this country.

In sum, tension, conflict, and violence inhere within diversity, particularly at points of expansion. Each new wave of immigration brought a new challenge to the stability of civil society and its shared understandings of justice, rights, respect, toleration, and the public good.

Why is every new surge of religious immigration not simply and quietly absorbed into civic culture? How does one explain the hostility and violence? Such acts invariably violate precisely the traditions of moral reasoning that the perpetrators claim to be defending. In their own terms, these acts are indefensible—indeed, unintelligible. What is clear (and what the fact of mistaken identity in the murder of the Sikh makes particularly plain) is that it is not primarily differences in doctrinal content and substantive logic that explain the forceful exclusion of rising religious minorities. These acts of violence are not religious debates carried too far but tensions inherent to the contest over social space and collective identity.

Thus, to make sense of the tension and conflict that attends the expansion of religious pluralism in American history, it is helpful to distinguish between substantive reason and social logic, between theoretical formulations and their social embodiment. A long line of scholars from Emile Durkheim to

Mary Douglas has shown that societies are, among other things, commonly held ways of ordering reality. If aspects of reality resist that ordering or fall outside of its categories, they are regarded as "impure" or "dirty."[1] While finding one expression in the idiom of hygiene, the problematic nature of people and things without social categories is hardly trivial. Such a situation requires the assertion and maintenance of categories at the very heart of social life and in so doing summons a society's most coercive forces. The people and things included within a social order must be strictly separated from those excluded. Defining and enforcing these bounds of inclusion and exclusion takes on an urgency disproportionate to their practical significance. Through this process of excluding outsiders, the shared order of a society is clarified and social solidarity is reinforced. Here again, this process is governed primarily by a social logic rooted in fear and manifested in collective rituals of boundary maintenance rather than embedded in the substantive reason inherent to particular moral and religious traditions.

Religion, with its capacity to place all meanings in a transcendent frame of reference, only intensifies the emotion and vested interests. At stake in the conflicts between established and emergent religious groups in U.S. history is the by no means trivial question of what it means to be an American. In such conflicts, the dominant culture typically maintains its status precisely by keeping a new minority faith marginal. In this context, acts of violence against religious minorities become intelligible, even predictable.

But this is not all that is going on.

The Life Course of Immigrant Religions

As a general rule, then, the inclusion of a new religious group within the American mainstream is not bestowed but won. Beneath each phase of expansion is the complicated history of groups that successfully contended for acceptance as members and participants in the social and political order. This is a dynamic and even idiosyncratic process that challenges not only the larger social order but also the coherence and identity of the challenging group itself.

How a faith community carried by a new wave of immigration is integrated into the social order is influenced by the content of the particular religion in question. Returning to the American case, Protestantism provided the founding myths for the nation and for this reason long enjoyed a de facto establishment that, in turn, provided civil religious legitimation and the institutional means (in schools and churches) for inculcating in succeeding generations the habits of civility basic to democratic citizenship. Though Catholicism and

Judaism worked out comparable narratives to reconcile their relationship to American culture, it took more than a century for those groups to become accepted by the Protestant majority. For all of the differences among Protestants, Catholics, and Jews, commonalities of language and an overlapping European heritage within the Judeo-Christian tradition could renew civil society and make it vital. The substantial Protestant bias in law explored in Courtney Bender and Jennifer Snow's chapter in this volume provides a window into this dynamic. The courts' tendencies to define religion, marriage, family law, and property rights in ways compatible with the form (individuation) and content (monotheism) of Protestant theology and experience were entrenched from the beginning. Congruent in many ways and incompatible in others, the Jewish and Catholic communities took decades of internal negotiation before becoming reconciled to some of these legal structures and practices. (Some observers speak rightly of the Protestantization of Judaism and Catholicism in this regard.) Reconciliation and inclusion may not have been a foregone conclusion, but enough commonality existed for these traditions to be workable. In the end, the public culture expanded and rebalanced and the communities of faith adapted and accommodated to prevailing social and cultural circumstances.

This backdrop raises important questions about the current wave of expansion in American diversity. Do Protestantism, Catholicism, and Judaism have a unique relationship to American civic culture? Is the vitality they contribute to civic culture something peculiar to these traditions? Can other faith communities participate in vital ways only insofar as they can imitate and re-create the relevant features of Protestantism? Or can the civic culture presupposed by American democratic institutions find congenial content in the very different traditions of Islam, Buddhism, Hinduism, and Sikhism and the communities that carry them?

We can begin to answer these questions by acknowledging that the experience of each new religious group in American culture is different. It could not be otherwise. Yet one can discern broad patterns in the way in which new religious groups are incorporated, with implications not only for the larger civic and political culture but also for these groups themselves. A life course model suggests four broad phases: introduction, recognition, negotiation, and establishment. These phases are ideal types, of course, analytically distinguishable but in reality overlapping. This is a heuristic model intended to help clarify certain tendencies of the complex cultural and political impact of post-1965 immigration.

PHASE 1 ° Introduction

The introductory phase of a new religious group in American culture is often quiet, with the group satisfied to find a niche on the margins and representatives of the dominant culture content to leave group members alone for the simple reason that they make few if any claims for themselves and pose no particular threat to mainstream economic or political interests. The formation of inwardly focused enclaves, through geographical proximity, language, and other symbolic markers, characterizes the orientation of the new group. However, to call this phase "quiet" is misleading in some cases. This internal focus often results from a minority group recognizing the limits of its welcome. Mormons, to take an obvious example, faced hostility from the outset. They saw their search for an isolated place free from intervention as much as a necessity as a choice. In most cases, there is a mix of both.

Examples of this inward-looking introductory phase can be found in the history of Catholic and Jewish immigrants, each of which clustered geographically and developed alternative parallel institutions to mainstream Protestant institutions. We can also find examples in the recent history of post-1965 immigrant religions. Prior to being pulled out of isolation by racially motivated violence in the early twenty-first century, the Sikh community had been a quietly prosperous minority. Similarly, Vietnamese Buddhists, in creating temples with traditional Vietnamese architecture and conducting services in the Vietnamese language, are trying to imagine what a Vietnamese Buddhism would be like absent the political domination of the Chinese. This is a unique kind of Buddhism growing on American soil, but it is enabled more than shaped by the American context. Tibetan Buddhism in America illuminates another of Buddhism's introductions to the United States. It was introduced to American culture in the 1950s not through large numbers of immigrants but rather through a few small teaching centers. These efforts produced no recognizable enclave: Tibetan Buddhists self-consciously maintained a geographically diffuse following. So in diverse ways, encounters between the mainstream culture and immigrant religious communities tend to be deferred and deflected in the introductory phase.

PHASE 2 ° Recognition

Groups in the introductory phase generally lack the interests, the resources, and the critical mass required to risk increased visibility before the American public and the American state. However, any number of changes internal or external to the group may drive it out of isolation to demand public recognition. One way that a group is characteristically pulled out of isolation is by being defined by the dominant culture as an enemy. The Japanese Buddhist community leaders during World War II offer an example of how being cast as enemies encourages leaders to make public claims to recognition. The leaders of the Japanese Buddhist community responded to Pearl Harbor and the anticipated reaction by internally encouraging members to be politically active while working externally to portray Japanese Buddhists as model citizens. This dynamic is also evident in the position taken by the Hindu International Council against Defamation, which petitioned the White House following Hinduism's absence at a September 16, 2001, government-sponsored prayer service. The authors of this petition argued that as "hard working people who contribute to the American society, economy, education and quality of life," Hindu citizens ought to be recognized as rightful occupants of the American religious landscape. Such efforts by spokespersons encourage both members and outsiders to think of group members as loyal citizens. In so doing, the group works to create new space for itself in the public sphere and tends to make politics more central to its identity. A similar dynamic appears to be at play in American Islam. While deeply ambivalent about U.S. culture and politics, mosque leaders agree on the importance of participation in American politics for purposes of protection. Since 9/11, American Muslim leaders see involvement in American politics as necessary, if not desirable, for securing fair treatment.

Yet these efforts to achieve recognition often coincide with a desire to avoid recognition and to escape notice as a minority. In fact, these claims for recognition are themselves ambivalent. On the one hand, leaders are demanding that their differences be taken into account; on the other, they argue that these differences should be reckoned with because they already fit very well within existing notions of citizenship. The group should be included, in other words, precisely because its members are not substantively different. In this way, demands for recognition are simultaneously efforts to avoid recognition—to hide, protect, and minimize difference. Here, in the form of organizational rhetoric, we find something akin to what Erving Goffman called passing.[2] Goffman argued that members of a stigmatized group usually find it in their interest to try to pass for "normal," to hide or disguise their stigma, whether it is a physical handicap, a questionable family background, or a minority religious affiliation. So the adoption by Japanese American Buddhist groups of the title "church" and even certain Protestant practices, like the use of "hymnbooks" and the singing of songs such as "Onward

Buddhist Soldiers" among members of the Buddhist Churches of America, can all be partly understood as efforts collectively to pass. This tendency toward Protestantization is invariably challenged, of course, initiating internal debates about the limits of compromise. So here too the possibilities for conflict multiply.

Claiming legal protection under the Free Exercise Clause of the First Amendment is another way that immigrant religions demand minimal recognition and state protection. In this way, often quite apart from the public voice of group leadership, members of immigrant religious groups initiate an encounter between themselves and the state. For example, Jewish and other prisoners whose religions include dietary restrictions have regularly brought suit against the government for failing to provide acceptable food. The act of turning to the courts for protection grants some legitimacy to the American state and implies a certain degree of integration into American society. Not surprisingly, these efforts to gain recognition tend to come first from native converts and prisoners, the members likely to be most familiar with the U.S. legal system and most integrated into U.S. society. Moreover, these cases are often furthered by organizations at some distance from the immigrant community, dedicated to the legal protection of religious freedom in general (the American Civil Liberties Union) or to particular kinds of religious freedoms (Home School Legal Defense Association) in addition to those dedicated to the protection of a particular group. These organizations have resources that allow an issue to gain a public hearing and to shape the way the issue is framed (often in terms of individual rights). Thus, the American Civil Liberties Union of Rhode Island, in challenging the charges brought against a Sikh man for carrying a *kirpan* (the small sword worn by Sikhs) on a Providence train on September 12, 2001, cited the man's "right to religious freedom."[3] The impact of these cases on the boundaries of inclusion has been mixed, sometimes broadening, sometimes narrowing the courts' definition of religion. In either instance, these cases raise the visibility of the minority religious group in the eyes of the public and the state.

In the recognition phase, groups make claims that are public in nature, and their focus is more outward than it is in the introduction phase, though this outwardness is defensive. Increasing public visibility and increasing interaction with the state make life in an enclave much more difficult to sustain. After moving into public recognition, the religious group's identity will necessarily be negotiated both internally and externally in relation to the broader culture and the state.

PHASE 3 ○ Negotiation

Without calling too much attention to it, the existence of books such as this one dedicated to post-1965 immigrant religions is significant. It suggests that these religions have moved beyond the introductory phase and perhaps even the recognition phase, entering into the process of negotiation with American culture. This negotiation has both an internal focus and an external concern.

An immigrant group's internal negotiation is related to the competing pulls of continuity and change, preservation and assimilation, that play off of each other in a new setting. The issues run to questions of how to maintain integrity in doctrine and/or belief, concerns about the fidelity or adaptability of ritual, and the desire to tell a coherent collective narrative that acknowledges the changes a community has experienced. We can see this process working itself out on a number of levels. The emergence of progressive Islam provides one example of internal negotiation at the intellectual/theological level. Sacred texts are read in light of the new place and social location within the university, with new purposes in mind giving rise to new interpretations— in this case, an interpretation that, drawing on the work of both modern western intellectuals and Islamic traditions, criticizes both certain forms of Islam and certain forms of modernity. Events outside of intellectual life gave progressive Islam a new appeal and opened up new forums. After 9/11, the relationship of Islam to the West took on heightened significance, both through traditional mosque-based dissemination and, as Muslim intellectuals found an expanded audience, through academic work and popular media. Mainstream conferences, journals, and newspaper and magazine articles have suddenly become prominent venues for discussing Islamic political theology.

Religious interpretations also find expression in the phenomenology of everyday life. For example, American Hindus living away from the sacralized geography of India face a profound challenge in their new setting. This is partly an intellectual challenge but, more importantly, is a challenge for practical religious life in a place where the physical locations of the sacred are far away. The Hindu response has been to reinterpret, both intellectually and ritually, the sacred geography so that the American continent finds its place in traditional Hindu cosmology, literally and figuratively merging the waters of great American rivers with the sacred rivers of India.

The Hindu case illustrates the importance of language as a site of internal negotiation. More than just a medium of communication, language is a way of expressing loyalties and taking up sides. As is the case for American Hindus, the naming of things is often bound up with ritual. Thus, the language of religious services, along with linguistic analogues such as the symbolism of architectural space and dress, are negotiated and contested within immigrant religious groups, particularly between generations, as younger practitioners tend to learn and speak English more readily than their elders. The language and symbolic ordering of religious life, alongside of and in tension with experiences in the broader culture, provide the context of negotiation at the level of experience, where members of the immigrant group feel their differences from outsiders, whether as pride, embarrassment, or revulsion, and then feed those differences back into the negotiation process in a loop as circular as the cycle of life, death, and rebirth itself.

Part of this process consists of these new immigrant groups' efforts to establish their loyalty to the mainstream in the face of suspicion and discrimination. The case of Sikhism again provides an interesting example. The Sikh community is held together by the Guru Granth (the sacred text), the practice of *langar* (sharing food), the Nishan Sahib (a triangular flag hung in the place of worship), and members' distinctive appearance. That appearance includes, for men, the so-called five Ks: *kes* (unshorn hair worn under a turban), *kanga* (comb), *kirpan* (sword), *karha* (steel bracelet), and *kaccha* (special undergarments). The standards of dress have raised questions in the eyes of authorities, both about the loyalty of Sikhs and about bureaucratic procedure. The turban has become problematic when other forms of headgear are normally associated with a role. For example, recent controversies have involved a high school student who would not remove his turban to wear a graduation cap, a construction worker who would not wear a hard hat, and a police officer whose turban violated department policy. The *kirpan* has faced slightly different challenges as the suspicion of men wearing turbans after 9/11 has combined with heightened security policies that place the *kirpan* into the category of prohibited objects. Each of these cases poses a complex set of questions to the Sikh community about what is essential to Sikh practice and what can be compromised.

Instances of negotiation often take on a life of their own, going far beyond the concerns of a particular individual. This is particularly likely when organizations dedicated to protecting members of a group from discrimination are involved. For example, when Amric Singh Rathour was fired from his position at the New York Police Department for wearing a turban, he turned to the Sikh Coalition, which wrote letters to city officials on his behalf, prepared and distributed a thirty-page media guide, and filed a lawsuit against the city. The Sikh Coalition was formed after September 11, 2001, to combat expected discrimination against Sikhs. While working to protect Sikh individuals, however, the organization has also taken on the more ambitious goal of public education. It attempts to inform the public about Sikhism's commitment to civic and human rights and to the democratic political order. In this way, the Sikh Coalition, like other organizations interested in defending members' rights, is contributing to the expansion of American civil religion, stretching the American "sacred canopy" and changing its colors.

If public affairs organizations of minority religions function to extend the scope of the dominant culture, the case of Latin American Christianity reminds us that this culture is not monolithic or without internal conflicts of its own. Nowhere is this more clear than in U.S. politics, which often pits religious conservatives promoting traditional family structures and laissez-faire capitalism against religious liberals who are less traditional in their views on family, have a less favorable view of the market, and tend to vote Democratic. According to the Hispanic Church and Public Life study, funded by the Pew Charitable Trust, Latin American immigrants sit astride the standard American political distinctions.[4] Latin American immigrants are largely Christian (90 percent) and tend to be religiously conservative and traditional in their beliefs about family life. However, they also favor more government intervention in the economy and usually vote for Democratic candidates. How the rapidly growing population of Latinos will change to fit the American religious and political landscape and how those landscapes will change to fit them are increasingly important issues with high political stakes. The U.S. political system tends to channel political debate into liberal-conservative oppositions. The structure of the two-party political system and U.S. political institutions push in this direction. Latin American Christians will doubtless face pressure to fit their politics within these categories. However, as a large and growing group of voters, Latin American Christians may also contribute to a realignment of American political life.

PHASE 4 ∘ Establishment

A group can be seen as reaching the establishment phase when new boundaries of American civic life have normalized around the group, when it has been accepted within the public imagination and its presence reinforced within public institutions. Both the Protestant and Judeo-Christian establishments were coercive cultural establishments of a kind; they were hard won and continually contested, but eventually they normalized. In this regard it is important to note that the terms of establishment will vary considerably, largely as a result of conditions intrinsic to the religious community itself. While is too early to say how any of the post-1965 immigrant groups will finally negotiate the terms of normalization, Buddhism and Islam illustrate the different ways that this process could unfold.

Though it had won some followers in the academy and in literary circles by the early 1960s, the presence of Buddhism in the United States was mostly insignificant. That changed quickly. By the late 1960s and early 1970s, many Americans became aware of Asian religions not just because of new immigration but also through the religious experimentation of the counterculture. A survey of the San Francisco Bay area conducted in 1973, for example, found that 30 percent of residents had not only heard of Zen Buddhism but knew something about it, and a sizable percentage of these respondents were attracted to it.[5] Transcendental Meditation, yoga, and ISKCON (the Hare Krishnas) all had roughly similar degrees of recognition and appeal. While San Francisco was hardly a barometer of the nation as a whole in 1973, the data suggest where and when the shift in public consciousness began. In the years that followed, the Dalai Lama came to enjoy celebrity status, and popular films and books portrayed Buddhism in a positive light. Today Buddhism is visible in the culture to an extent far greater than the actual proportion of Buddhists in the population (less than 1 percent).

Part of this visibility and acceptance can be traced to a lack of desire among Buddhists to turn Buddhism into a public religion. Indeed, Buddhism and most other Asian faith communities have made few claims on the reordering of public and political life. Moreover, Buddhism's absence of strict doctrinal codes, its sympathy with liberal criticisms of organized and authoritarian religion, and its affinity with a culture of subjectivism have created a broad context of receptiveness.[6] In some cases, of course, even a mostly private religion will become involved in public conflicts, as in a construction project and or in education, yet even here the conflicts tend to be localized and contained. By and large, Buddhism, along with Hinduism and Sikhism, has taken a low-profile strategy vis-à-vis public culture in general and the political world in particular. Buddhism has ventured out visibly (and then rather tentatively) only to engage the Tibet cause, though many members of the groups energized by that issue are not Buddhists.

Islam in America is a different story. Though it was fairly quietistic politically through the last three decades of the twentieth century, by tradition it is less inclined to remain a private faith. Take, for example, the recent proliferation of Islamic public affairs organizations. The formation of antidefamation and public advocacy groups to monitor public discourse represents an important step toward religious establishment. The Jewish Anti-Defamation League is the model of this kind of organization. Founded in 1913, the Anti-Defamation League exists explicitly to shape public portrayals of Jews and employs considerable organizational and financial resources toward that end. (The league's annual budget is $45 million.) The Catholic League for Religious and Civil Rights, along with more policy-oriented groups such as the U.S. Conference of Catholic Bishops, perform a similar function for American Catholics.

Muslims have formed a number of antidefamation groups, most of them since 1990. The Council on American-Islamic Relations (CAIR) was established in 1994 to "promote an accurate image of Islam and Muslims in America" through moral persuasion and public opinion pressure. The group has already claimed several notable victories. In 1996, under pressure from CAIR, Simon and Schuster withdrew a world religions textbook that unfavorably depicted the Prophet Muhammad. In 1998, Nike agreed to remove the word "Allah" from the side of a shoe after a CAIR Action Alert ignited worldwide Muslim protests. In 2001, United Airlines changed its uniform policy to allow employees to wear a *hijab* or a turban as part of their uniform in response to pressure from the organization.[7]

In addition to these sorts of policing organizations, American Muslims have founded groups focused on mobilizing and informing Muslim voters, influencing policy decisions, and gathering data and conducting research. *The North American Muslim Resource Guide* lists fifty-three Muslim public affairs organizations in the United States, including antidefamation groups, think tanks, and lobbying organizations ranging in focus from local concerns to issues of international politics.[8] The Federal Election Commission listed five active Muslim political action committees in 2004.

The increasing presence of Islamic organizations in American public life suggests that talk of an "Abrahamic" America is not purely imaginary. In fact, some of the institutional groundwork has been laid for a move in this direction. Conversely, there is no guarantee that increasing visibility of Islam in American public life will lead to its acceptance. It seems equally likely that participation might give rise to new conflicts between Muslims and other religious groups that previously could ignore each other. Whether Judeo-Christian America will yield to Judeo-Christian-Islamic America remains an open question.

The Question of Education

While not explicitly discussed in this volume, education is a critical arena where these larger questions are worked out. Schools, of course, not only are institutions for passing on skills and integrating the young into the labor market but also are sites of social, moral, political, and cultural formation. Cumulatively, their function is to reproduce the national culture across generations. Through education, children come to internalize the boundaries that separate "us" from "them" and the cultural markers that distinguish each. From the vantage point of the dominant culture, the work of boundary maintenance becomes explicit in the schools. For this reason, school standards and textbooks are deeply contested by different faith and ethnic communities. Claims and counterclaims about what is American, what should be included in the curriculum, and who deserves attention, respect, and consideration are at stake. At the same time, schools are the social institutions in which the immigrant community works through its concerns about preservation and assimilation, its tensions between continuity and change.

This situation creates a quandary for immigrant groups and religious minorities. How do members participate in a least-common-denominator public life and still reproduce their distinctive cultures, sustaining solidarity from generation to generation? Both Catholics and Jews responded to this challenge by creating alternatives and supplements to the Protestant-dominated public schools of the nineteenth and early twentieth centuries. The great school wars of the mid–nineteenth century between Catholics and the Protestant establishment testify to all that is at stake.

How recent immigrant religions will engage these challenges remains unclear. Will they create after-school and weekend religious education courses? Will they set up separate schools? Will they school their children at home? At the same time, how will public schools accommodate the presence of more and more children from the Hindu, Sikh, Buddhist, and Muslim communities?

By all appearances, Muslims have been the most active in creating educational institutions and making claims on the public schools. Part of this effort seeks to increase the scope of education in public schools to include teaching about major religions in general and Islam in particular. The Council on Islamic Education (CIE), which is "devoted to raising the standards of teaching religion in schools," is the leading Islamic organization on this front. The CIE operates out of a multiculturalist framework, arguing that "in the public forum of the classroom . . . knowledge gained by individuals of diverse heritages validates and tempers their experience of learning about themselves and others."[9] In this spirit, the CIE tries to convince textbook manufacturers, school districts, and teachers to spend more time teaching about Islam and to do so in ways that assume neither the superiority of Christianity nor the stagnation of Islam.

American Muslims' ambivalence about American culture and public schooling for their children goes beyond concerns about the content of formal education. Immigrant parents recognize that without intentional efforts to instruct children in the ways of the faith, their children will not learn to inhabit Islam (as they did as children) as an all-embracing culture.

Mosques have long tried to fill this void by holding religious education classes on weekends. Although these classes may succeed in teaching the Koran, they are unlikely to reproduce a culture among children who spend five days each week in public schools. In fact, it is this culture of public schools to which many Muslims most object. Khaled Husein, a Palestinian engineer whose three children attend New York's Islamic Al Noor School, put the point this way: "You don't have to be a psychologist or an expert to see there is something wrong at public schools . . . big competition and pressure on kids to be the best dressed, the best looking, the slimmest."[10] Thus, Islamic educational efforts are animated by more than simply the desire to pass on religious doctrine and belief. They also constitute a recognition that the culture of Islam is at odds with some of the dominant cultural features of American youth culture generally. "We want [school] to be a place where they don't have to assimilate," said Majida Zeiter, an Islamic studies teacher in northern Virginia. "We teach them the history and good values and what it takes to be a good Muslim."[11]

In recent decades, the appeal of these arguments, along with Muslim immigration, have made full-time private Muslim schools increasingly popular. The National Center on Education Statistics has collected data on Islamic private schools since the 1991–92 school year, when 4,482 students attended 44 Islamic private schools. By the time of the 1999–2000 survey, these figures had grown dramatically, with the number of students in Islamic schools increasing to 11,412 and the number of schools to 152.[12] This rate of growth greatly outstripped that of private schools generally, which expanded by only 5 percent over the same period.

The growth of private Islamic schools has created opportunities for supporting organizations. For example, the Council of Islamic Schools of North America was founded in 1990 to develop and implement accreditation standards for Islamic private schools. Accrediting organizations tend to protect schools from challenges, but the legitimacy granted by accrediting organizations comes at the cost of a degree of imposed uniformity, since standards are typically not made from scratch but are at least partially borrowed, and the most readily available and publicly legitimate model is the one developed by Christian private schools. In court cases, because Islamic schools are so new, they are interpreted in light of cases involving other religious minorities; as a result, Islamic schools tend to hire lawyers with experience defending Christian sectarian education. In short, for a number of institutional reasons, Islamic schools likely will not chart an entirely new path but will follow a model created by other minority religions that have used parochial schools to sustain their unique identities.

While the success of Islamic private schools in sustaining a unique cultural identity remains an open question (even privately schooled children encounter the broader culture), private schools in principle provide a context in which the uniqueness of Islamic culture, including its standards of appearance and sexuality, might be sustained and even flourish. However, what do such schools mean for democracy?

Islamic schools have given rise to worries, first among them the concerns that Americans have long harbored about the existence of religious schools. Public schools have borne the weighty hopes of John Dewey and many others that they would be models and carriers of pluralist democracy. A similar and perhaps more realistic expectation has been that public schools would serve as a homogenizing force, cultivating a certain degree of homogeneity necessary for democracy to function. These objections are wide ranging and have diverse historical strands, but they generally share a belief in an Enlightenment solution to religious diversity—religions can peacefully coexist insofar as they are privatized. Public schools, in this view, serve both to create a public space in which different people can participate and to exclude religious commitments from that space. Schools that seek to instruct children in one particular religious tradition necessarily pose a threat to democracy.

However, if we do not assume that publicly held religious commitments are necessarily at odds with democratic citizenship, then we find ourselves on much less sure ground with respect to the consequences of Islamic schools for democracy. An answer will depend on exactly what is taught in history, social studies, and Islamic studies courses and on the culture developed in Islamic schools. At this point, we have little more than anecdotal evidence on any of these counts. These schools are in the very early stages, as are the supporting organizations growing up around them. More fundamentally, re-membering that schools do not so much produce culture as reproduce culture, the future shape of Islamic education will depend on how American Islam as a whole positions itself with respect to American democracy and how American democracy positions itself with respect to Islam. In short, the implications of Islamic education for American democracy will likely hinge on whether Muslims will claim insider status within America and be able to do so plausibly.

Change and Continuity

As we have said, establishment is a particular configuration of power, and this configuration is never without challenges and conflicting pressures. The traditions that enjoy influence in social and political life and whose legitimacy is critical to the vitality of public institutions do so under the heading "for the time being." For this reason, "establishment" is never stasis. The post-1965 era offers eloquent testimony to this reality. The last decades of the twentieth century and the first years of the twenty-first have been a time of incredible flux during which the terms of older establishments have destabilized and what will replace them remains undecided.

The force of this larger point is made by the case of evangelical Protestantism. Though much altered internally from the colonial period to the mid–nineteenth century, it held a proprietary place in American social life if not a dominant role in the shaping of the nation's public institutions. Since the nineteenth century, it has followed a long trajectory from the center of cultural formation to the periphery, enduring a century-long schism from its liberal/progressive wing and a combination of withdrawal and eviction from its leading role in public schools, higher learning, social services, and the arts. Contemporary evangelicalism of course continues to do very well institutionally—it maintains some political clout, and its success in popular commerce may be unrivaled. Yet evangelicalism flourishes mainly as a subculture on the margins of cultural formation. Though highly committed to U.S. political ideals, over the past three decades the American evangelical population has shown increasing disaffection from governing institutions, consistent resentment toward elites in all realms of public life, and strong disapproval of the direction of the nation. Nowhere are these dynamics seen more clearly than through the prism of education: evangelicals' exodus from the public schools in favor of sectarian alternatives (home schooling among them) represents a recognition that they are outside the mainstream of American civic culture. The relationship of contemporary evangelicalism to civil society is, then, at the very least, ambivalent. While evangelicals are still part of a civic and political establishment, the terms of that establishment have altered in ways that were unimaginable a century ago.

At this stage, the question is not so much whether but how Buddhism, Hinduism, Sikhism, and Islam will be integrated within the civic, political, and cultural establishment. The nature of their relationship to the dominant order remains to be determined. How will the dialectic pressures alter the internal dynamics of each faith community? Belief, ritual, structures of authority, and social practices will face the relentless pressures of assimilation. Through it all, the negotiation between faith communities—new and old—and political institutions and ideals persists unabated, the contingencies of civil society remain as fragile as ever, and the experiment of American democracy, tentatively and apprehensively, continues to unfold.

NOTES

1. Mary Douglas, *Purity and Danger* (London: Routledge, 1966).

2. Erving Goffman, *Stigma: Notes on the Management of Spoiled Identity* (New York: Aronson, 1963).

3. American Civil Liberties Union, "ACLU Calls on Providence Police to Dismiss Case against Sikh Arrested at Train Station," press release, October 16, 2001, <http://www.aclu.org/immigrants/discrim/11595prs20011016.html>.

4. <http://www.nd.edu/~latino/research/pubs/HispChurchesEnglishWEB.pdf>.

5. Robert Wuthnow, *The Consciousness Reformation* (Berkeley: University of California Press, 1976).

6. Steven Tipton, *Getting Saved from the Sixties: Moral Meaning in Conversion and Cultural Change* (Berkeley: University of California Press, 1982); Wuthnow, *Consciousness Reformation*.

7. See <http://www.cair-net.org>.

8. Mohamed Nimer, *The North American Muslim Resource Guide* (New York: Routledge, 2002).

9. <http://www.cie.org>.

10. Tara Bahrampour, "Where Islam Meets 'Brave New World,'" *New York Times*, November 11, 2001, 4A.23.

11. Valerie Strauss and Emily Wax, "Where Two Worlds Collide: Muslim Schools Face Tension of Islamic, U.S. Views," *Washington Post*, February 25, 2002, A1.

12. More recent survey data are not yet available, but observers expect that the numbers are currently much higher, with some estimating the existence of as many as six hundred Islamic schools with thirty thousand students.

ACKNOWLEDGMENTS

Many thanks to Professor Peter Berger of Boston University, who conceived of this project, helped to secure funding for it, and headquartered it at his Institute on Culture, Religion, and World Affairs (CURA). Many thanks also to the Smith-Richardson Foundation, for stretching beyond its traditional areas of interest to fund this research, and especially to Mark Steinmeyer, the foundation's senior program officer on domestic public policy, for convincing his colleagues to wade into the controversial waters of American religion. (We hope they are liking getting wet.) Laurel Whalen, CURA's administrator, took expert care of the project's finances. Stephen Dawson did much of the heavy lifting as our project administrator, helping to organize two workshops and seeing this volume into print. Karen Nardella and Neil O'Callaghan provided much-appreciated administrative support in Boston University's Department of Religion.

BIBLIOGRAPHY

Ahlstrom, Sydney E. *A Religious History of the American People*. New Haven: Yale University Press, 1972.

Albanese, Catherine L. *America: Religions and Religion*. 3rd ed. Belmont, Calif.: Wadsworth, 1999.

Audi, Robert, and Nicholas Wolterstorff. *Religion in the Public Square: The Place of Religious Convictions in Political Debate*. Lanham, Md.: Rowman and Littlefield, 1997.

Bellah, Robert N. *The Broken Covenant: Civil Religion in Time of Trial*. New York: Seabury, 1975.

Benhabib, Seyla, ed. *Democracy and Difference: Contesting the Boundaries of the Political*. Princeton: Princeton University Press, 1996.

Bloom, Harold. *The American Religion: The Emergence of the Post-Christian Nation*. New York: Simon and Schuster, 1992.

Brimelow, Peter. *Alien Nation: Common Sense about America's Immigration Disaster*. New York: Random House, 1985.

Buenker, John D., and Lorman A. Ratner, eds. *Multiculturalism in the United States: A Comparative Guide to Acculturation and Ethnicity*. New York: Greenwood, 1992.

Butler, Jon. *Awash in a Sea of Faith: Christianizing the American People*. Cambridge: Harvard University Press, 1990.

Carnes, Tony, and Fenggang Yang, eds. *Asian American Religions: The Making and Remaking of Borders and Boundaries*. New York: New York University Press, 2004.

Carroll, Bret E. *The Routledge Historical Atlas of Religion in America*. New York: Routledge, 2000.

Carter, Stephen L. *The Culture of Disbelief: How American Laws and Politics Trivialize Religious Devotion*. New York: Basic Books, 1993.

Casanova, José. "Civil Society and Religion: Retrospective Reflections on Catholicism and Prospective Reflections on Islam." *Social Research* 68.4 (2001): 1041–80.

——. *Public Religions in the Modern World*. Chicago: University of Chicago Press, 1994.

Coward, Harold, John R. Hinnells, and Raymond Brady Williams, eds. *The South Asian Religious Diaspora in Britain, Canada, and the United States*. Albany: SUNY Press, 2000.

Curry, Thomas J. *The First Freedoms: Church and State in America to the Passage of the First Amendment*. New York: Oxford University Press, 1986.

Dinnerstein, Leonard. *Antisemitism in America*. New York: Oxford University Press, 1994.

Dionne, E. J., Jr., and John J. DiIulio. *What's God Got to Do with the American Experiment?: Essays on Religion and Politics.* Washington, D.C.: Brookings Institution, 2000.

Dolan, Jay P. *The American Catholic Experience: A History from Colonial Times to the Present.* Garden City, N.Y.: Doubleday, 1985.

Douglass, R. Bruce, ed. *A Nation under God?: Essays on the Future of Religion in American Public Life.* Lanham, Md.: Rowman and Littlefield, 2000.

Ebaugh, Helen Rose, and Janet Saltzman Chafetz. *Religion and the New Immigrants: Continuities and Adaptations in Immigrant Congregations.* Walnut Creek, Calif.: AltaMira, 2000.

Eck, Diana L. *A New Religious America: How a "Christian Country" Has Become the World's Most Religiously Diverse Nation.* San Francisco: HarperSanFrancisco, 2001.

Eck, Diana L., and the Pluralism Project at Harvard University. *On Common Ground: World Religions in America.* New York: Columbia University Press, 1997.

Evans, Bette Novit. *Interpreting the Free Exercise of Religion: The Constitution and American Pluralism.* Chapel Hill: University of North Carolina Press, 1997.

Farkas, Steve. *For Goodness' Sake: Why So Many Want Religion to Play a Greater Role in American Life.* New York: Public Agenda Foundation, 2001.

Fields, Rick. *How the Swans Came to the Lake: A Narrative History of Buddhism in America.* Boston: Shambhala, 1992.

Gaustad, Edwin S. *A Religious History of America.* San Francisco: HarperCollins, 1990.

Glazer, Nathan. *We Are All Multiculturalists Now.* Cambridge: Harvard University Press, 1997.

Gray, John. *Two Faces of Liberalism.* New York: New Press, 2000.

Hackett, David G. *Religion and American Culture: A Reader.* New York: Routledge, 1995.

Haddad, Yvonne Yazbeck. *Islamic Values in the United States.* New York: Oxford University Press, 1987.

———. *The Muslims of America.* New York: Oxford University Press, 1991.

———, ed. *Muslims in the West: From Sojourners to Citizens.* New York: Oxford University Press, 2002.

Haddad, Yvonne Yazbeck, Jane I. Smith, and John L. Esposito, eds. *Religion and Immigration: Christian, Jewish, and Muslim Experiences in the United States.* Walnut Creek, Calif.: AltaMira, 2003.

Hamburger, Phillip. *Separation of Church and State.* Cambridge: Harvard University Press, 2002.

Hatch, Nathan O. *The Democratization of American Christianity.* New Haven: Yale University Press, 1989.

Heclo, Hugh, and Wilfred M. McClay, eds. *Religion Returns to the Public Square: Faith and Policy in America.* Washington, D.C.: Woodrow Wilson Center Press, 2003.

Herberg, Will. *Protestant-Catholic-Jew.* Garden City, N.Y.: Doubleday, 1955.

Hibri, Azizah Y al-, Jean Bethke Elshtain, Charles C. Haynes, and Os Guinness. *Religion in American Public Life: Living with Our Deepest Differences.* New York: Norton, 2001.

Howe, Mark DeWolfe. *The Garden and the Wilderness: Religion and Government in American Constitutional History.* Chicago: University of Chicago Press, 1965.

Hunter, James Davison. *Before the Shooting Begins: Searching for Democracy in America's Culture Wars*. New York: Free Press, 1994.

———. *Culture Wars: The Struggle to Define America*. New York: Basic Books, 1991.

Hutchison, William R. *Religious Pluralism in America: The Contentious History of a Founding Ideal*. New Haven: Yale University Press, 2003.

Iwamura, Jane Naomi, and Paul Spickard. *Revealing the Sacred in Asian and Pacific America*. New York: Routledge, 2003.

Jackson, Carl T. *The Oriental Religions and American Thought: Nineteenth-Century Explorations*. Westport, Conn.: Greenwood, 1981.

———. *Vedanta for the West: The Ramakrishna Movement in the United States*. Bloomington: Indiana University Press, 1994.

Jelen, Ted G., ed. *Sacred Markets, Sacred Canopies: Essays on Religious Markets and Religious Pluralism*. Lanham, Md.: Rowman and Littlefield, 2002.

Jensen, Joan M. *Passage from India: Asian Indian Immigrants in North America*. New Haven: Yale University Press, 1988.

Kosmin, Barry A., and Seymour P. Lachman. *One Nation under God: Religion in Contemporary American Society*. New York: Harmony Books, 1993.

Kosmin, Barry A., Egon Meyer, and Ariela Keysar. *American Religious Identification Survey*. New York: Graduate Center of the City University of New York, 2001.

Kwon, Ho-Youn, Kwang Chung Kim, and R. Stephen Warner, eds. *Korean Americans and Their Religions: Pilgrims and Missionaries from a Different Shore*. New York: New York University Press, 2001.

Lawrence, Bruce B. *New Faiths, Old Fears: Muslims and Other Asian Immigrants in American Religious Life*. New York: Columbia University Press, 2002.

Leonard, Karen I. *Making Ethnic Choices: California's Punjabi Mexican Americans*. Philadelphia: Temple University Press, 1992.

———. *The South Asian Americans*. Westport, Conn.: Greenwood, 1997.

Leonard, Karen I., Alex Stepick, Manuel A. Vasquez, and Jennifer Holdaway, eds. *Immigrant Faiths: Transforming Religious Life in America*. Walnut Creek, Calif.: AltaMira, 2005.

Lippy, Charles H. *Pluralism Comes of Age: American Religious Culture in the Twentieth Century*. Armonk, N.Y.: Sharpe, 2000.

Lubarsky, Sandra B. *Tolerance and Transformation: Jewish Approaches to Religious Pluralism*. West Orange, N.J.: Cincinnati Hebrew Union College Press, 1990.

Mallon, Elias D. *Neighbors: Muslims in North America*. New York: Friendship Press, 1989.

Mann, Gurinder Singh, Paul David Numrich, and Raymond B. Williams. *Buddhists, Hindus, and Sikhs in America*. New York: Oxford University Press, 2002.

Marty, Martin. *The Protestant Voice in American Pluralism*. Athens: University of Georgia Press, 2004.

Mazur, Eric Michael. *The Americanization of Religious Minorities: Confronting the Constitutional Order*. Baltimore: Johns Hopkins University Press, 1999.

McConkey, Dale, and Peter Augustine Lawlor, eds. *Faith, Morality and Civil Society*. Lanham, Md.: Lexington Books, 2003.

McElroy, James Harmon. *American Beliefs: What Keeps a Big Country and a Diverse People United*. Chicago: Dee, 1999.

McGraw, Barbara A., and Jo Renee Formicola, eds. *Taking Religious Pluralism Seriously: Spiritual Politics on America's Sacred Ground*. Waco, Tex.: Baylor University Press, 2005.

McGreevy, John T. *Catholicism and American Freedom: A History*. New York: Norton, 2003.

Metcalf, Barbara. *Making Muslim Space in North America and Europe*. Berkeley: University of California Press, 1996.

Min, Pyong Gap, and Jung Ha Kim, eds. *Religions in Asian America: Building Faith Communities*. Walnut Creek, Calif.: AltaMira, 2002.

Monsma, Stephen V., and J. Christopher Soper. *The Challenge of Pluralism: Church and State in Five Democracies*. Lanham, Md.: Rowman and Littlefield, 1997.

Moore, R. Laurence. *Religious Outsiders and the Making of Americans*. New York: Oxford University Press, 1986.

Neuhaus, Richard John. *The Naked Public Square: Religion and Democracy in America*. 2nd ed. Grand Rapids, Mich.: Eerdmans, 1986.

Noll, Mark A., ed. *Religion and American Politics*. New York: Oxford University Press, 1990.

Numrich, Paul David. *Old Wisdom in the New World: Americanization in Two Immigrant Theravada Buddhist Temples*. Knoxville: University of Tennessee Press, 1996.

Orsi, Robert A. *Gods of the City: Religion and the American Urban Landscape*. Bloomington: Indiana University Press, 1999.

Porterfield, Amanda. *The Transformation of American Religion: The Story of a Late-Twentieth-Century Awakening*. New York: Oxford University Press, 2001.

Prebish, Charles S., and Kenneth K. Tanaka. *The Faces of Buddhism in America*. Berkeley: University of California Press, 1998.

Prothero, Stephen. *American Jesus: How the Son of God Became a National Icon*. New York: Farrar, Straus, and Giroux, 2003.

Rawls, John. *Political Liberalism*. New York: Columbia University Press, 1993.

Richardson, E. Allen. *Strangers in This Land: Pluralism and the Response to Diversity in the United States*. New York: Pilgrim Press, 1988.

Roof, Wade Clark. *Spiritual Marketplace: Baby Boomers and the Remaking of American Religion*. Princeton: Princeton University Press, 1999.

Rosenblum, Nancy L., ed. *Obligations of Citizenship and Demands of Faith*. Princeton: Princeton University Press, 2000.

Sarna, Jonathan D. *Minority Faiths and the American Protestant Mainstream*. Urbana: University of Illinois Press, 1998.

Schlesinger, Arthur M., Jr. *The Disuniting of America*. New York: Norton, 1998.

Seager, Richard. *Buddhism in America*. New York: Columbia University Press, 1999.

Skillen, James W. *Recharging the American Experiment: Principled Pluralism for Genuine Civic Community*. Grand Rapids, Mich.: Baker Books, 1994.

Smith, Jane. *Islam in America*. New York: Columbia University Press, 1999.

Sowell, Thomas. *Ethnic America: A History*. New York: Basic Books, 1981.

Takaki, Ronald. *Strangers from a Different Shore: A History of Asian Americans*. New York: Penguin, 1989.

Taylor, Charles. *Multiculturalism: Examining the Politics of Recognition*. Edited by Amy Gutmann. Princeton: Princeton University Press, 1994.

Tweed, Thomas A., ed. *Retelling U.S. Religious History*. Berkeley: University of California Press, 1997.

Tweed, Thomas A., and Stephen Prothero, eds. *Asian Religions in America: A Documentary History*. New York: Oxford University Press, 1999.

Walzer, Michael. *What It Means to Be an American: Essays on the American Experience*. New York: Marsilio, 1992.

Warner, R. Stephen, and Judith G. Wittner, eds. *Gatherings in Diaspora: Religious Communities and the New Immigration*. Philadelphia: Temple University Press, 1998.

Williams, Peter W. *America's Religions: Traditions and Cultures*. New York: Macmillan, 1990.

Williams, Raymond Brady. *Religions of Immigrants from India and Pakistan: New Threads in the American Tapestry*. Cambridge: Cambridge University Press, 1988.

——, ed. *A Sacred Thread: Modern Transmission of Hindu Traditions in India and Abroad*. Chambersburg, Pa.: Anima, 1992.

Williams, Rhys H., ed. *Cultural Wars in American Politics: Critical Reviews of a Popular Myth*. New York: Aldine de Gruyter, 1997.

Wolfe, Alan. *One Nation after All: What Americans Really Think about God, Country, Family, Racism, Welfare, Immigration, Homosexuality, Work, the Right, the Left, and Each Other*. New York: Viking, 1998.

——. *The Transformation of American Religion: How We Actually Live Our Faith*. New York: Free Press, 2003.

Wuthnow, Robert. *After Heaven: Spirituality in America since the 1950s*. Berkeley: University of California Press, 1998.

——. *America and the Challenges of Religious Diversity*. Princeton: Princeton University Press, 2005.

——. *The Restructuring of American Religion: Society and Faith since World War II*. Princeton: Princeton University Press, 1988.

Yetman, Norman R., ed. *Majority and Minority: The Dynamics of Race and Ethnicity in American Life*. 4th ed. Boston: Allyn and Bacon, 1985.

Yoo, David K., ed. *New Spiritual Homes: Religion and Asian Americans*. Honolulu: University of Hawaii Press, 1999.

CONTRIBUTORS

IHSAN BAGBY is an associate professor of Islamic studies at the University of
Kentucky. He specializes in Islam in America and is the coauthor of the first
comprehensive study of mosques in the United States, *The Mosque in America:
A National Portrait* (Washington, D.C.: Council on American-Islamic Relations,
2001). He is active in the Council on American-Islamic Relations, the Muslim
Alliance in North America, and the Islamic Society of North America.

COURTNEY BENDER is an assistant professor in the Departments of Religion and
Sociology at Columbia University and is the author of *Heaven's Kitchen: Living
Religion at God's Love We Deliver* (Chicago: University of Chicago Press, 2003).
Her latest project is *Worlds of Experience*, a study of the religious experiences of
contemporary mystics and spiritual practitioners in Cambridge, Massachusetts.

STEPHEN DAWSON holds a Ph.D. in the study of religion from Boston University and
teaches philosophy and religion at Lynchburg College. He is at work on a book
project that combines religious history and constitutional law and is tentatively
titled *A Facsimile of Grace: The Protestant Roots of American Constitutionalism*.

HIEN DUC DO is an associate professor in the Department of Social Science at San
Jose State University and is a past president of the Association of Asian American
Studies. The author of *The Vietnamese Americans* (Westport, Conn.: Greenwood,
1999), he also served as associate producer of *Viet Nam: At the Crossroads* (KTEH,
1994), a one-hour documentary film that aired nationally on PBS and won the
1994 CINE Golden Eagle Award.

DAVID FRANZ is a graduate fellow at the Institute for Advanced Studies in Culture at
the University of Virginia.

JAMES DAVISON HUNTER is the LaBrosse-Levinson Distinguished Professor in
Religion, Culture, and Social Theory and serves as executive director of the
Institute for Advanced Studies in Culture at the University of Virginia. His eight
books include *Evangelicalism: The Coming Generation* (Chicago: University of Chicago
Press, 1987) and *Culture Wars: The Struggle to Define America* (New York: Basic Books,
1991). In 2004, President George W. Bush appointed Hunter to a six-year term on
the National Council of the National Endowment for the Humanities.

PREMA A. KURIEN is an associate professor of sociology at Syracuse University. She
is the author of *Kaleidoscopic Ethnicity: International Migration and the Reconstruction
of Community Identities in India* (New Brunswick, N.J.: Rutgers University Press,
2002) and served as the editor of a special 2004 issue of the *International Journal of*

Sociology and Social Policy on the impact of immigrants on American institutions. She is at work on a second book, *Multiculturalism and Immigrant Religion: The Development of an American Hinduism.*

GURINDER SINGH MANN is the Kundan Kaur Kapany Professor of Sikh Studies at the University of California, Santa Barbara. He is the author of *Sikhism* (Upper Saddle River, N.J.: Prentice Hall, 2003) and *The Making of Sikh Scripture* (New York: Oxford University Press, 2001) and is coauthor of *Buddhists, Hindus, and Sikhs in America* (New York: Oxford University Press, 2001). He is also the sole contributor of entries on Sikhism for the *Encyclopedia Britannica.*

VASUDHA NARAYANAN is a professor of religion at the University of Florida and previously served as president of the American Academy of Religion. She has written or edited six books, including *Hinduism* (New York: Oxford University Press, 2004) and *The Vernacular Veda* (Columbia: University of South Carolina Press, 1994). She is active in the University of Florida's Center for the Study of Hindu Traditions.

STEPHEN PROTHERO is the chair of the Department of Religion and director of the Graduate Division of Religious and Theological Studies at Boston University. He has written or edited five books, including most recently *American Jesus: How the Son of God Became a National Icon* (New York: Farrar, Straus, and Giroux, 2003), and has contributed to a variety of newspapers and magazines, including the *Wall Street Journal*, Salon.com, and the *New York Times Magazine.*

OMID SAFI is an associate professor of Islamic studies at the University of North Carolina at Chapel Hill. He serves as cochair of the Study of Islam section at the American Academy of Religion and is the editor of *Progressive Muslims: On Justice, Gender, and Pluralism* (Oxford, Eng.: Oneworld, 2003) and the author of *The Politics of Knowledge in Premodern Islam* (Chapel Hill: University of North Carolina Press, 2006).

JENNIFER SNOW holds a Ph.D. in American religious history from Columbia University and is administrator and associate program director of Progressive Christians Uniting in Los Angeles.

ROBERT A. F. THURMAN, a former Tibetan Buddhist monk, is the Jey Tsong Khapa Professor of Indo-Tibetan Buddhist Studies and chair of the Department of Religion at Columbia University. He is a prolific translator and writer of both scholarly and popular works, among them *Essential Tibetan Buddhism* (San Francisco: HarperSanFrancisco, 1995) and *Inner Revolution: Life, Liberty, and the Pursuit of Real Happiness* (New York: Riverhead, 1998). He is also the cofounder, with actor Richard Gere, of Tibet House, a New York City–based nonprofit organization dedicated to preserving the living culture of Tibet. In 1997, *Time* magazine tapped Thurman as one of its twenty-five most influential Americans.

R. STEPHEN WARNER is a professor of sociology at the University of Illinois at Chicago and previously served as president of the Association for the Sociology of Religion. He has written or edited four books, including *A Church of Our Own: Disestablishment and Diversity in American Religion* (New Brunswick, N.J.: Rutgers University Press, 2005) and *Gatherings in Diaspora: Religious Communities and the*

New Immigration (Philadelphia: Temple University Press, 1998). His many articles include the widely cited "Work in Progress: Toward a New Paradigm for the Sociological Study of Religion in the United States," *American Journal of Sociology* 98 (1993): 1044–93.

DUNCAN RYÛKEN WILLIAMS is an associate professor of Japanese Buddhism at the University of California, Berkeley. He is the editor of two books and the author of *The Other Side of Zen: A Social History of Sōtō Zen: Buddhism in Tokugawa Japan* (Princeton: Princeton University Press, 2005). His current projects include *Camp Dharma*, a study of Japanese American Buddhism during World War II, and *Hot Water Buddha*, a study of Buddhist influences on hot springs in Japan.

Fatwas, 49, 55
Federal Bureau of Investigation, 12, 63, 64, 73, 74
Federation of Hindu Associations, 126, 127
Filipino Catholics, 239, 240
Finke, Roger, 187
First Amendment, 1, 7, 185, 188, 198, 201, 209, 213, 214, 219, 220, 222; Free Exercise and Establishment Clauses, 15, 181, 182, 183, 184, 185, 186, 187, 188, 189, 194, 195, 197, 203, 204, 213, 220, 223, 224, 263; jurisprudence, 181–229
Five Ks: *kaccha*, 161, 265; *kanga*, 161, 265; *karha*, 161, 166, 265; *kes*, 161, 265; *kirpan*, 161, 166, 191, 192, 198, 263, 265
Foundation for the Preservation of Mahayana Tradition, 103, 109
Four-Three-Oh v. BAPS, 191, 203

Gandhi, Mahatma, 56, 158
Ganesh, 128, 196, 197
Ganesha Temple, 5, 157
Ganga (Ganges) River, 147, 148
Gargi, Sister, 152, 153
Garuda, 140, 152
Gay marriage, 12
"Genteel multiculturalism," 14; in American Hinduism, 120, 121, 126, 133
Gere, Richard, 12, 107
Ghettoization, 32, 82
Gore, Al, 9
Govinda, Lama Anagarika, 100, 101
Graham, Billy, 10
Graham, Franklin, 10, 55
Greenawalt, Kent, 181, 198, 199
Gurdwaras, 10, 160–74 passim
Guru Granth (text), 161, 162, 163, 166, 168, 169, 170, 265

Hadith, 51, 53
Hamburger, Philip, 185, 194

Hare Krishnas, 190, 200, 201, 203
Hawaii, 7, 71, 74; Buddhists in public schools in, 6
Herberg, Will, 3, 5, 7, 8, 9, 10, 122; *Protestant, Catholic, Jew* (book), 3, 7
Hijab, 40, 268
Hindu Americans, 14, 119–38, 186, 187, 191, 194, 196, 237, 246, 248, 264; as model minorities, 127; and religious identity, 124, 127, 147; from upper castes, 121
Hindu International Council against Defamation (HICAD), 119, 128, 133, 262
Hinduism, 4, 8, 9, 10, 11, 13, 119–59, 181, 185, 187, 196, 200, 202; within academia, 128, 132; as anti-Islamic, 131; caste system of, 7, 125, 129, 130; description of, 124; in diaspora, 126; as opposite of Islam, 120; and orthopraxy, 125, 139; as stereotyped, 128; Vedantic, 99, 112; and women, 130
Hinduism Today (newspaper), 121
Hindu organizations, 13, 121, 126, 127, 130
Hindu Temple of Atlanta, 155–58
Hindus, 7, 9, 10, 11, 13, 15, 16, 48, 73, 75, 162; percentage of population of in India, 121
Hindu temples, 5, 6, 10, 140, 142, 149–53, 156, 157; first in America, 14
Hispanic American Christians, 241, 242, 248, 266
Hispanic Church and American Public Life project, 248, 266
Historically Sunni African American Mosques (HSAAM), 27, 28, 30, 33, 36
Homosexuality: in Islam, 25, 36
Hunter, James Davison, 15, 37, 46, 124
Huntington, Samuel, 11

Imams, 48, 189
Immigrants: and American identity, 3;

Reardon, Alima Delores, 192, 193
Recognition phase, 15, 37, 124, 261–63
Rehnquist Court, 184, 185
Reincarnation, 97, 113
Religious Freedom Restoration Act of
   1993 (RFRA), 184
Republicans, 1, 39, 247, 248
Resistance, 12, 64, 123, 124; in Islam, 23,
   35, 36
Reynolds v. United States, 181
Rinpoche, Chagdud, 108, 109
Rinpoche, Chetsang, 108, 110
Rinpoche, Deshung, 102, 110
Rinpoche, Dudjom, 104, 109
Rinpoche, Gelek, 108, 109
Rinpoche, Kalu, 102, 103
Rinpoche, Lama Zopa, 103, 104, 108, 109
Rinpoche, Penor, 108, 109
Rinpoche, Sakya Trichen, 104, 108, 110
Rinpoche, Tai Situ, 108, 109, 110
Rinpoche, Trungpa, 102, 103, 104, 108
Roman Catholics. *See* Catholics

Sacralization of landscape: by American
   Hindus, 69–70, 139–59, 264; by
   Oregon Buddhists, 69
Sacred canopy, 23, 24, 38, 75, 114, 119,
   134, 266
Sacred geography, 139–59, 264; in
   Hindu rituals, 144; in Sikhism, 162,
   174
Safi, Omid, 11, 46
Said, Edward, 49, 53
Salafi movement, 35, 36; return to ways
   of *al-salaf al-saleh*, 45; thought, 28, 45,
   47, 48
Sanghas, 97, 113
Sankaranti festivals, 125, 140, 155, 156
Sankirtan, 198, 200, 201, 203
Sanskrit, 97, 139, 142, 143, 144, 155
Sarasvati River, 141, 148
Saudi Arabia, 45, 132
Scalia, Antonin, 183, 213, 214, 221, 222
School prayer, 7, 12

Secular humanism, 53
Secularism, 24, 101, 209
Secularization, 8, 34, 101, 256
September 11, 2001. *See* 9/11
Sera Monastic University, 103, 113
Sethuraman, J., 142, 143
Seva, 156, 157
Seventh-Day Adventists, 182, 213, 248
Seven Years in Tibet, 101, 107
Sharia, 50, 51, 55
Sherbert v. Verner, 182, 183, 184, 213, 214
Shiite Muslims, 45, 54
Shintoism, 63, 65
Shiva, Lord, 148, 150, 151, 152, 153, 154
Sikhism, 4, 8, 10, 14, 160–77, 181; and
   gender equality, 168; as stereotyped,
   128
Sikh Mediawatch and Resource Task
   Force (SMART), 173
Sikhs, 6, 10, 12, 15, 16, 50, 64, 72, 73, 75,
   121, 160–77, 198, 258; American
   population of, 4; and identity, 161;
   world population of, 161
Singh, Guru Gobind, 161, 162
Slavery, 133; biblical view of, 14
Snow, Jennifer, 15, 221, 260
Sodhi, Balbir Singh, 14, 72
Soka Gakkai International. *See* Buddhism
South Africa, 46, 53
South Asians, 50, 72
Spiritual marketplace, 5, 15
Sri Lanka, 94, 95, 96, 151
"Sri Venkatesha America Vaibhava
   Stotram" (poem), 142, 143
Sufis, 29, 45, 46, 47, 54, 112
Sunna, 28, 45, 47, 48
Sunni Muslims, 7, 27, 54
Sutras, 66, 88, 90
Swastika symbol, 69, 72

Tablighi Jamaat, 29, 35, 36
Taliban, 43, 132
Tantric Buddhism, 94, 95, 96, 97, 99
Taoism. *See* Daoism